A Tale of the Secret Saint

2

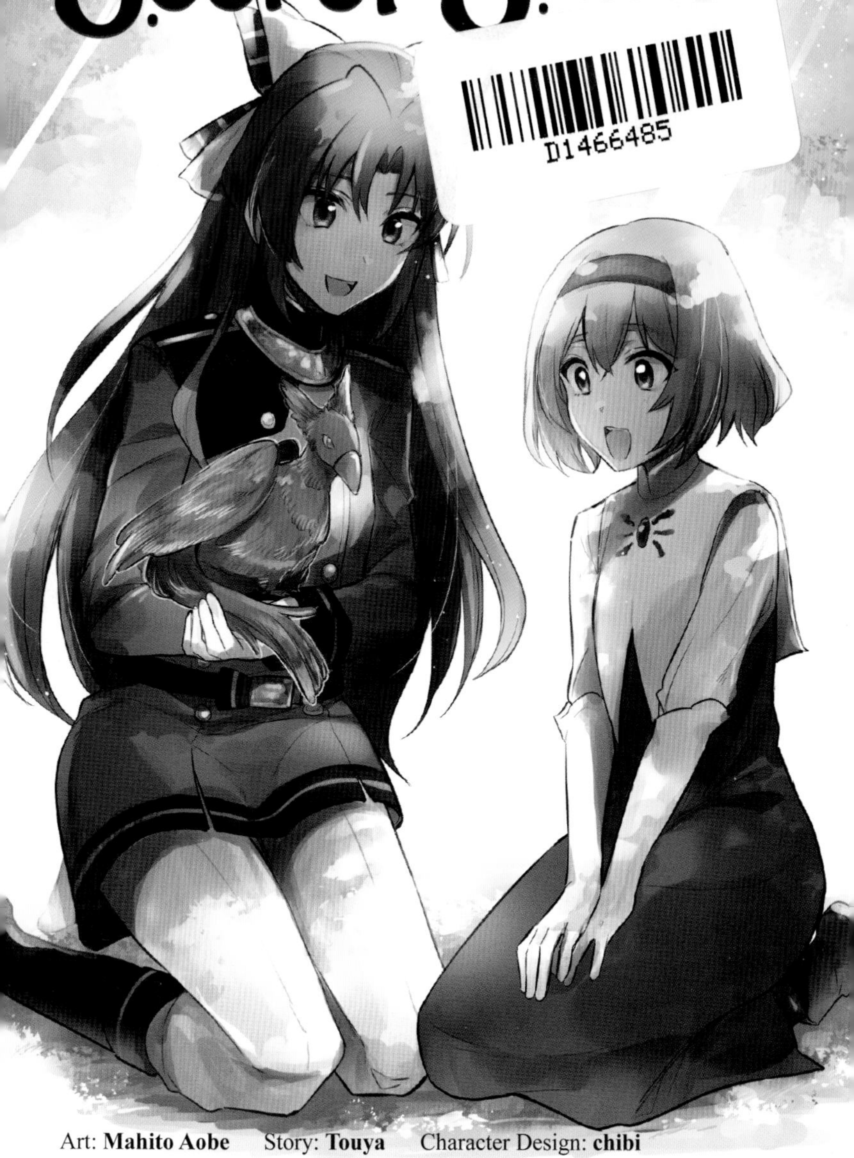

Art: **Mahito Aobe** Story: **Touya** Character Design: **chibi**

CONTENTS

A Tale of the Secret Saint

Presented by Touya / chibi / Mahito Aobe

Volume Two

CHARACTERS

A Tale of the Secret Saint

FIA RUUD

Youngest daughter of the knightly Ruud family. Member of the First Knight Brigade. Although she's regained her past life's powers, she believes she'll be killed if the demon lord's servant discovers that the Great Saint was reborn. She keeps her powers a secret and becomes a knight.

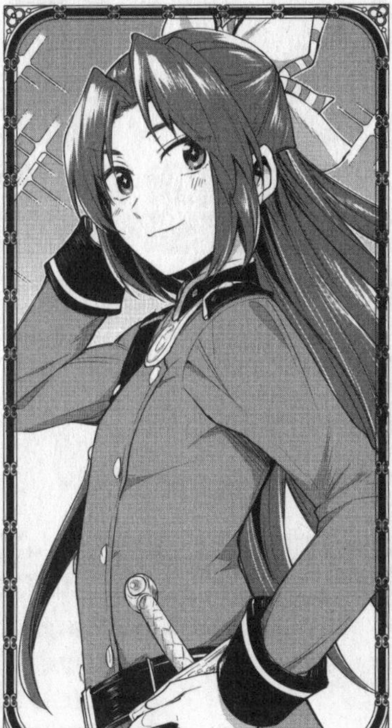

ZAVILIA

Fia's familiar. The world's only black dragon. One of the continent's Three Great Beasts.

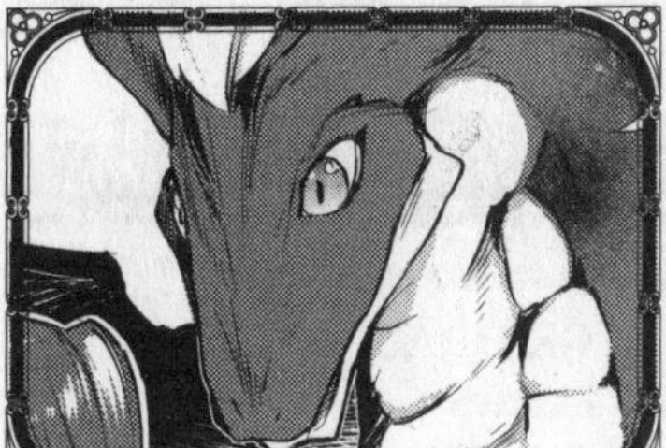

STORY

Fia longs to become a knight. However, when she is attacked by a black dragon, the most powerful monster in the world, and finds herself on the brink of death, she remembers her past life as a Great Saint.

Her mighty Saint abilities are potent enough to form a pact with the black dragon. She escapes death, but if the right hand of the demon lord learns she has been reborn, she could be killed. Fia hides her powers and resolves to become a knight.

Fia aces the knight exam with her powers and is assigned to the First Knight Brigade. When she accompanies another brigade on a monster extermination mission, they are attacked! The flummoxed brigade has never fought such a monster before, but newly knighted Fia takes command. Then Cyril, Captain of the First Knight Brigade, rushes onto the scene...

DESMOND
RONAN

Captain of the Second Knight Brigade and Commandant of the military police. An earl and the head of a noble family. This so-called "Tiger of Náv" lost his trust in women when his younger brother stole his fiancée.

SAVIZ
NÁV

Commander of the Náv Black Dragon Knights. As the younger brother of the king, he's next in line for the throne.

CYRIL
SUTHERLAND

Captain of the First Knight Brigade. A duke and the head of a noble family, he's second in line to the throne. No one in the Knight Brigades can match the swordplay of this "Dragon of Náv."

NÁV KINGDOM BLACK DRAGON KNIGHT BRIGADES

COMMANDER SAVIZ NÁV

First Knight Brigade (protects the royal family)
Second Knight Brigade (guards the royal castle)
Third Mage Knight Brigade (mages)
Fourth Monster Tamer Knight Brigade (monster tamers)
Fifth Knight Brigade (guards the royal capital)
Sixth Knight Brigade (monster extermination near the capital)

⋮

Twentieth Knight Brigade (patrols the border)

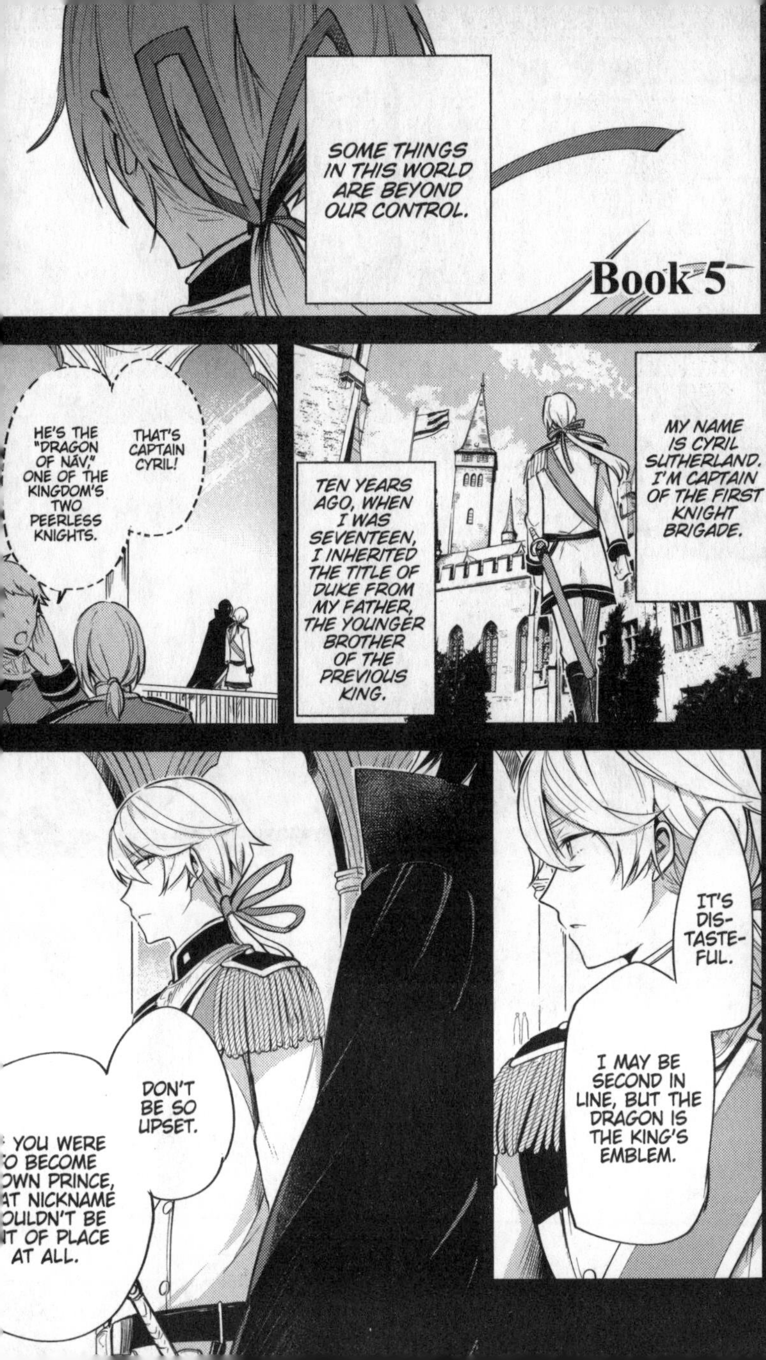
SOME THINGS IN THIS WORLD ARE BEYOND OUR CONTROL.
Book 5
MY NAME IS CYRIL SUTHERLAND. I'M CAPTAIN OF THE FIRST KNIGHT BRIGADE.
TEN YEARS AGO, WHEN I WAS SEVENTEEN, I INHERITED THE TITLE OF DUKE FROM MY FATHER, THE YOUNGER BROTHER OF THE PREVIOUS KING.
THAT'S CAPTAIN CYRIL!
HE'S THE "DRAGON OF NÄV," ONE OF THE KINGDOM'S TWO PEERLESS KNIGHTS.
IT'S DISTASTEFUL.
I MAY BE SECOND IN LINE, BUT THE DRAGON IS THE KING'S EMBLEM.
DON'T BE SO UPSET.
YOU WERE O BECOME OWN PRINCE, AT NICKNAME OULDN'T BE T OF PLACE AT ALL.

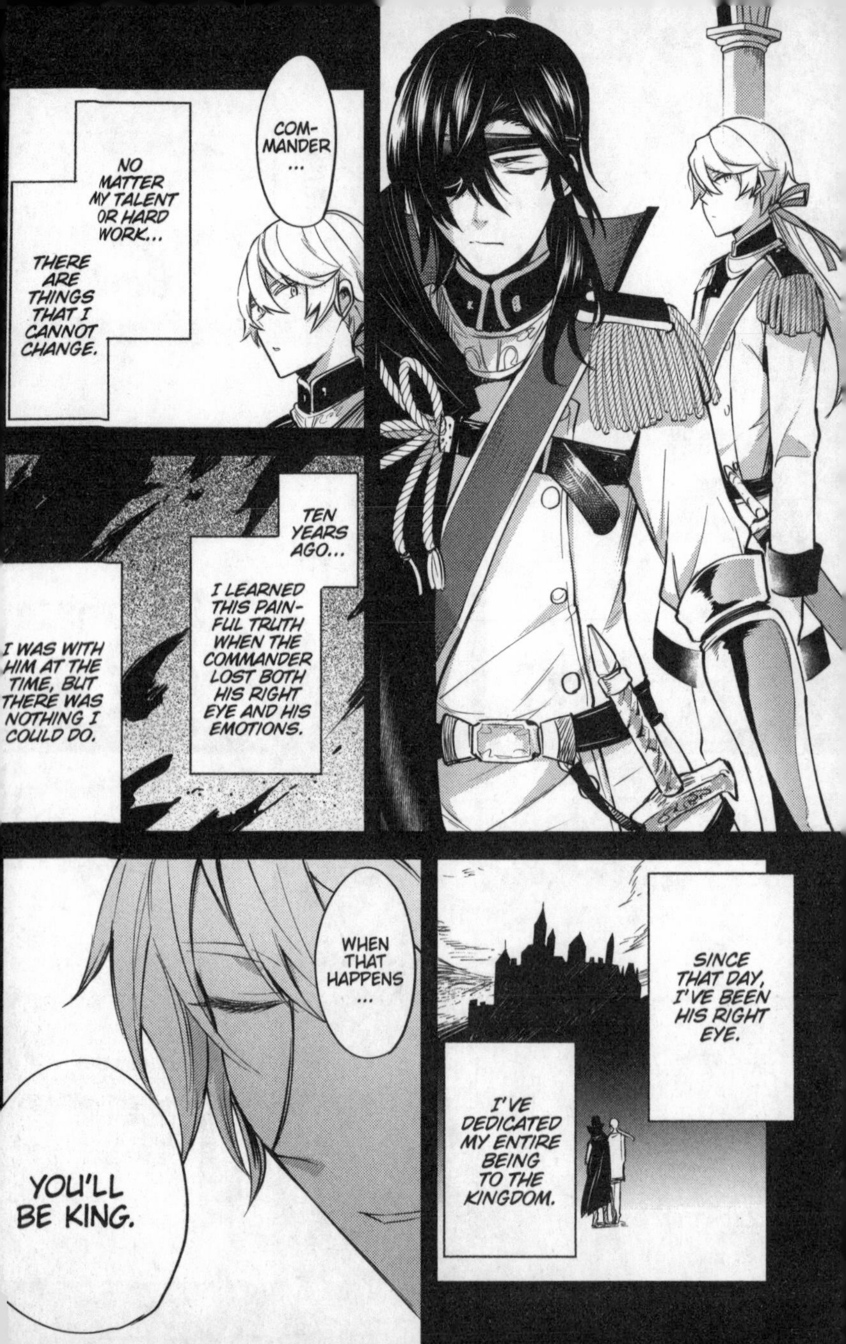
COM-MANDER...
NO MATTER MY TALENT OR HARD WORK...
THERE ARE THINGS THAT I CANNOT CHANGE.
TEN YEARS AGO...
I LEARNED THIS PAIN-FUL TRUTH WHEN THE COMMANDER LOST BOTH HIS RIGHT EYE AND HIS EMOTIONS.
I WAS WITH HIM AT THE TIME, BUT THERE WAS NOTHING I COULD DO.
SINCE THAT DAY, I'VE BEEN HIS RIGHT EYE.
I'VE DEDICATED MY ENTIRE BEING TO THE KINGDOM.
WHEN THAT HAPPENS...
YOU'LL BE KING.

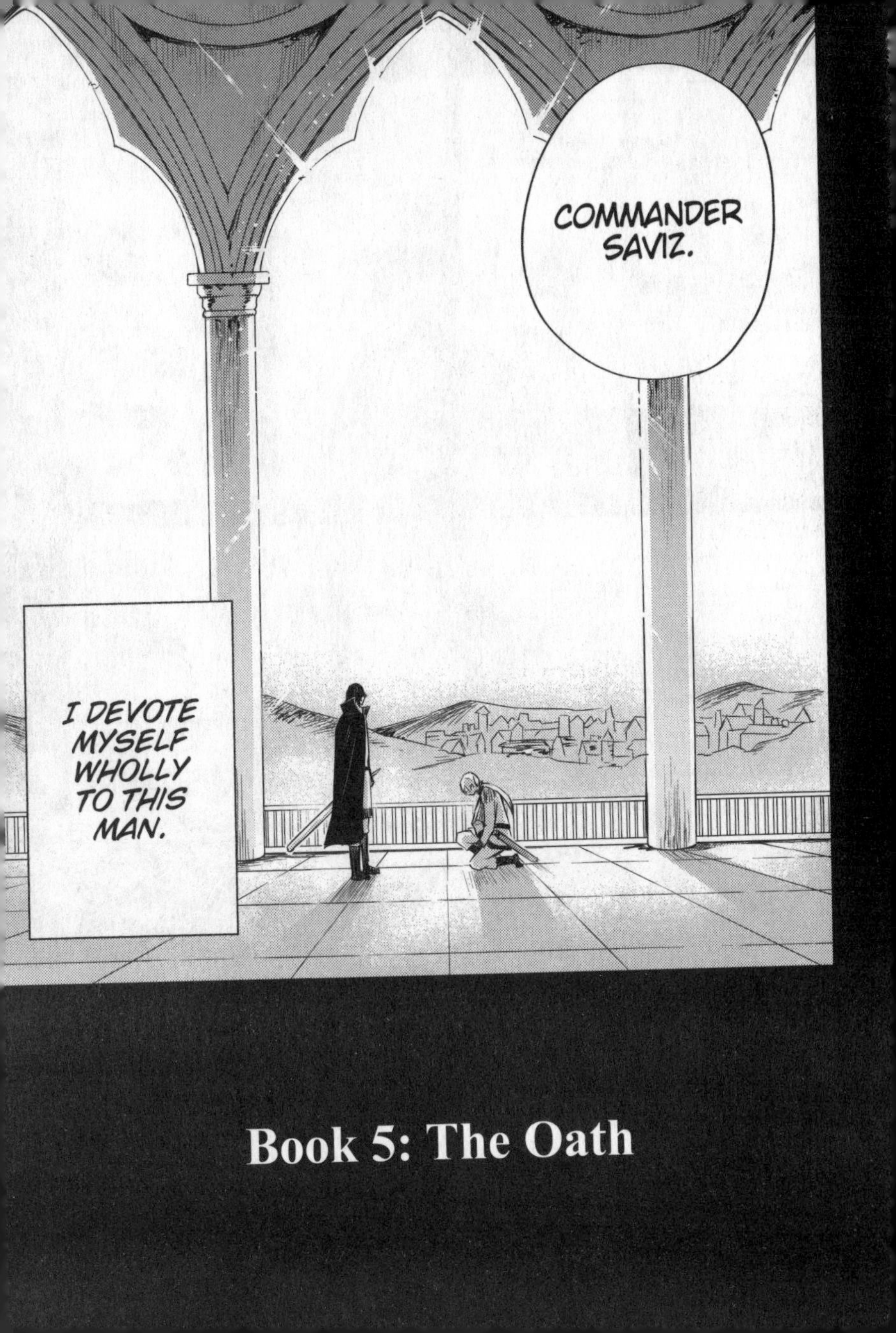
COMMANDER SAVIZ.
I DEVOTE MYSELF WHOLLY TO THIS MAN.

Book 5: The Oath

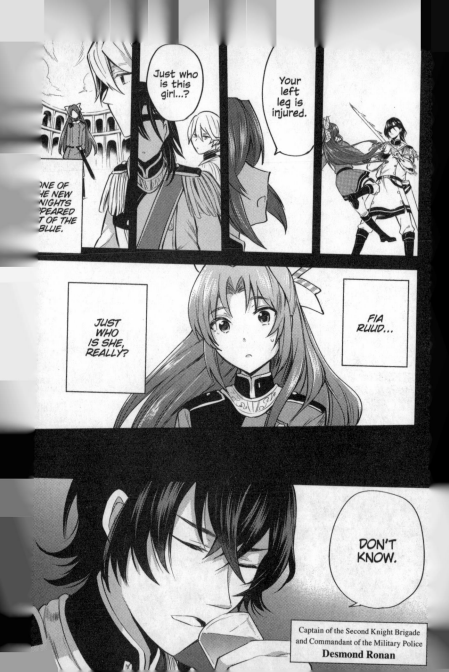

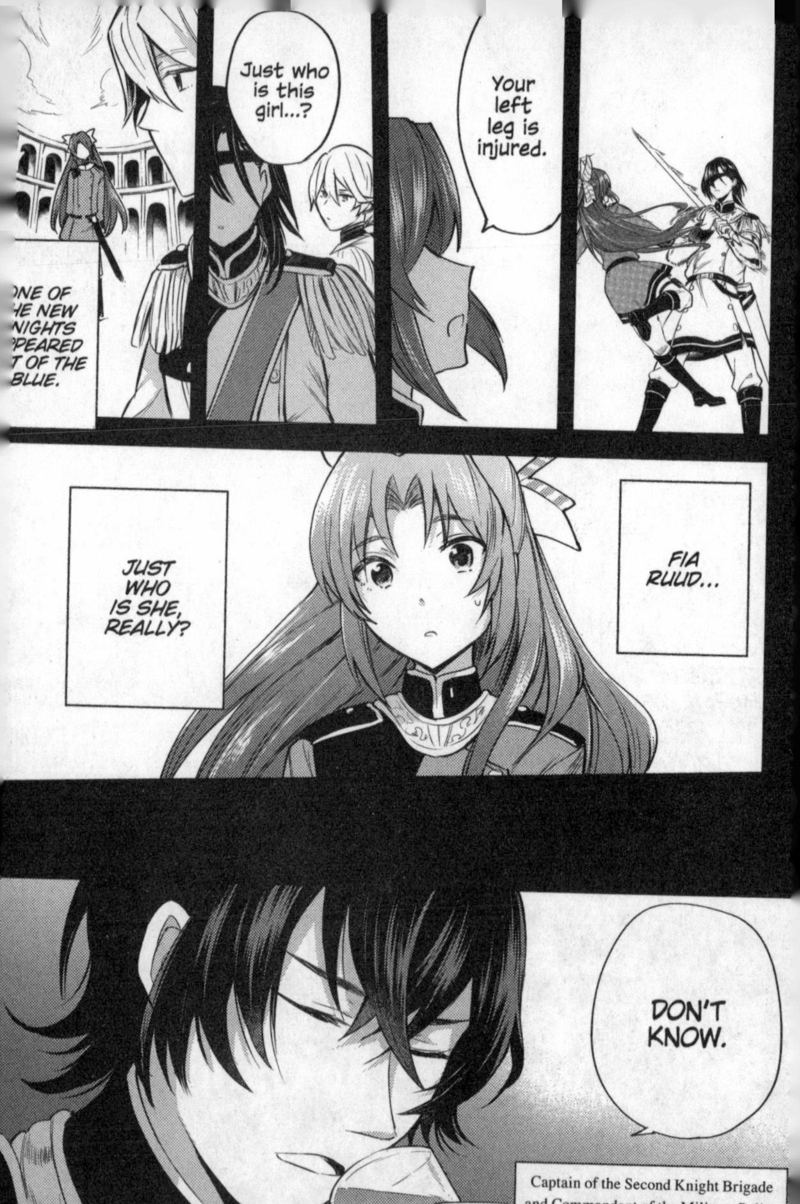
Your left leg is injured.
Just who is this girl...?
ONE OF HE NEW NIGHTS PPEARED T OF THE BLUE.
FIA RUUD...
JUST WHO IS SHE, REALLY?
DON'T KNOW.
Captain of the Second Knight Brigade and Commandant of the Military Police
Desmond Ronan

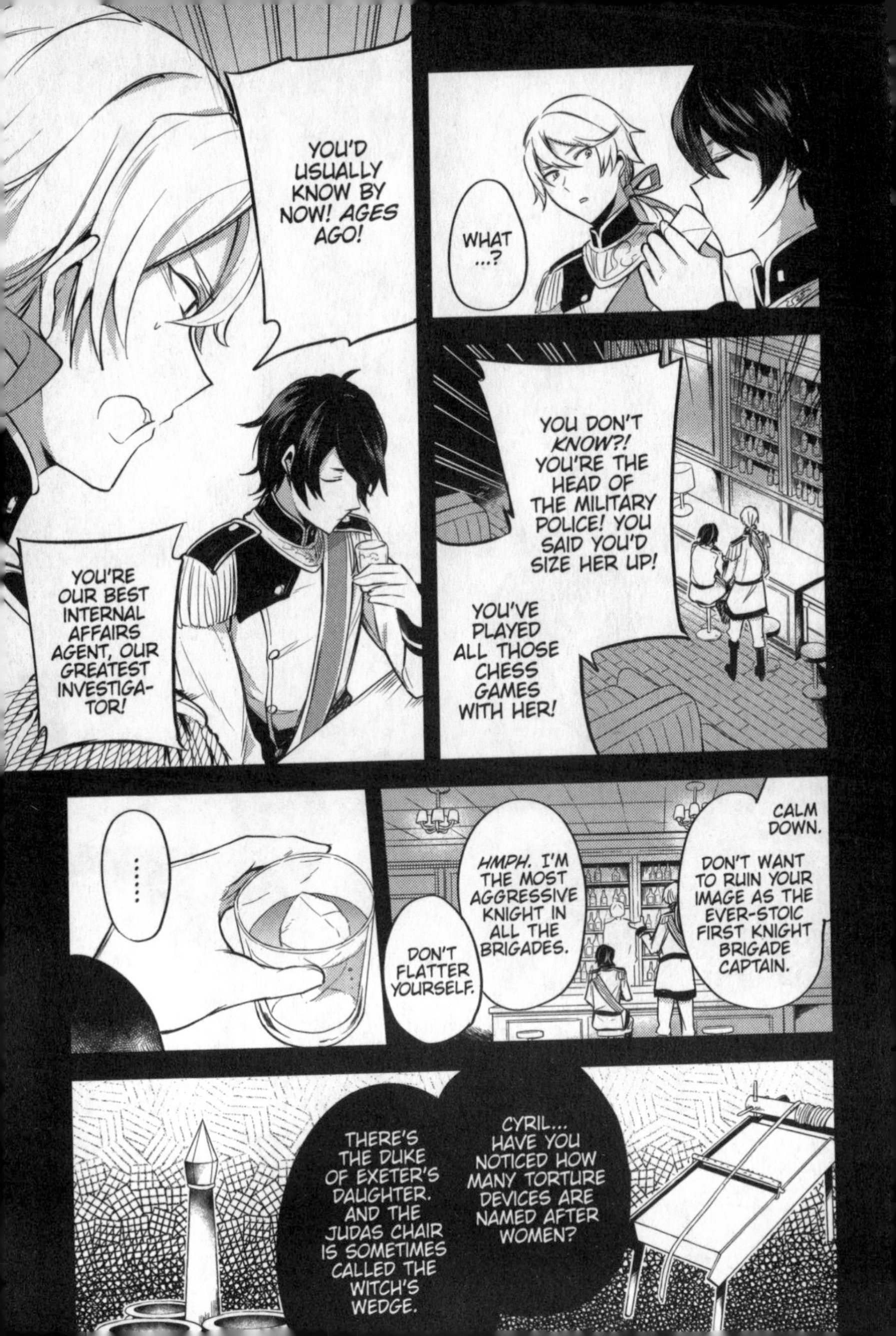
WHAT ...?
YOU DON'T *KNOW*?! YOU'RE THE HEAD OF THE MILITARY POLICE! YOU SAID YOU'D SIZE HER UP!
YOU'VE PLAYED ALL THOSE CHESS GAMES WITH HER!
YOU'D USUALLY KNOW BY NOW! *AGES AGO!*
YOU'RE OUR BEST INTERNAL AFFAIRS AGENT, OUR GREATEST INVESTIGA-TOR!
CALM DOWN.
DON'T WANT TO RUIN YOUR IMAGE AS THE EVER-STOIC FIRST KNIGHT BRIGADE CAPTAIN.
HMPH. I'M THE MOST AGGRESSIVE KNIGHT IN ALL THE BRIGADES.
DON'T FLATTER YOURSELF.
......
CYRIL... HAVE YOU NOTICED HOW MANY TORTURE DEVICES ARE NAMED AFTER WOMEN?
THERE'S THE DUKE OF EXETER'S DAUGHTER. AND THE JUDAS CHAIR IS SOMETIMES CALLED THE WITCH'S WEDGE.

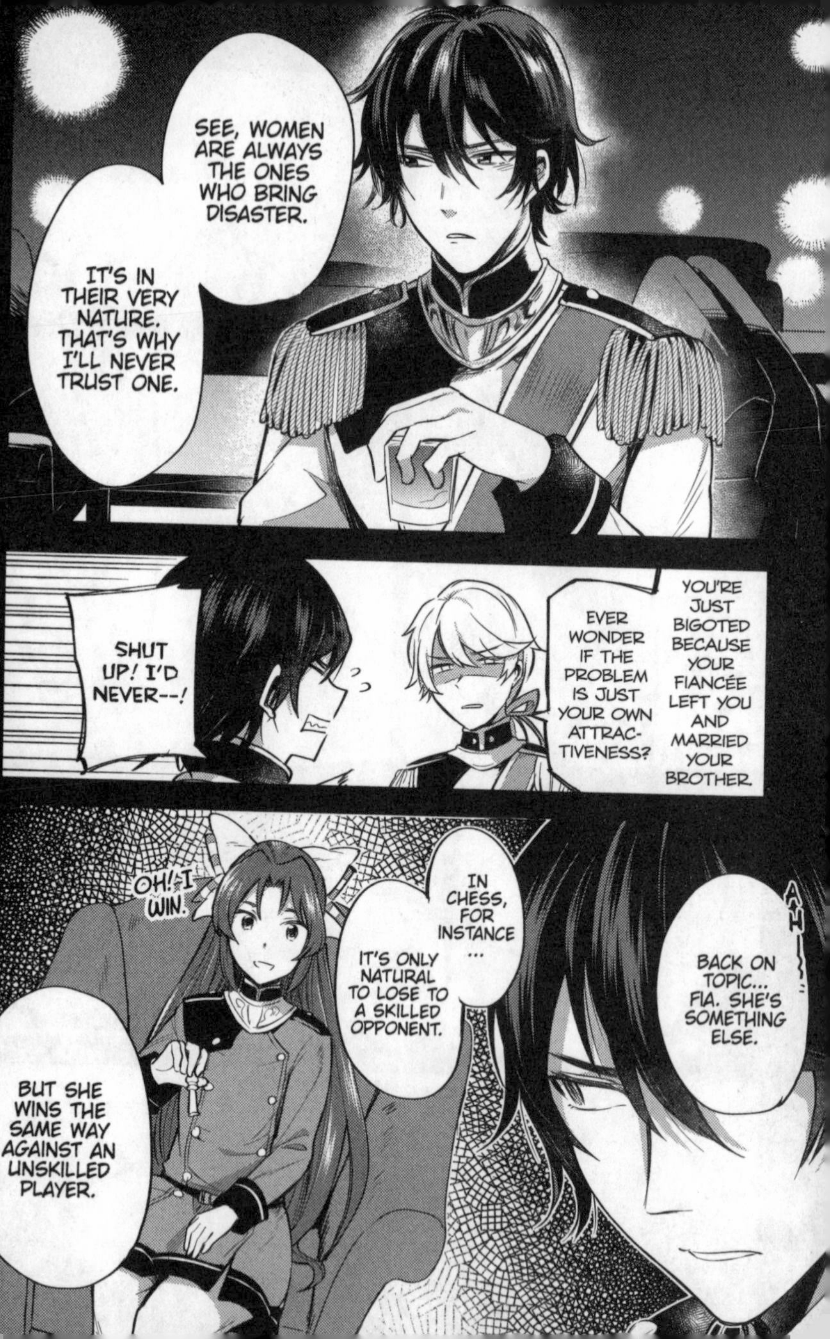
SEE, WOMEN ARE ALWAYS THE ONES WHO BRING DISASTER.
IT'S IN THEIR VERY NATURE. THAT'S WHY I'LL NEVER TRUST ONE.
YOU'RE JUST BIGOTED BECAUSE YOUR FIANCÉE LEFT YOU AND MARRIED YOUR BROTHER.
EVER WONDER IF THE PROBLEM IS JUST YOUR OWN ATTRACTIVENESS?
SHUT UP! I'D NEVER--!
AAH~
BACK ON TOPIC... FIA. SHE'S SOMETHING ELSE.
IN CHESS, FOR INSTANCE...
IT'S ONLY NATURAL TO LOSE TO A SKILLED OPPONENT.
OH! I WIN.
BUT SHE WINS THE SAME WAY AGAINST AN UNSKILLED PLAYER.

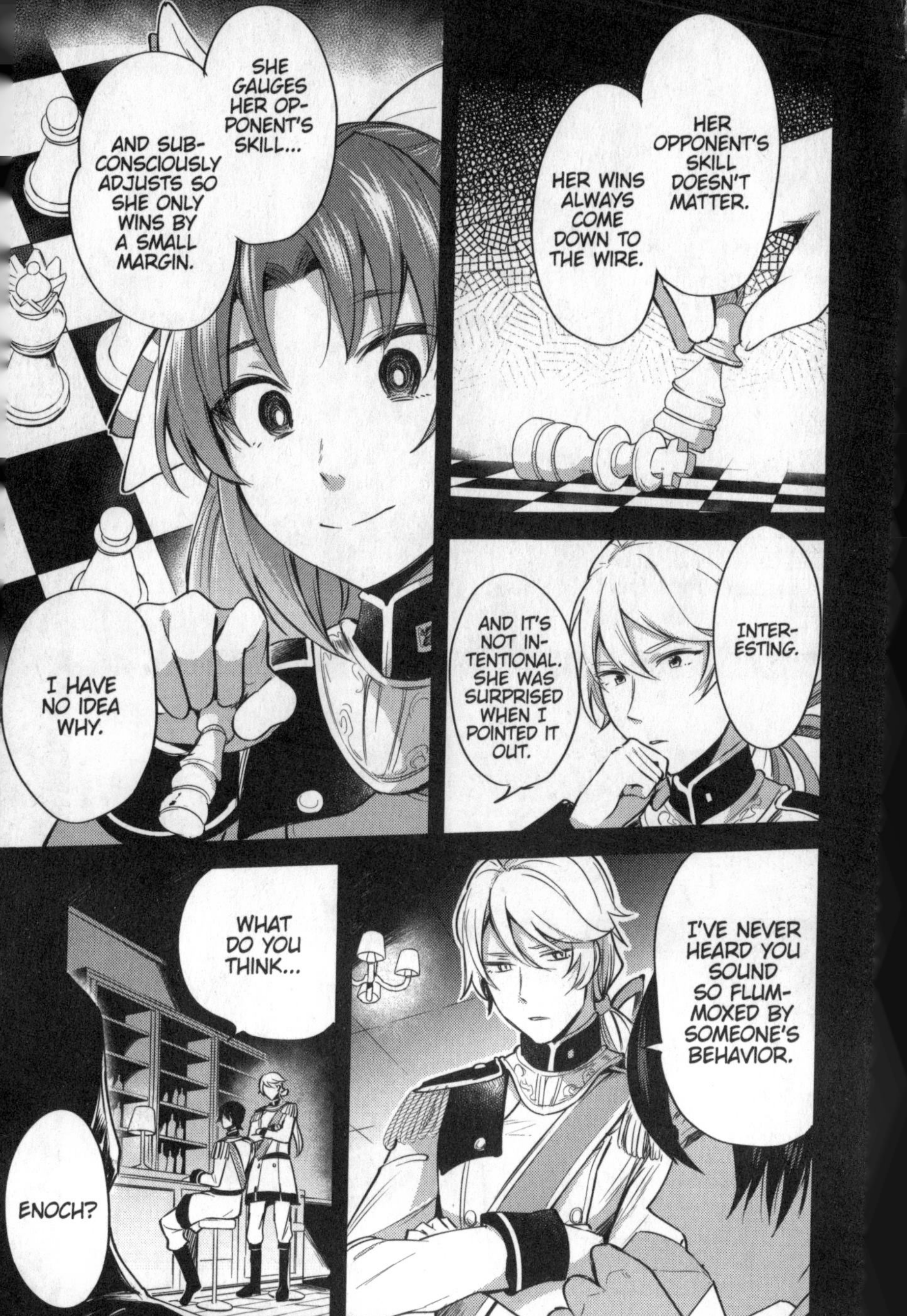
HER OPPONENT'S SKILL DOESN'T MATTER.
HER WINS ALWAYS COME DOWN TO THE WIRE.
INTER-ESTING.
AND IT'S NOT IN-TENTIONAL. SHE WAS SURPRISED WHEN I POINTED IT OUT.
SHE GAUGES HER OP-PONENT'S SKILL...
AND SUB-CONSCIOUSLY ADJUSTS SO SHE ONLY WINS BY A SMALL MARGIN.
I HAVE NO IDEA WHY.
I'VE NEVER HEARD YOU SOUND SO FLUM-MOXED BY SOMEONE'S BEHAVIOR.
WHAT DO YOU THINK...
ENOCH?

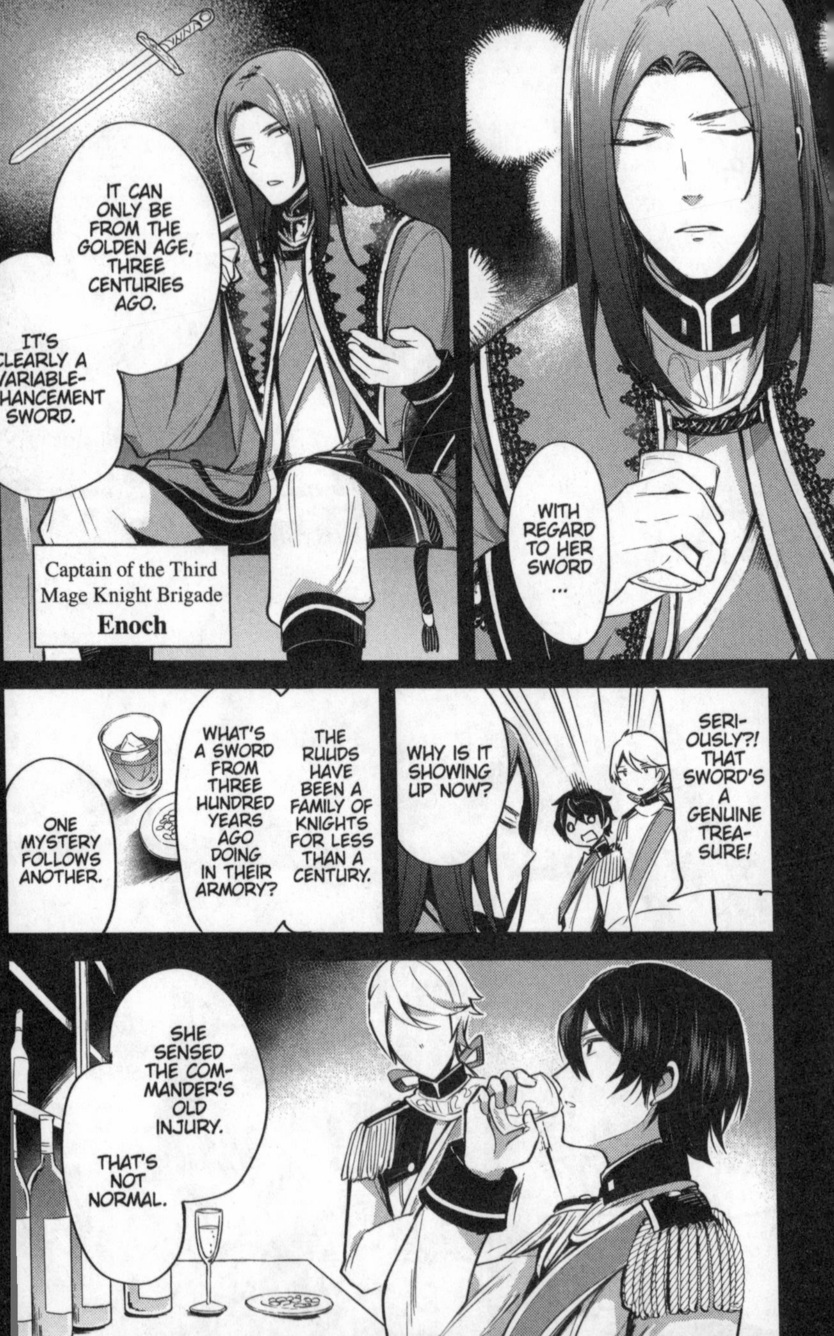
WITH REGARD TO HER SWORD ...
IT CAN ONLY BE FROM THE GOLDEN AGE, THREE CENTURIES AGO.
IT'S CLEARLY A VARIABLE-ENHANCEMENT SWORD.
Captain of the Third Mage Knight Brigade
Enoch
SERIOUSLY?! THAT SWORD'S A GENUINE TREASURE!
WHY IS IT SHOWING UP NOW?
THE RUUDS HAVE BEEN A FAMILY OF KNIGHTS FOR LESS THAN A CENTURY.
WHAT'S A SWORD FROM THREE HUNDRED YEARS AGO DOING IN THEIR ARMORY?
ONE MYSTERY FOLLOWS ANOTHER.
SHE SENSED THE COMMANDER'S OLD INJURY.
THAT'S NOT NORMAL.

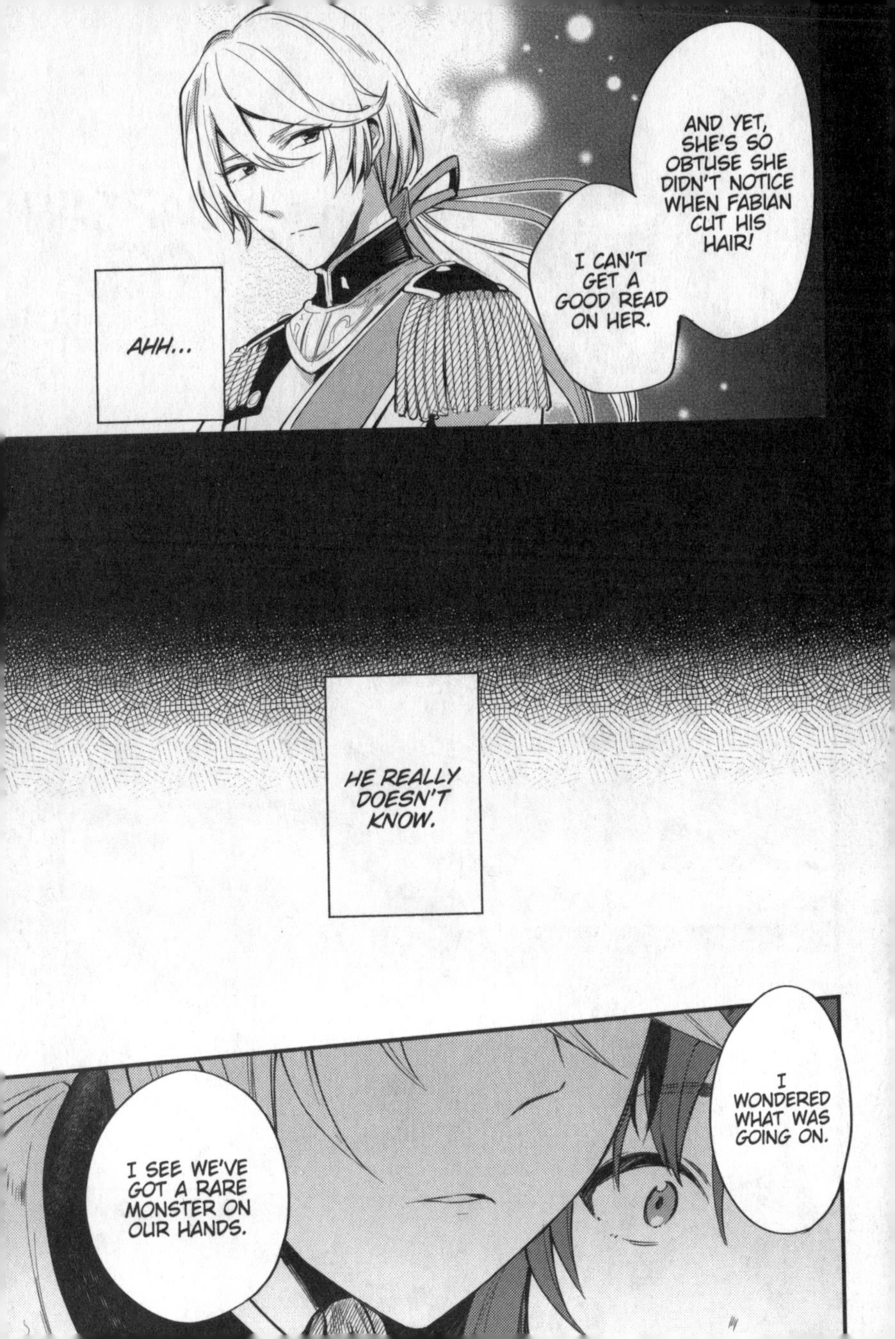
AND YET, SHE'S SO OBTUSE SHE DIDN'T NOTICE WHEN FABIAN CUT HIS HAIR!
I CAN'T GET A GOOD READ ON HER.
AHH...
HE REALLY DOESN'T KNOW.
I WONDERED WHAT WAS GOING ON.
I SEE WE'VE GOT A RARE MONSTER ON OUR HANDS.

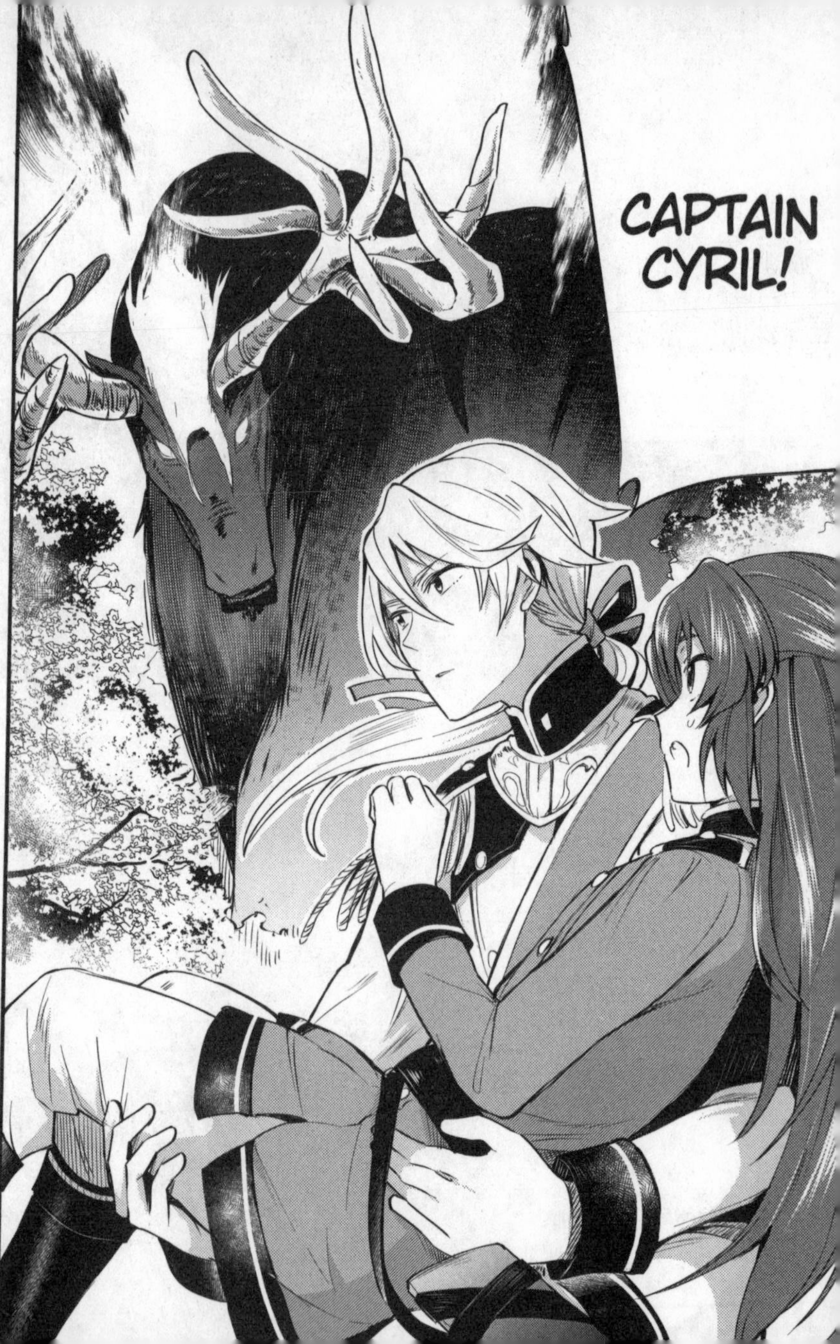
CAPTAIN CYRIL!

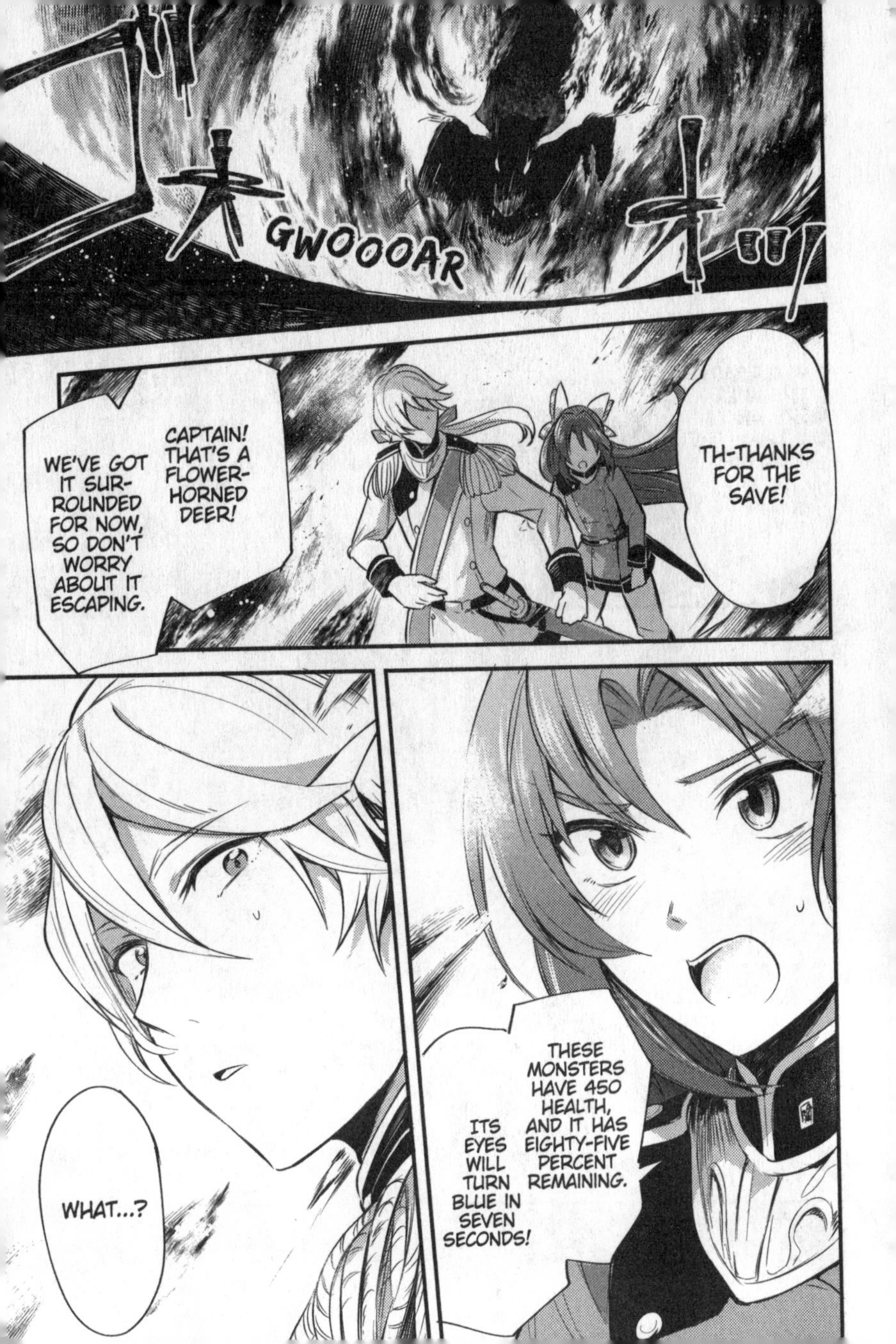
GWOOOAR
TH-THANKS FOR THE SAVE!
CAPTAIN! THAT'S A FLOWER-HORNED DEER!
WE'VE GOT IT SUR-ROUNDED FOR NOW, SO DON'T WORRY ABOUT IT ESCAPING.
THESE MONSTERS HAVE 450 HEALTH, AND IT HAS EIGHTY-FIVE PERCENT REMAINING.
ITS EYES WILL TURN BLUE IN SEVEN SECONDS!
WHAT...?

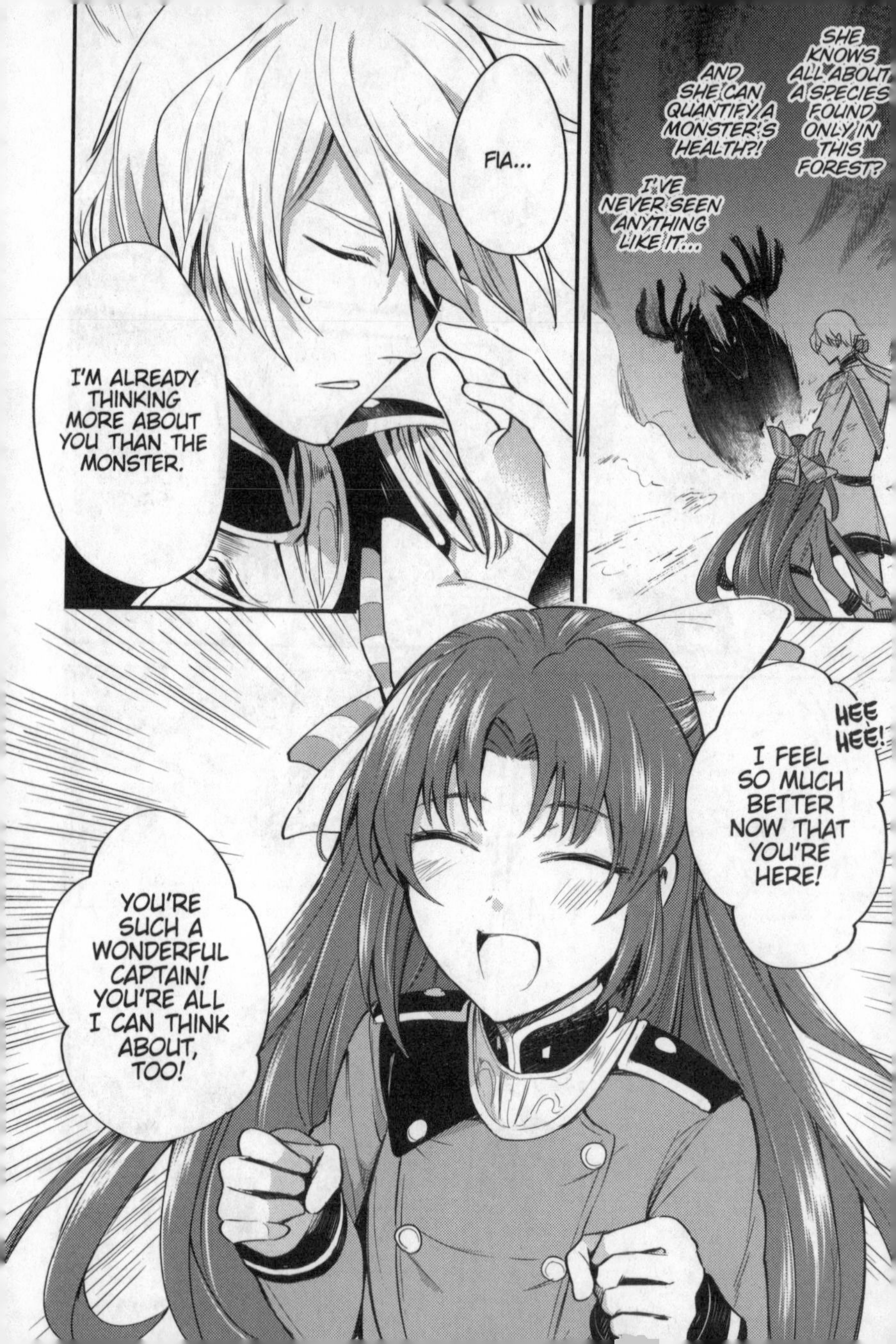
SHE KNOWS ALL ABOUT A SPECIES FOUND ONLY IN THIS FOREST?
AND SHE CAN QUANTIFY A MONSTER'S HEALTH?!
I'VE NEVER SEEN ANYTHING LIKE IT...
FIA...
I'M ALREADY THINKING MORE ABOUT YOU THAN THE MONSTER.
HEE HEE!
I FEEL SO MUCH BETTER NOW THAT YOU'RE HERE!
YOU'RE SUCH A WONDERFUL CAPTAIN! YOU'RE ALL I CAN THINK ABOUT, TOO!

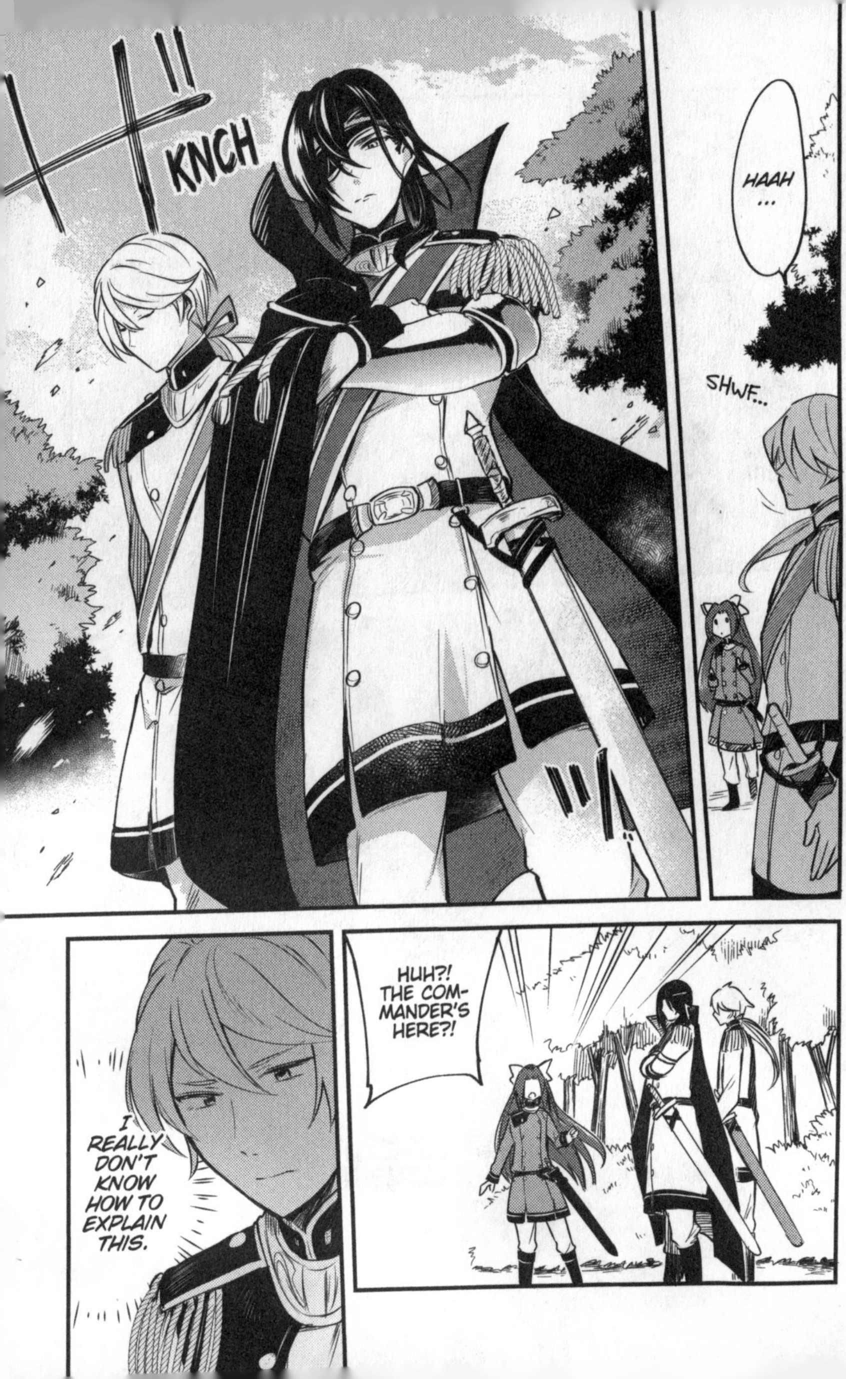
HAAH ...
SHWF...
KNCH
HUH?! THE COM- MANDER'S HERE?!
I REALLY DON'T KNOW HOW TO EXPLAIN THIS.

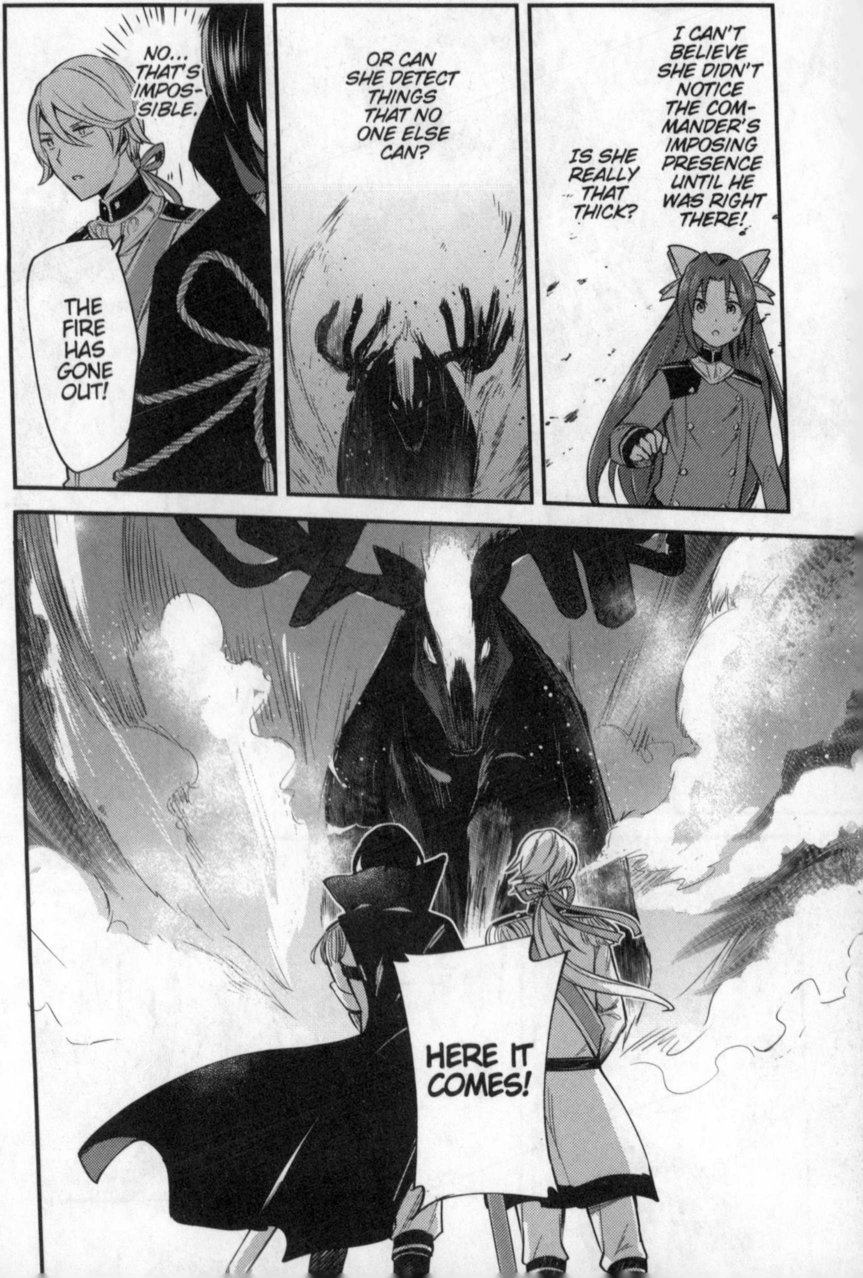
I CAN'T BELIEVE SHE DIDN'T NOTICE THE COM-MANDER'S IMPOSING PRESENCE UNTIL HE WAS RIGHT THERE!
IS SHE REALLY THAT THICK?
OR CAN SHE DETECT THINGS THAT NO ONE ELSE CAN?
NO... THAT'S IMPOS-SIBLE.
THE FIRE HAS GONE OUT!
HERE IT COMES!

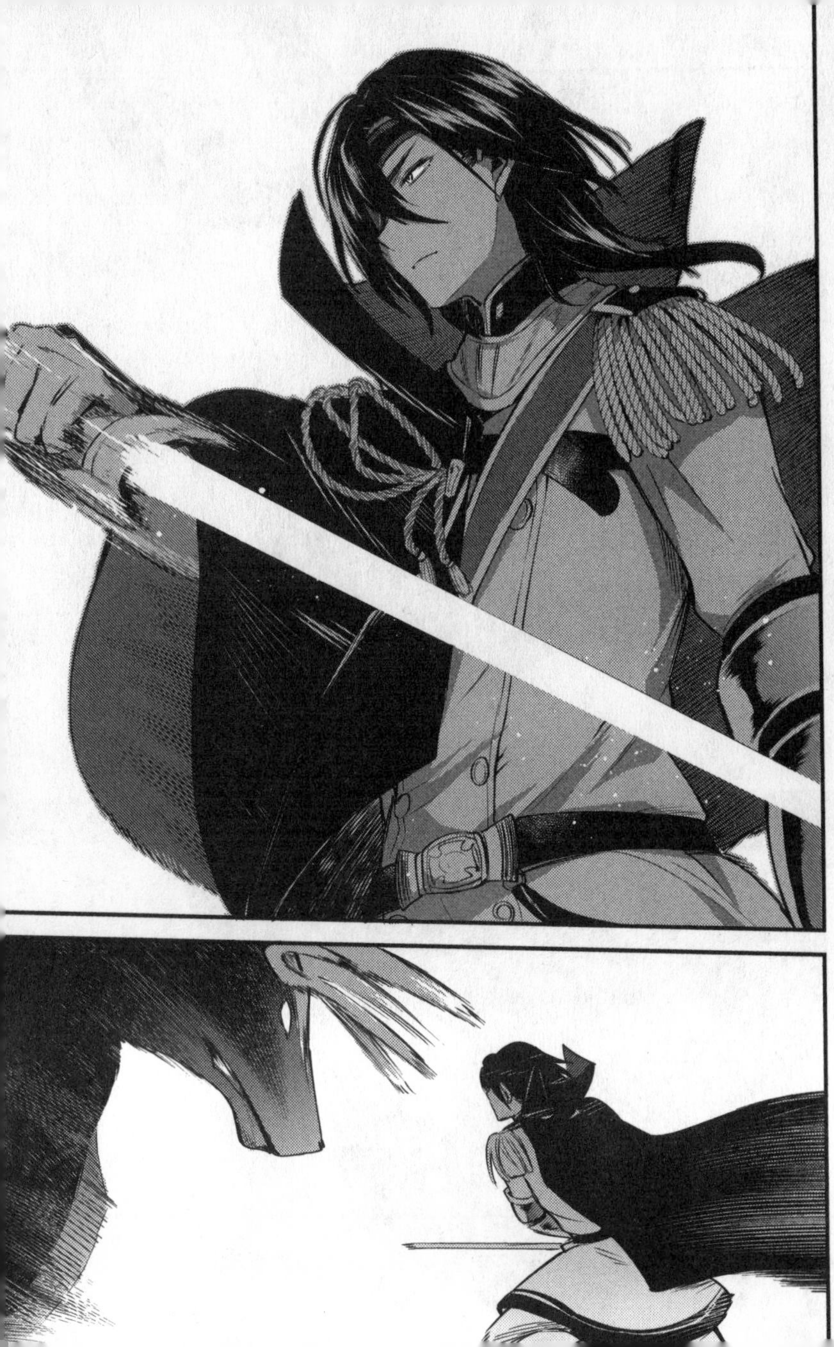

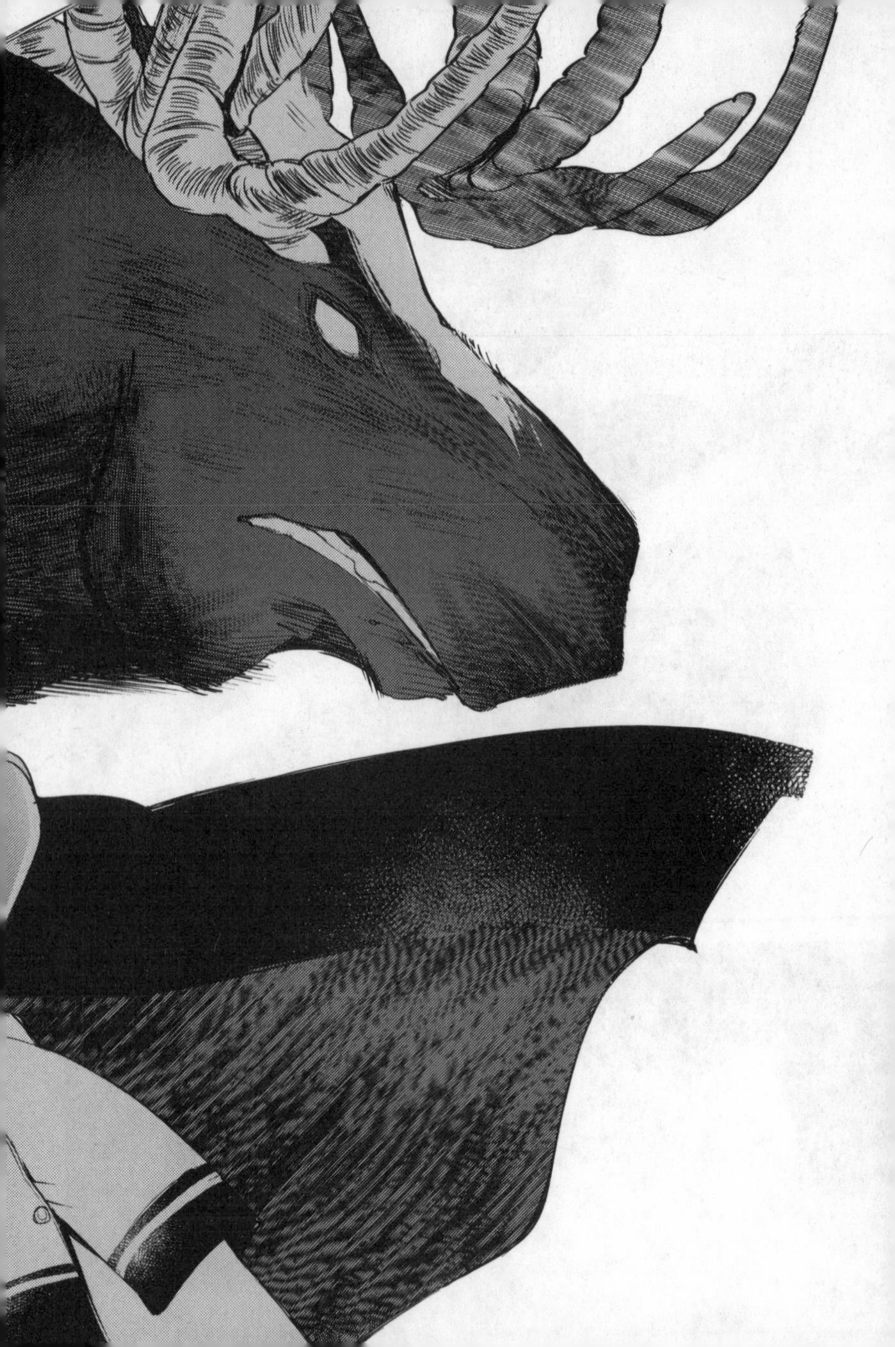

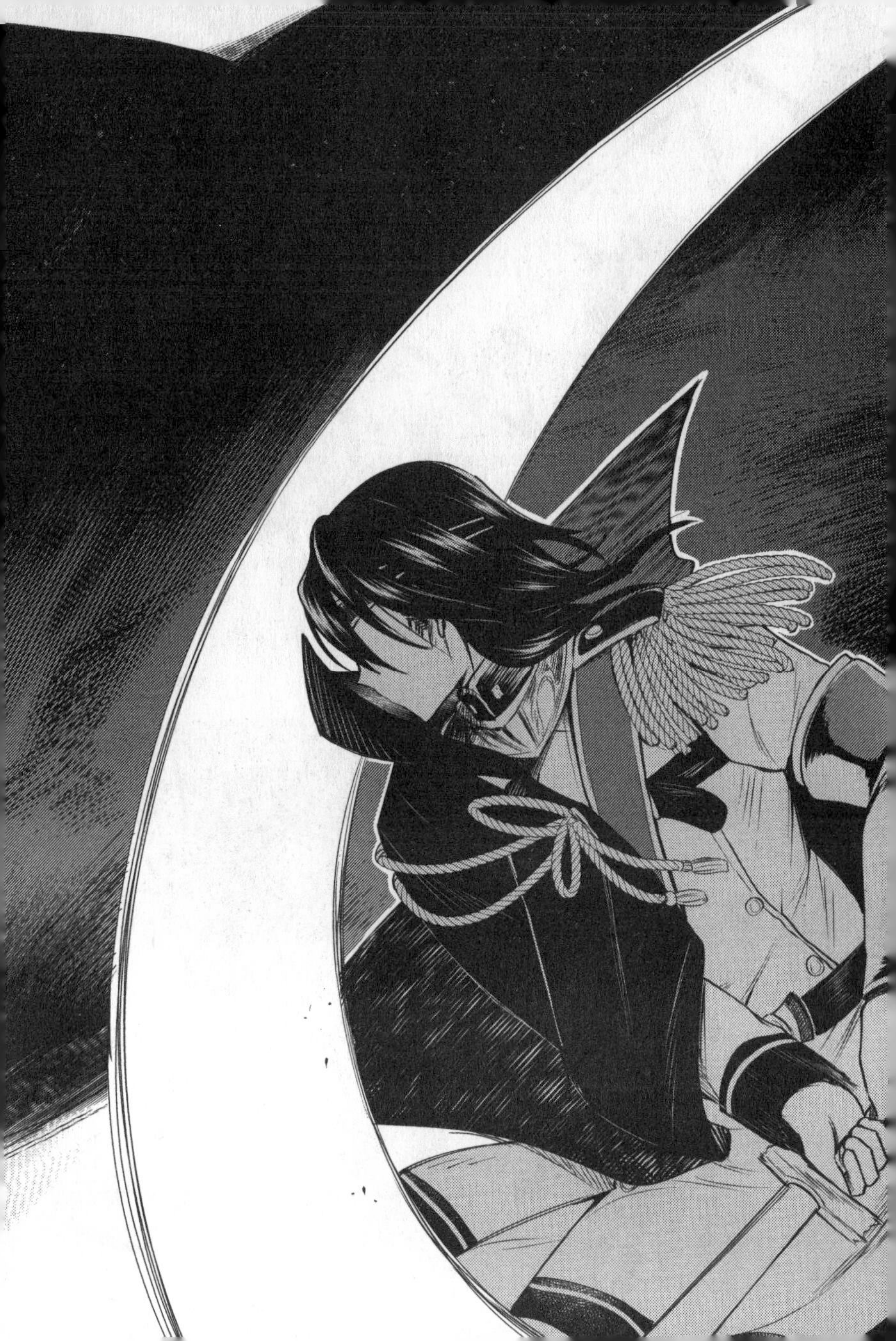

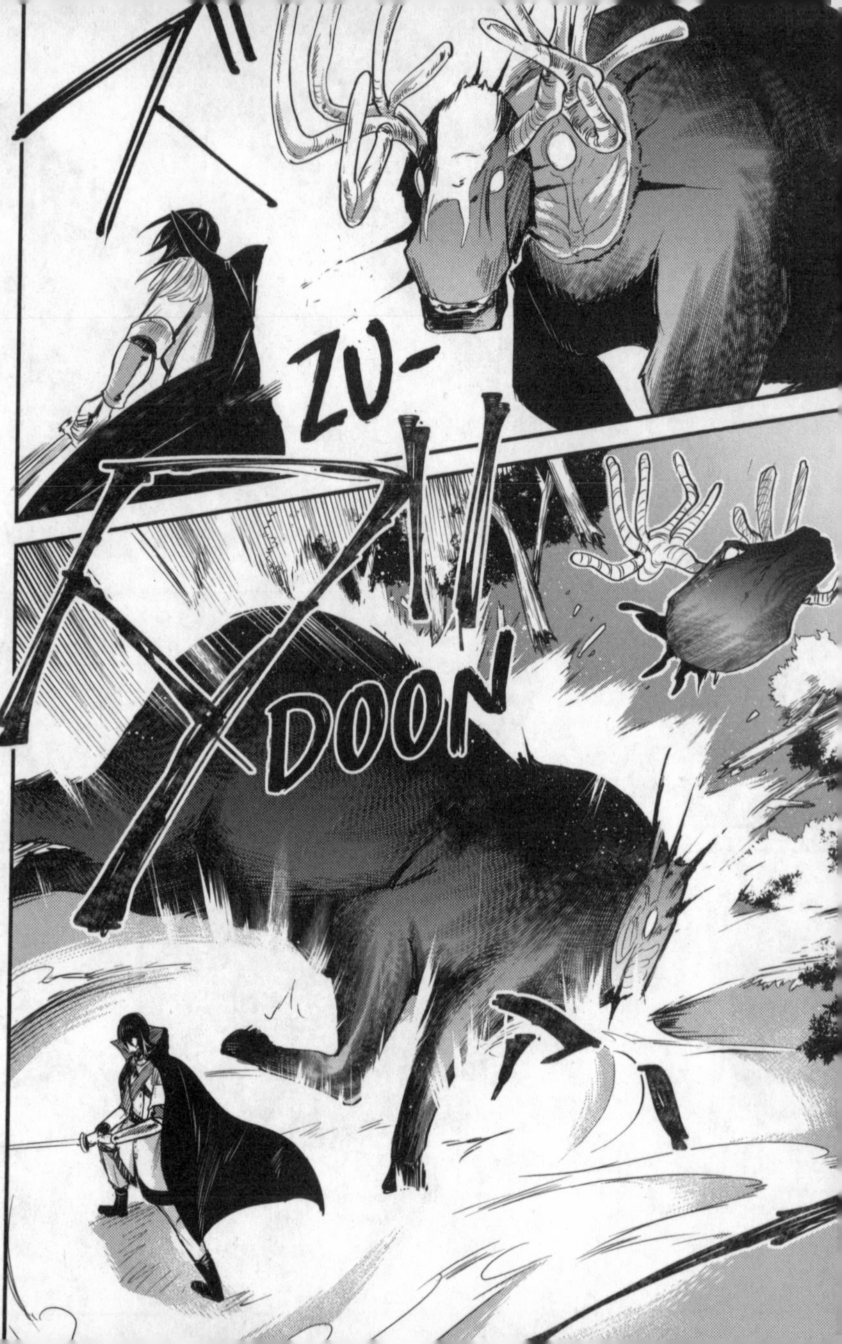
ZU-
DOON

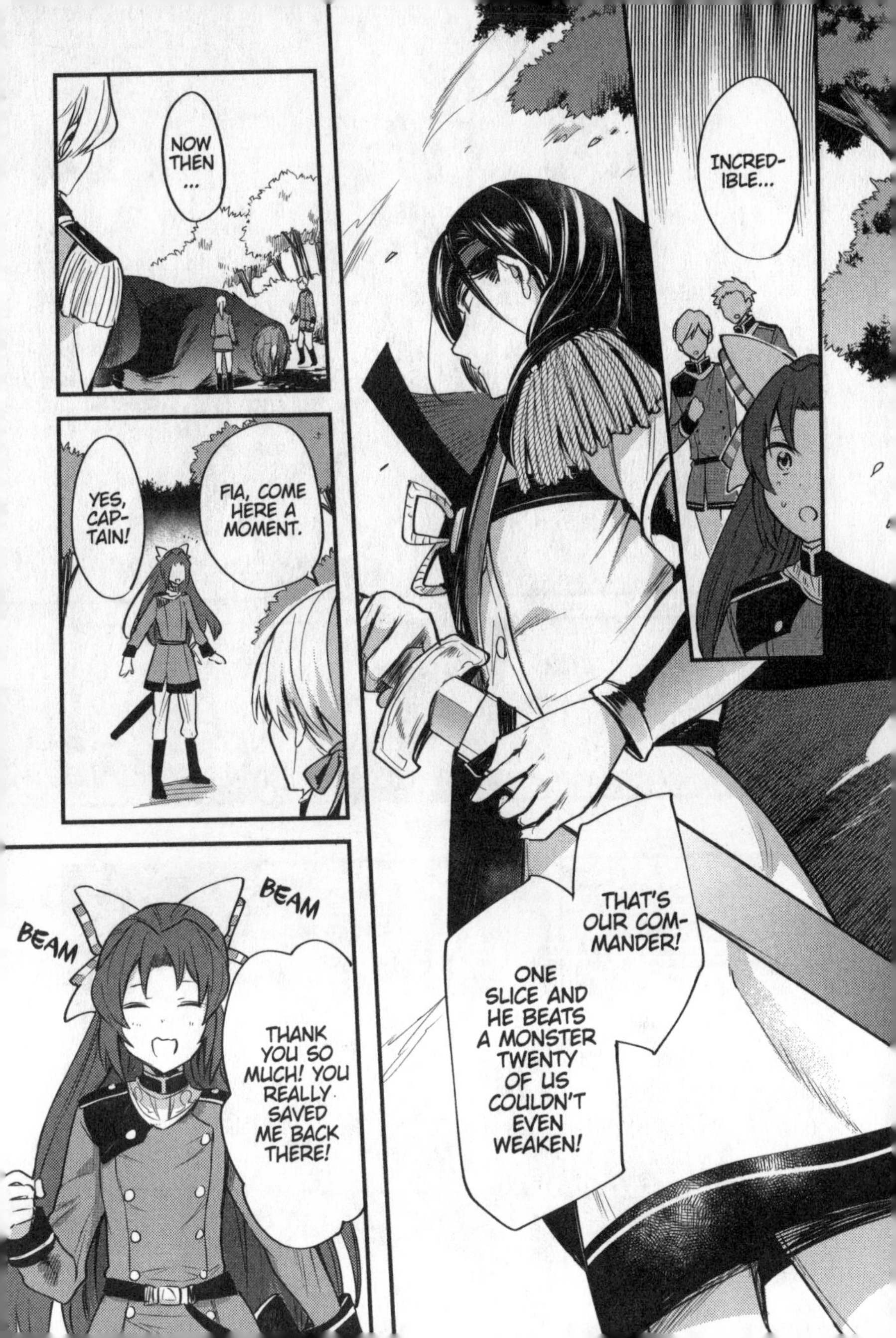
INCRED-IBLE...
THAT'S OUR COM-MANDER!
ONE SLICE AND HE BEATS A MONSTER TWENTY OF US COULDN'T EVEN WEAKEN!
NOW THEN ...
FIA, COME HERE A MOMENT.
YES, CAP-TAIN!
BEAM
BEAM
THANK YOU SO MUCH! YOU REALLY SAVED ME BACK THERE!

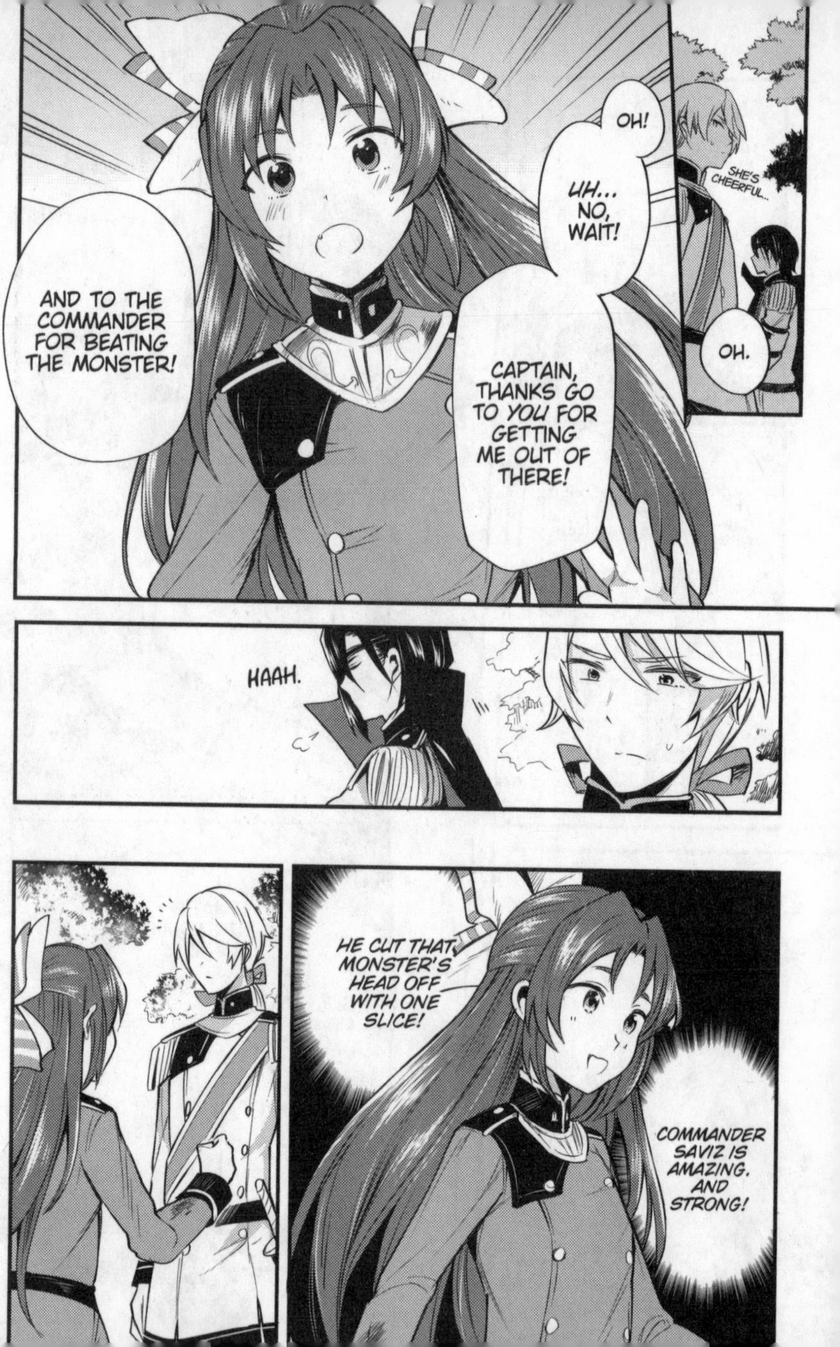
SHE'S CHEERFUL...
OH.
OH!
UH... NO, WAIT!
CAPTAIN, THANKS GO TO YOU FOR GETTING ME OUT OF THERE!
AND TO THE COMMANDER FOR BEATING THE MONSTER!
HAAH.
HE CUT THAT MONSTER'S HEAD OFF WITH ONE SLICE!
COMMANDER SAVIZ IS AMAZING. AND STRONG!

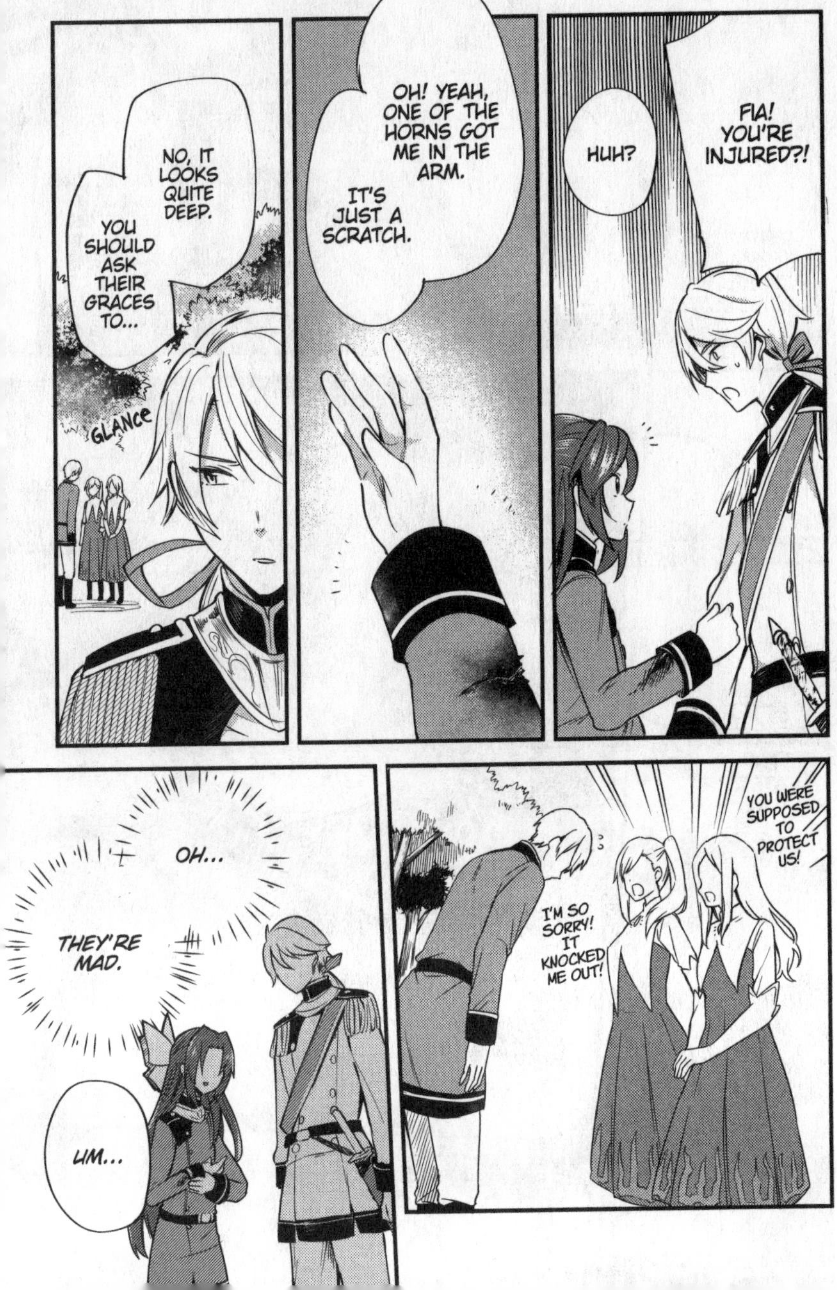
FIA! YOU'RE INJURED?!
HUH?
OH! YEAH, ONE OF THE HORNS GOT ME IN THE ARM.
IT'S JUST A SCRATCH.
NO, IT LOOKS QUITE DEEP.
YOU SHOULD ASK THEIR GRACES TO...
GLANCE
YOU WERE SUPPOSED TO PROTECT US!
I'M SO SORRY! IT KNOCKED ME OUT!
OH...
THEY'RE MAD.
UM...

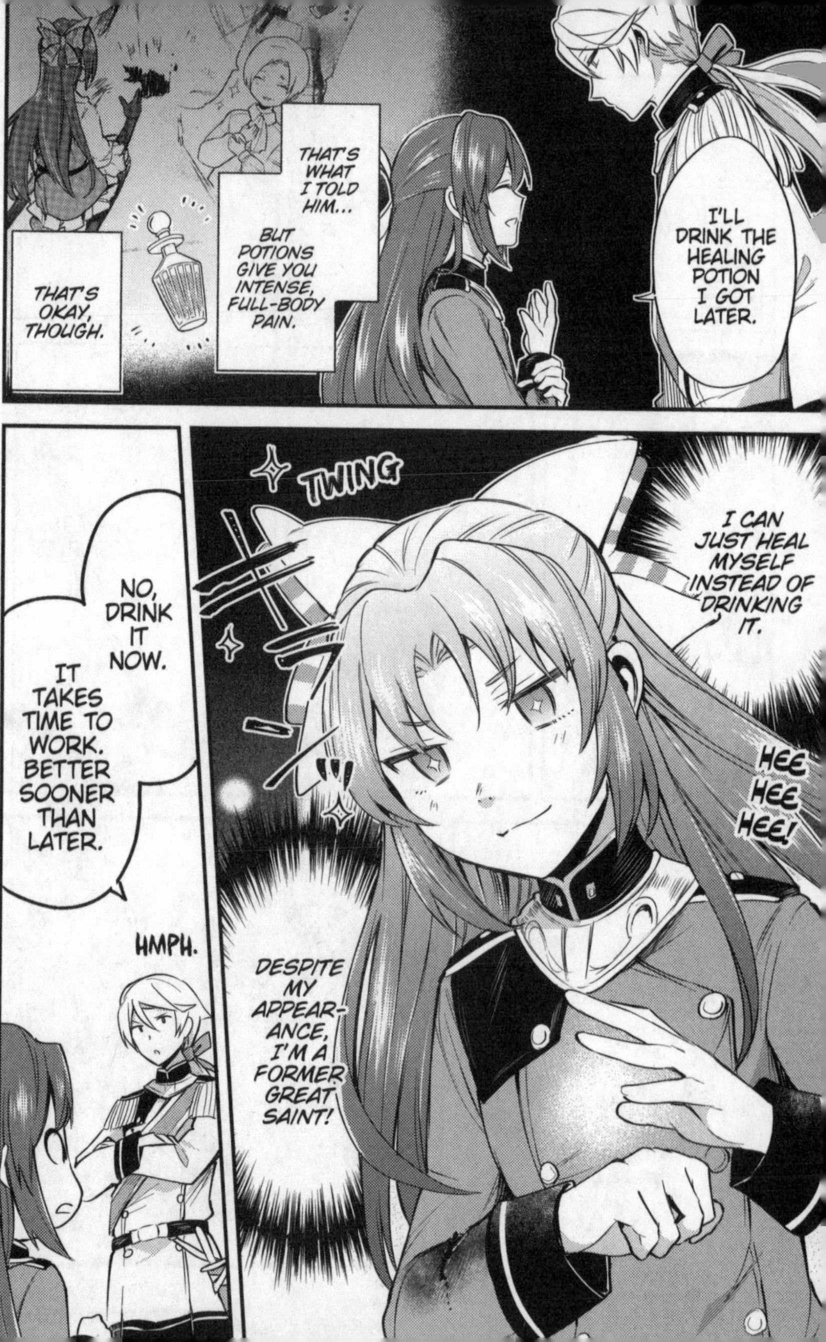
I'LL DRINK THE HEALING POTION I GOT LATER.
THAT'S WHAT I TOLD HIM...
BUT POTIONS GIVE YOU INTENSE, FULL-BODY PAIN.
THAT'S OKAY, THOUGH.
TWING
I CAN JUST HEAL MYSELF INSTEAD OF DRINKING IT.
HEE HEE HEE!
DESPITE MY APPEARANCE, I'M A FORMER GREAT SAINT!
NO, DRINK IT NOW.
IT TAKES TIME TO WORK. BETTER SOONER THAN LATER.
HMPH.

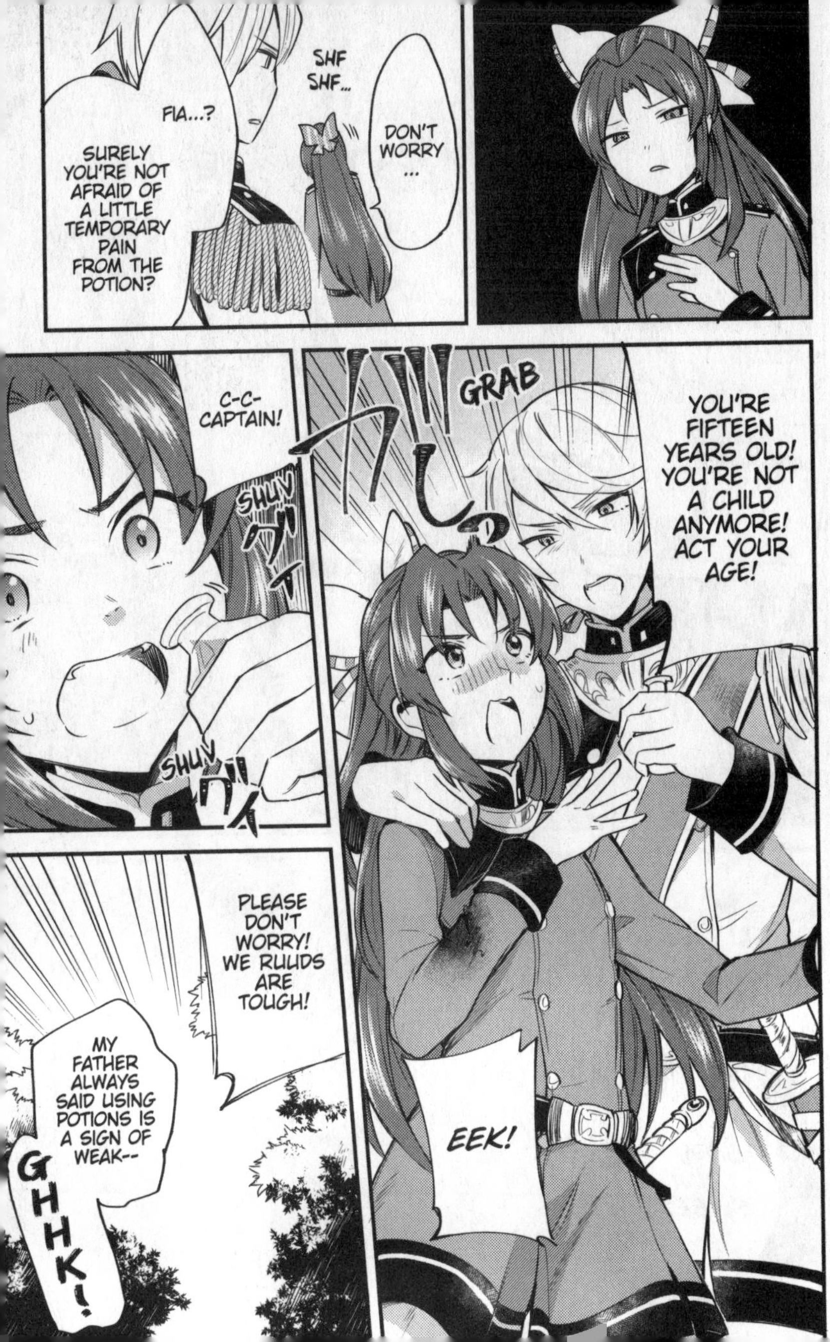
SHF SHF...
DON'T WORRY ...
FIA...?
SURELY YOU'RE NOT AFRAID OF A LITTLE TEMPORARY PAIN FROM THE POTION?
GRAB
YOU'RE FIFTEEN YEARS OLD! YOU'RE NOT A CHILD ANYMORE! ACT YOUR AGE!
EEK!
C-C-CAPTAIN!
SHUV
SHUV
PLEASE DON'T WORRY! WE RUUDS ARE TOUGH!
MY FATHER ALWAYS SAID USING POTIONS IS A SIGN OF WEAK--
GHHK!

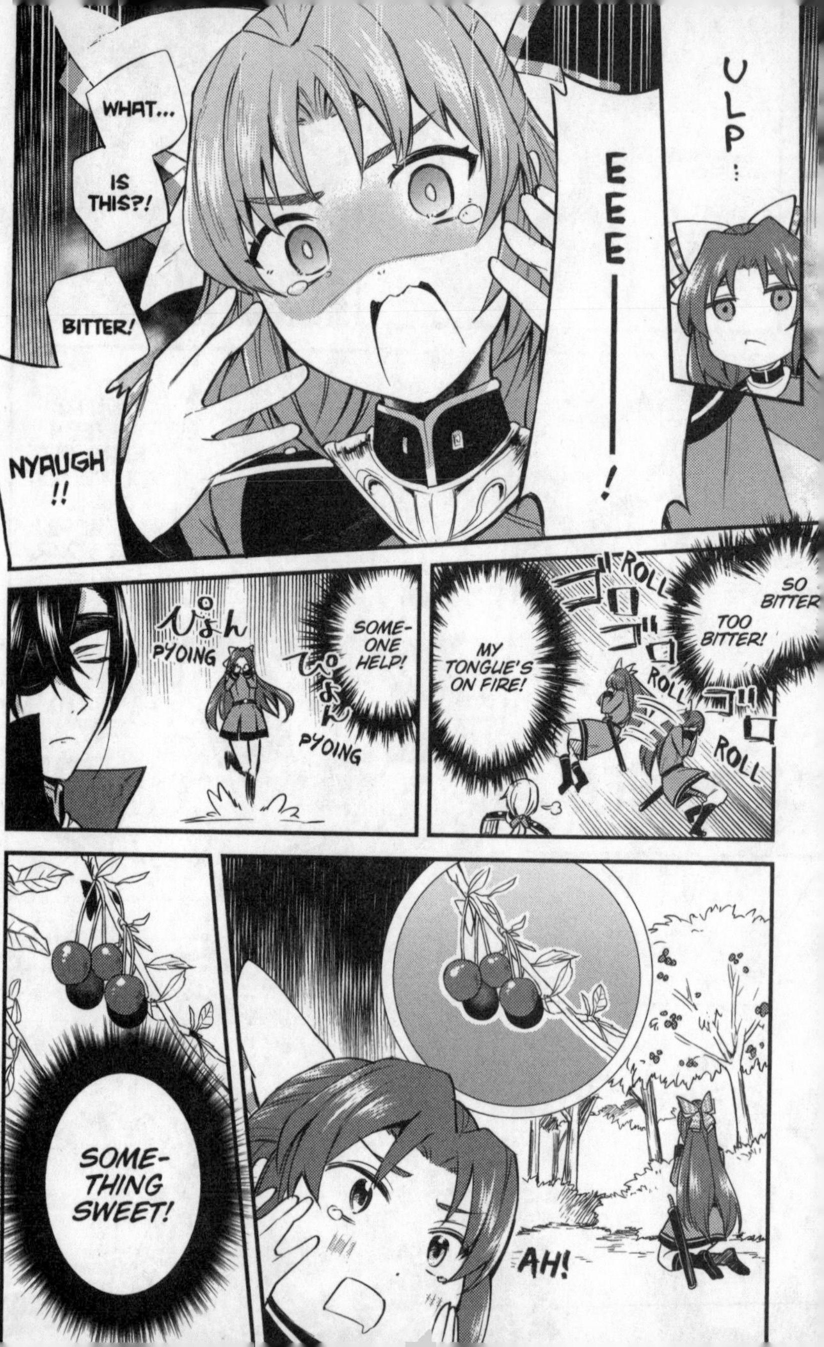
ULP...
EEE—!
WHAT... IS THIS?!
BITTER!
NYAUGH!!
SO BITTER
TOO BITTER!
ゴロ ROLL
ゴロ ROLL
ゴロ ROLL
MY TONGUE'S ON FIRE!
SOME-ONE HELP!
ぴょん PYOING
ぴょん PYOING
AH!
SOME-THING SWEET!

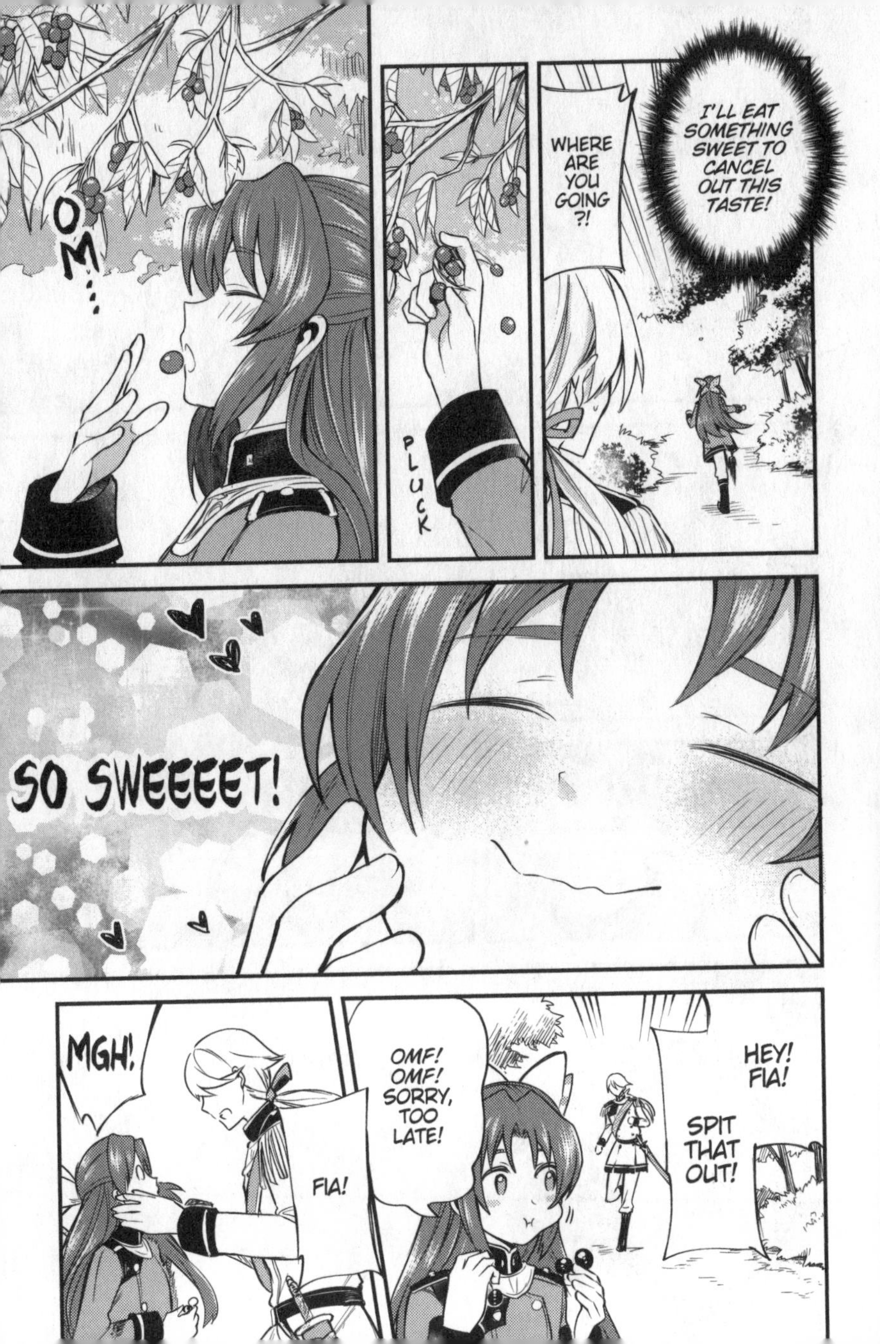
I'LL EAT SOMETHING SWEET TO CANCEL OUT THIS TASTE!
WHERE ARE YOU GOING ?!
PLUCK
OM...
SO SWEEEEET!
HEY! FIA!
SPIT THAT OUT!
OMF! OMF! SORRY, TOO LATE!
MGH!
FIA!

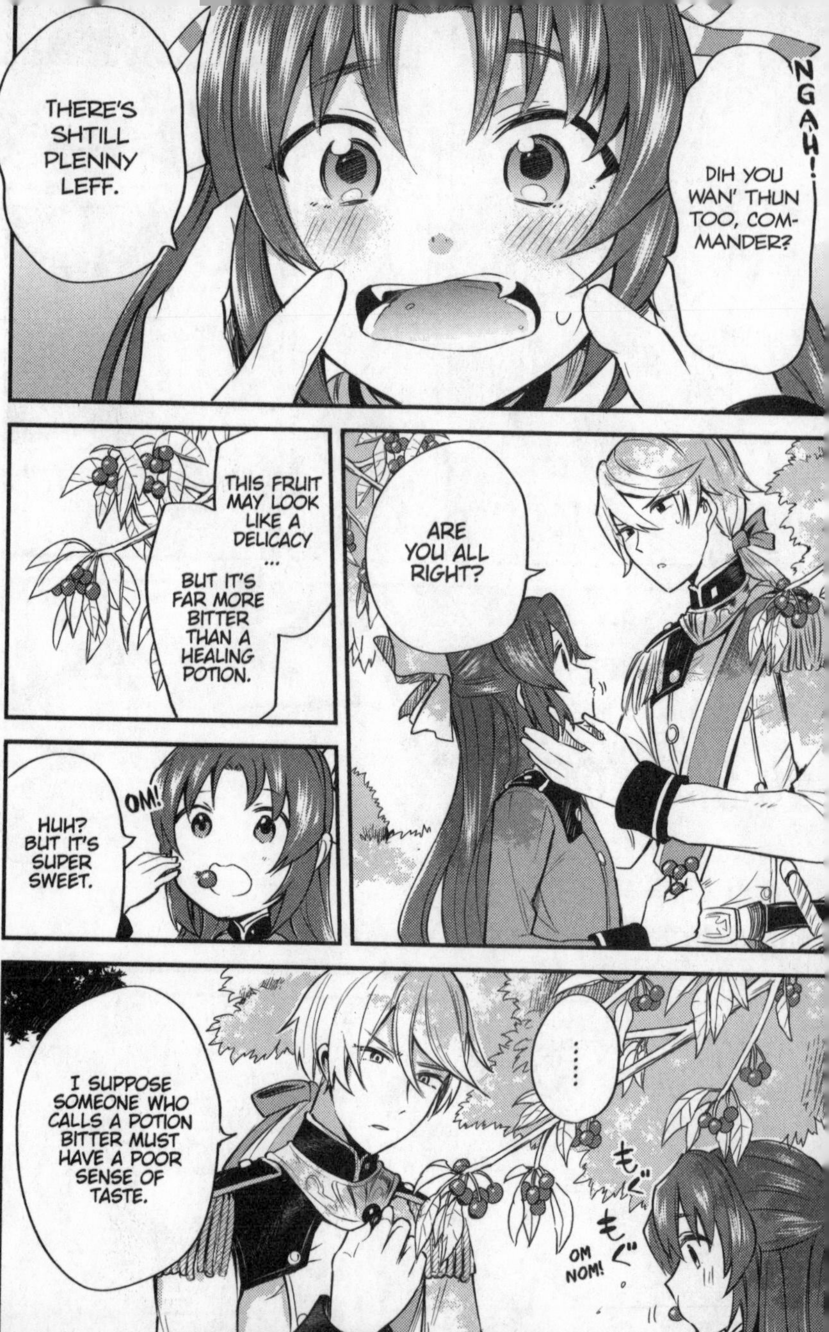
NGAH!
DIH YOU WAN' THUN TOO, COM-MANDER?
THERE'S SHTILL PLENNY LEFF.
ARE YOU ALL RIGHT?
THIS FRUIT MAY LOOK LIKE A DELICACY ...
BUT IT'S FAR MORE BITTER THAN A HEALING POTION.
OM!
HUH? BUT IT'S SUPER SWEET.
......
もぐ もぐ
OM NOM!
I SUPPOSE SOMEONE WHO CALLS A POTION BITTER MUST HAVE A POOR SENSE OF TASTE.

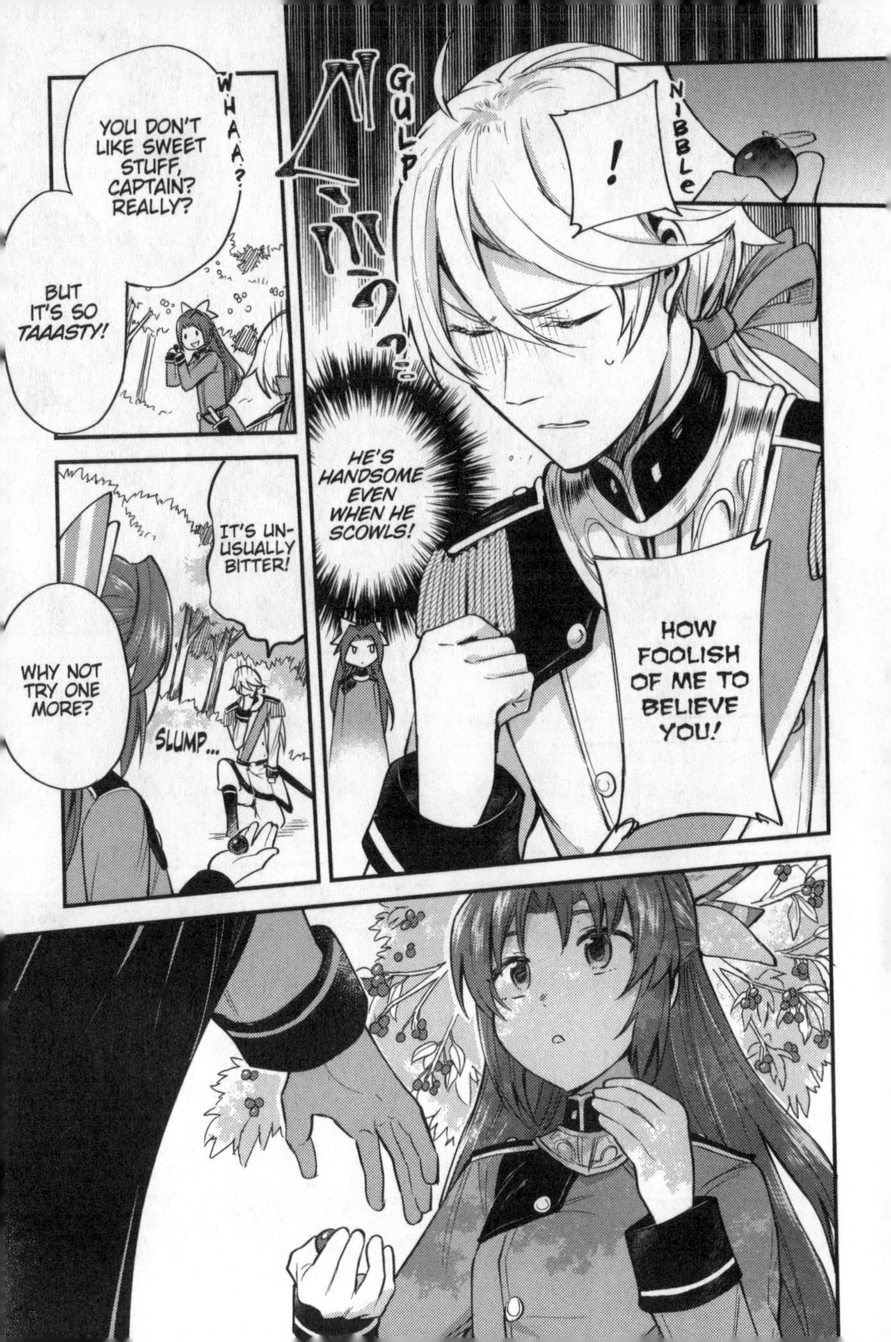
NIBBLE
!
GULP
HE'S HANDSOME EVEN WHEN HE SCOWLS!
HOW FOOLISH OF ME TO BELIEVE YOU!
WHAAA?
YOU DON'T LIKE SWEET STUFF, CAPTAIN? REALLY?
BUT IT'S SO *TAAASTY!*
IT'S UN-USUALLY BITTER!
SLUMP...
WHY NOT TRY ONE MORE?

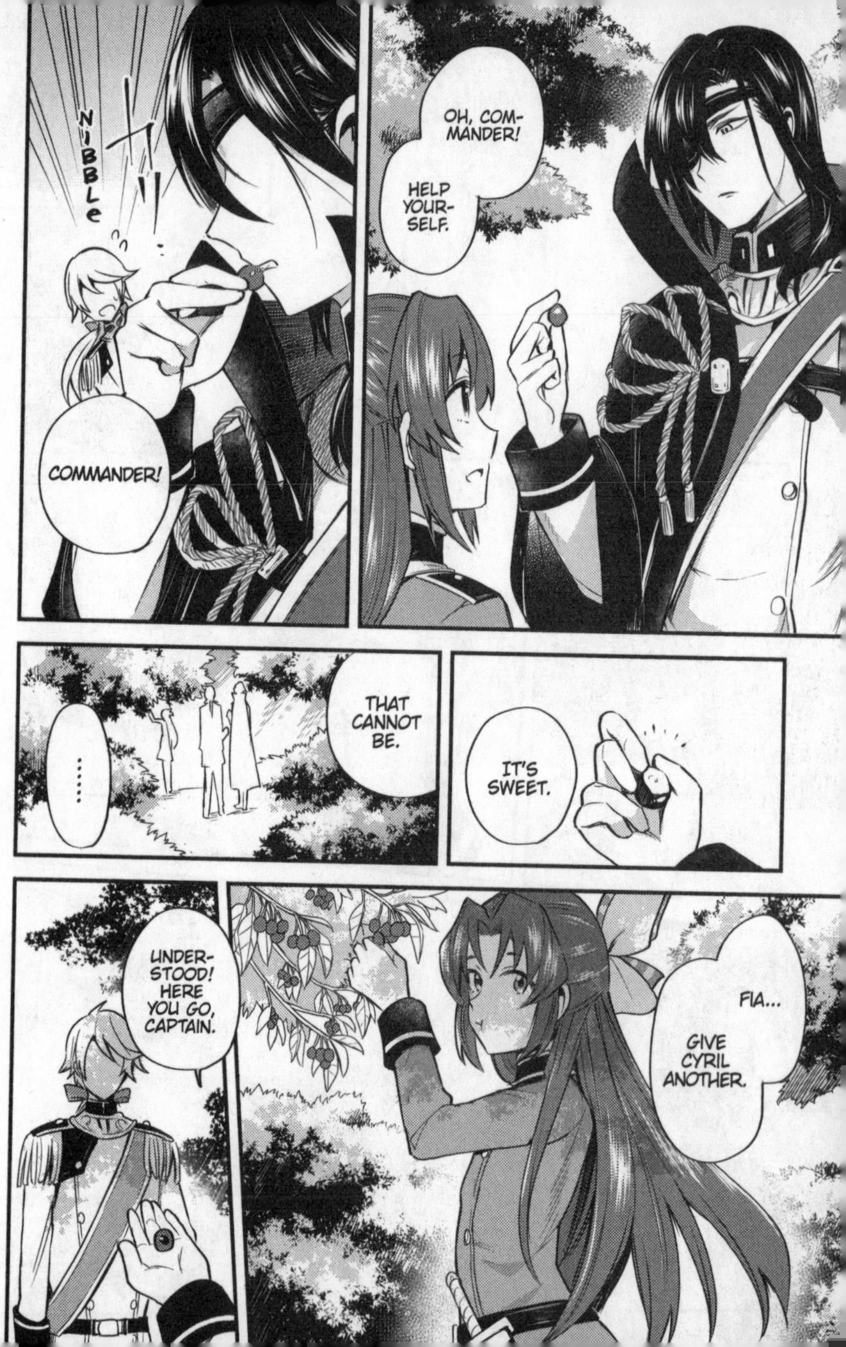

OH, COM-MANDER!
HELP YOUR-SELF.
NIBBLE
COMMANDER!
IT'S SWEET.
THAT CANNOT BE.
......
FIA...
GIVE CYRIL ANOTHER.
UNDER-STOOD! HERE YOU GO, CAPTAIN.

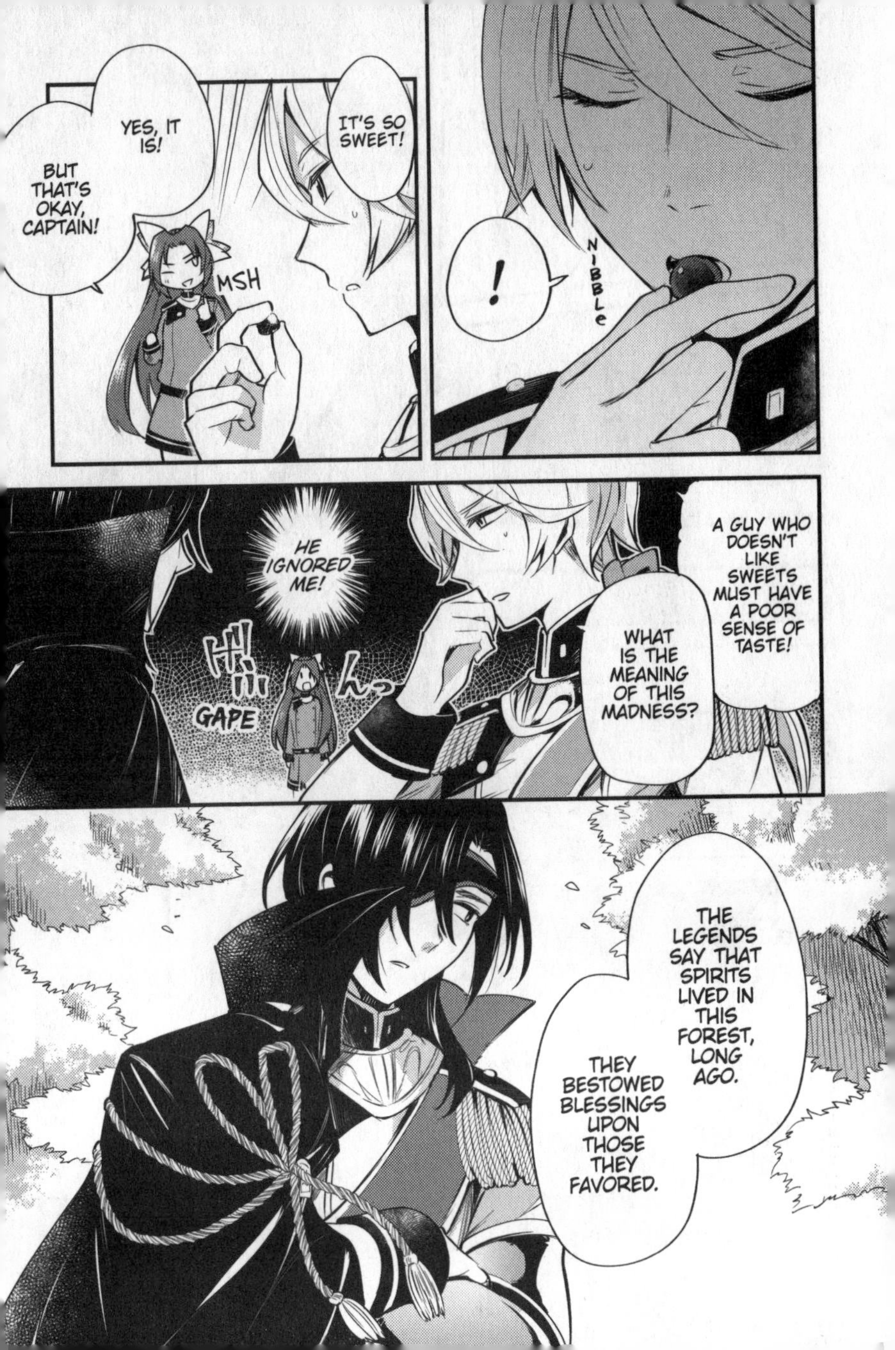
!
NIBBLE
IT'S SO SWEET!
YES, IT IS!
BUT THAT'S OKAY, CAPTAIN!
MSH
A GUY WHO DOESN'T LIKE SWEETS MUST HAVE A POOR SENSE OF TASTE!
WHAT IS THE MEANING OF THIS MADNESS?
HE IGNORED ME!
GAPE
THE LEGENDS SAY THAT SPIRITS LIVED IN THIS FOREST, LONG AGO.
THEY BESTOWED BLESSINGS UPON THOSE THEY FAVORED.

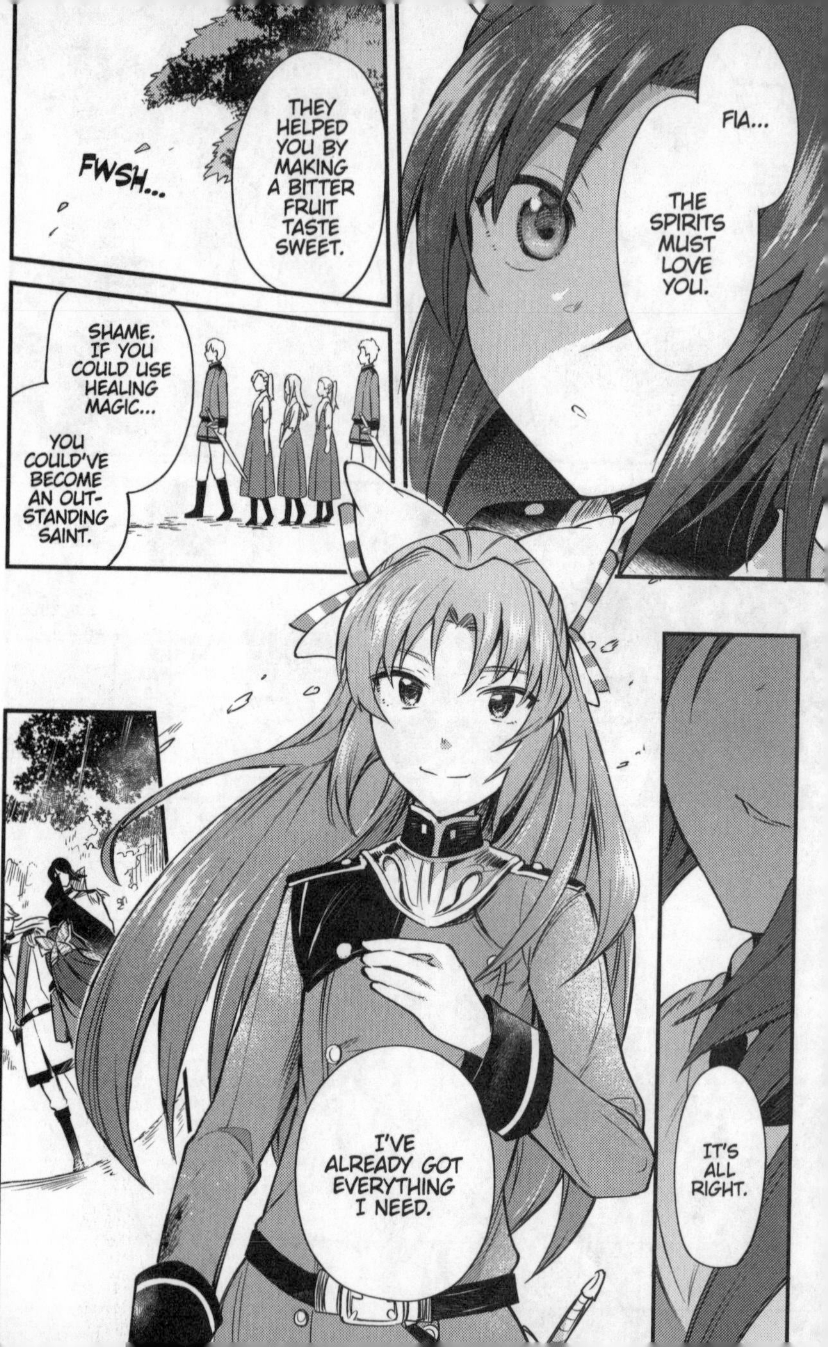
FIA...
THE SPIRITS MUST LOVE YOU.
THEY HELPED YOU BY MAKING A BITTER FRUIT TASTE SWEET.
FWSH...
SHAME. IF YOU COULD USE HEALING MAGIC...
YOU COULD'VE BECOME AN OUT-STANDING SAINT.
IT'S ALL RIGHT.
I'VE ALREADY GOT EVERYTHING I NEED.

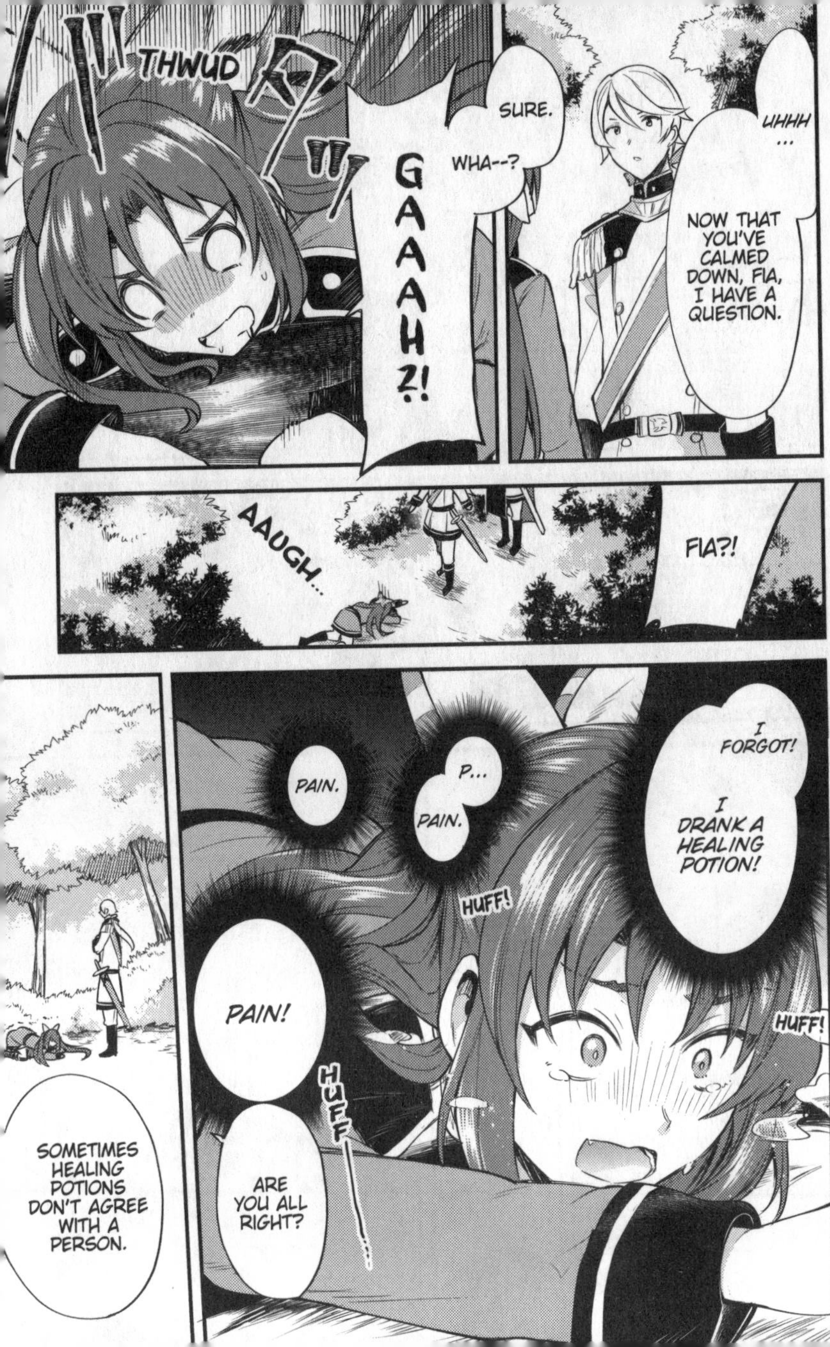
UHHH ...
NOW THAT YOU'VE CALMED DOWN, FIA, I HAVE A QUESTION.
SURE.
WHA--?
THWUD
GAAAAH?!
FIA?!
AAUGH...
I FORGOT!
I DRANK A HEALING POTION!
HUFF!
P... PAIN.
PAIN.
HUFF!
PAIN!
HUFF
ARE YOU ALL RIGHT?
SOMETIMES HEALING POTIONS DON'T AGREE WITH A PERSON.

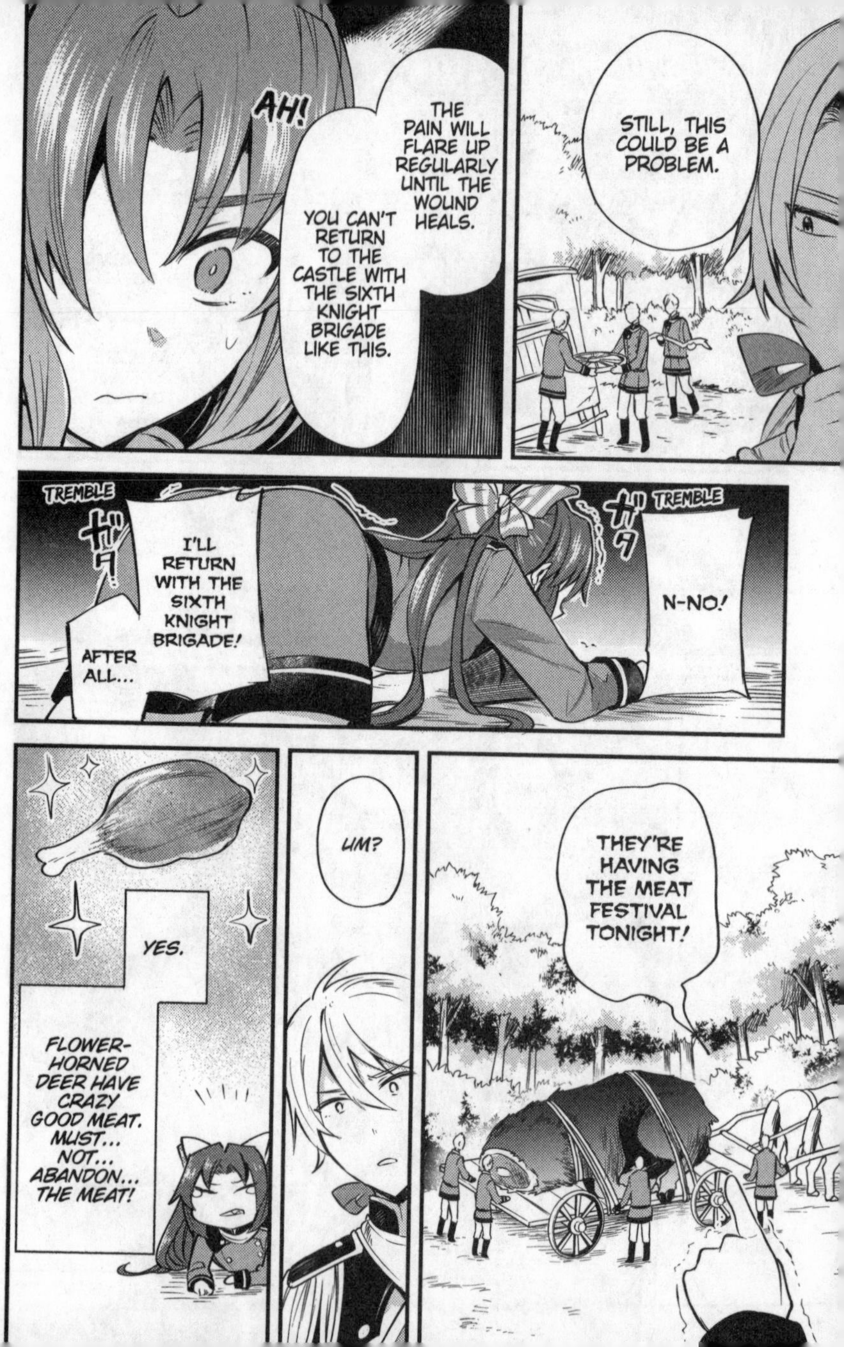
STILL, THIS COULD BE A PROBLEM.
AH!
THE PAIN WILL FLARE UP REGULARLY UNTIL THE WOUND HEALS.
YOU CAN'T RETURN TO THE CASTLE WITH THE SIXTH KNIGHT BRIGADE LIKE THIS.
TREMBLE
N-NO!
TREMBLE
I'LL RETURN WITH THE SIXTH KNIGHT BRIGADE!
AFTER ALL...
THEY'RE HAVING THE MEAT FESTIVAL TONIGHT!
UM?
YES.
FLOWER-HORNED DEER HAVE CRAZY GOOD MEAT. MUST... NOT... ABANDON... THE MEAT!

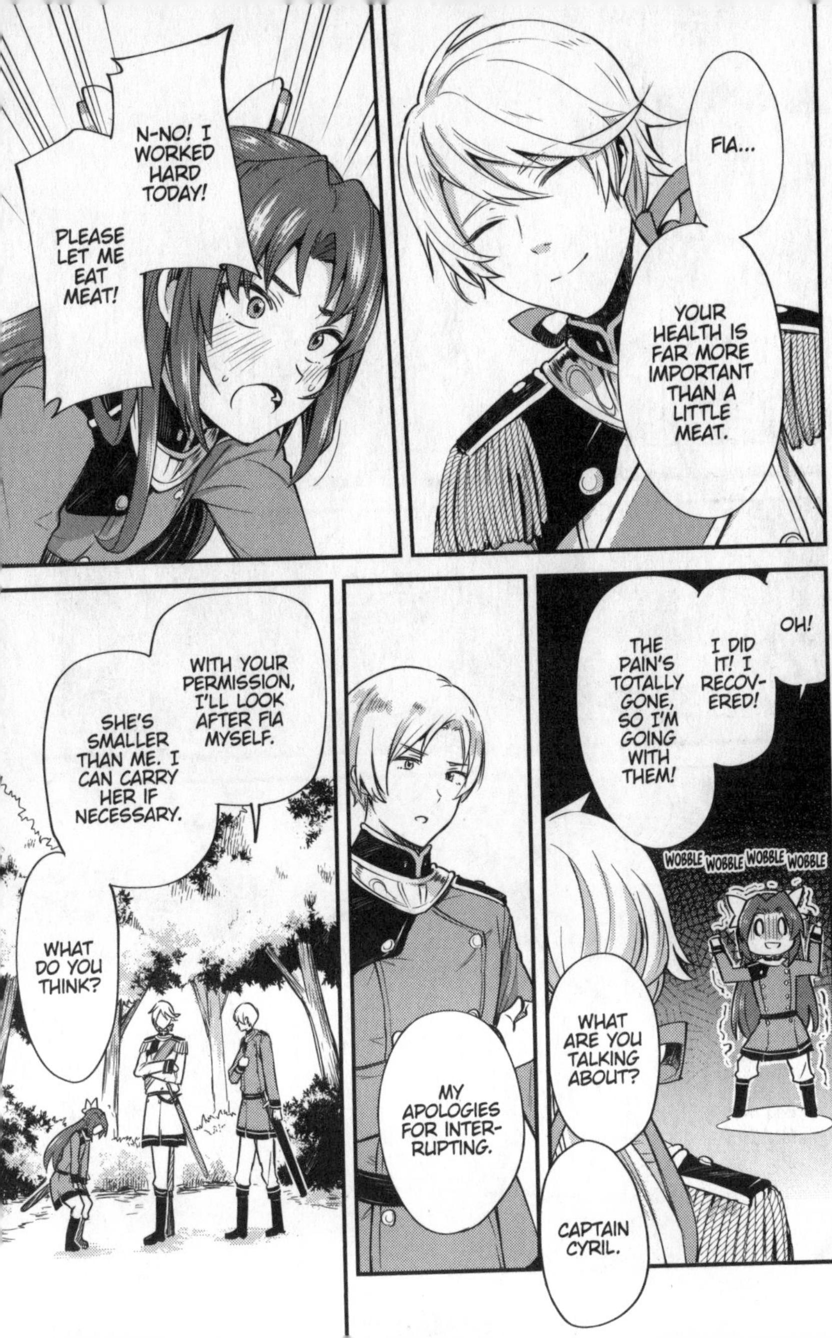
FIA...
YOUR HEALTH IS FAR MORE IMPORTANT THAN A LITTLE MEAT.
N-NO! I WORKED HARD TODAY!
PLEASE LET ME EAT MEAT!
OH!
I DID IT! I RECOVERED!
THE PAIN'S TOTALLY GONE, SO I'M GOING WITH THEM!
WOBBLE WOBBLE WOBBLE WOBBLE
WHAT ARE YOU TALKING ABOUT?
MY APOLOGIES FOR INTERRUPTING.
CAPTAIN CYRIL.
WITH YOUR PERMISSION, I'LL LOOK AFTER FIA MYSELF.
SHE'S SMALLER THAN ME. I CAN CARRY HER IF NECESSARY.
WHAT DO YOU THINK?

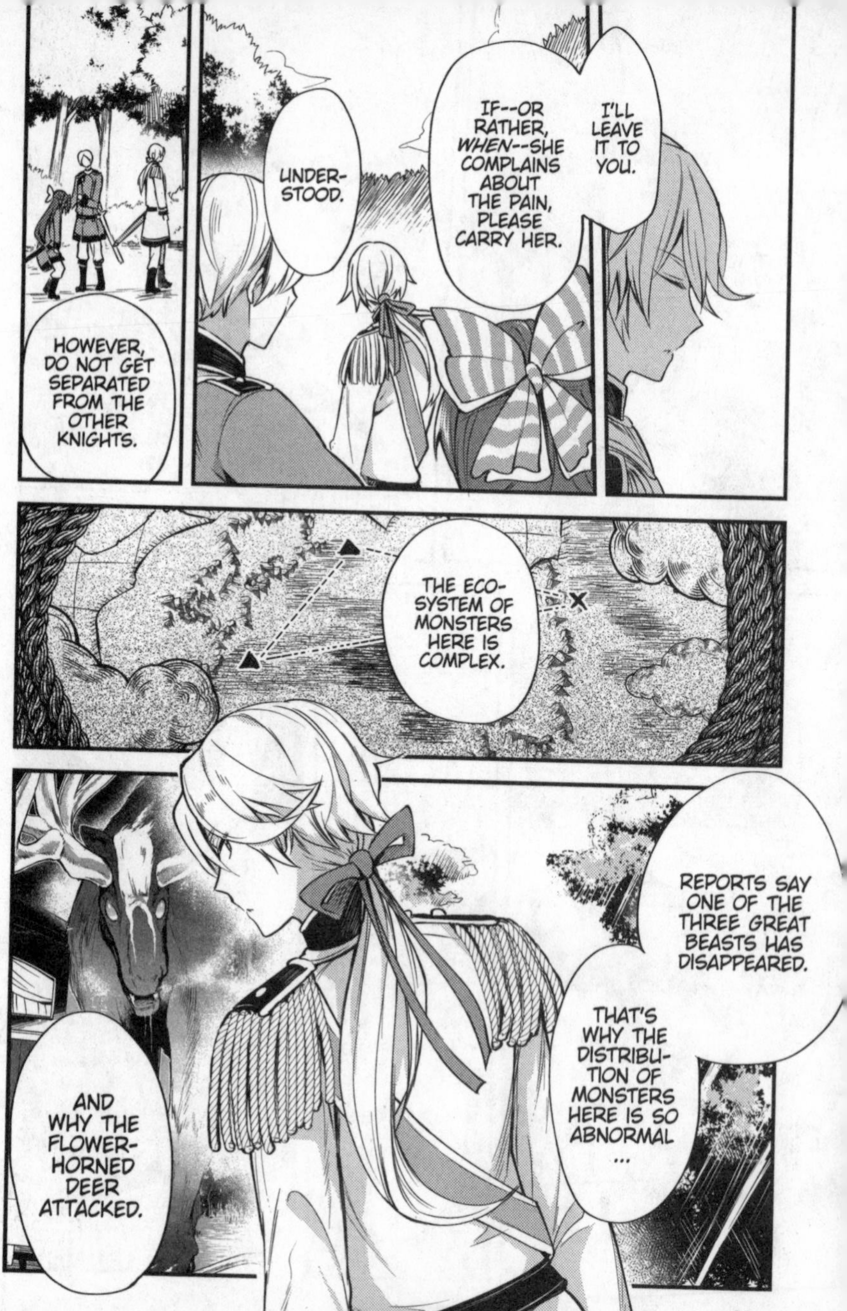
I'LL LEAVE IT TO YOU.
IF--OR RATHER, *WHEN*--SHE COMPLAINS ABOUT THE PAIN, PLEASE CARRY HER.
UNDER-STOOD.
HOWEVER, DO NOT GET SEPARATED FROM THE OTHER KNIGHTS.
THE ECO-SYSTEM OF MONSTERS HERE IS COMPLEX.
REPORTS SAY ONE OF THE THREE GREAT BEASTS HAS DISAPPEARED.
THAT'S WHY THE DISTRIBU-TION OF MONSTERS HERE IS SO ABNORMAL ...
AND WHY THE FLOWER-HORNED DEER ATTACKED.

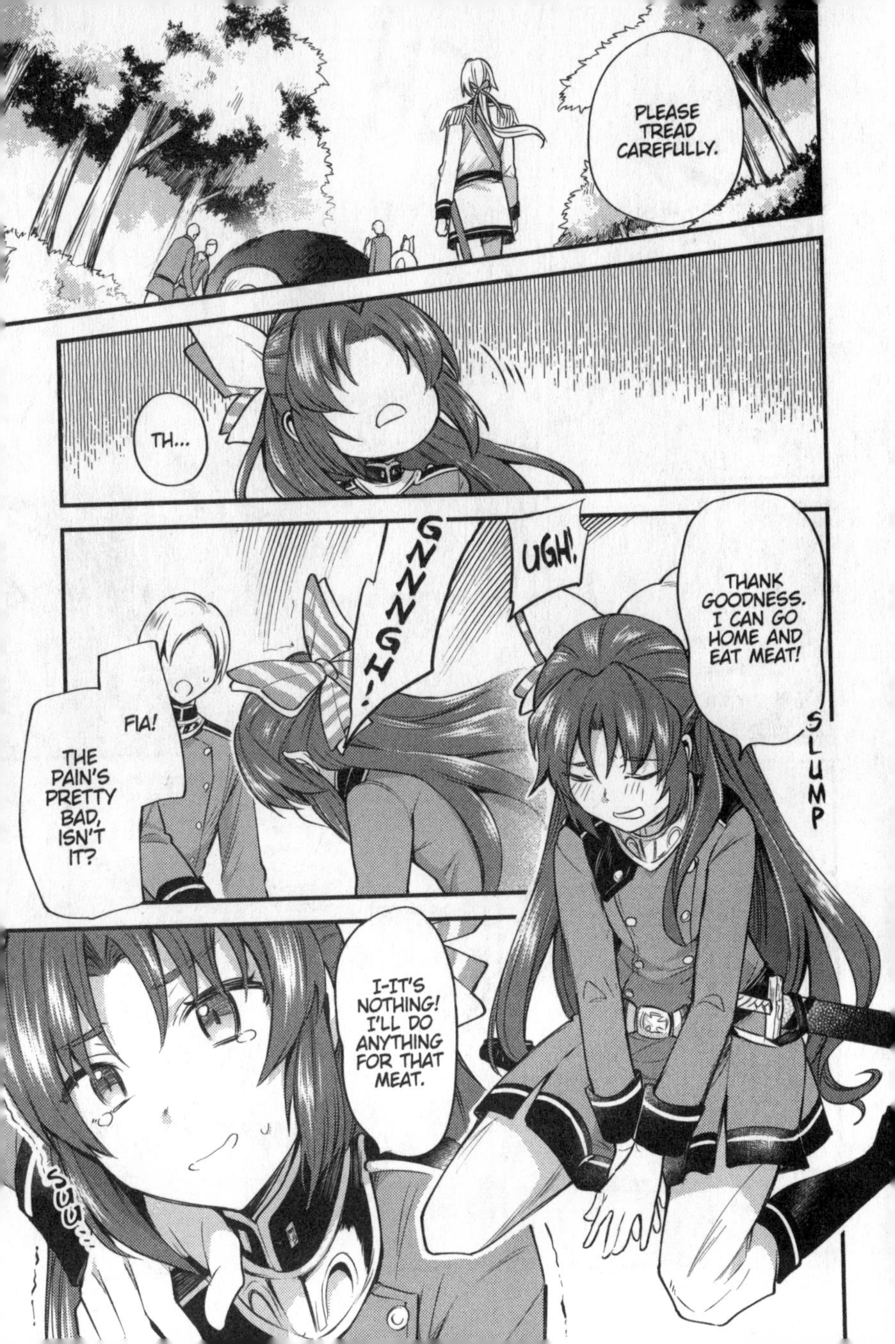
PLEASE TREAD CAREFULLY.
TH...
THANK GOODNESS. I CAN GO HOME AND EAT MEAT!
SLUMP
UGH!
GNNNGH!
FIA!
THE PAIN'S PRETTY BAD, ISN'T IT?
I-IT'S NOTHING! I'LL DO ANYTHING FOR THAT MEAT.
SUUU...

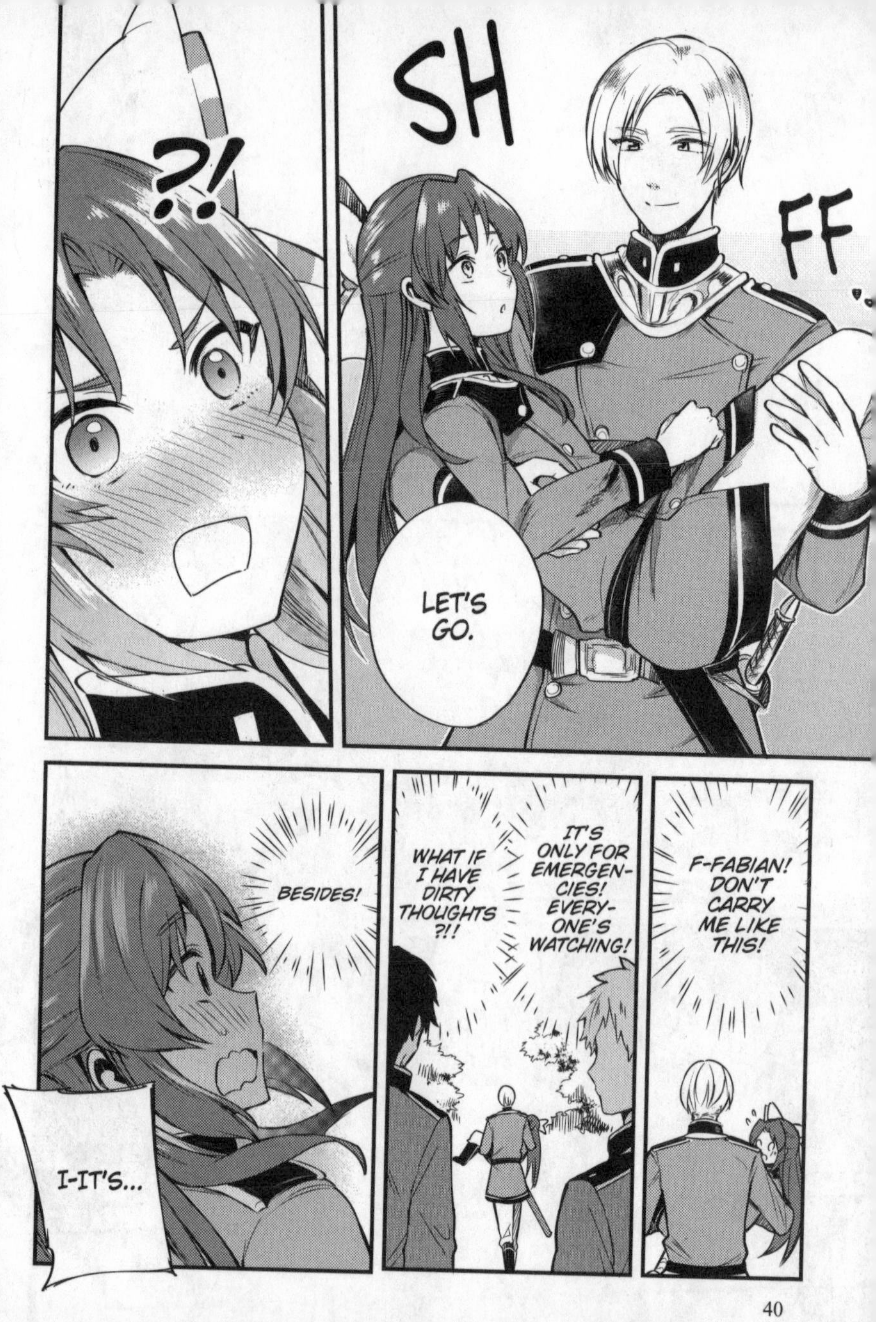
SH
FF
LET'S GO.
?!
F-FABIAN! DON'T CARRY ME LIKE THIS!
IT'S ONLY FOR EMERGENCIES! EVERYONE'S WATCHING!
WHAT IF I HAVE DIRTY THOUGHTS?!!
BESIDES!
I-IT'S...

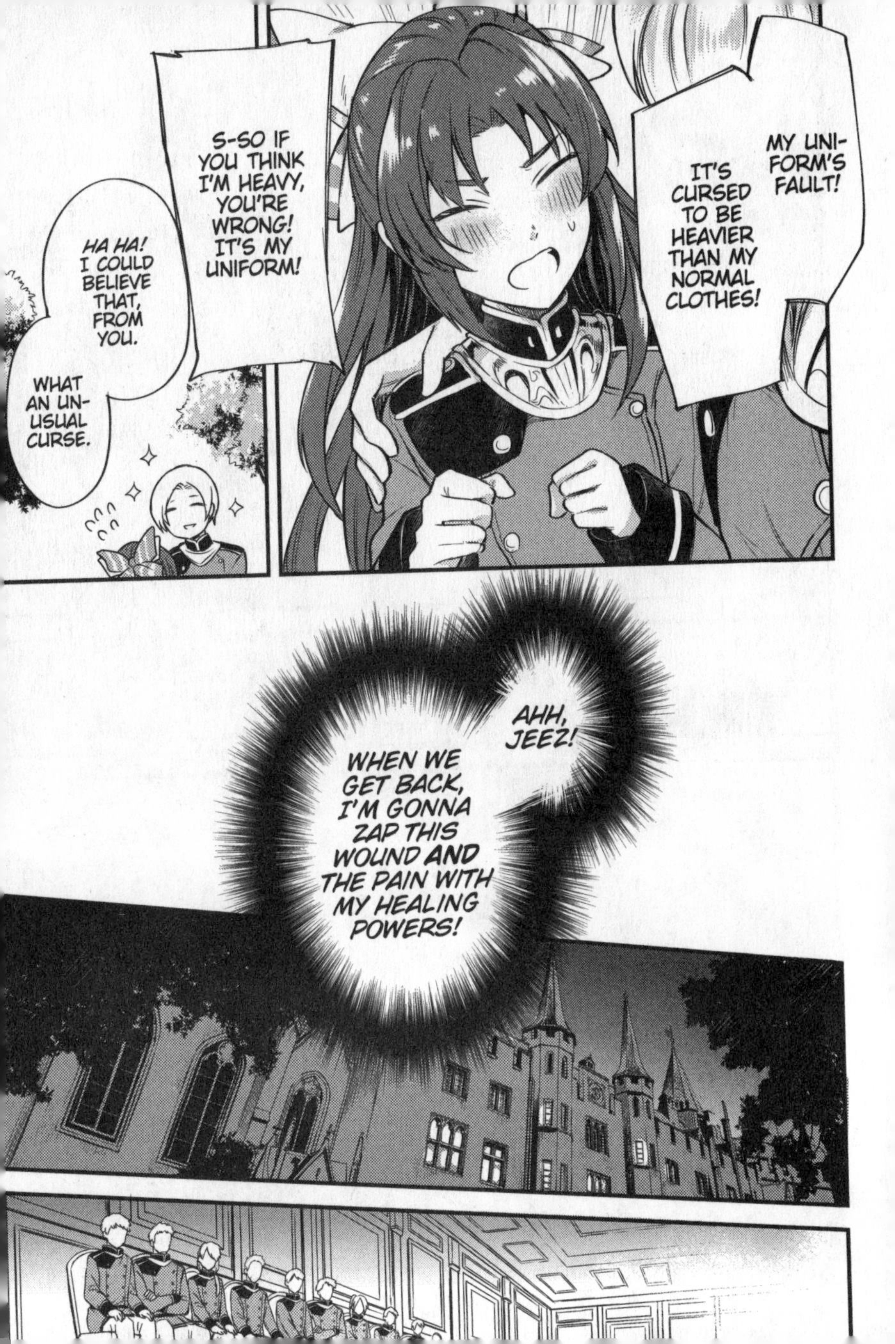
MY UNIFORM'S FAULT!
IT'S CURSED TO BE HEAVIER THAN MY NORMAL CLOTHES!
S-SO IF YOU THINK I'M HEAVY, YOU'RE WRONG! IT'S MY UNIFORM!
HA HA! I COULD BELIEVE THAT, FROM YOU.
WHAT AN UNUSUAL CURSE.
AHH, JEEZ!
WHEN WE GET BACK, I'M GONNA ZAP THIS WOUND AND THE PAIN WITH MY HEALING POWERS!

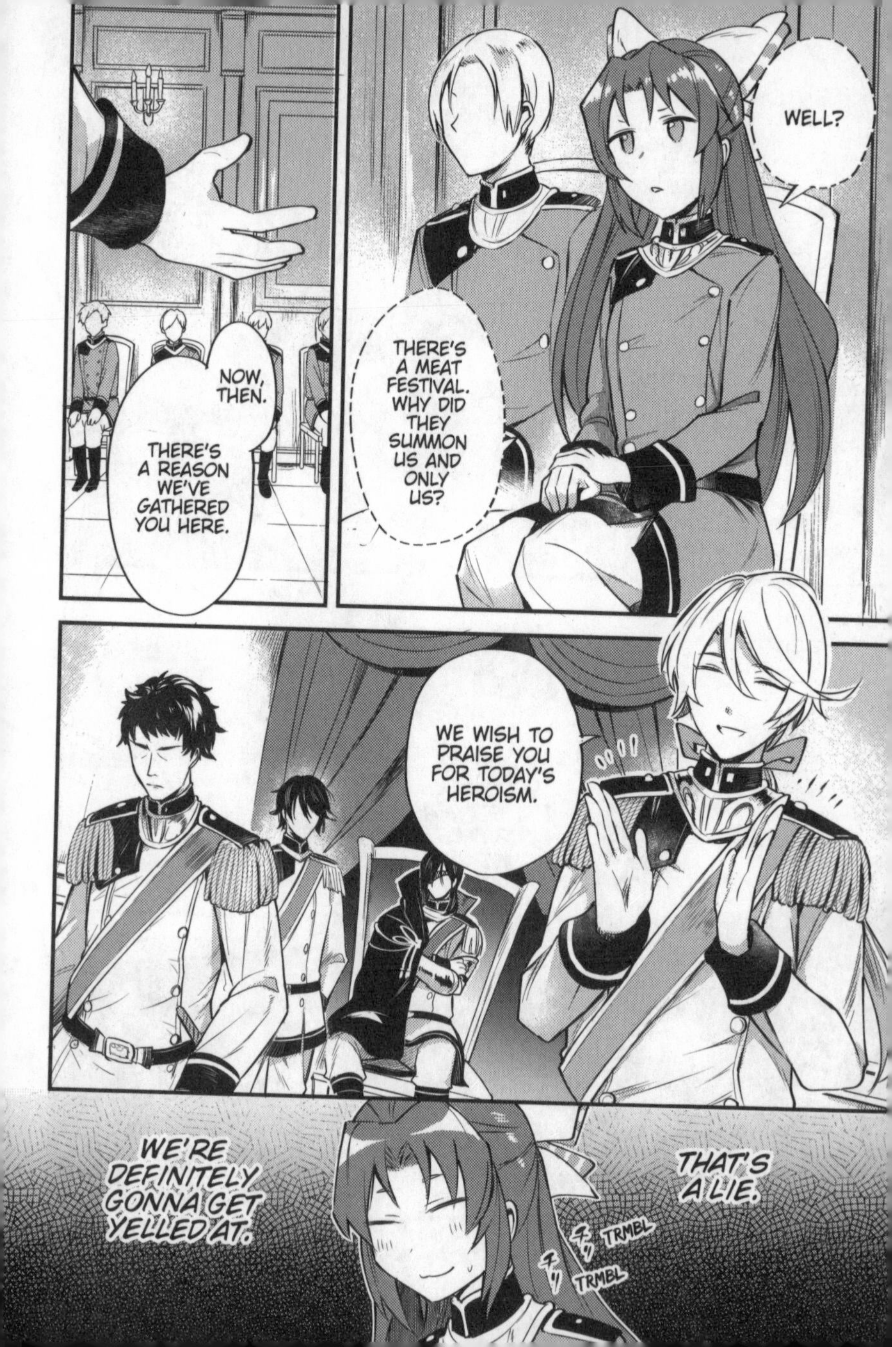
WELL?
THERE'S A MEAT FESTIVAL. WHY DID THEY SUMMON US AND ONLY US?
NOW, THEN.
THERE'S A REASON WE'VE GATHERED YOU HERE.
WE WISH TO PRAISE YOU FOR TODAY'S HEROISM.
THAT'S A LIE.
TRMBL
TRMBL
WE'RE DEFINITELY GONNA GET YELLED AT.

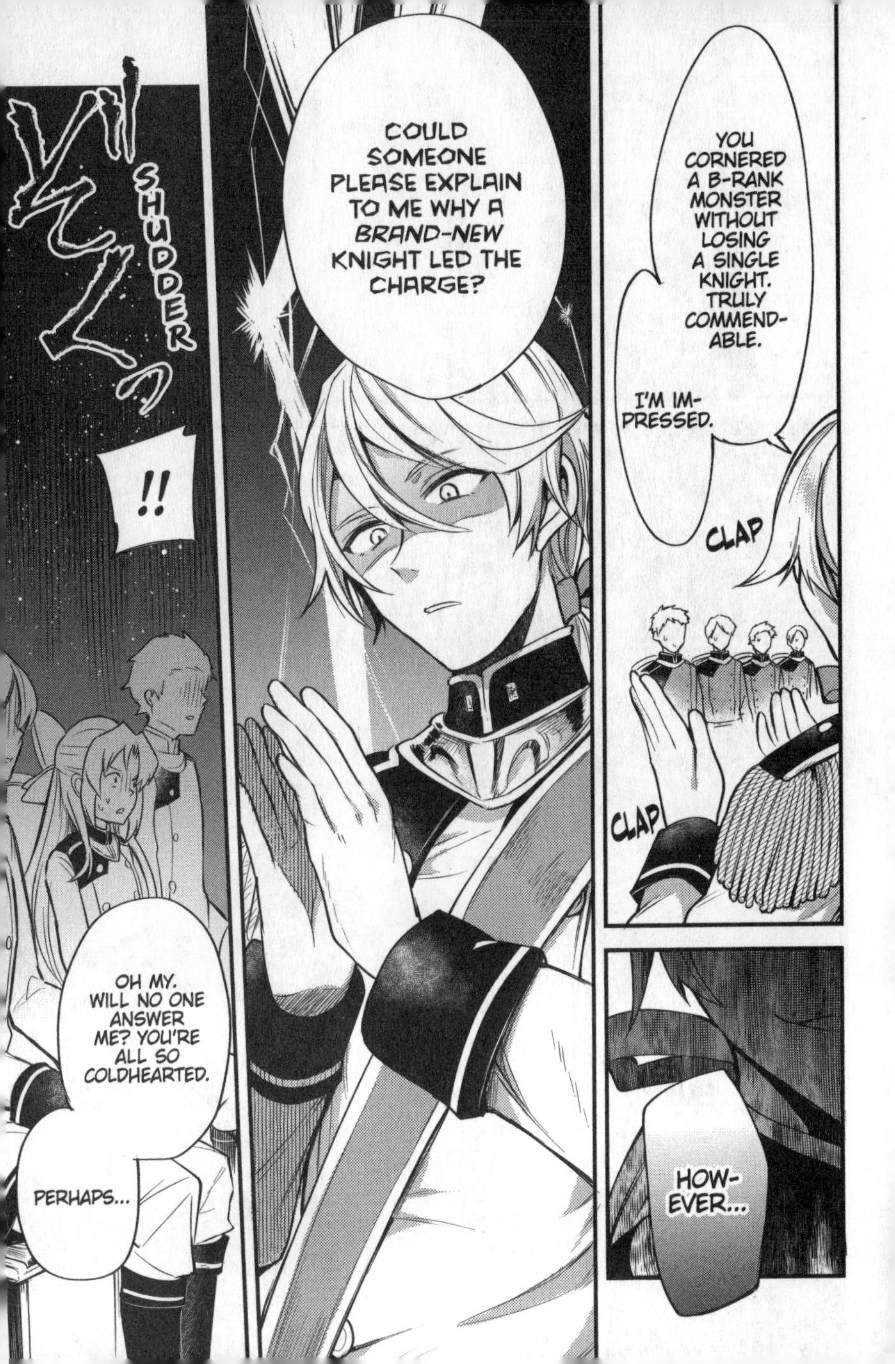
YOU CORNERED A B-RANK MONSTER WITHOUT LOSING A SINGLE KNIGHT. TRULY COMMEND-ABLE.
I'M IM-PRESSED.
CLAP
CLAP
HOW-EVER...
COULD SOMEONE PLEASE EXPLAIN TO ME WHY A BRAND-NEW KNIGHT LED THE CHARGE?
SHUDDER
!!
OH MY. WILL NO ONE ANSWER ME? YOU'RE ALL SO COLDHEARTED.
PERHAPS...

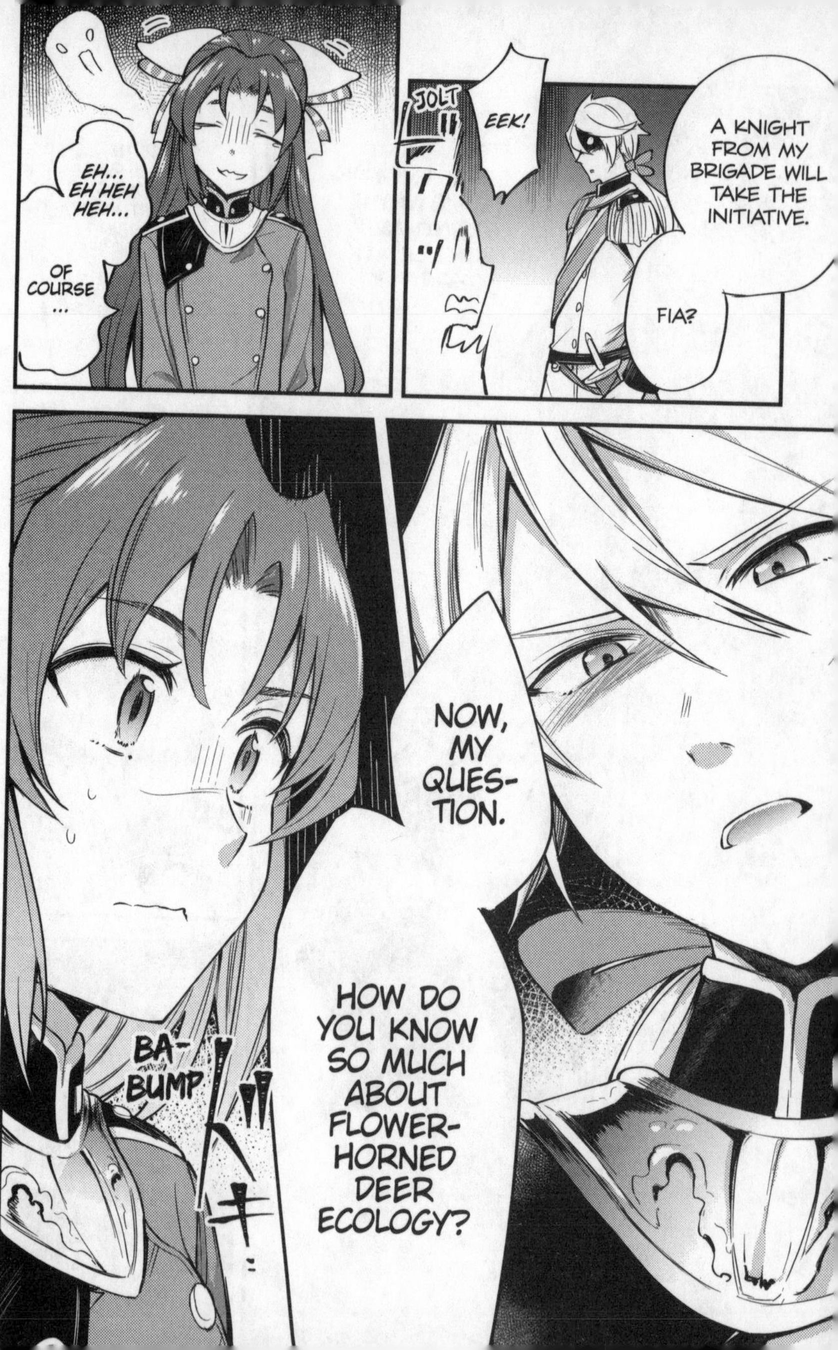
A KNIGHT FROM MY BRIGADE WILL TAKE THE INITIATIVE.
EEK!
JOLT
FIA?
EH... EH HEH HEH...
OF COURSE ...
NOW, MY QUES-TION.
HOW DO YOU KNOW SO MUCH ABOUT FLOWER-HORNED DEER ECOLOGY?
BA-BUMP

A Tale of the
Secret
Saint

A Tale of the
Secret
Saint

Book 6: Meat Festival

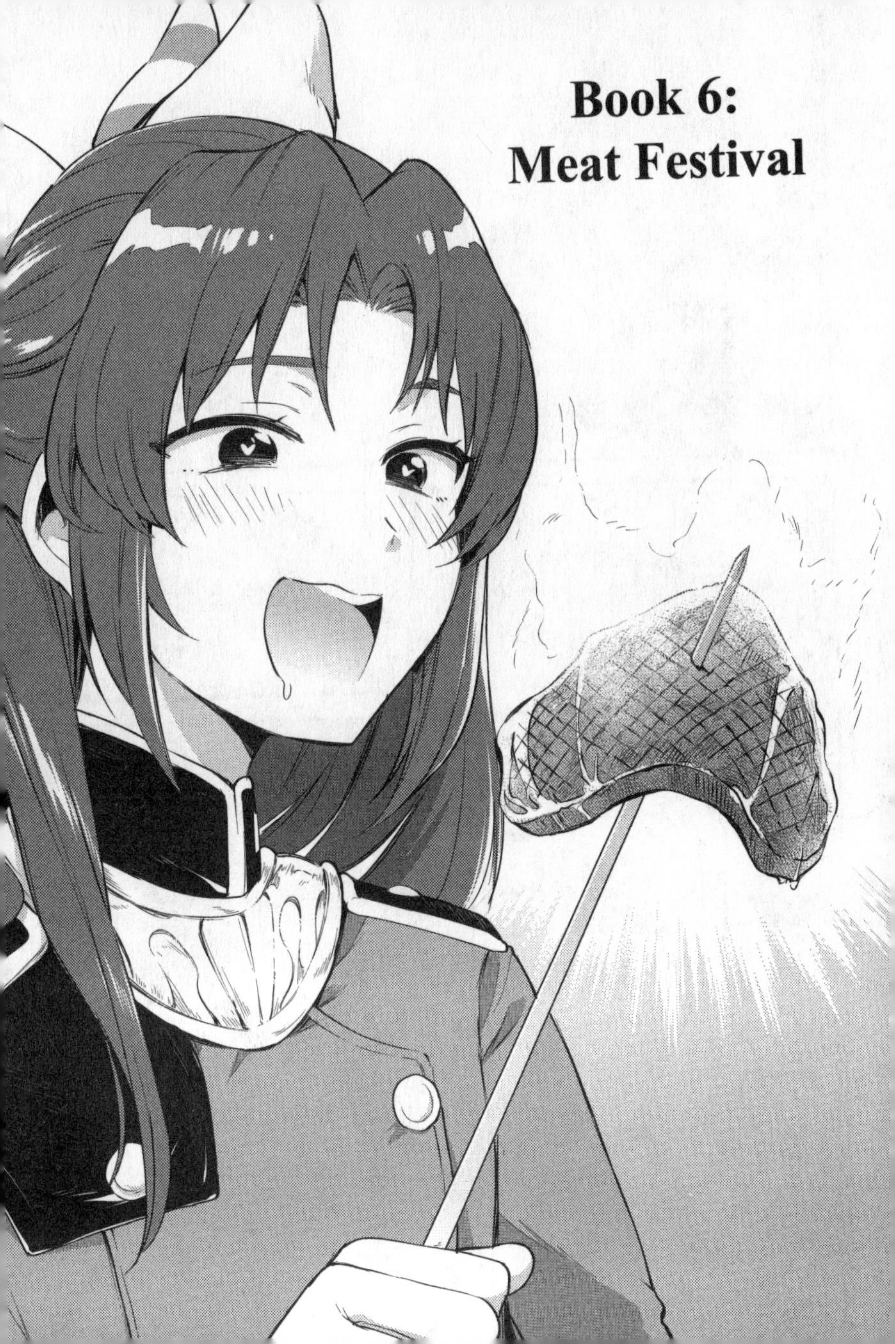

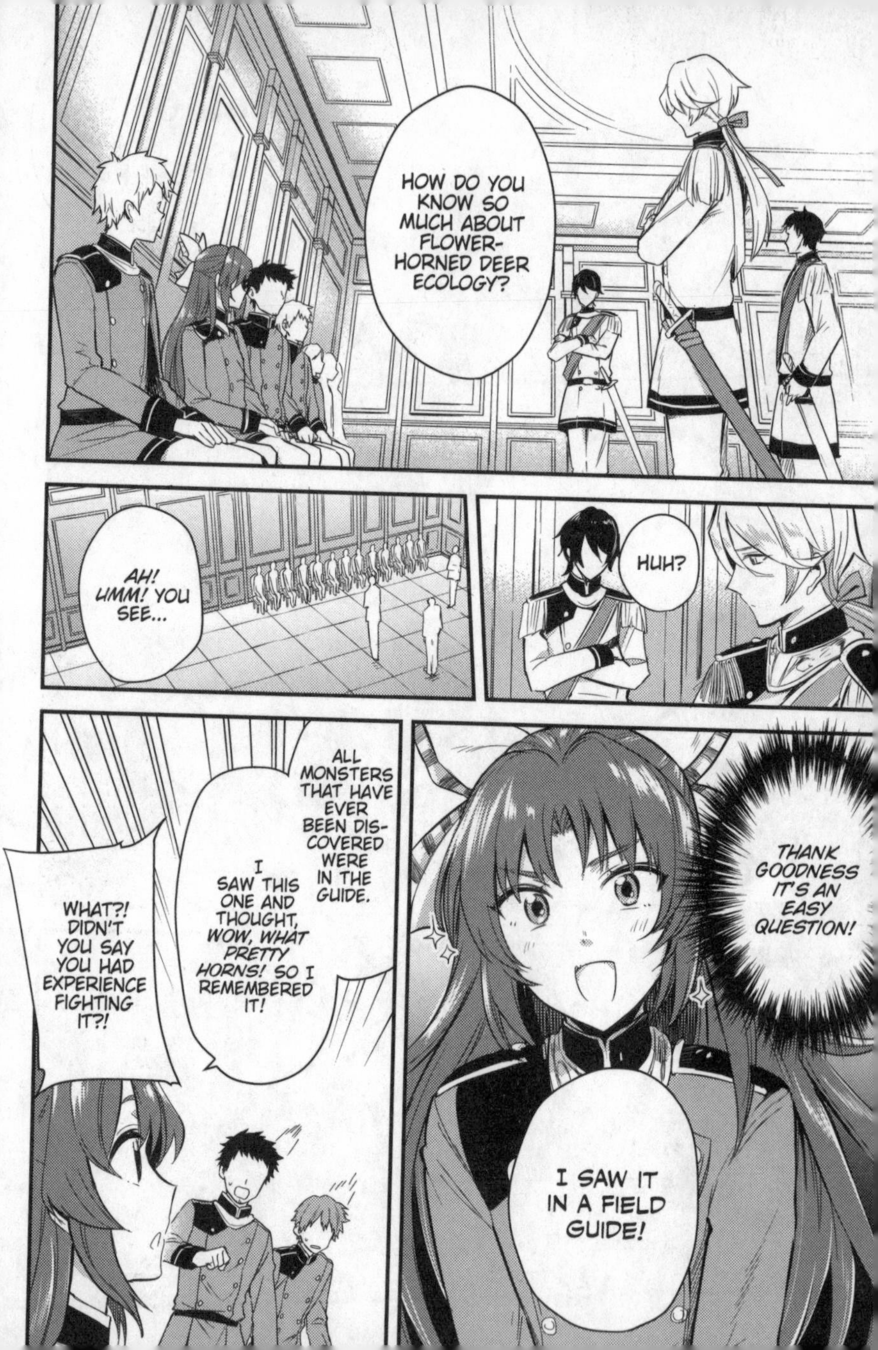
HOW DO YOU KNOW SO MUCH ABOUT FLOWER-HORNED DEER ECOLOGY?
HUH?
AH! UMM! YOU SEE...
THANK GOODNESS IT'S AN EASY QUESTION!
I SAW IT IN A FIELD GUIDE!
ALL MONSTERS THAT HAVE EVER BEEN DIS-COVERED WERE IN THE GUIDE.
I SAW THIS ONE AND THOUGHT, *WOW, WHAT PRETTY HORNS!* SO I REMEMBERED IT!
WHAT?! DIDN'T YOU SAY YOU HAD EXPERIENCE FIGHTING IT?!

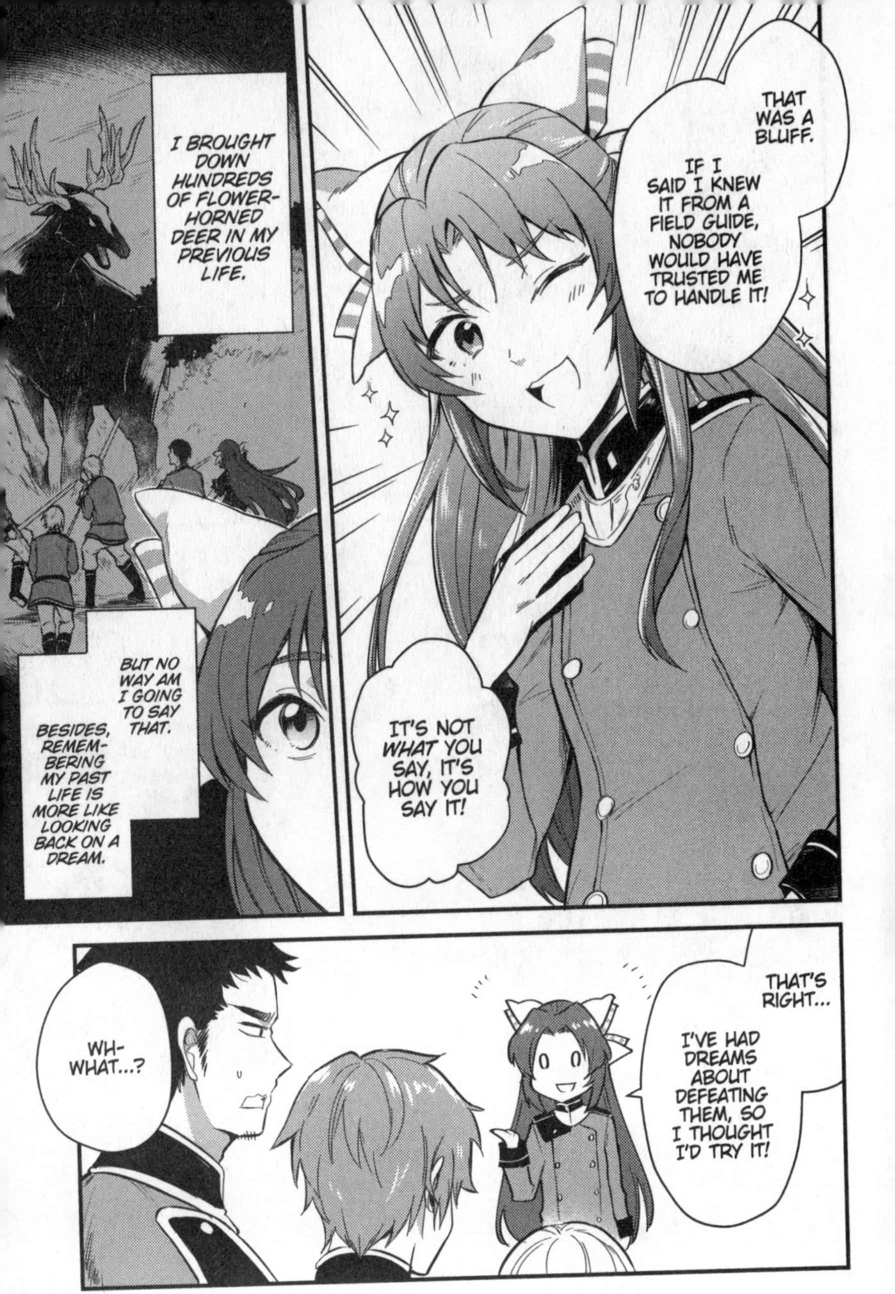
THAT WAS A BLUFF.
IF I SAID I KNEW IT FROM A FIELD GUIDE, NOBODY WOULD HAVE TRUSTED ME TO HANDLE IT!
IT'S NOT *WHAT* YOU SAY, IT'S HOW YOU SAY IT!
I BROUGHT DOWN HUNDREDS OF FLOWER-HORNED DEER IN MY PREVIOUS LIFE.
BUT NO WAY AM I GOING TO SAY THAT.
BESIDES, REMEMBERING MY PAST LIFE IS MORE LIKE LOOKING BACK ON A DREAM.
THAT'S RIGHT...
I'VE HAD DREAMS ABOUT DEFEATING THEM, SO I THOUGHT I'D TRY IT!
WH-WHAT...?

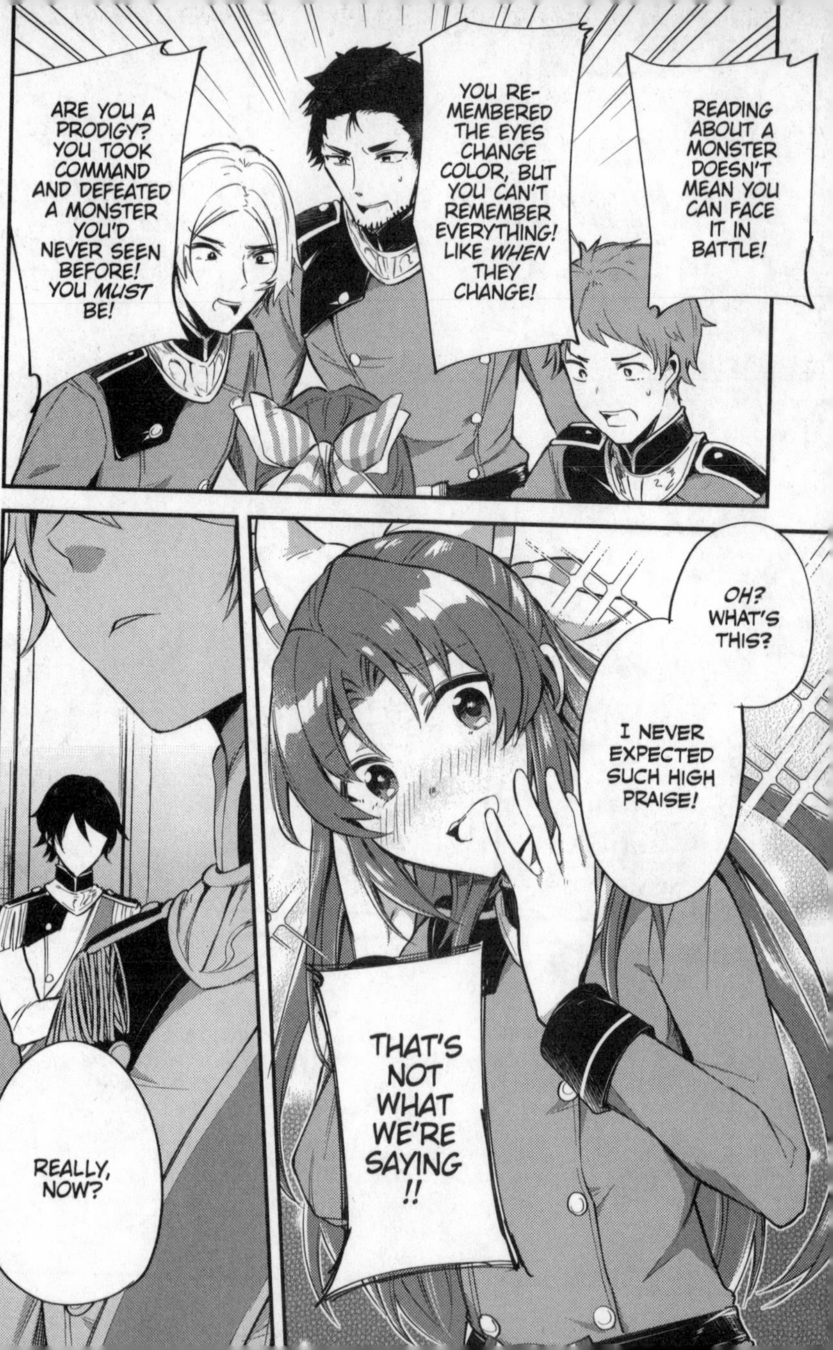
READING ABOUT A MONSTER DOESN'T MEAN YOU CAN FACE IT IN BATTLE!
YOU RE-MEMBERED THE EYES CHANGE COLOR, BUT YOU CAN'T REMEMBER EVERYTHING! LIKE *WHEN* THEY CHANGE!
ARE YOU A PRODIGY? YOU TOOK COMMAND AND DEFEATED A MONSTER YOU'D NEVER SEEN BEFORE! YOU *MUST* BE!
OH? WHAT'S THIS?
I NEVER EXPECTED SUCH HIGH PRAISE!
THAT'S NOT WHAT WE'RE SAYING!!
REALLY, NOW?

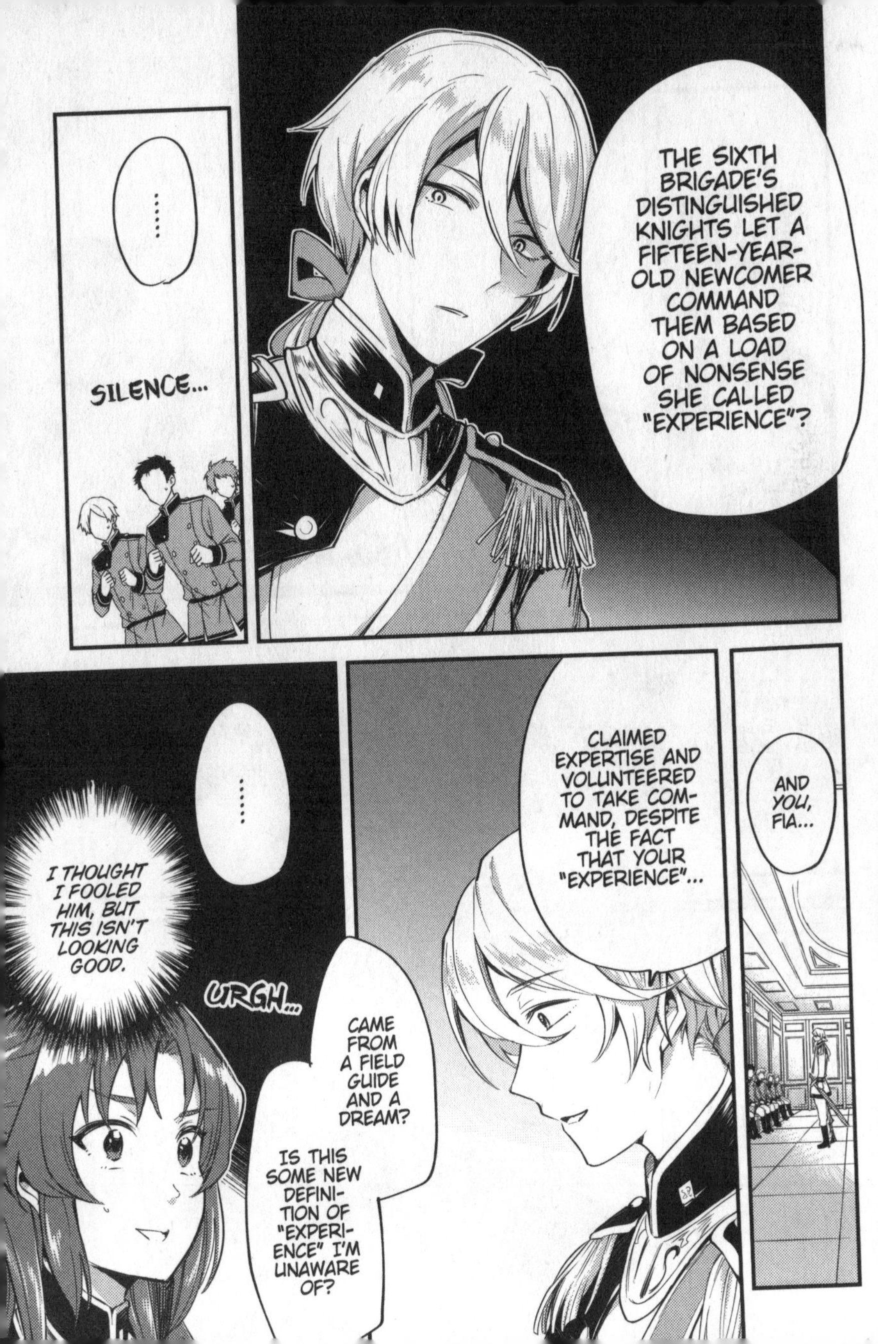
THE SIXTH BRIGADE'S DISTINGUISHED KNIGHTS LET A FIFTEEN-YEAR-OLD NEWCOMER COMMAND THEM BASED ON A LOAD OF NONSENSE SHE CALLED "EXPERIENCE"?
......
SILENCE...
AND YOU, FIA...
CLAIMED EXPERTISE AND VOLUNTEERED TO TAKE COMMAND, DESPITE THE FACT THAT YOUR "EXPERIENCE"...
CAME FROM A FIELD GUIDE AND A DREAM?
IS THIS SOME NEW DEFINITION OF "EXPERIENCE" I'M UNAWARE OF?
......
I THOUGHT I FOOLED HIM, BUT THIS ISN'T LOOKING GOOD.
URGH...

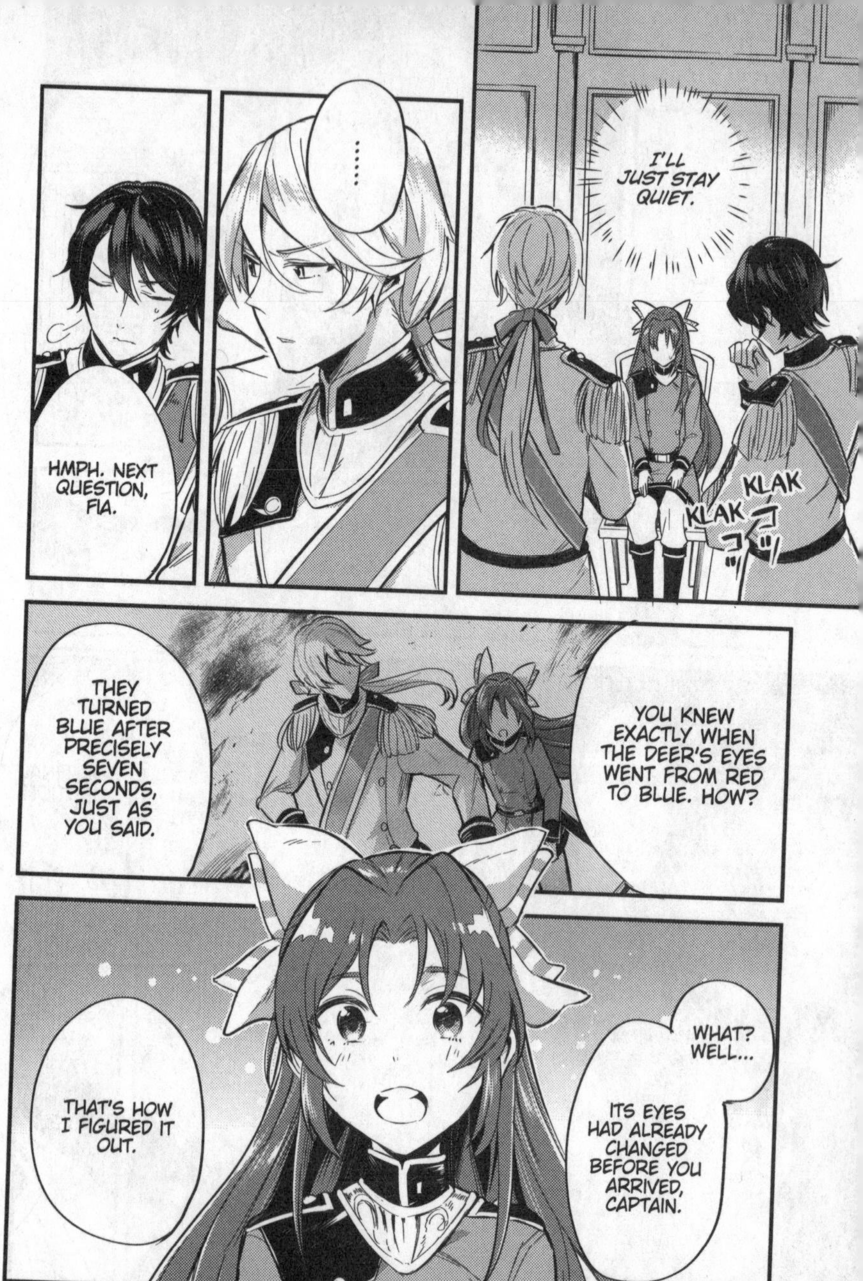
I'LL JUST STAY QUIET.
KLAK KLAK
......
HMPH. NEXT QUESTION, FIA.
YOU KNEW EXACTLY WHEN THE DEER'S EYES WENT FROM RED TO BLUE. HOW?
THEY TURNED BLUE AFTER PRECISELY SEVEN SECONDS, JUST AS YOU SAID.
WHAT? WELL...
ITS EYES HAD ALREADY CHANGED BEFORE YOU ARRIVED, CAPTAIN.
THAT'S HOW I FIGURED IT OUT.

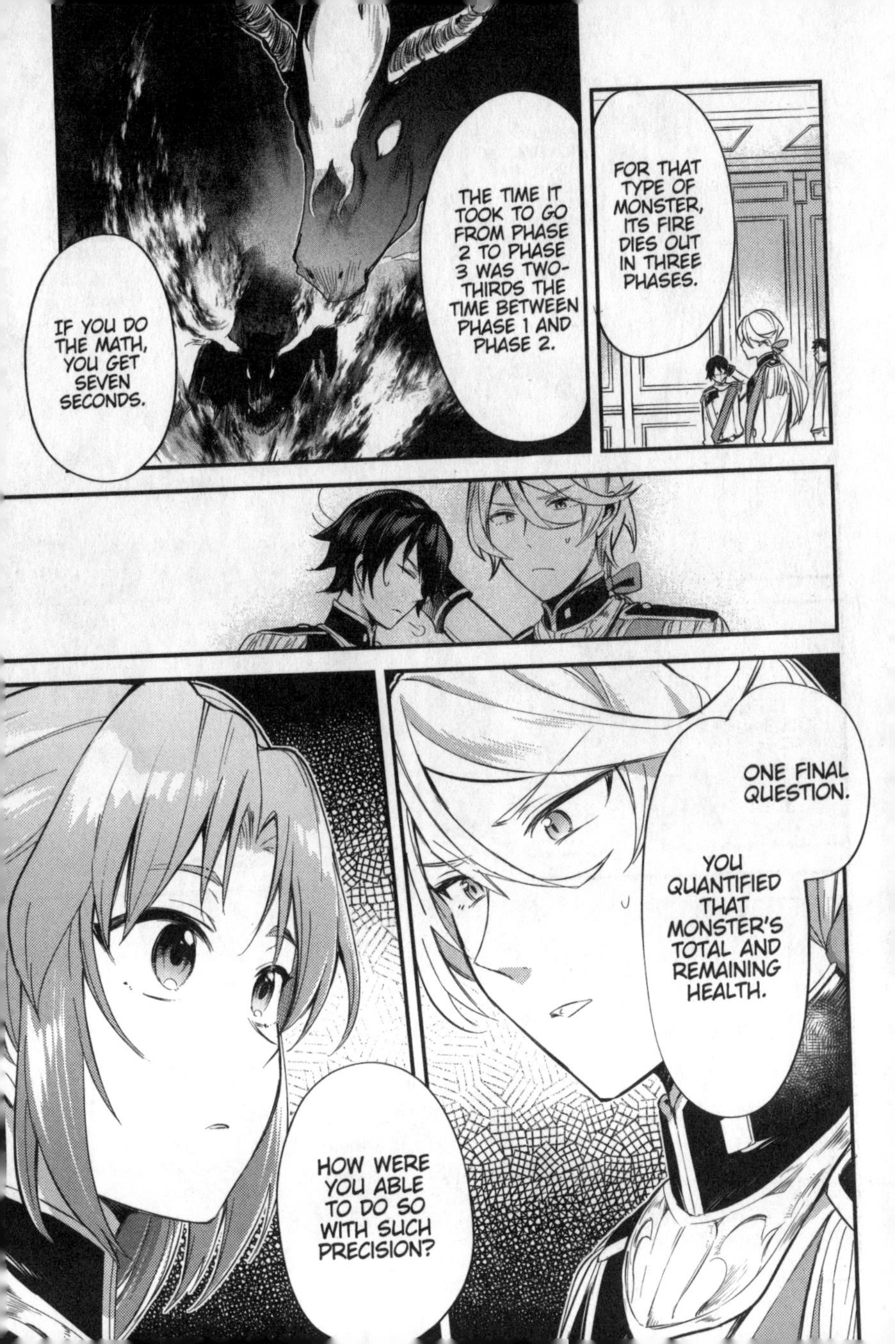
FOR THAT TYPE OF MONSTER, ITS FIRE DIES OUT IN THREE PHASES.
THE TIME IT TOOK TO GO FROM PHASE 2 TO PHASE 3 WAS TWO-THIRDS THE TIME BETWEEN PHASE 1 AND PHASE 2.
IF YOU DO THE MATH, YOU GET SEVEN SECONDS.
ONE FINAL QUESTION.
YOU QUANTIFIED THAT MONSTER'S TOTAL AND REMAINING HEALTH.
HOW WERE YOU ABLE TO DO SO WITH SUCH PRECISION?

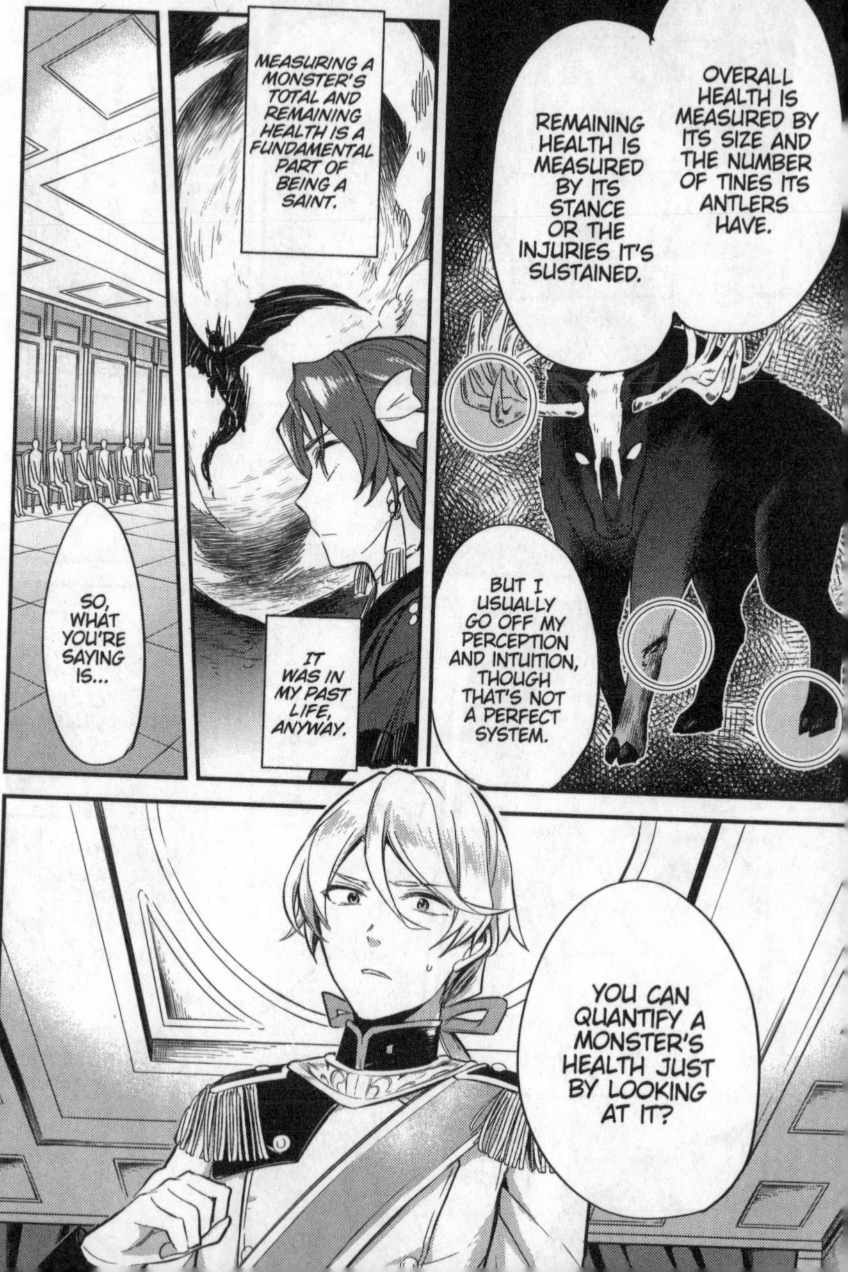
OVERALL HEALTH IS MEASURED BY ITS SIZE AND THE NUMBER OF TINES ITS ANTLERS HAVE.
REMAINING HEALTH IS MEASURED BY ITS STANCE OR THE INJURIES IT'S SUSTAINED.
BUT I USUALLY GO OFF MY PERCEPTION AND INTUITION, THOUGH THAT'S NOT A PERFECT SYSTEM.
MEASURING A MONSTER'S TOTAL AND REMAINING HEALTH IS A FUNDAMENTAL PART OF BEING A SAINT.
IT WAS IN MY PAST LIFE, ANYWAY.
SO, WHAT YOU'RE SAYING IS...
YOU CAN QUANTIFY A MONSTER'S HEALTH JUST BY LOOKING AT IT?

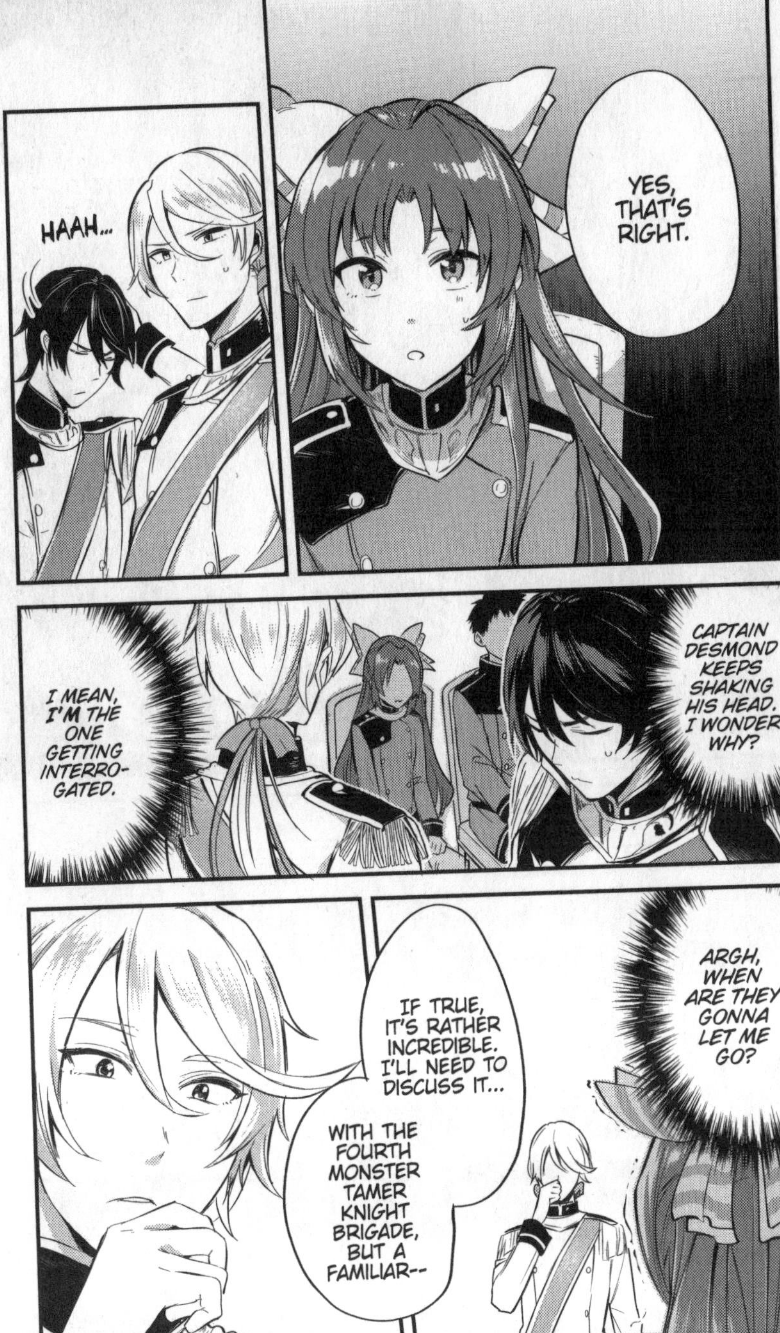
YES, THAT'S RIGHT.
HAAH...
CAPTAIN DESMOND KEEPS SHAKING HIS HEAD. I WONDER WHY?
I MEAN, *I'M* THE ONE GETTING INTERRO-GATED.
ARGH, WHEN ARE THEY GONNA LET ME GO?
IF TRUE, IT'S RATHER INCREDIBLE. I'LL NEED TO DISCUSS IT...
WITH THE FOURTH MONSTER TAMER KNIGHT BRIGADE, BUT A FAMILIAR--

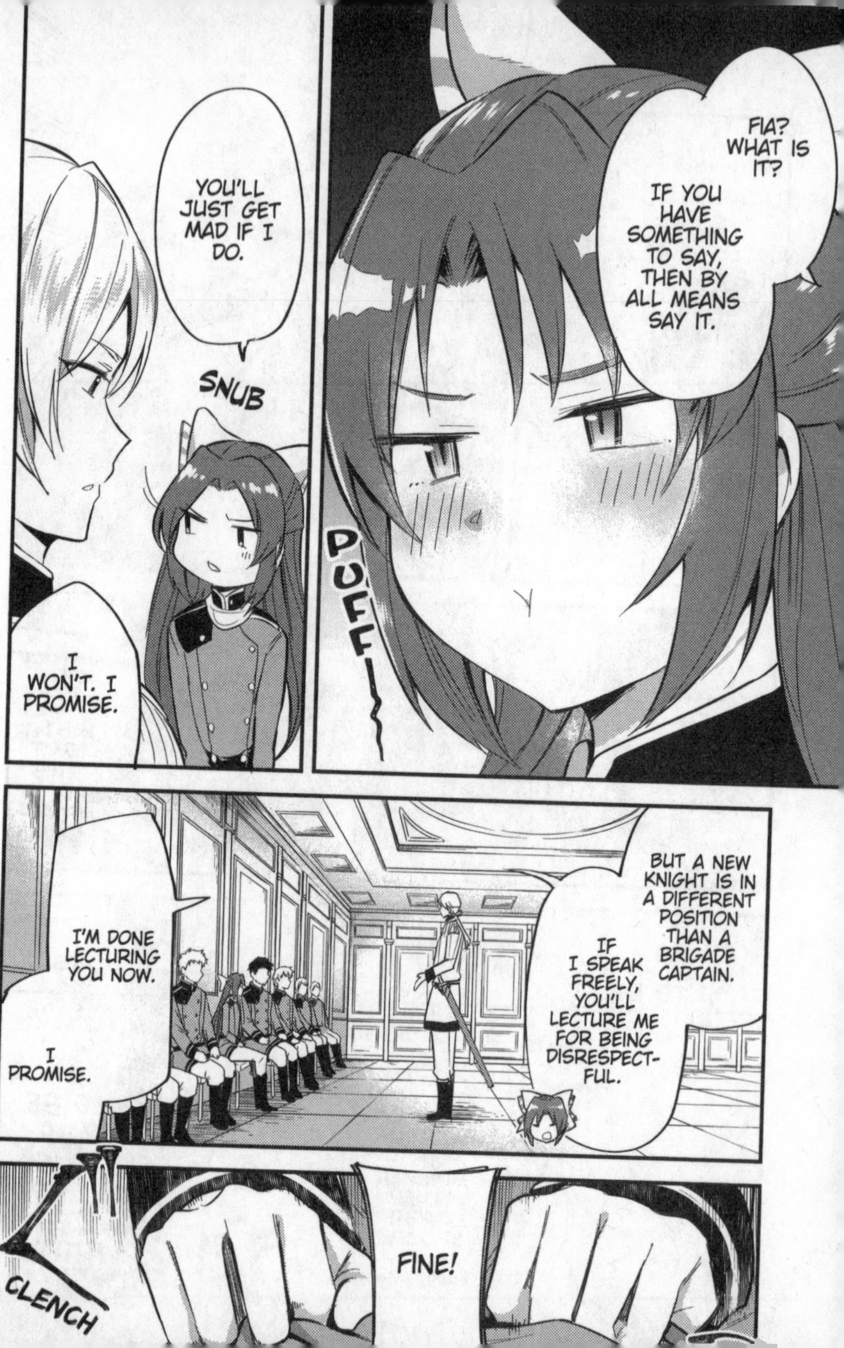
FIA? WHAT IS IT?
IF YOU HAVE SOMETHING TO SAY, THEN BY ALL MEANS SAY IT.
PUFF
YOU'LL JUST GET MAD IF I DO.
SNUB
I WON'T. I PROMISE.
BUT A NEW KNIGHT IS IN A DIFFERENT POSITION THAN A BRIGADE CAPTAIN.
IF I SPEAK FREELY, YOU'LL LECTURE ME FOR BEING DISRESPECT-FUL.
I'M DONE LECTURING YOU NOW.
I PROMISE.
FINE!
CLENCH

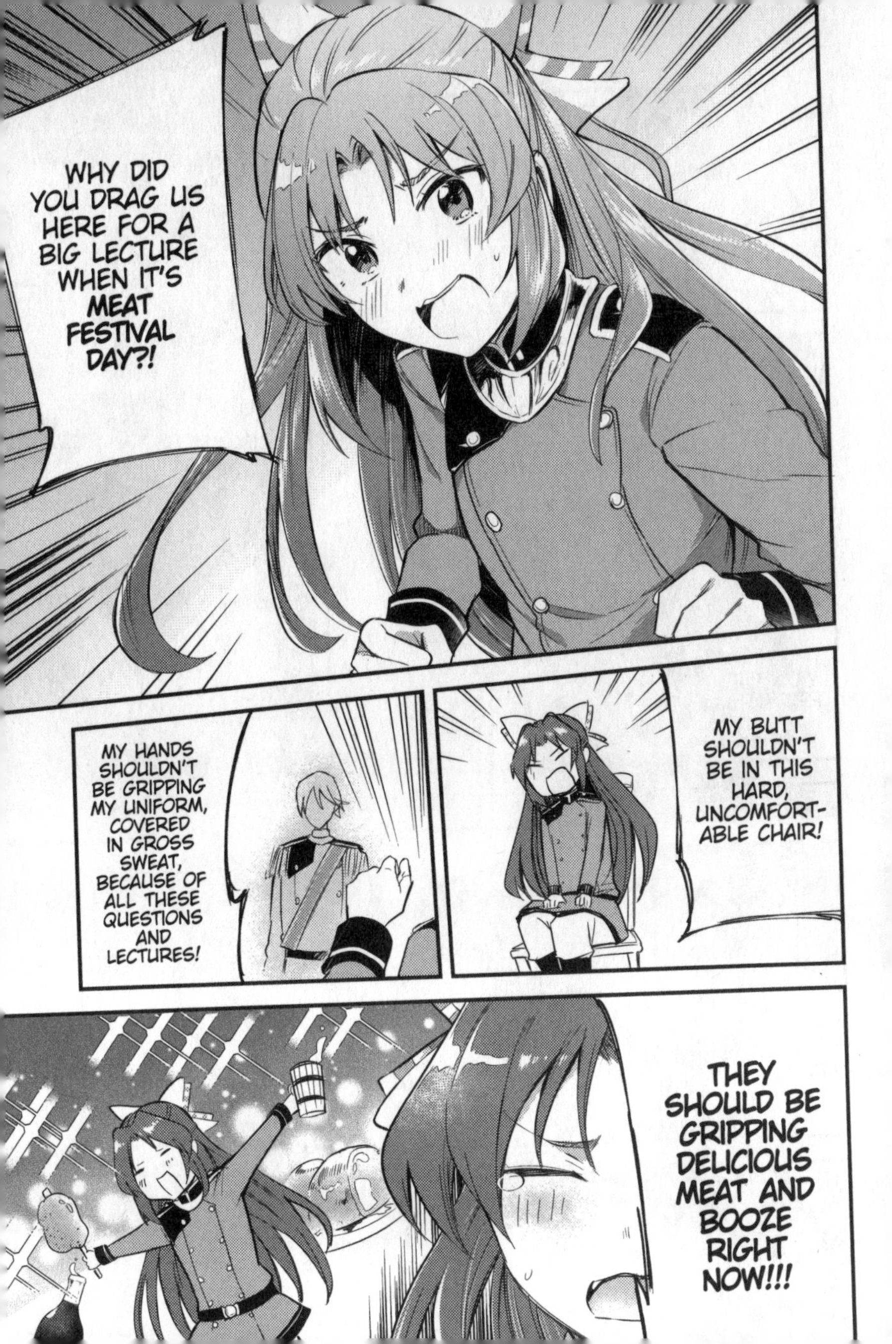
WHY DID YOU DRAG US HERE FOR A BIG LECTURE WHEN IT'S MEAT FESTIVAL DAY?!
MY BUTT SHOULDN'T BE IN THIS HARD, UNCOMFORTABLE CHAIR!
MY HANDS SHOULDN'T BE GRIPPING MY UNIFORM, COVERED IN GROSS SWEAT, BECAUSE OF ALL THESE QUESTIONS AND LECTURES!
THEY SHOULD BE GRIPPING DELICIOUS MEAT AND BOOZE RIGHT NOW!!!

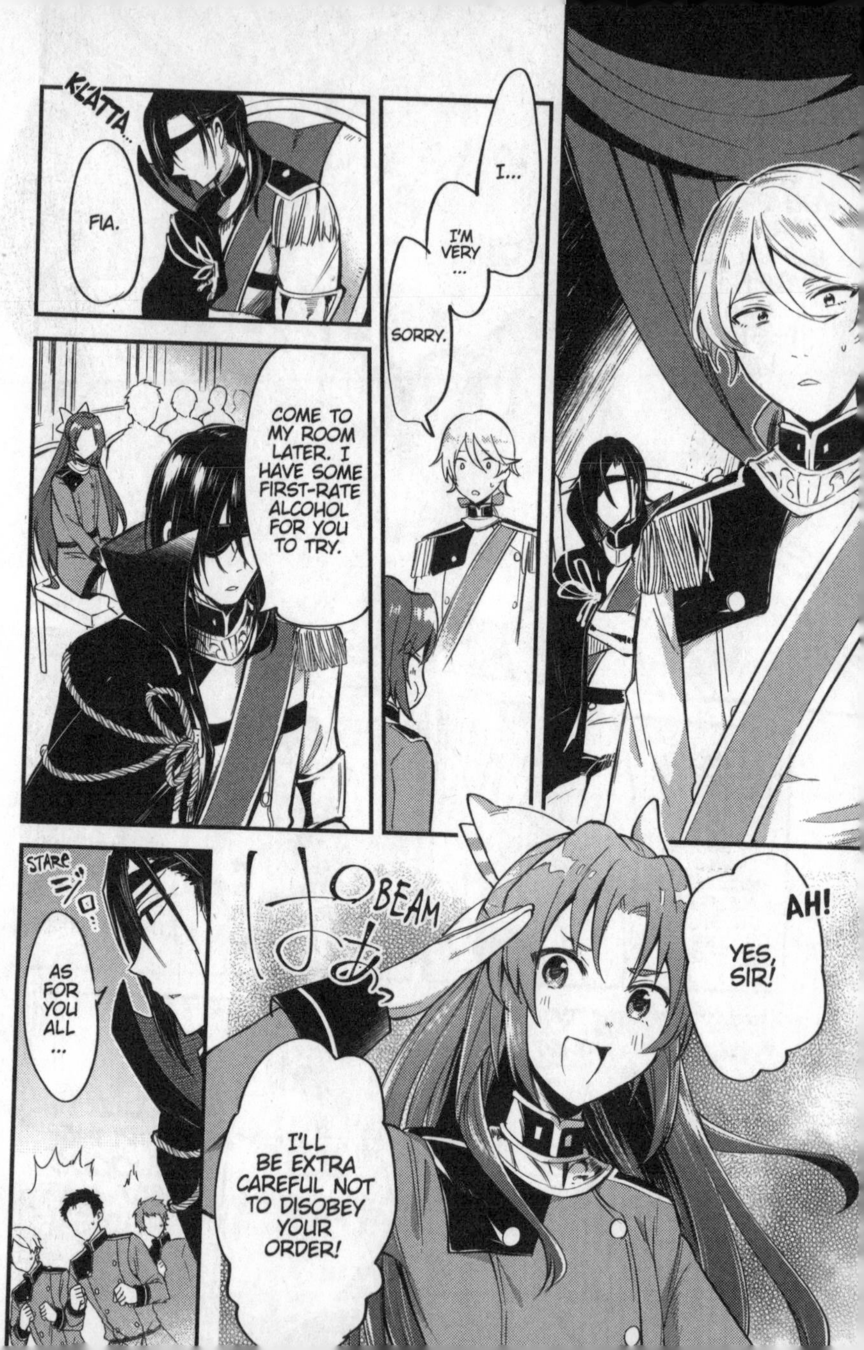
I...
I'M VERY ...
SORRY.
K-LATTA...
FIA.
COME TO MY ROOM LATER. I HAVE SOME FIRST-RATE ALCOHOL FOR YOU TO TRY.
AH!
YES, SIR!
BEAM
I'LL BE EXTRA CAREFUL NOT TO DISOBEY YOUR ORDER!
STARE
AS FOR YOU ALL ...

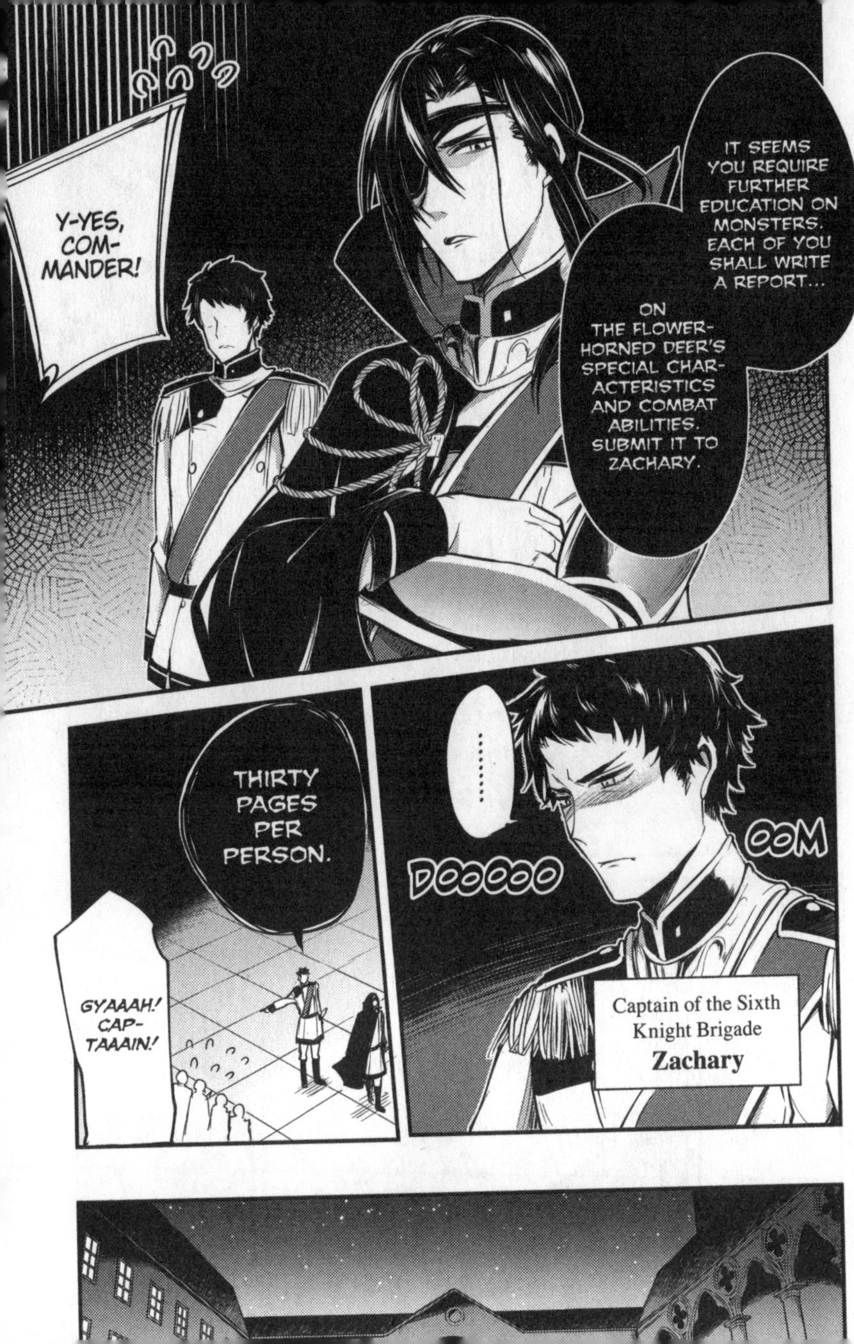
IT SEEMS YOU REQUIRE FURTHER EDUCATION ON MONSTERS. EACH OF YOU SHALL WRITE A REPORT...
ON THE FLOWER-HORNED DEER'S SPECIAL CHAR-ACTERISTICS AND COMBAT ABILITIES. SUBMIT IT TO ZACHARY.
Y-YES, COM-MANDER!
......
DOOOOOOOM
Captain of the Sixth Knight Brigade
Zachary
THIRTY PAGES PER PERSON.
GYAAAH! CAP-TAAAIN!

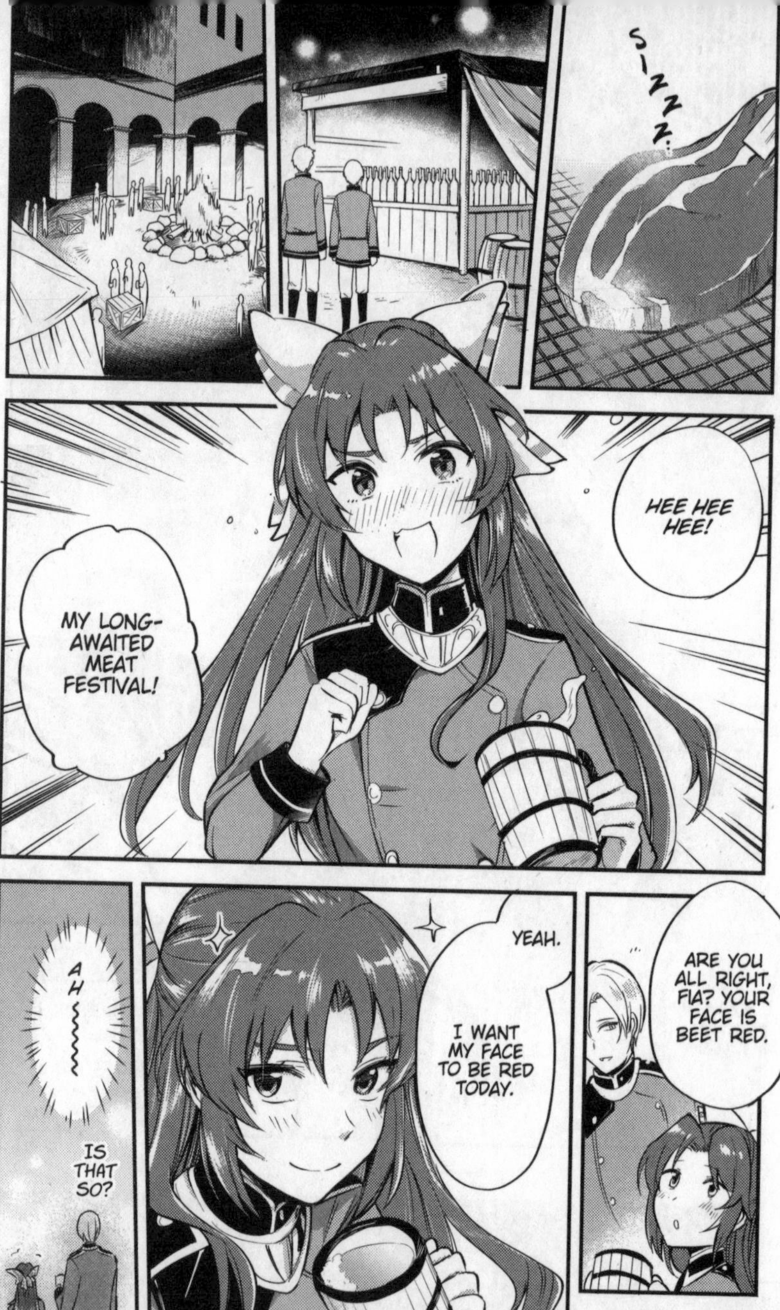
SIZZZ...
HEE HEE HEE!
MY LONG-AWAITED MEAT FESTIVAL!
ARE YOU ALL RIGHT, FIA? YOUR FACE IS BEET RED.
YEAH.
I WANT MY FACE TO BE RED TODAY.
AH~~
IS THAT SO?

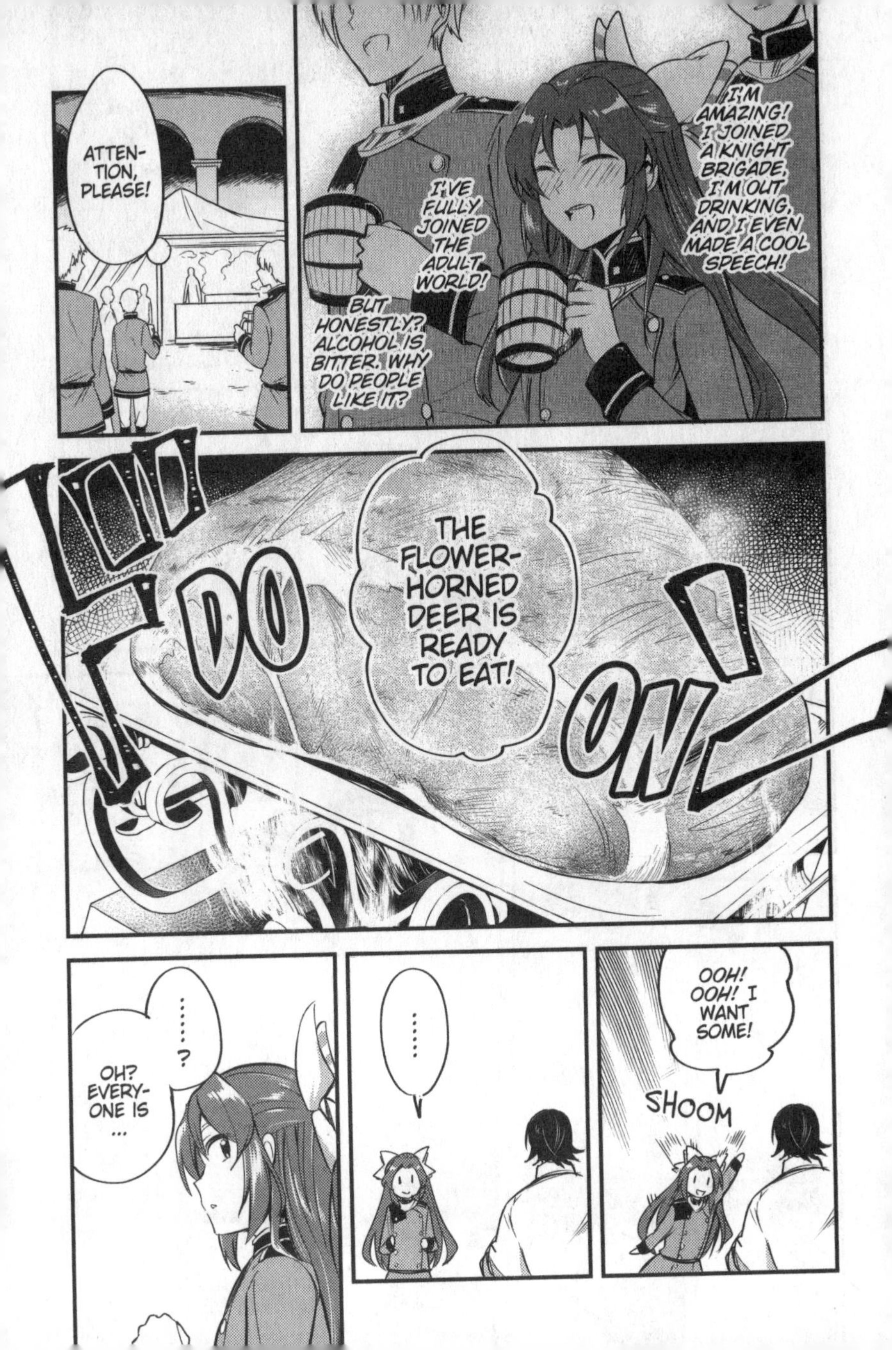
I'M AMAZING! I JOINED A KNIGHT BRIGADE, I'M OUT DRINKING, AND I EVEN MADE A COOL SPEECH!
I'VE FULLY JOINED THE ADULT WORLD!
BUT HONESTLY? ALCOHOL IS BITTER. WHY DO PEOPLE LIKE IT?
ATTEN-TION, PLEASE!
DO DO ON!
THE FLOWER-HORNED DEER IS READY TO EAT!
OOH! OOH! I WANT SOME!
SHOOM
......
......?
OH? EVERY-ONE IS ...

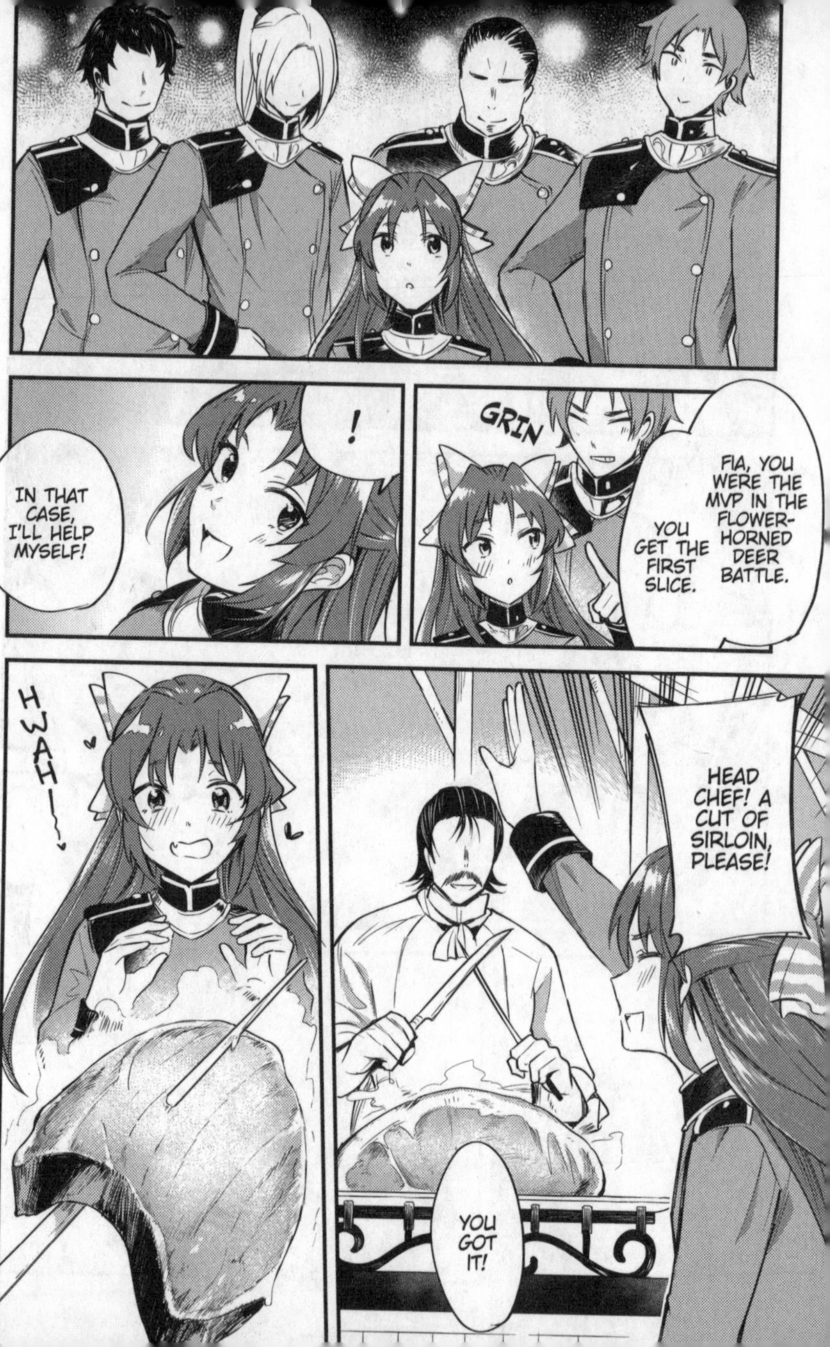
GRIN
FIA, YOU WERE THE MVP IN THE FLOWER-HORNED DEER BATTLE.
YOU GET THE FIRST SLICE.
!
IN THAT CASE, I'LL HELP MYSELF!
HEAD CHEF! A CUT OF SIRLOIN, PLEASE!
YOU GOT IT!
HWAH!~

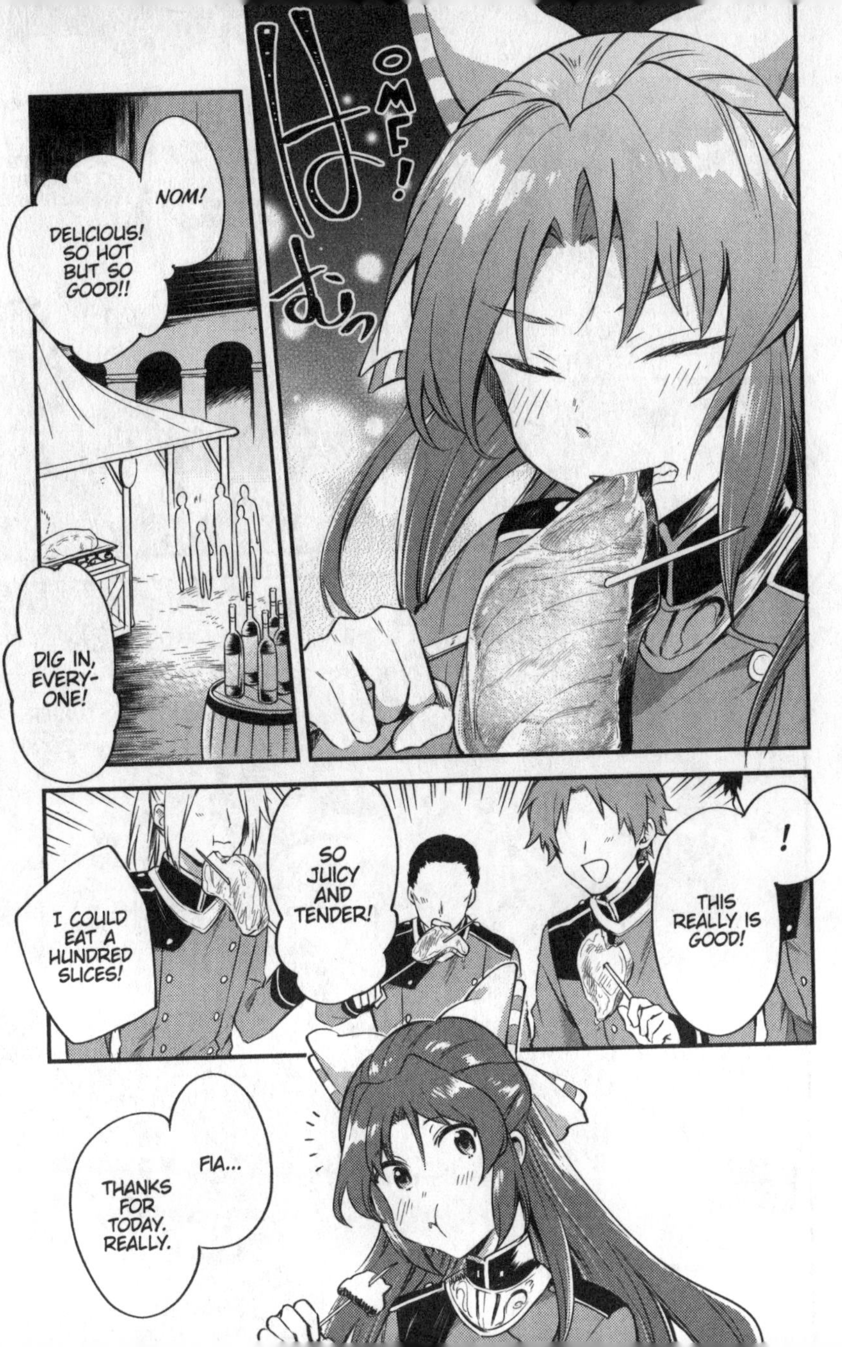
OMF!
NOM!
DELICIOUS! SO HOT BUT SO GOOD!!
DIG IN, EVERYONE!
!
THIS REALLY IS GOOD!
SO JUICY AND TENDER!
I COULD EAT A HUNDRED SLICES!
FIA...
THANKS FOR TODAY. REALLY.

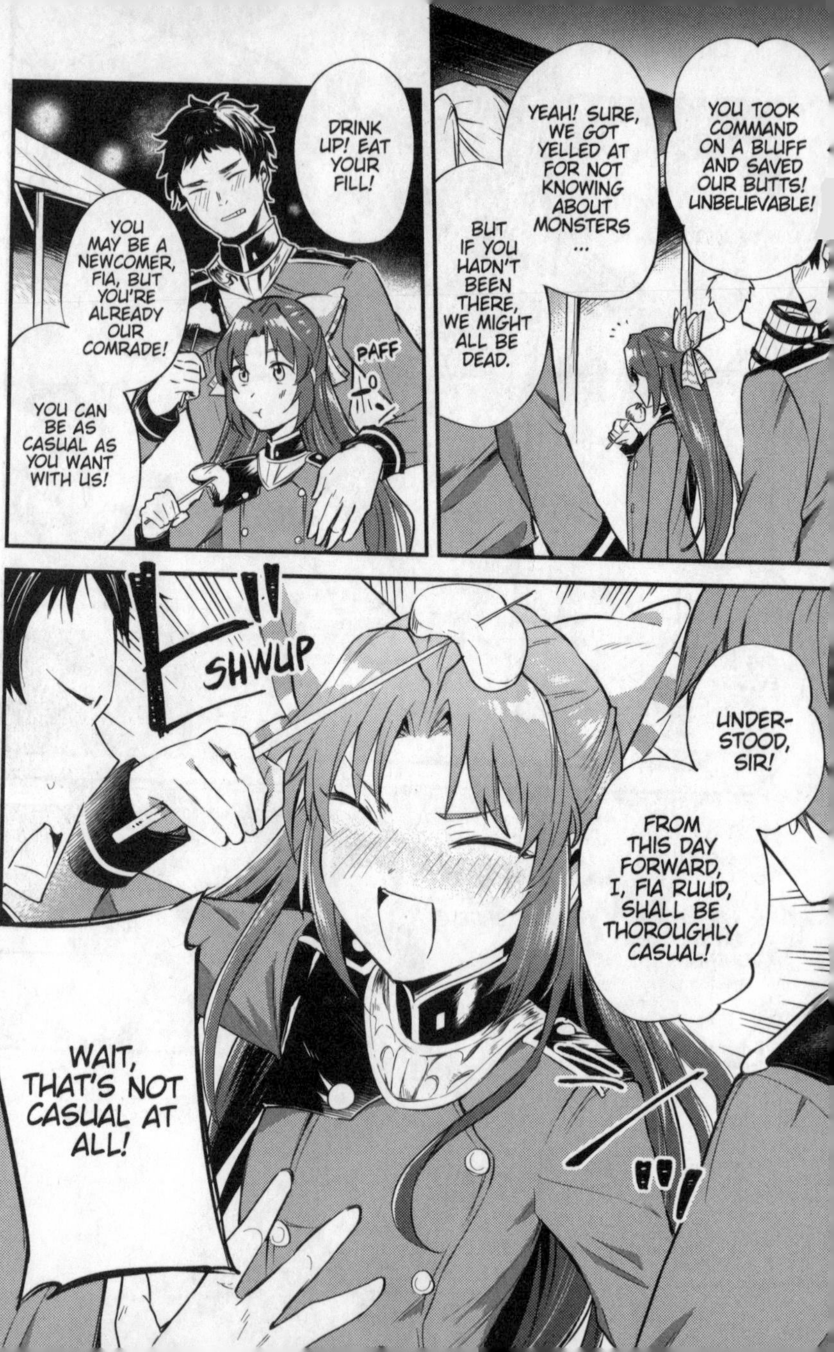
YOU TOOK COMMAND ON A BLUFF AND SAVED OUR BUTTS! UNBELIEVABLE!
YEAH! SURE, WE GOT YELLED AT FOR NOT KNOWING ABOUT MONSTERS ...
BUT IF YOU HADN'T BEEN THERE, WE MIGHT ALL BE DEAD.
DRINK UP! EAT YOUR FILL!
YOU MAY BE A NEWCOMER, FIA, BUT YOU'RE ALREADY OUR COMRADE!
PAFF
YOU CAN BE AS CASUAL AS YOU WANT WITH US!
UNDER-STOOD, SIR!
FROM THIS DAY FORWARD, I, FIA RUUD, SHALL BE THOROUGHLY CASUAL!
SHWUP
WAIT, THAT'S NOT CASUAL AT ALL!

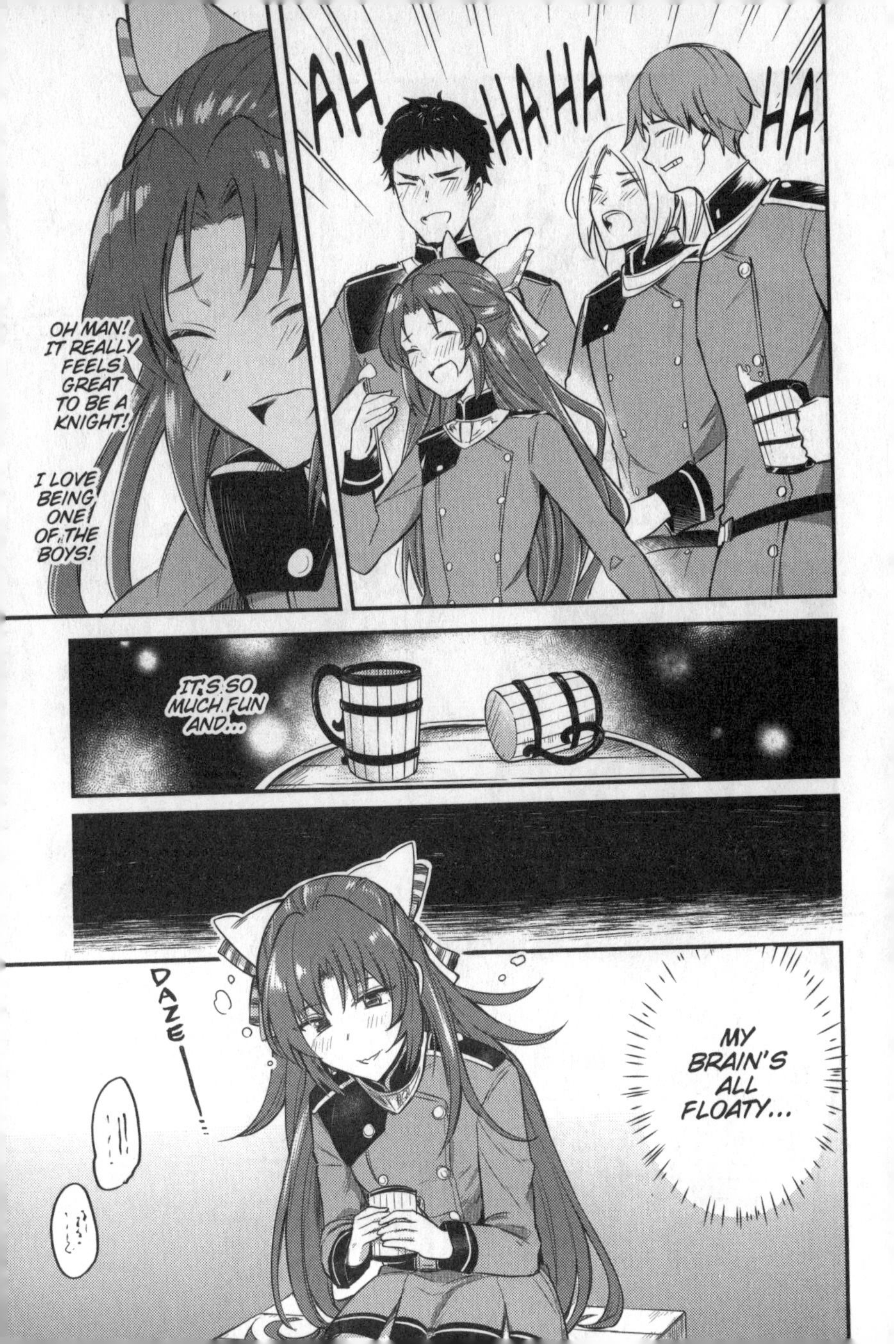

AH HAHAHA HA
OH MAN! IT REALLY FEELS GREAT TO BE A KNIGHT!
I LOVE BEING ONE OF THE BOYS!
IT'S SO MUCH FUN AND...
MY BRAIN'S ALL FLOATY...
DAZE—!!

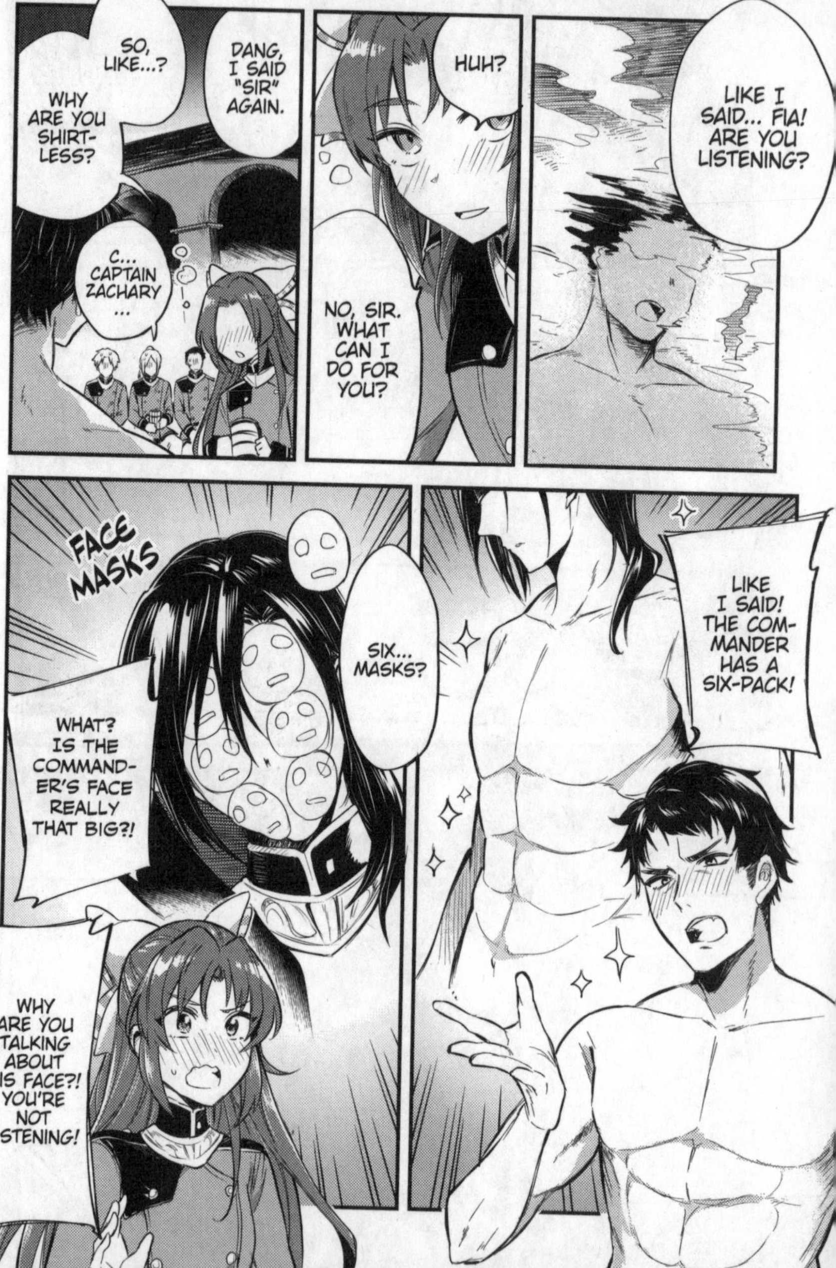
LIKE I SAID... FIA! ARE YOU LISTENING?
HUH?
NO, SIR. WHAT CAN I DO FOR YOU?
DANG, I SAID "SIR" AGAIN.
SO, LIKE...?
WHY ARE YOU SHIRT-LESS?
C... CAPTAIN ZACHARY ...
LIKE I SAID! THE COM-MANDER HAS A SIX-PACK!
SIX... MASKS?
FACE MASKS
WHAT? IS THE COMMAND-ER'S FACE REALLY THAT BIG?!
WHY ARE YOU TALKING ABOUT HIS FACE?! YOU'RE NOT LISTENING!

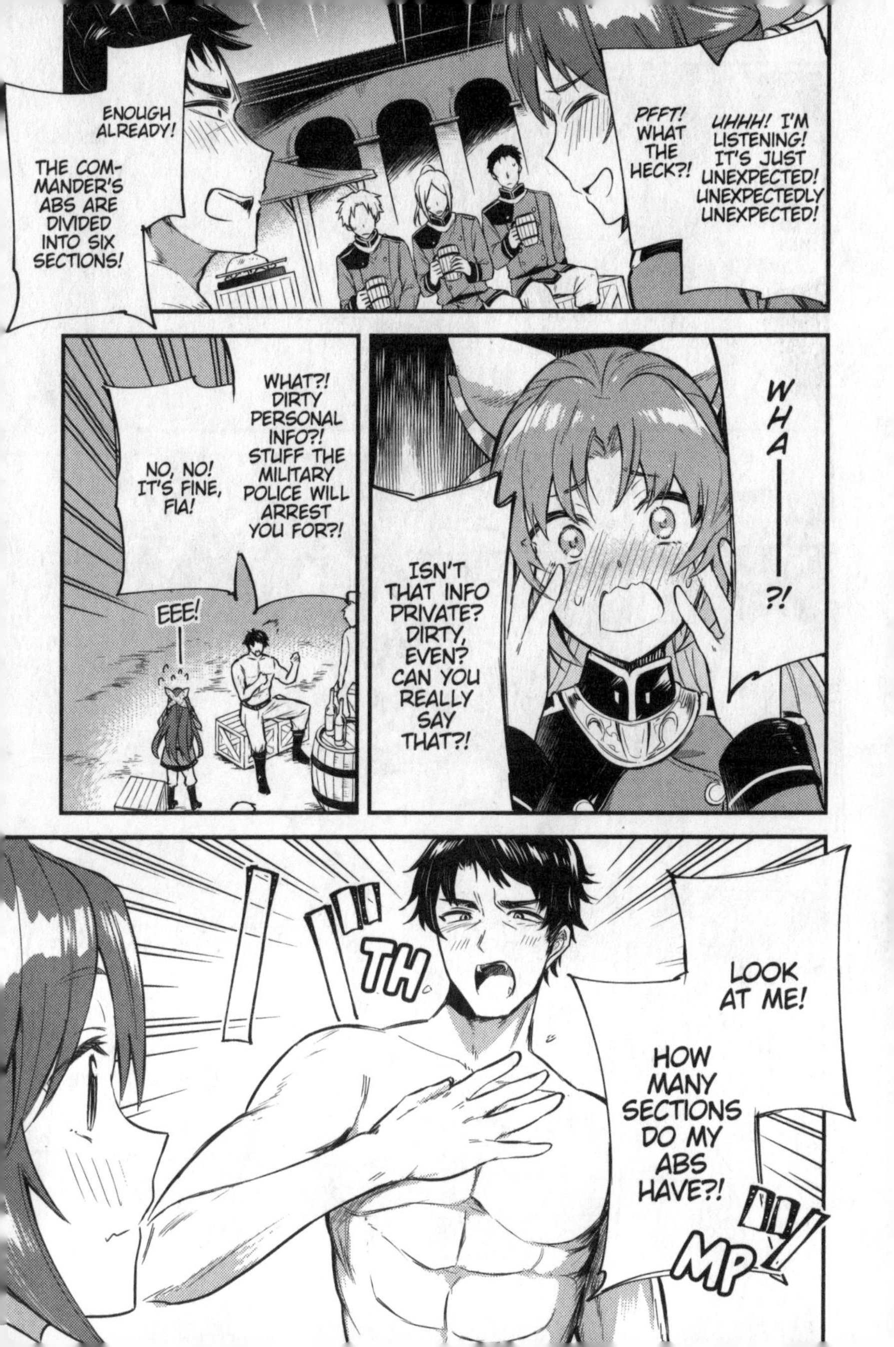
UHHH! I'M LISTENING! IT'S JUST UNEXPECTED! UNEXPECTEDLY UNEXPECTED!
PFFT! WHAT THE HECK?!
ENOUGH ALREADY!
THE COM-MANDER'S ABS ARE DIVIDED INTO SIX SECTIONS!
WHA—?!
ISN'T THAT INFO PRIVATE? DIRTY, EVEN? CAN YOU REALLY SAY THAT?!
WHAT?! DIRTY PERSONAL INFO?! STUFF THE MILITARY POLICE WILL ARREST YOU FOR?!
NO, NO! IT'S FINE, FIA!
EEE!
LOOK AT ME!
HOW MANY SECTIONS DO MY ABS HAVE?!
TH
MP

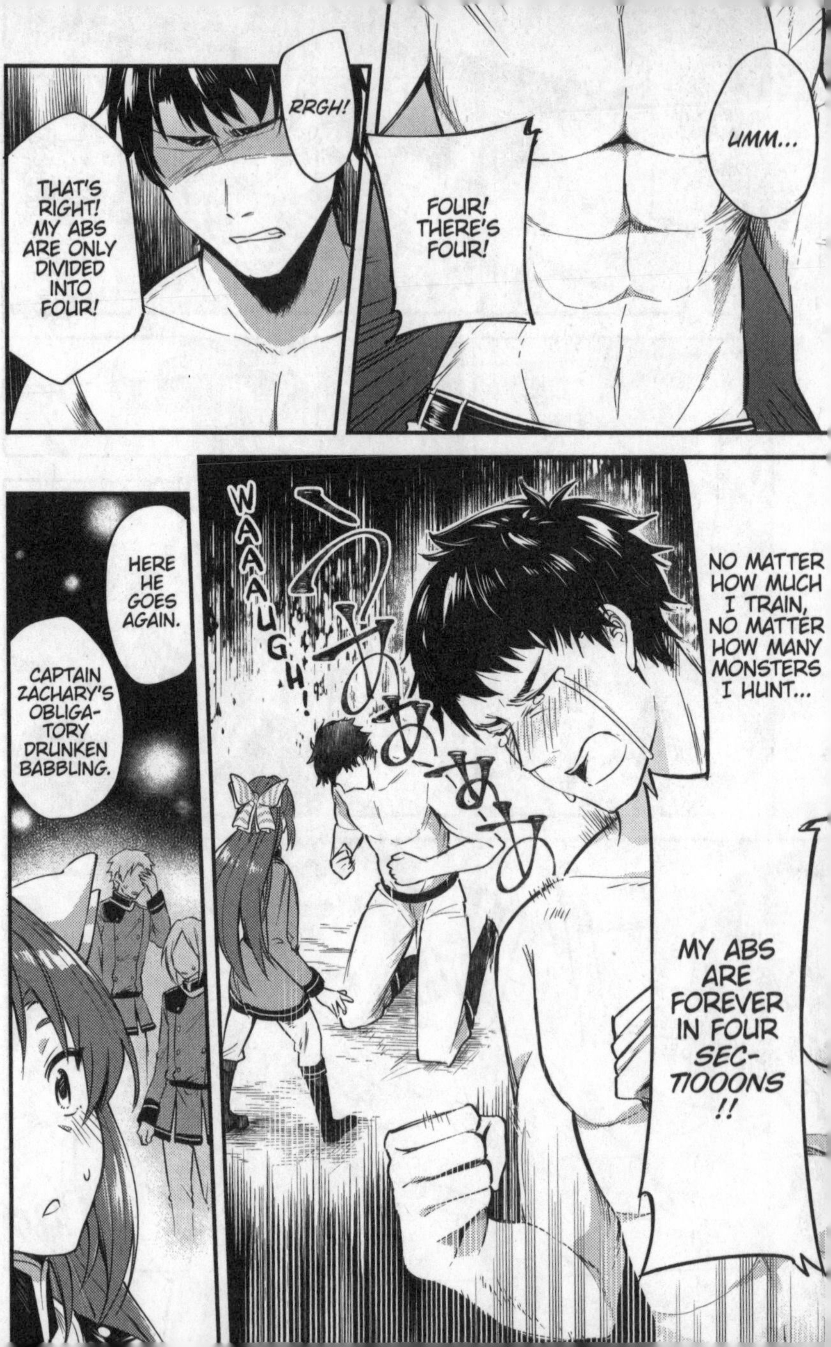
UMM...
FOUR! THERE'S FOUR!
RRGH!
THAT'S RIGHT! MY ABS ARE ONLY DIVIDED INTO FOUR!
NO MATTER HOW MUCH I TRAIN, NO MATTER HOW MANY MONSTERS I HUNT...
MY ABS ARE FOREVER IN FOUR SEC-TIOOONS!!
WAAAAUGH!
HERE HE GOES AGAIN.
CAPTAIN ZACHARY'S OBLIGA-TORY DRUNKEN BABBLING.

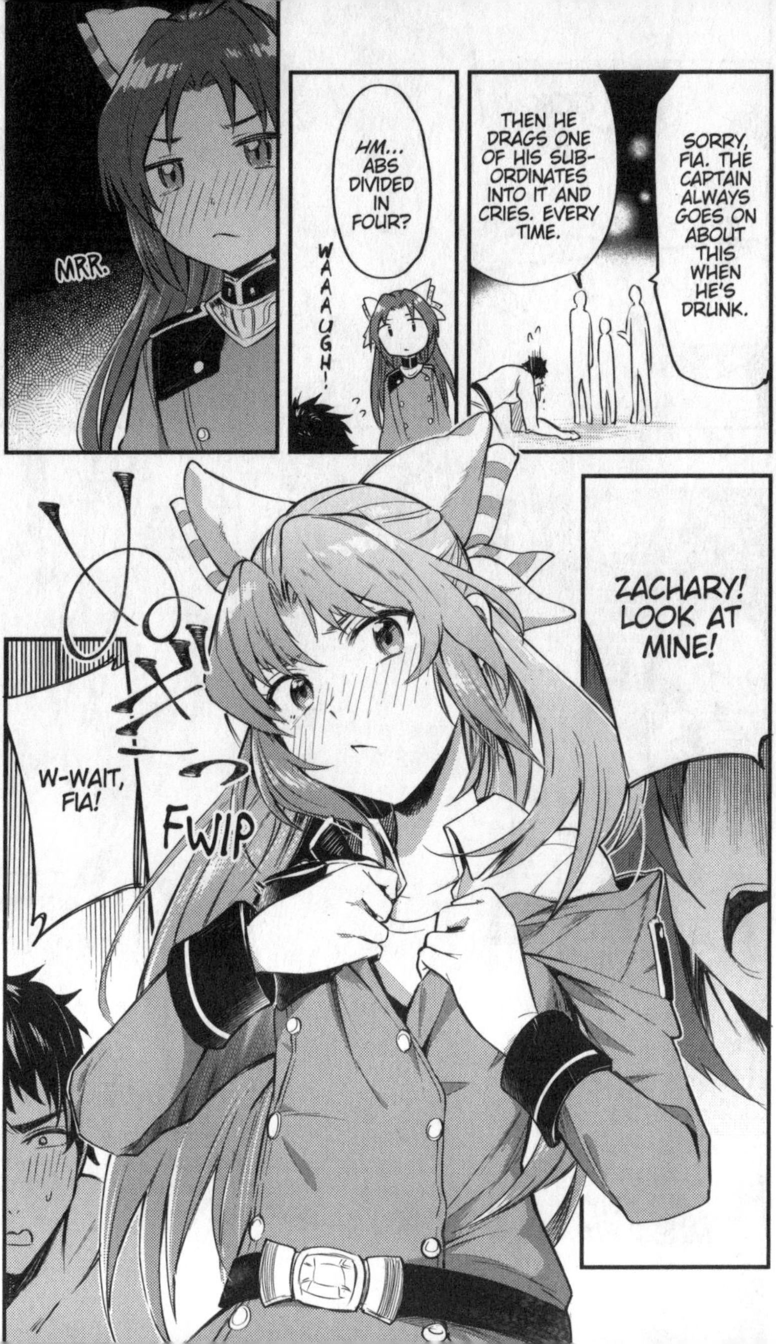
SORRY, FIA. THE CAPTAIN ALWAYS GOES ON ABOUT THIS WHEN HE'S DRUNK.
THEN HE DRAGS ONE OF HIS SUB-ORDINATES INTO IT AND CRIES. EVERY TIME.
HM... ABS DIVIDED IN FOUR?
WAAAAUGH!
MRR.
ZACHARY! LOOK AT MINE!
FWIP
W-WAIT, FIA!

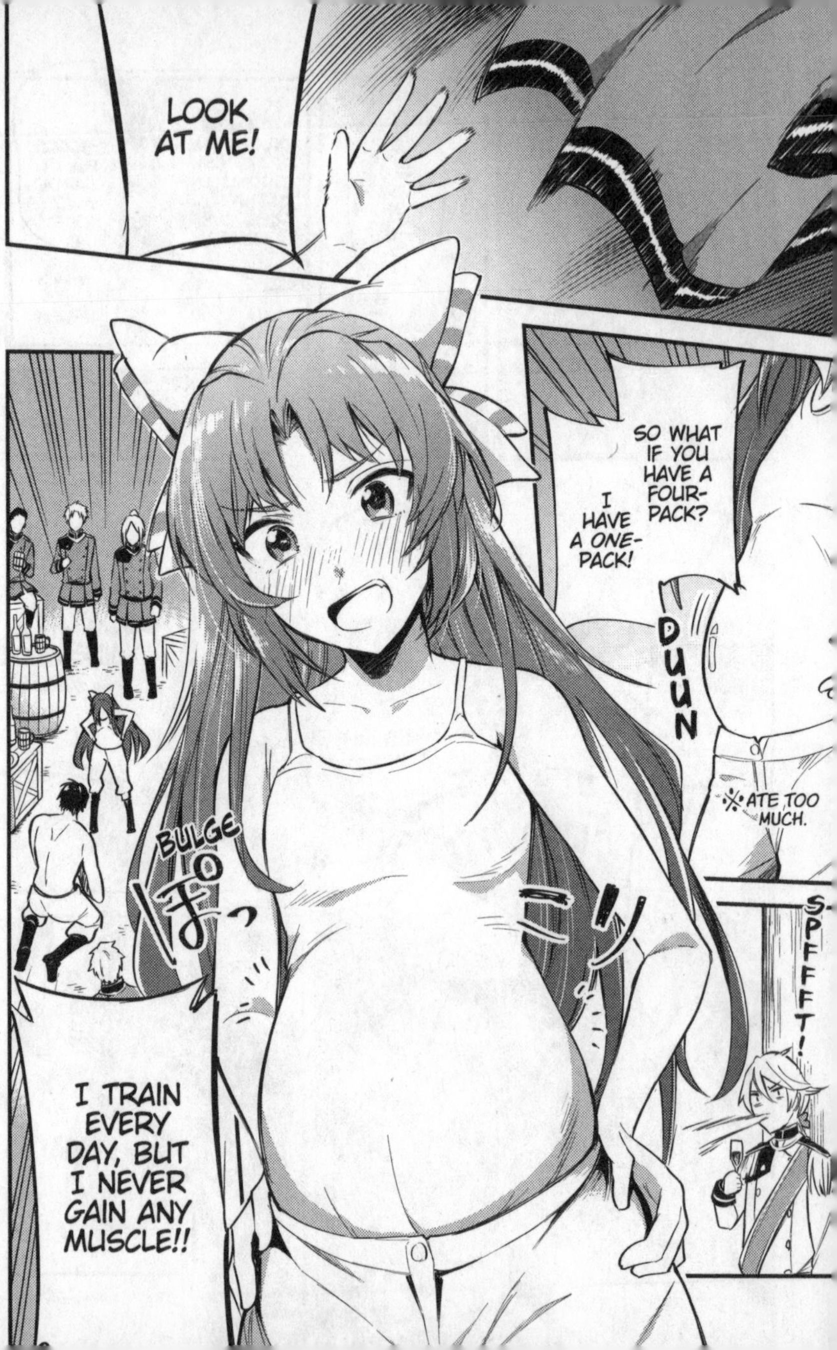
LOOK AT ME!
SO WHAT IF YOU HAVE A FOUR-PACK?
I HAVE A ONE-PACK!
DUUN
※ATE TOO MUCH.
SPFFFT!
BULGE
I TRAIN EVERY DAY, BUT I NEVER GAIN ANY MUSCLE!!

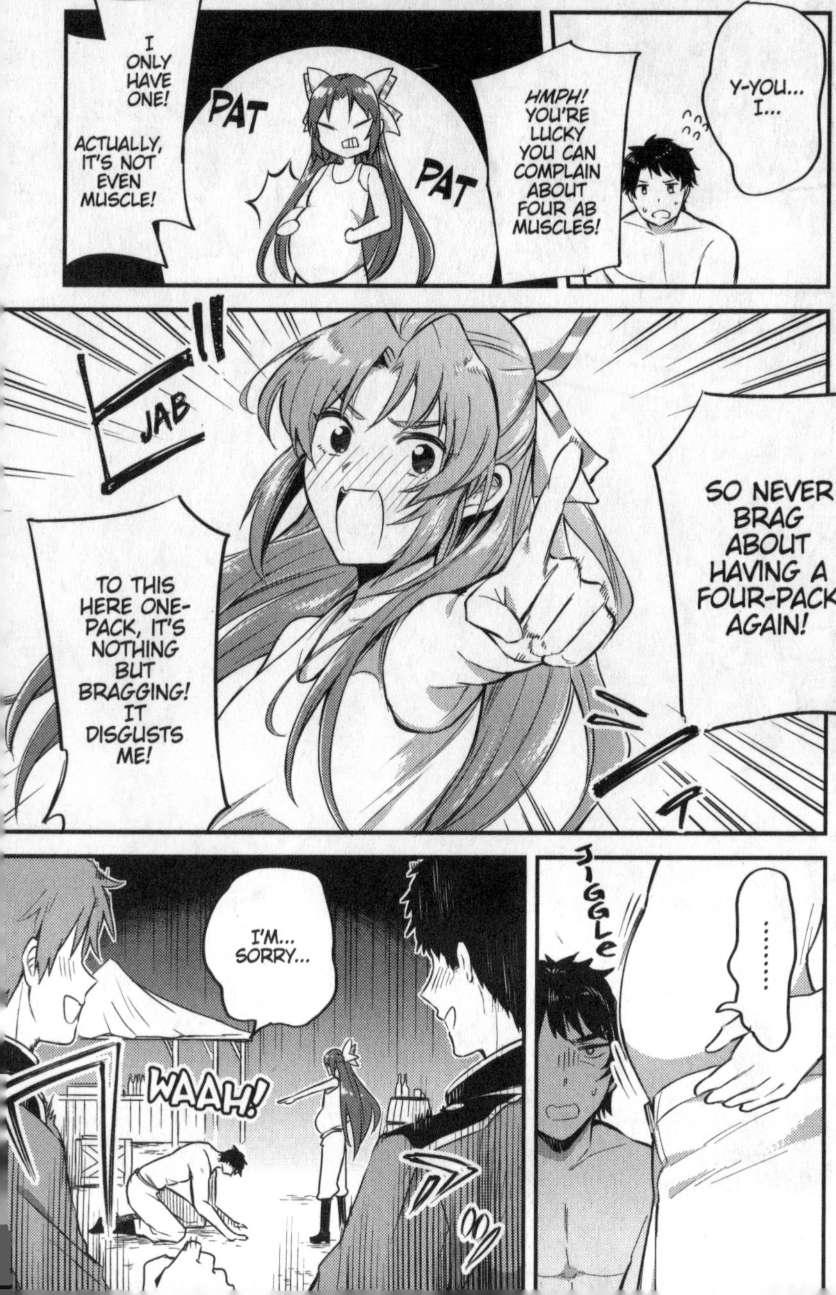
Y-YOU... I...
HMPH! YOU'RE LUCKY YOU CAN COMPLAIN ABOUT FOUR AB MUSCLES!
PAT
PAT
I ONLY HAVE ONE!
ACTUALLY, IT'S NOT EVEN MUSCLE!
SO NEVER BRAG ABOUT HAVING A FOUR-PACK AGAIN!
JAB
TO THIS HERE ONE-PACK, IT'S NOTHING BUT BRAGGING! IT DISGUSTS ME!
JIGGLE
......
I'M... SORRY...
WAAH!

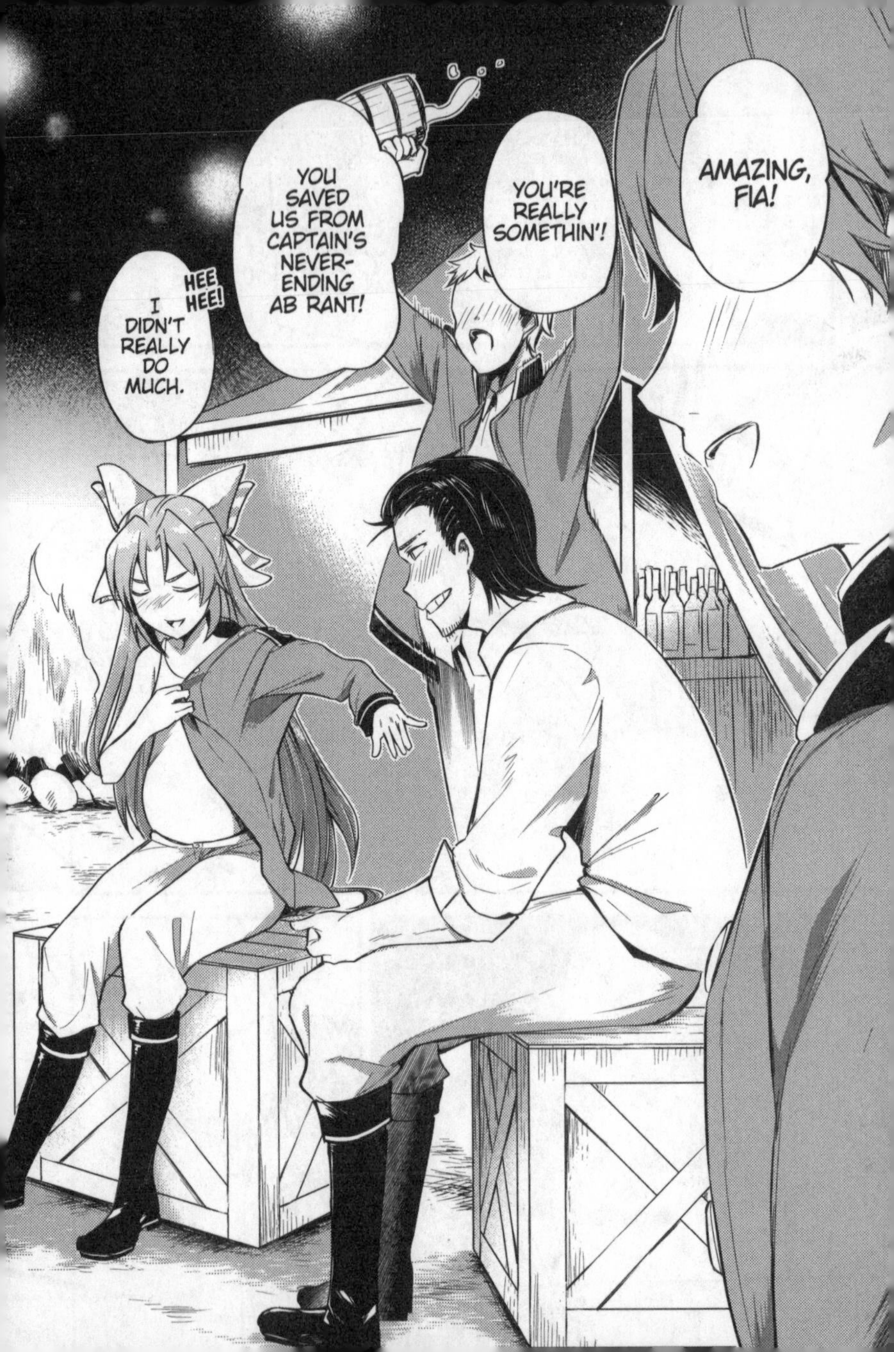
AMAZING, FIA!
YOU'RE REALLY SOMETHIN'!
YOU SAVED US FROM CAPTAIN'S NEVER-ENDING AB RANT!
HEE HEE!
I DIDN'T REALLY DO MUCH.

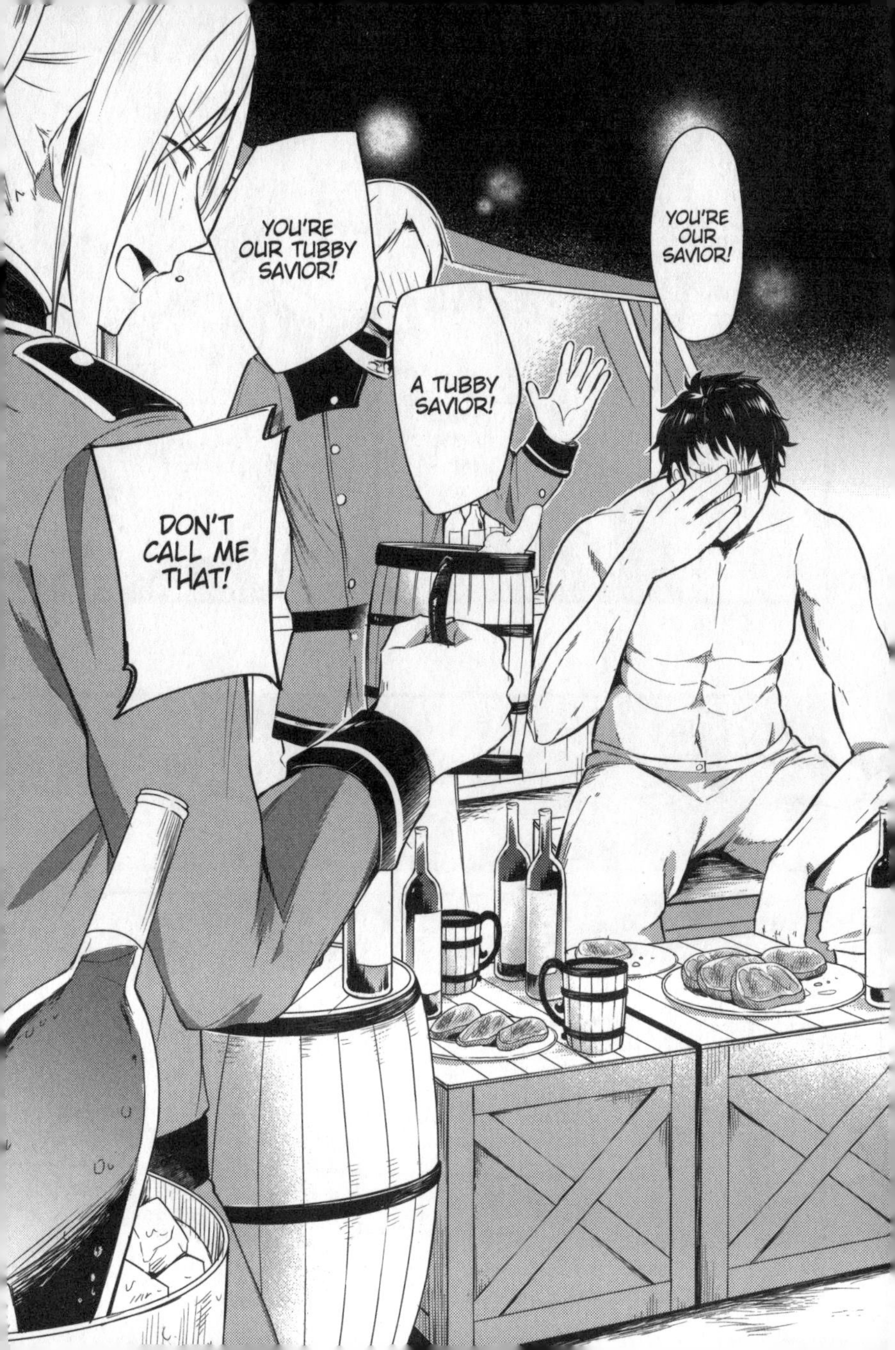
YOU'RE OUR SAVIOR!
YOU'RE OUR TUBBY SAVIOR!
A TUBBY SAVIOR!
DON'T CALL ME THAT!

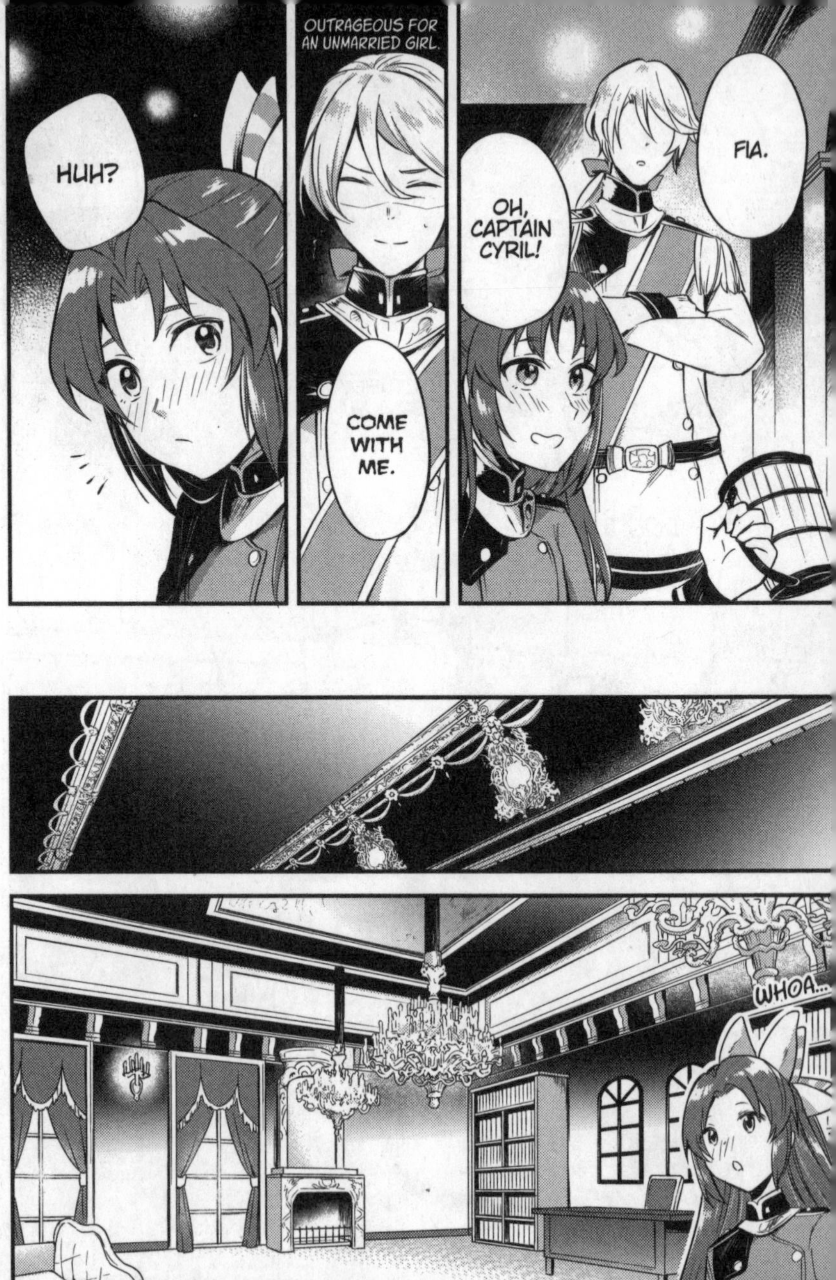
FIA.
OH, CAPTAIN CYRIL!
OUTRAGEOUS FOR AN UNMARRIED GIRL.
COME WITH ME.
HUH?
WHOA...

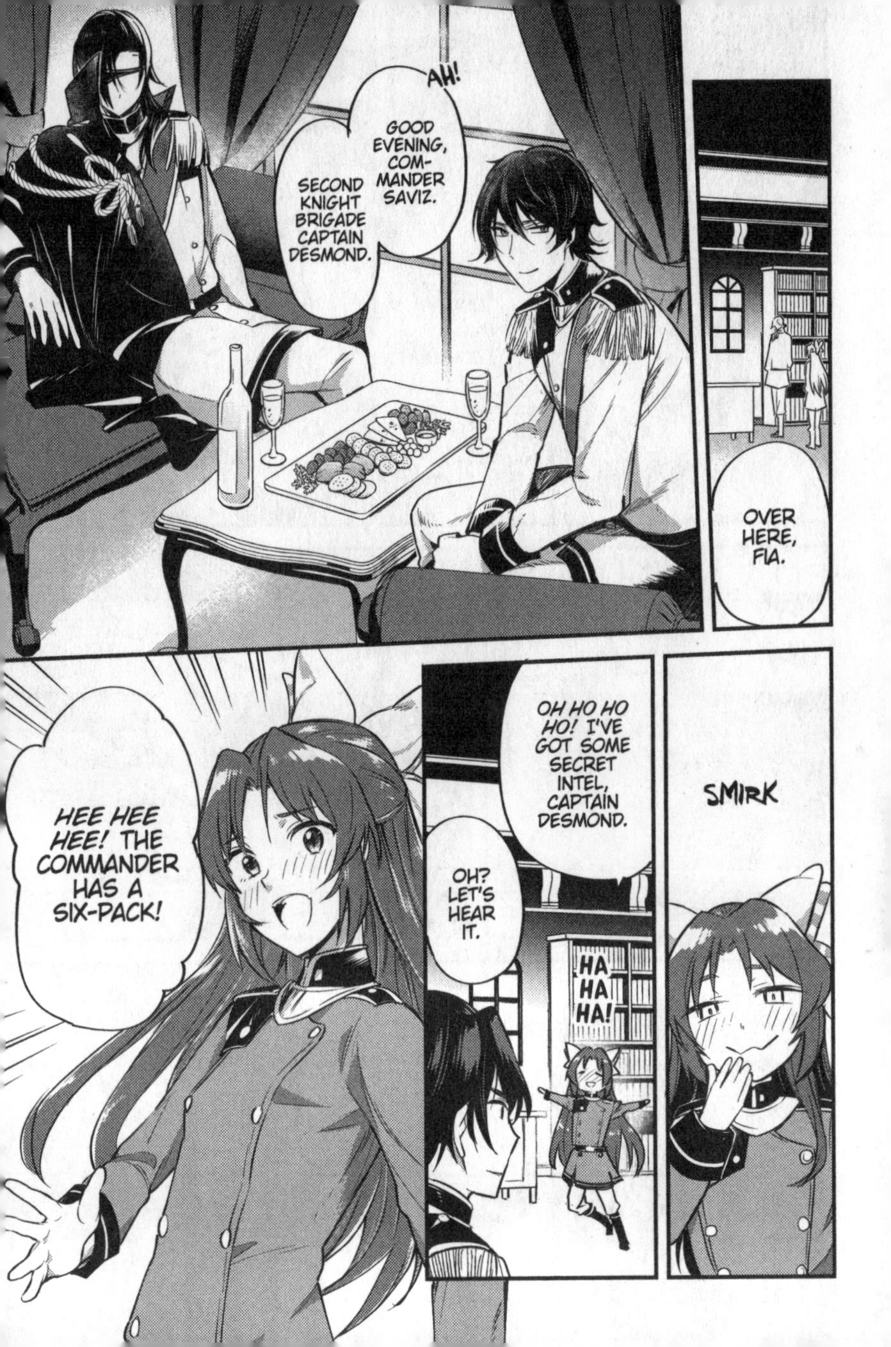
OVER HERE, FIA.
AH!
GOOD EVENING, COMMANDER SAVIZ.
SECOND KNIGHT BRIGADE CAPTAIN DESMOND.
SMIRK
OH HO HO HO! I'VE GOT SOME SECRET INTEL, CAPTAIN DESMOND.
OH? LET'S HEAR IT.
HA HA HA!
HEE HEE HEE! THE COMMANDER HAS A SIX-PACK!

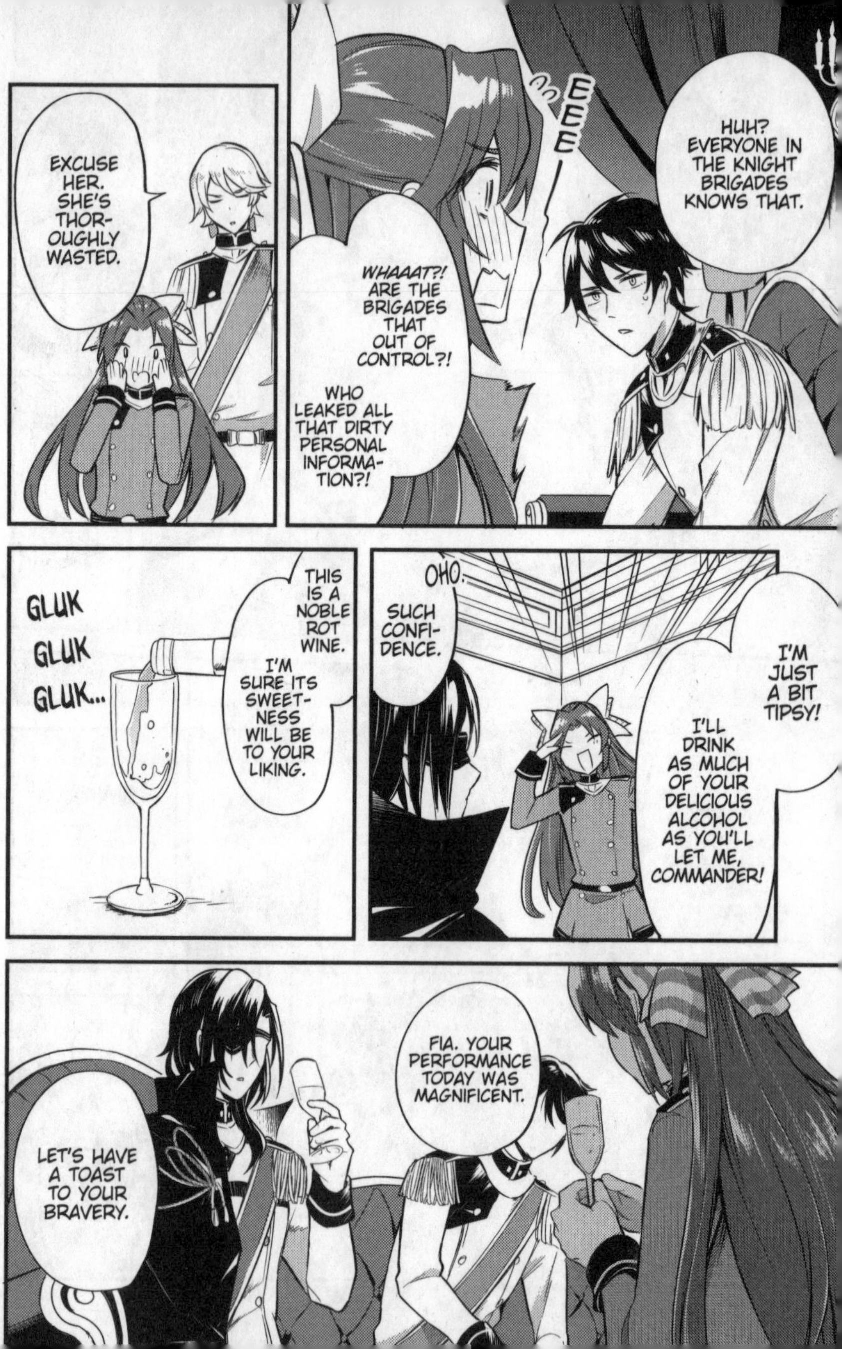
HUH? EVERYONE IN THE KNIGHT BRIGADES KNOWS THAT.
EEE—
WHAAAT?! ARE THE BRIGADES THAT OUT OF CONTROL?!
WHO LEAKED ALL THAT DIRTY PERSONAL INFORMATION?!
EXCUSE HER. SHE'S THOROUGHLY WASTED.
I'M JUST A BIT TIPSY!
I'LL DRINK AS MUCH OF YOUR DELICIOUS ALCOHOL AS YOU'LL LET ME, COMMANDER!
OHO.
SUCH CONFIDENCE.
THIS IS A NOBLE ROT WINE.
I'M SURE ITS SWEETNESS WILL BE TO YOUR LIKING.
GLUK GLUK GLUK...
FIA. YOUR PERFORMANCE TODAY WAS MAGNIFICENT.
LET'S HAVE A TOAST TO YOUR BRAVERY.

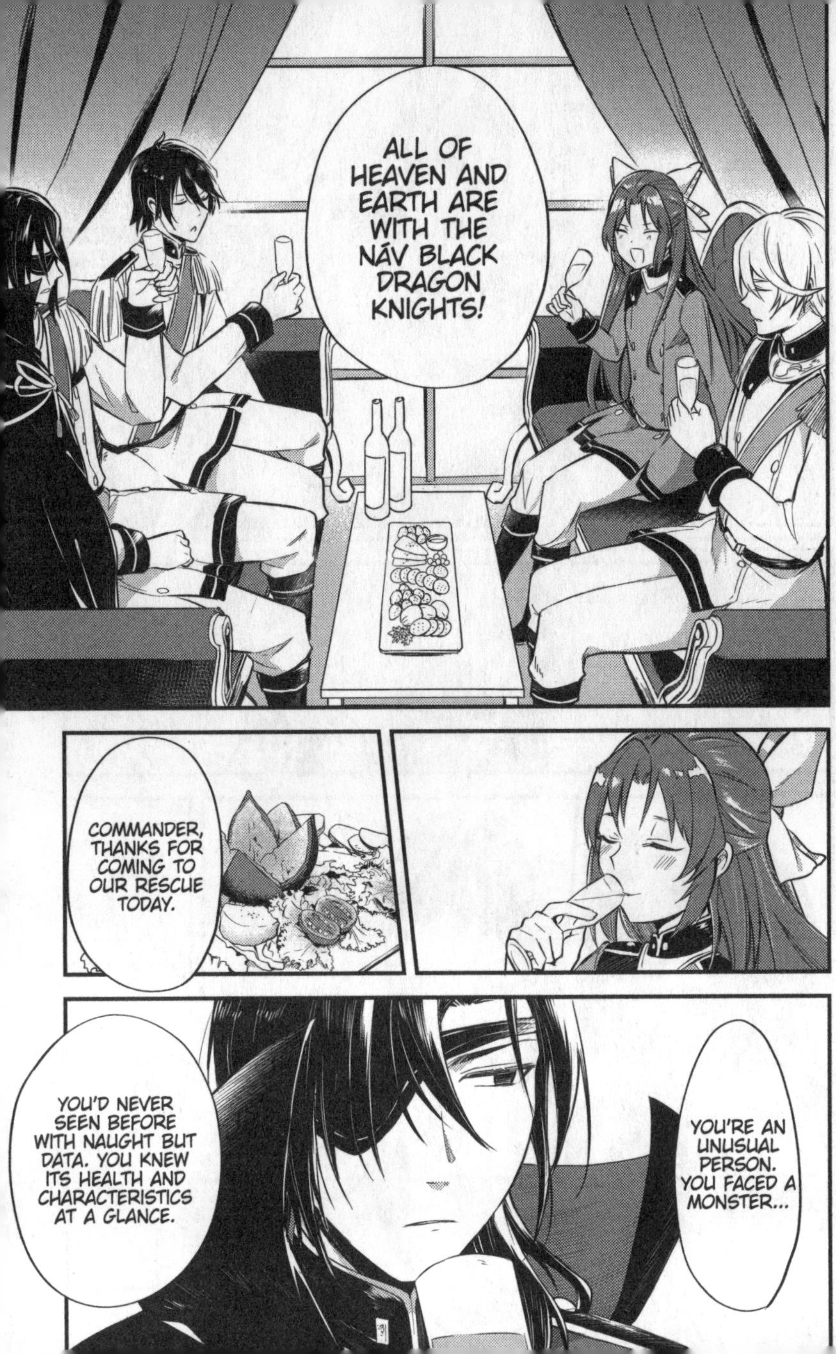
ALL OF HEAVEN AND EARTH ARE WITH THE NÁV BLACK DRAGON KNIGHTS!
COMMANDER, THANKS FOR COMING TO OUR RESCUE TODAY.
YOU'RE AN UNUSUAL PERSON. YOU FACED A MONSTER...
YOU'D NEVER SEEN BEFORE WITH NAUGHT BUT DATA. YOU KNEW ITS HEALTH AND CHARACTERISTICS AT A GLANCE.

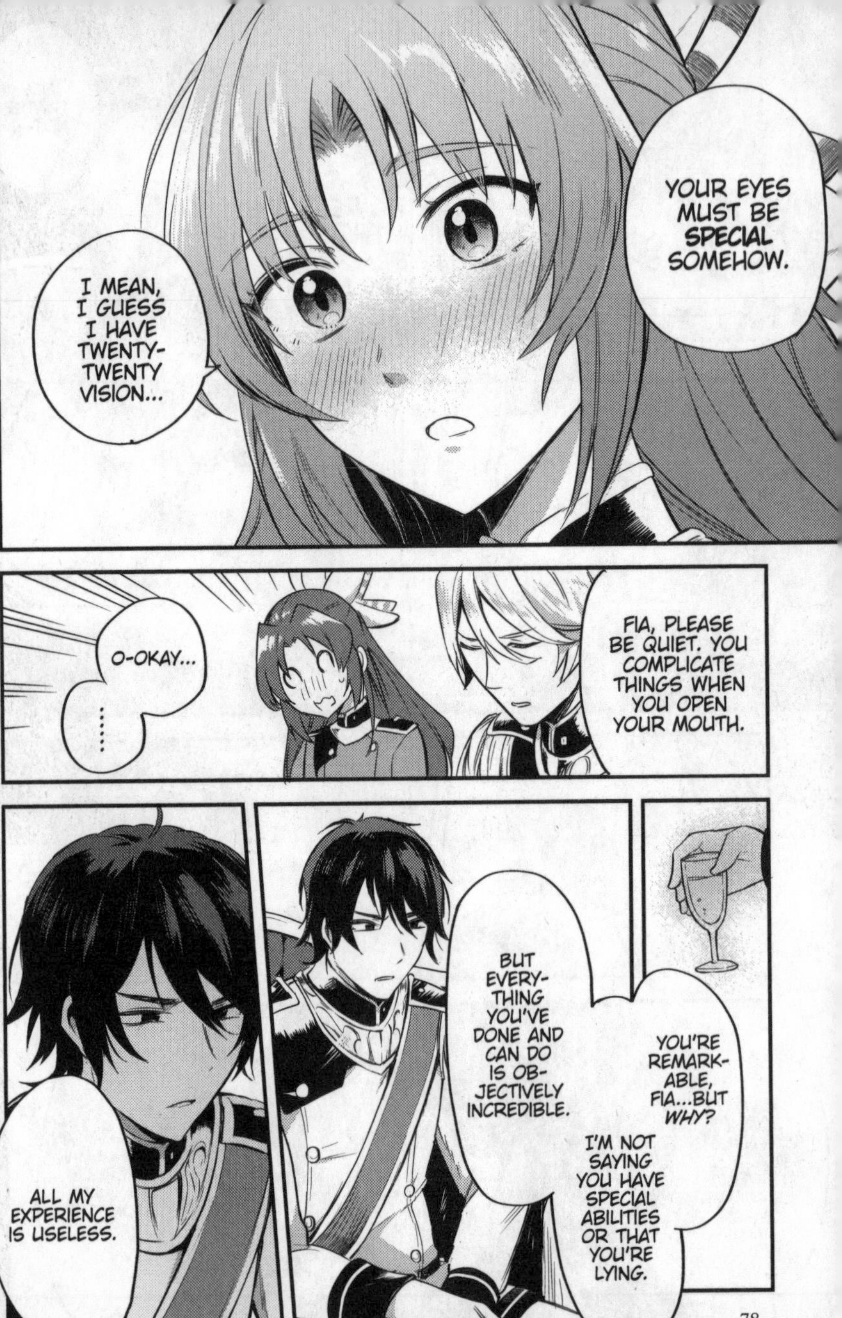
YOUR EYES MUST BE **SPECIAL** SOMEHOW.
I MEAN, I GUESS I HAVE TWENTY-TWENTY VISION...
FIA, PLEASE BE QUIET. YOU COMPLICATE THINGS WHEN YOU OPEN YOUR MOUTH.
O-OKAY...
......
YOU'RE REMARKABLE, FIA...BUT *WHY?*
I'M NOT SAYING YOU HAVE SPECIAL ABILITIES OR THAT YOU'RE LYING.
BUT EVERYTHING YOU'VE DONE AND CAN DO IS OBJECTIVELY INCREDIBLE.
ALL MY EXPERIENCE IS USELESS.

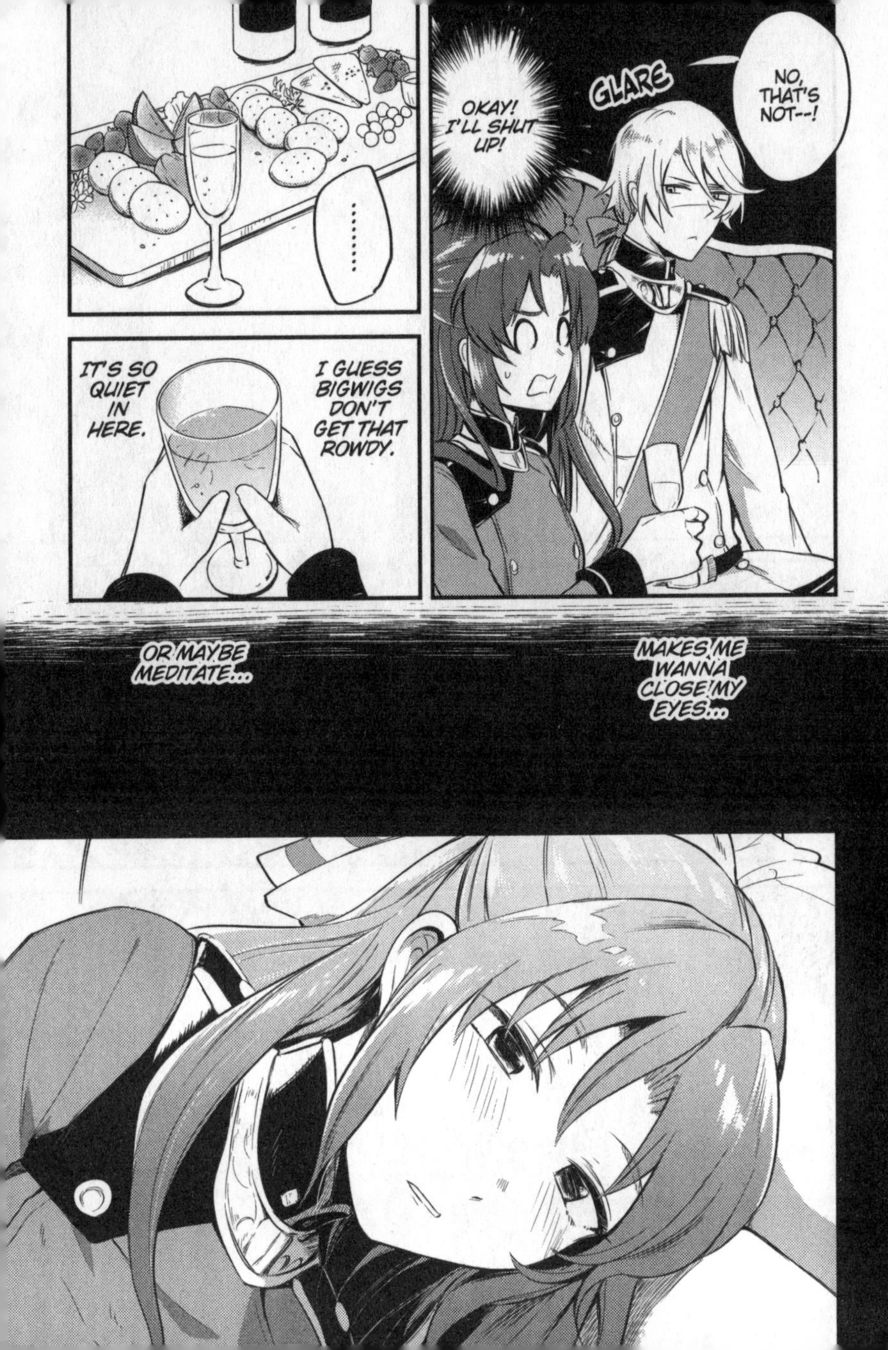
NO, THAT'S NOT--!
GLARE
OKAY! I'LL SHUT UP!
......
I GUESS BIGWIGS DON'T GET THAT ROWDY.
IT'S SO QUIET IN HERE.
MAKES ME WANNA CLOSE MY EYES...
OR MAYBE MEDITATE...

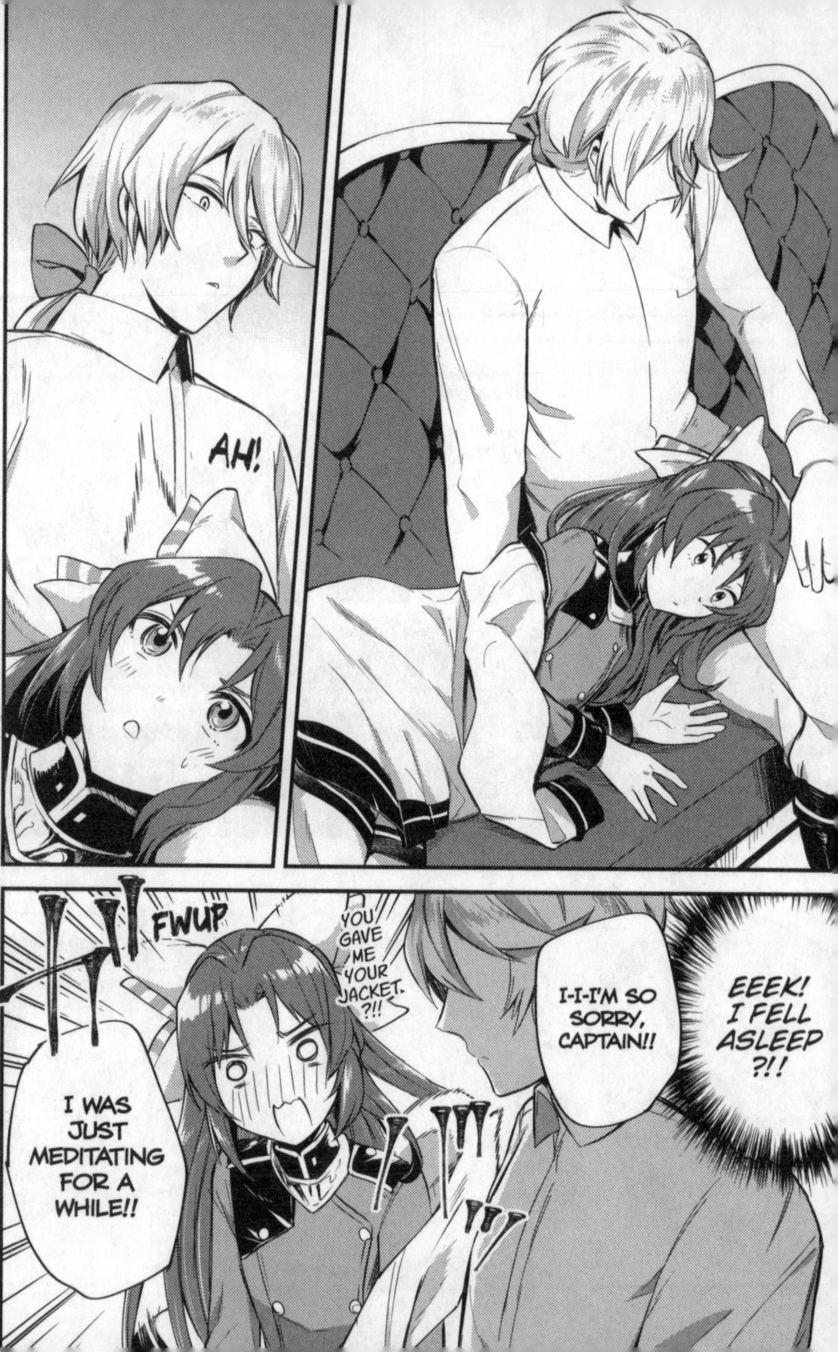
AH!
EEEK! I FELL ASLEEP ?!!
I-I-I'M SO SORRY, CAPTAIN!!
YOU GAVE ME YOUR JACKET. ?!!
FWUP
I WAS JUST MEDITATING FOR A WHILE!!

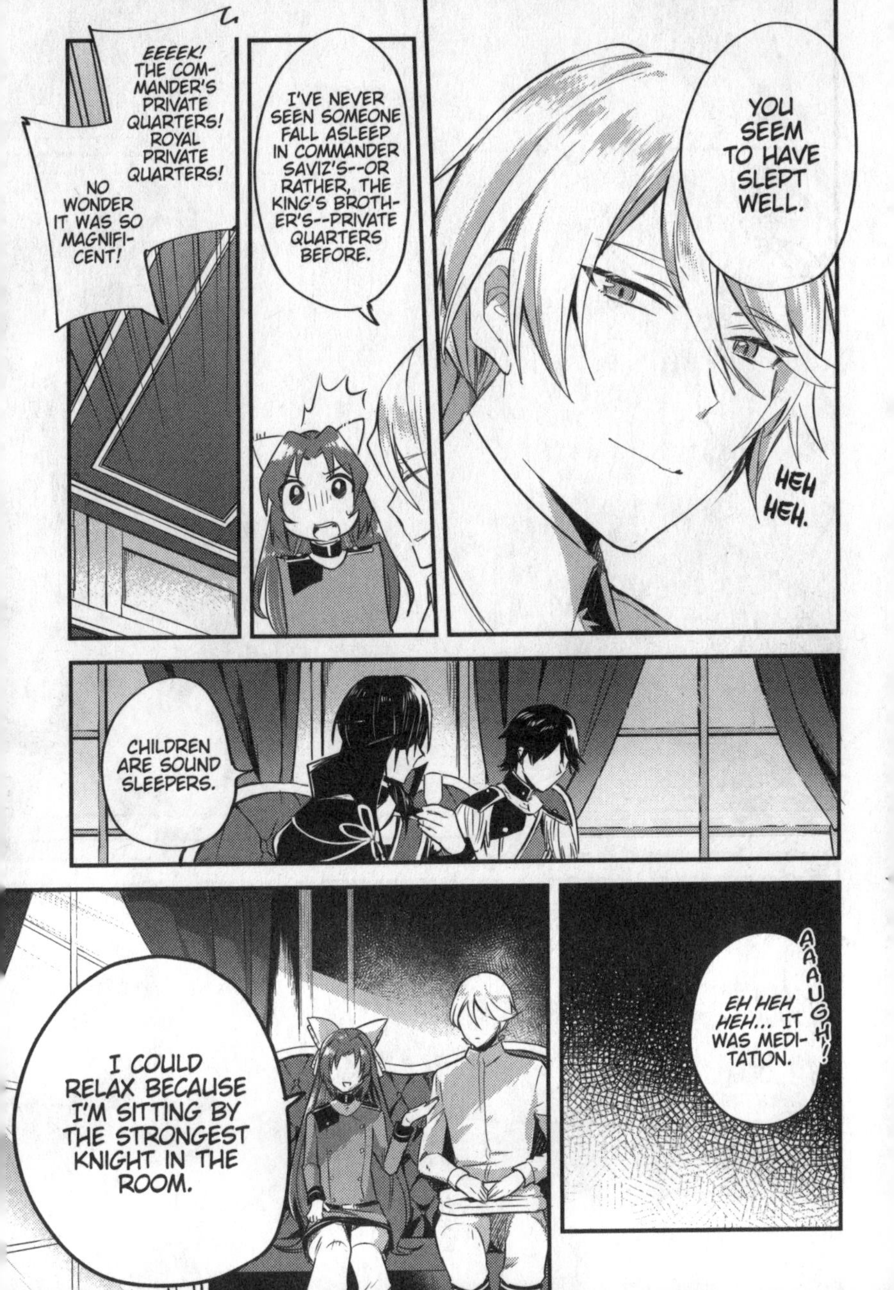
YOU SEEM TO HAVE SLEPT WELL.
HEH HEH.
I'VE NEVER SEEN SOMEONE FALL ASLEEP IN COMMANDER SAVIZ'S--OR RATHER, THE KING'S BROTHER'S--PRIVATE QUARTERS BEFORE.
EEEEK! THE COMMANDER'S PRIVATE QUARTERS! ROYAL PRIVATE QUARTERS!
NO WONDER IT WAS SO MAGNIFICENT!
CHILDREN ARE SOUND SLEEPERS.
AAAUGH!
EH HEH HEH... IT WAS MEDITATION.
I COULD RELAX BECAUSE I'M SITTING BY THE STRONGEST KNIGHT IN THE ROOM.

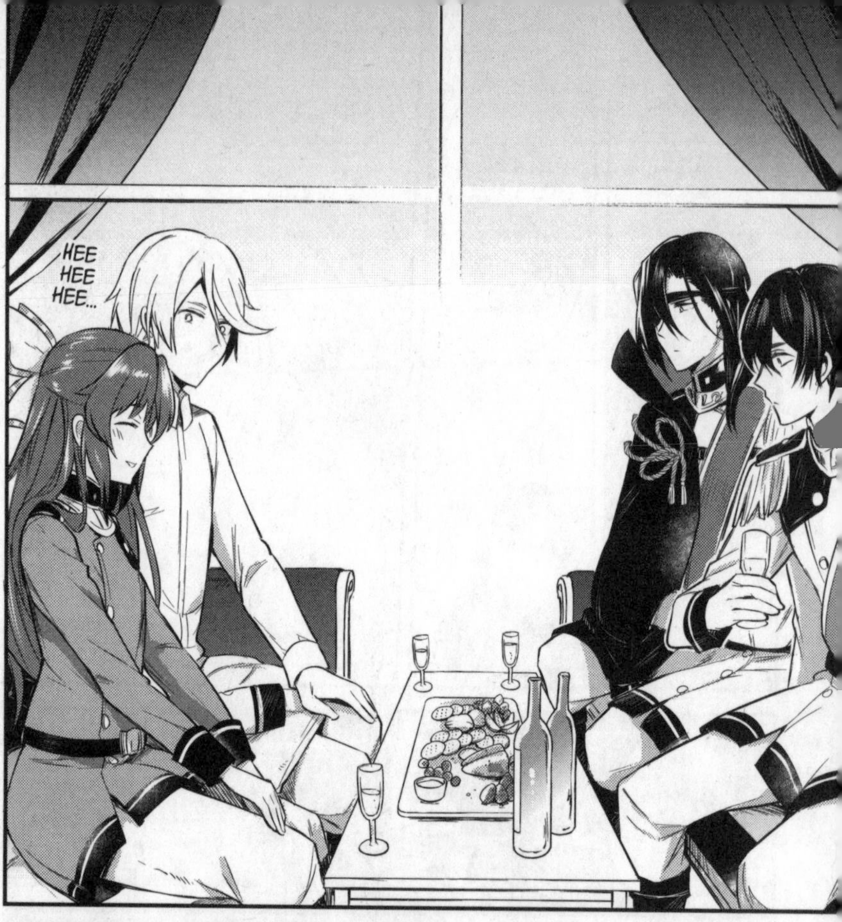
HEE HEE HEE...
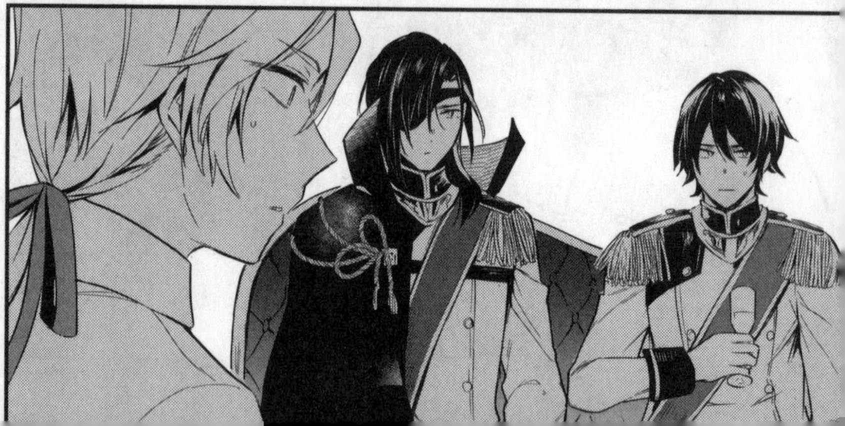

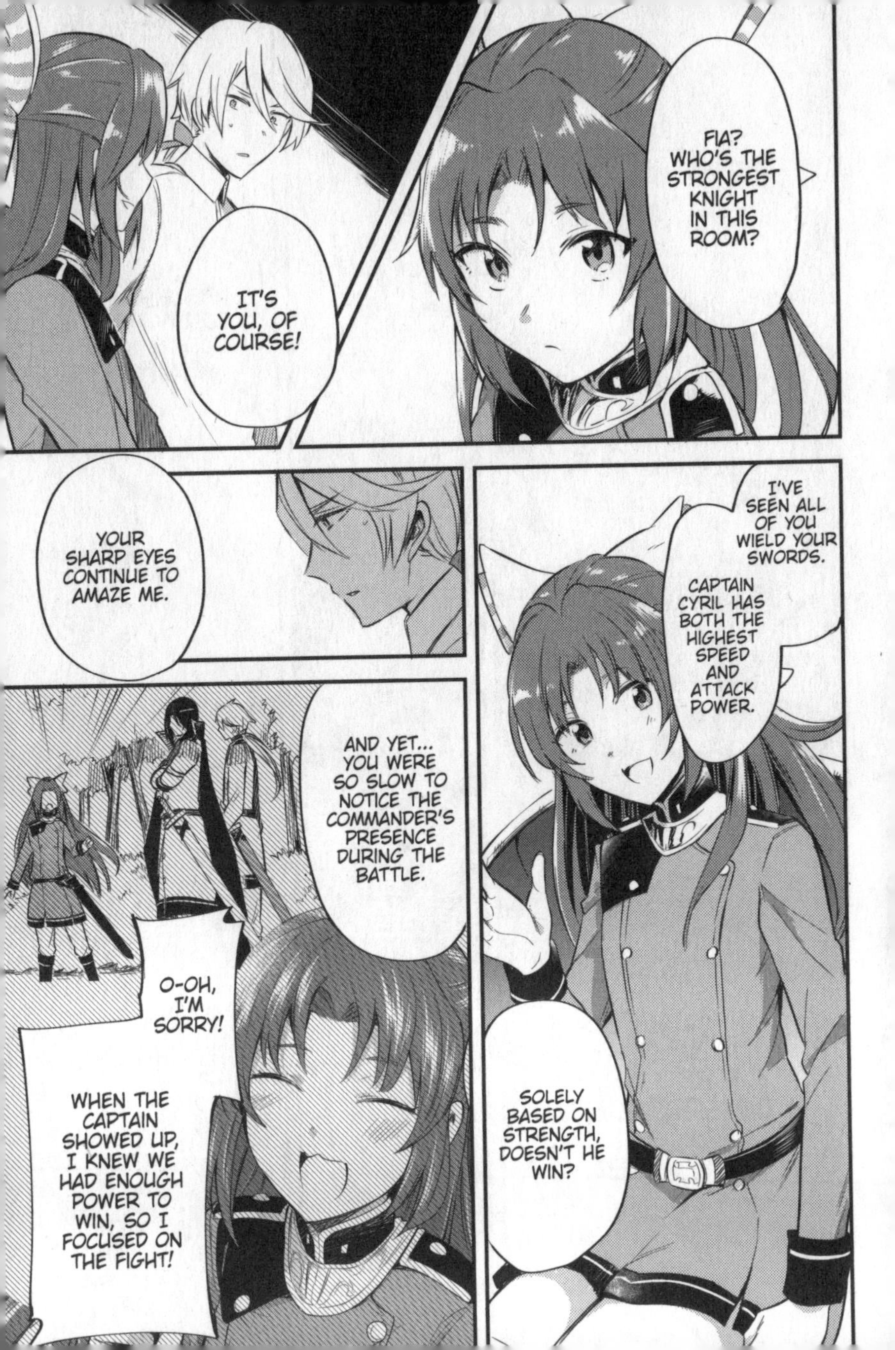
FIA? WHO'S THE STRONGEST KNIGHT IN THIS ROOM?
IT'S YOU, OF COURSE!
I'VE SEEN ALL OF YOU WIELD YOUR SWORDS.
CAPTAIN CYRIL HAS BOTH THE HIGHEST SPEED AND ATTACK POWER.
SOLELY BASED ON STRENGTH, DOESN'T HE WIN?
YOUR SHARP EYES CONTINUE TO AMAZE ME.
AND YET... YOU WERE SO SLOW TO NOTICE THE COMMANDER'S PRESENCE DURING THE BATTLE.
O-OH, I'M SORRY!
WHEN THE CAPTAIN SHOWED UP, I KNEW WE HAD ENOUGH POWER TO WIN, SO I FOCUSED ON THE FIGHT!

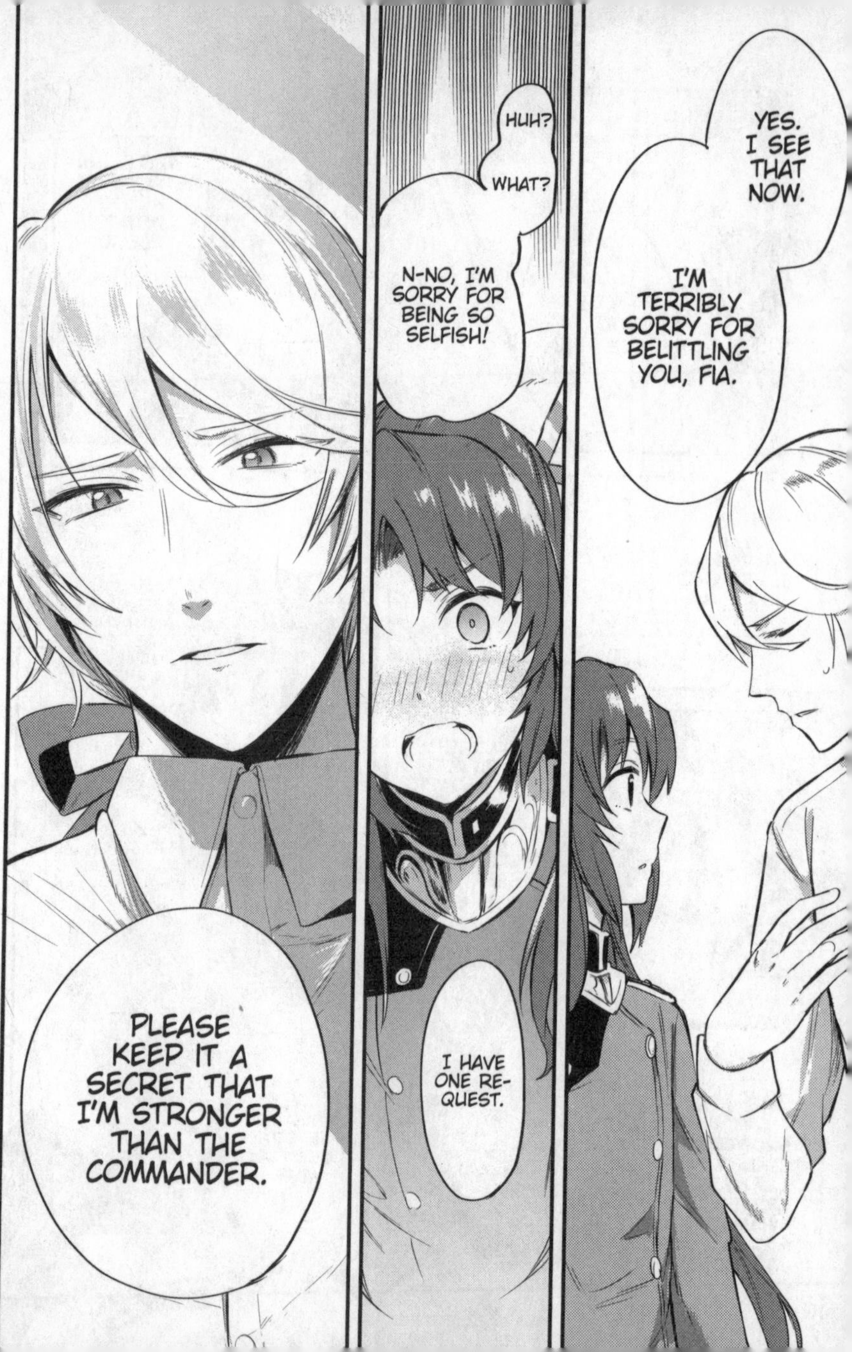
YES. I SEE THAT NOW.
I'M TERRIBLY SORRY FOR BELITTLING YOU, FIA.
HUH?
WHAT?
N-NO, I'M SORRY FOR BEING SO SELFISH!
I HAVE ONE RE-QUEST.
PLEASE KEEP IT A SECRET THAT I'M STRONGER THAN THE COMMANDER.

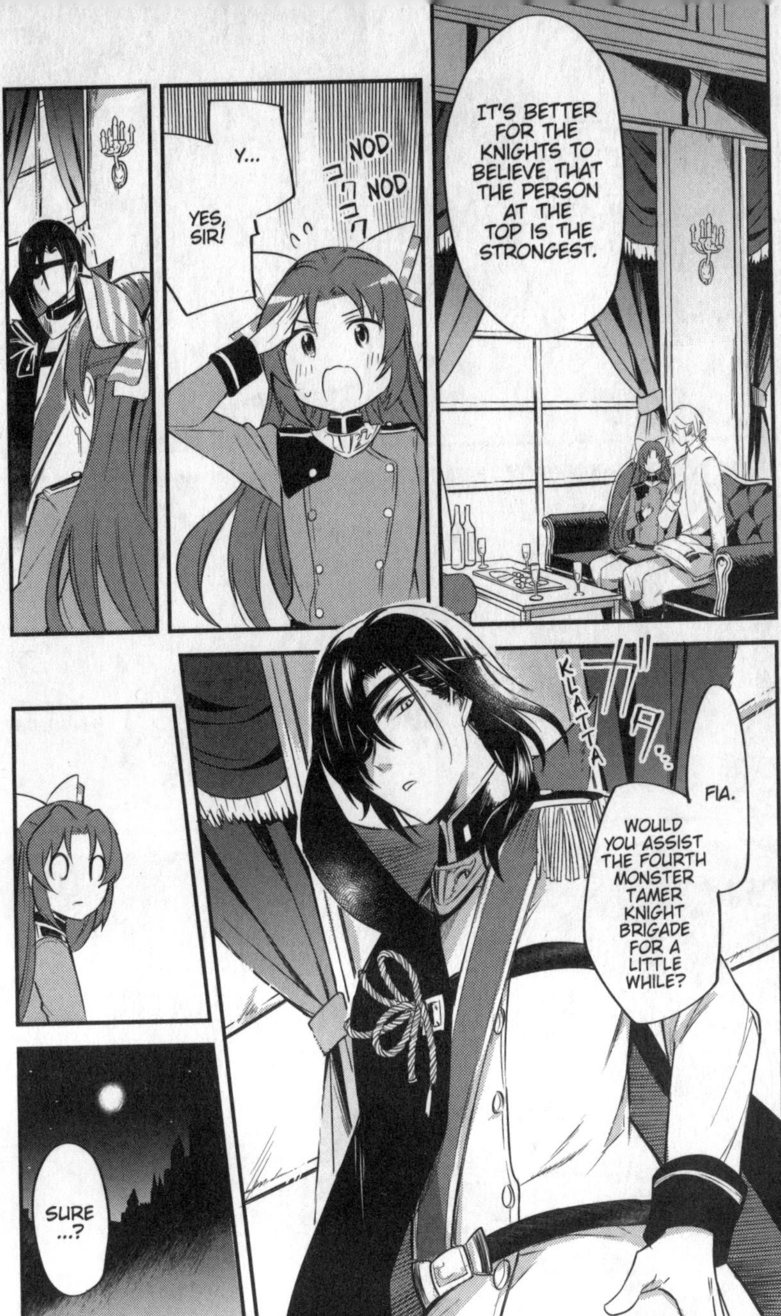

IT'S BETTER FOR THE KNIGHTS TO BELIEVE THAT THE PERSON AT THE TOP IS THE STRONGEST.
NOD NOD
Y...
YES, SIR!
KLATTA
FIA.
WOULD YOU ASSIST THE FOURTH MONSTER TAMER KNIGHT BRIGADE FOR A LITTLE WHILE?
SURE ...?

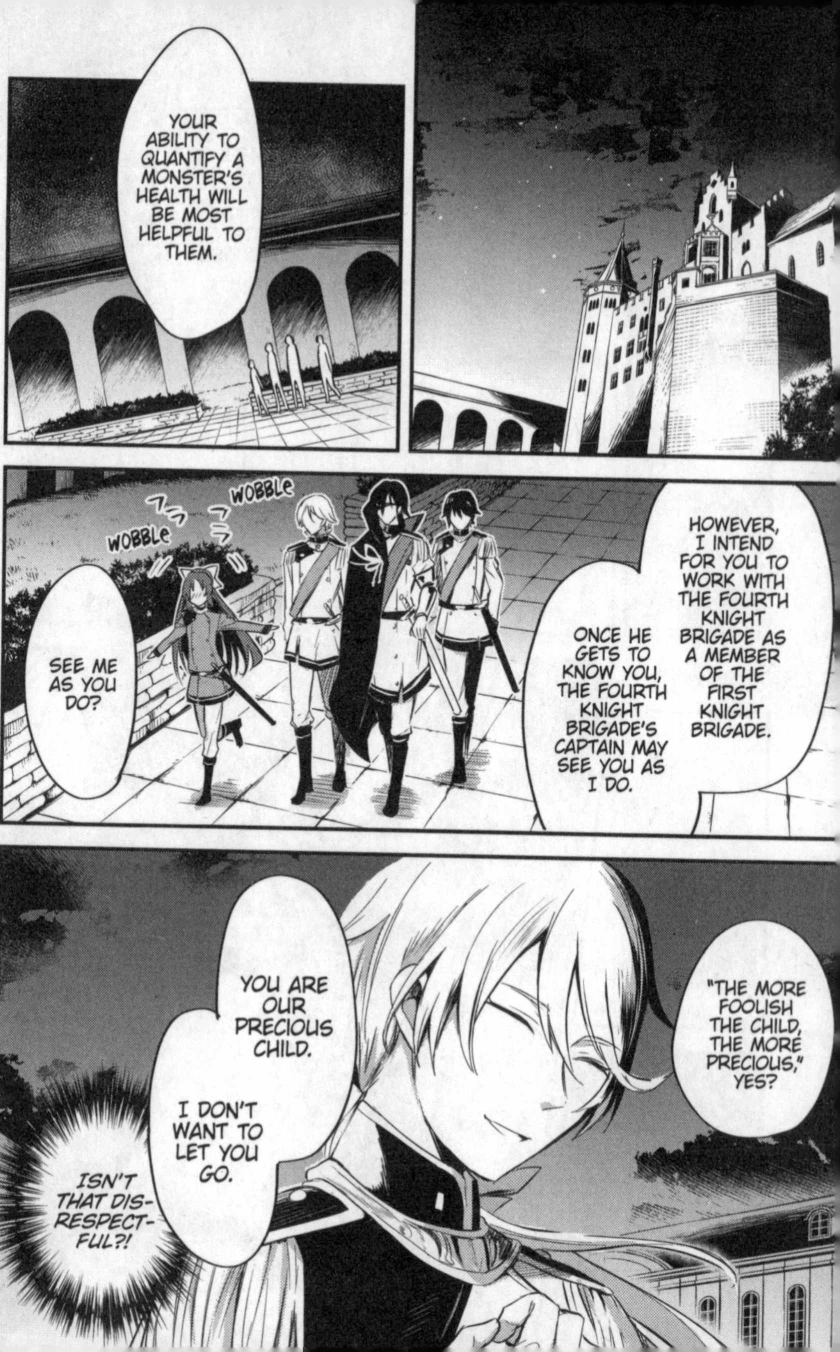
YOUR ABILITY TO QUANTIFY A MONSTER'S HEALTH WILL BE MOST HELPFUL TO THEM.
HOWEVER, I INTEND FOR YOU TO WORK WITH THE FOURTH KNIGHT BRIGADE AS A MEMBER OF THE FIRST KNIGHT BRIGADE.
ONCE HE GETS TO KNOW YOU, THE FOURTH KNIGHT BRIGADE'S CAPTAIN MAY SEE YOU AS I DO.
WOBBLE
WOBBLE
SEE ME AS YOU DO?
"THE MORE FOOLISH THE CHILD, THE MORE PRECIOUS," YES?
YOU ARE OUR PRECIOUS CHILD.
I DON'T WANT TO LET YOU GO.
ISN'T THAT DIS-RESPECTFUL?!

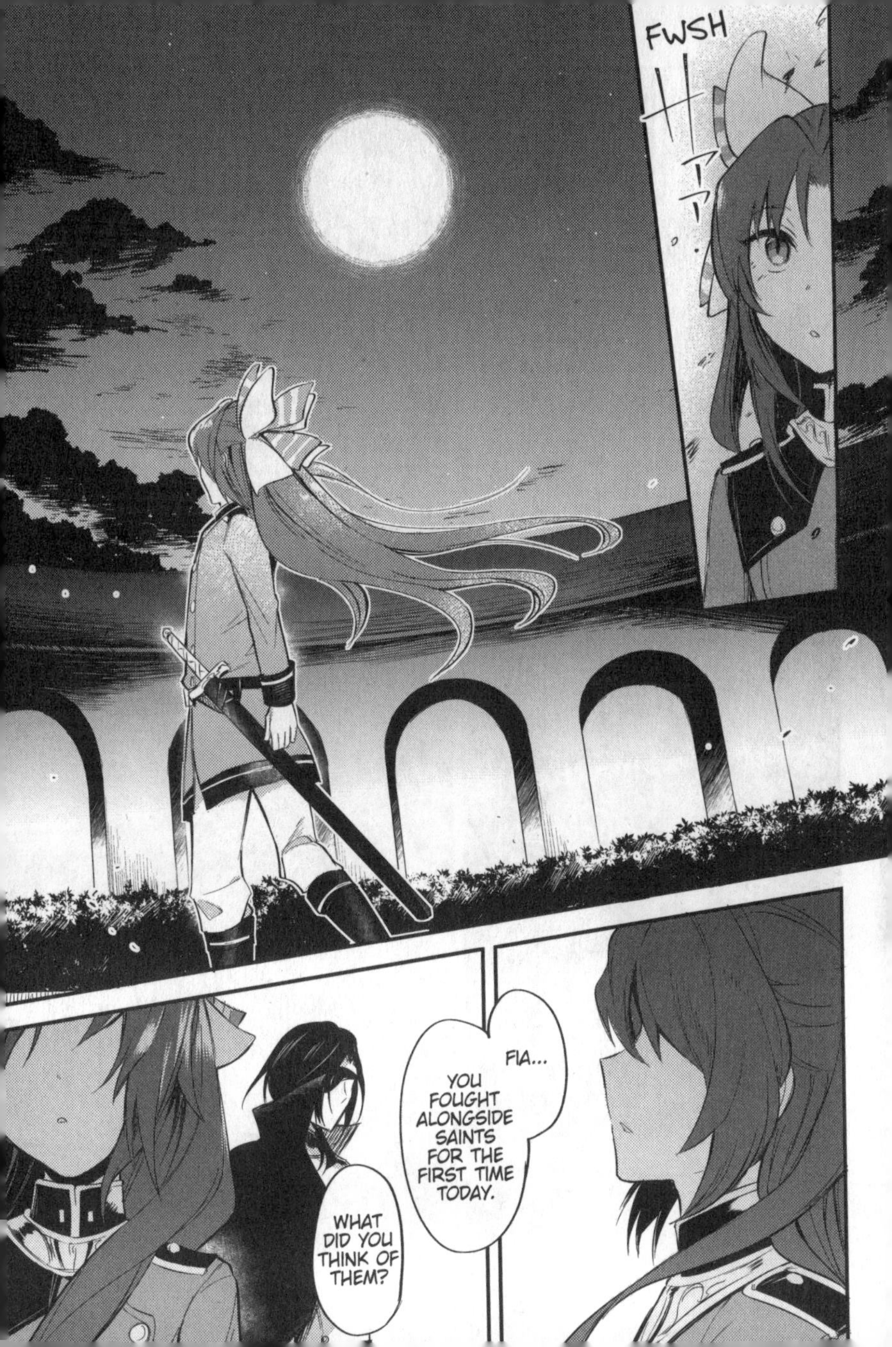
FWSH
FIA...
YOU FOUGHT ALONGSIDE SAINTS FOR THE FIRST TIME TODAY.
WHAT DID YOU THINK OF THEM?

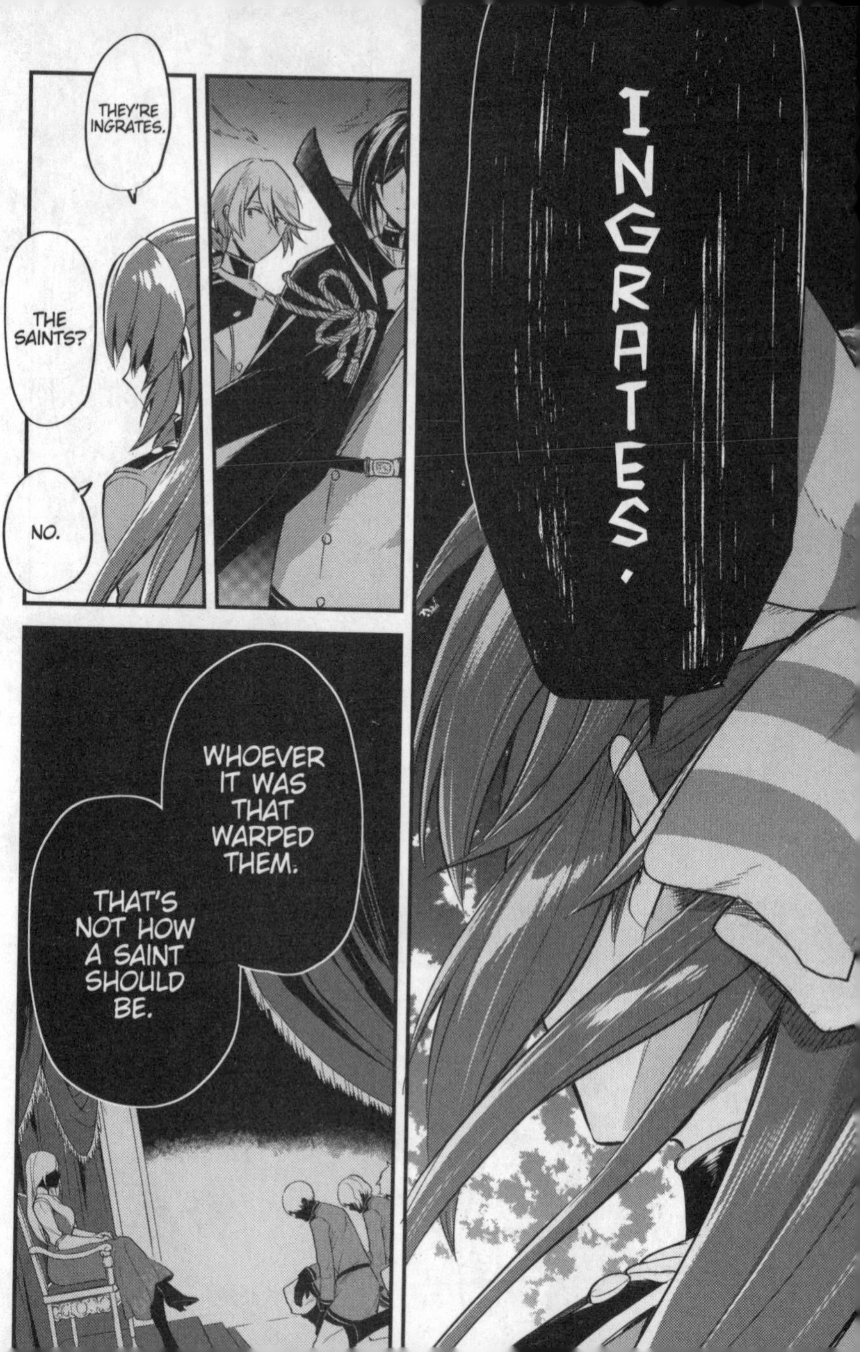
INGRATES.
THEY'RE INGRATES.
THE SAINTS?
NO.
WHOEVER IT WAS THAT WARPED THEM.
THAT'S NOT HOW A SAINT SHOULD BE.

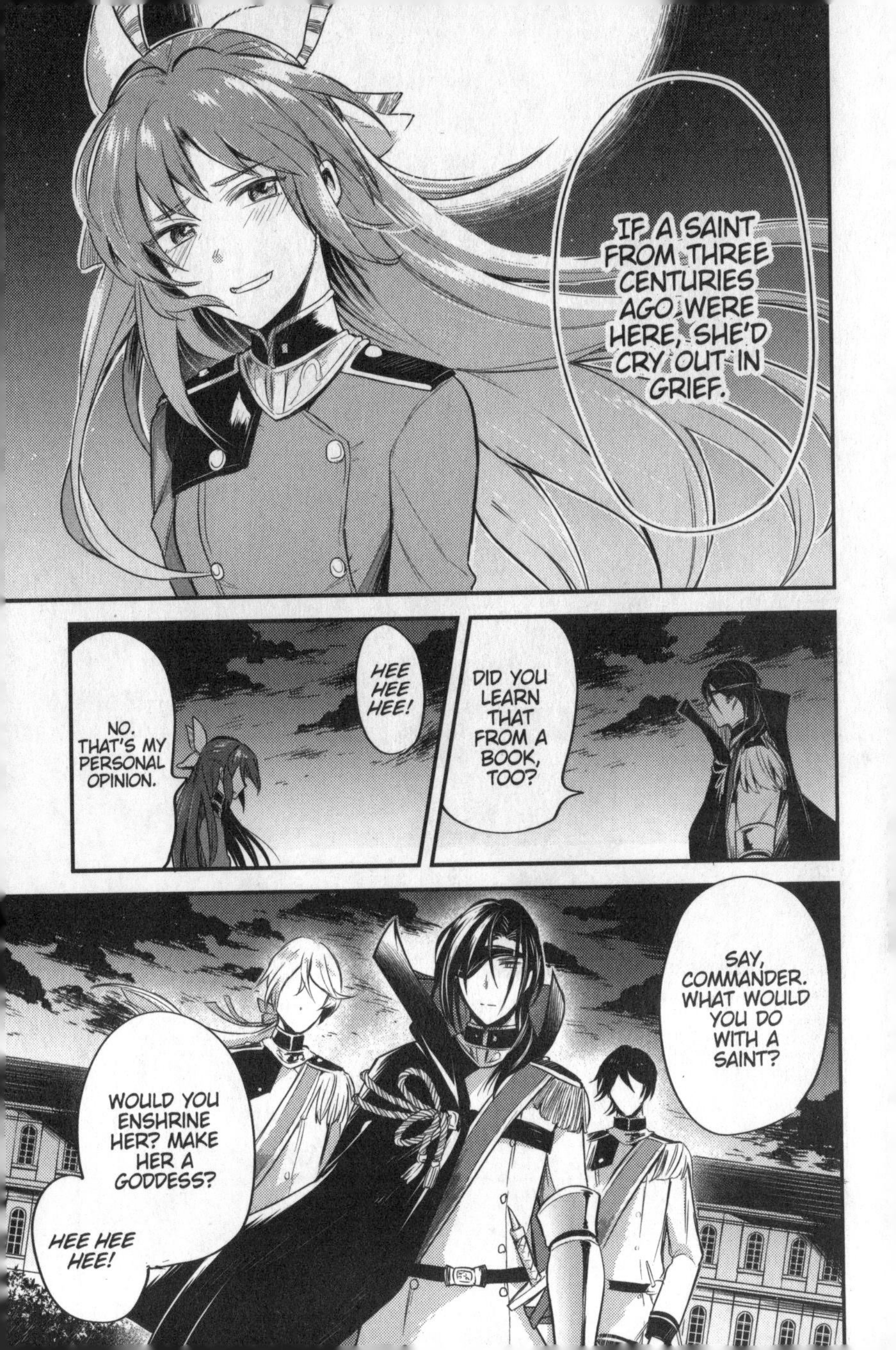
IF A SAINT FROM THREE CENTURIES AGO WERE HERE, SHE'D CRY OUT IN GRIEF.
DID YOU LEARN THAT FROM A BOOK, TOO?
HEE HEE HEE!
NO. THAT'S MY PERSONAL OPINION.
SAY, COMMANDER. WHAT WOULD YOU DO WITH A SAINT?
WOULD YOU ENSHRINE HER? MAKE HER A GODDESS?
HEE HEE HEE!

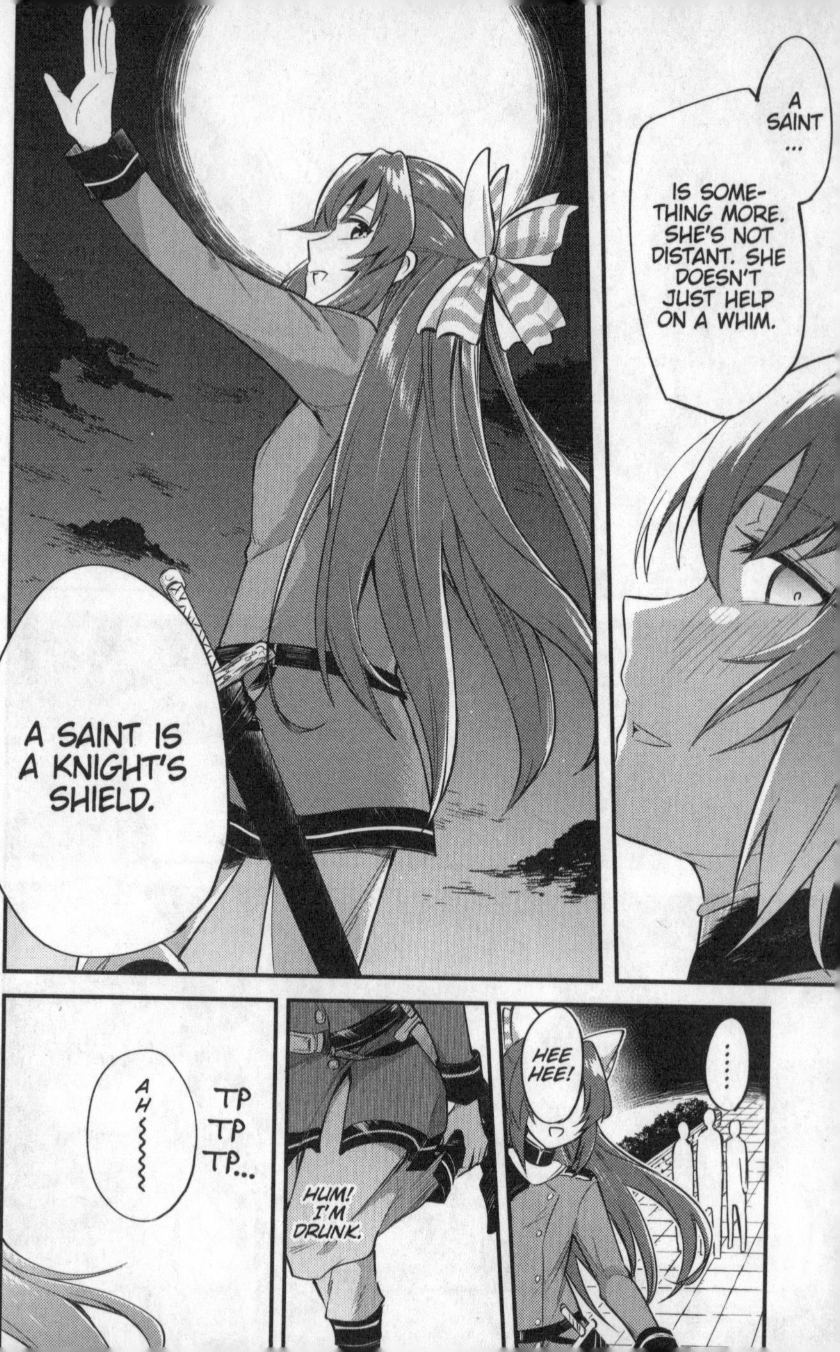
A SAINT ...
IS SOMETHING MORE. SHE'S NOT DISTANT. SHE DOESN'T JUST HELP ON A WHIM.
A SAINT IS A KNIGHT'S SHIELD.
......
HEE HEE!
HUM! I'M DRUNK.
TP TP TP...
AH~~~

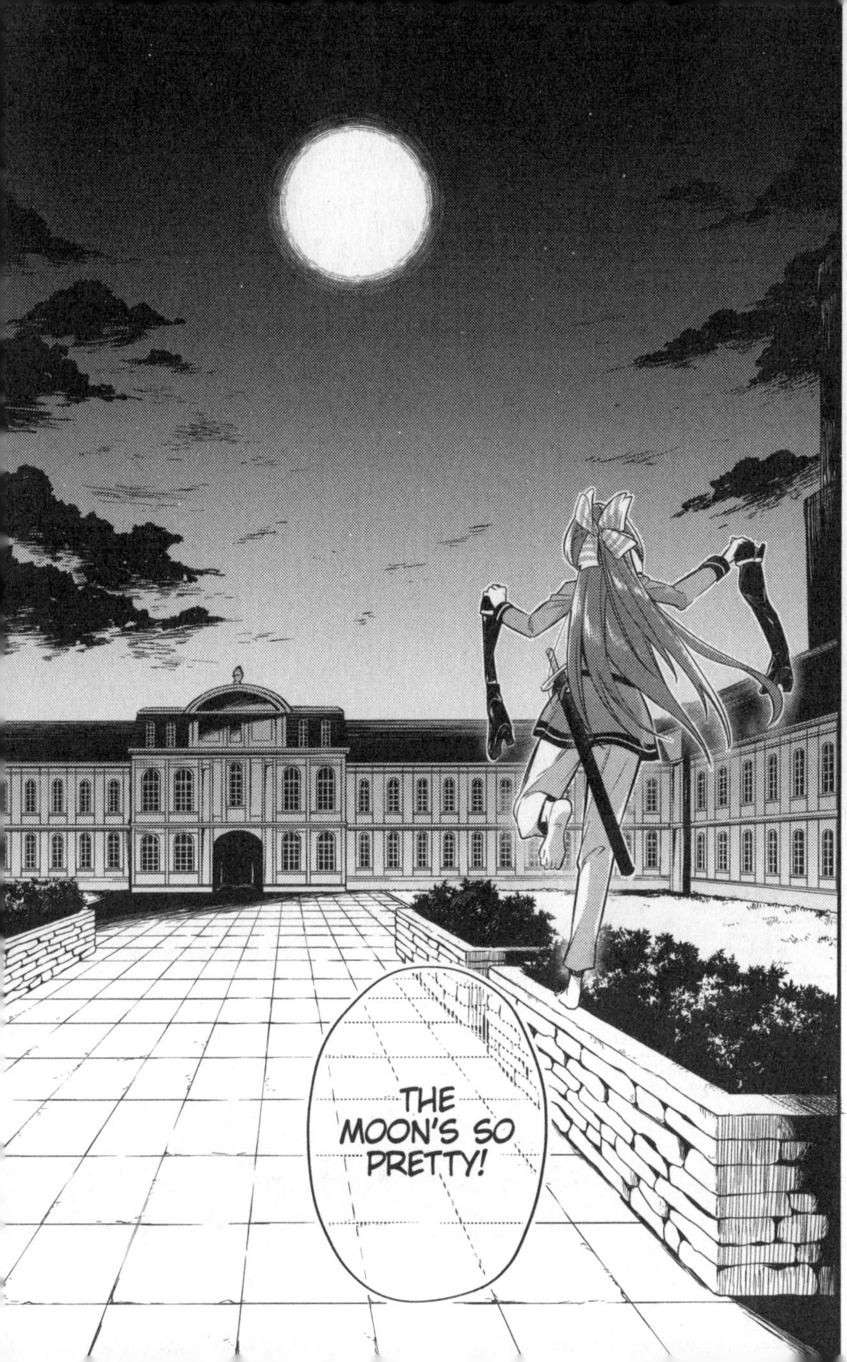
THE MOON'S SO PRETTY!

A Tale of the Secret Saint

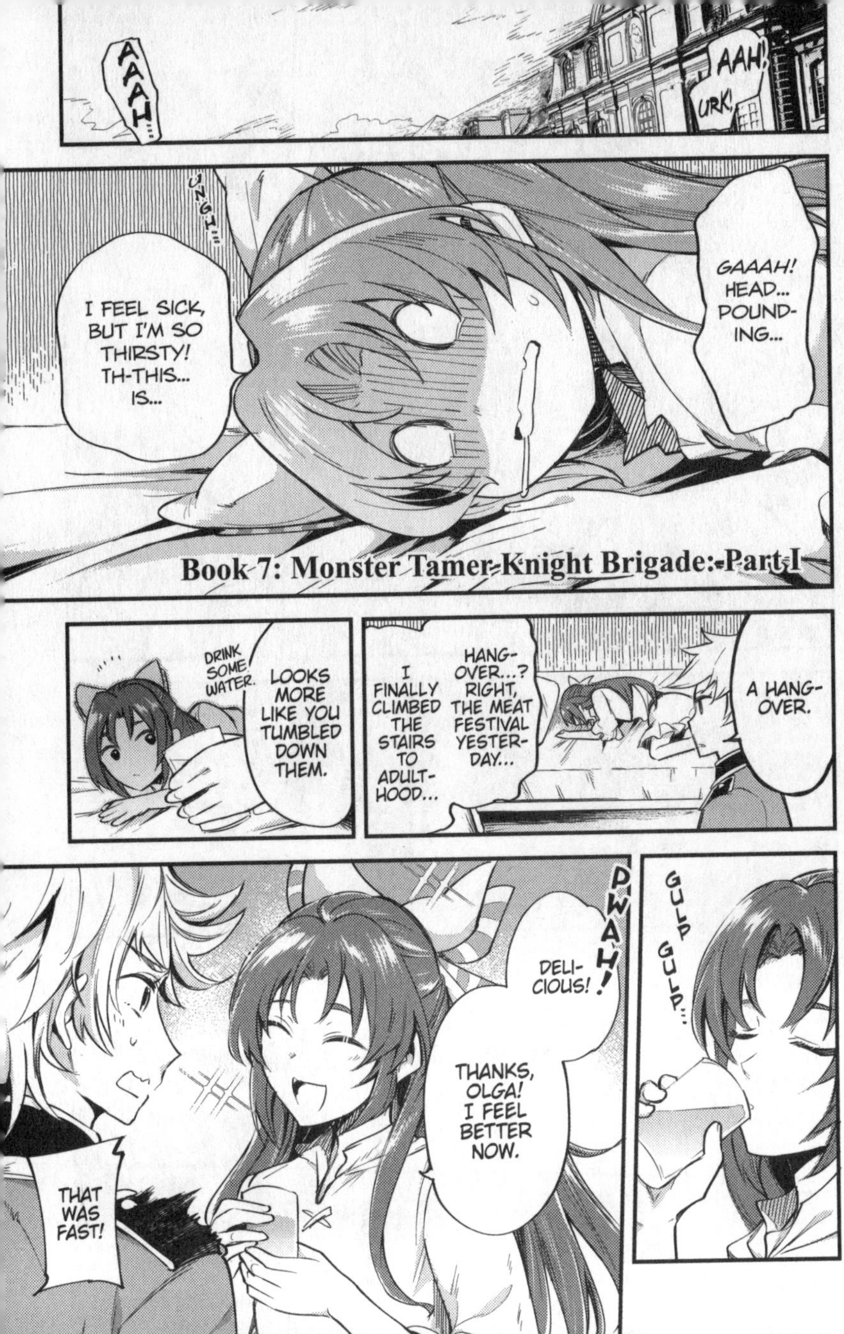
AAH!
URK!
AAAH...
GAAAH! HEAD... POUND-ING...
UNGH...
I FEEL SICK, BUT I'M SO THIRSTY! TH-THIS... IS...
Book 7: Monster Tamer Knight Brigade: Part I
A HANG-OVER.
HANG-OVER...? RIGHT, THE MEAT FESTIVAL YESTER-DAY...
I FINALLY CLIMBED THE STAIRS TO ADULT-HOOD...
LOOKS MORE LIKE YOU TUMBLED DOWN THEM.
DRINK SOME WATER.
...
GULP GULP...
PWAH!
DELI-CIOUS!
THANKS, OLGA! I FEEL BETTER NOW.
THAT WAS FAST!

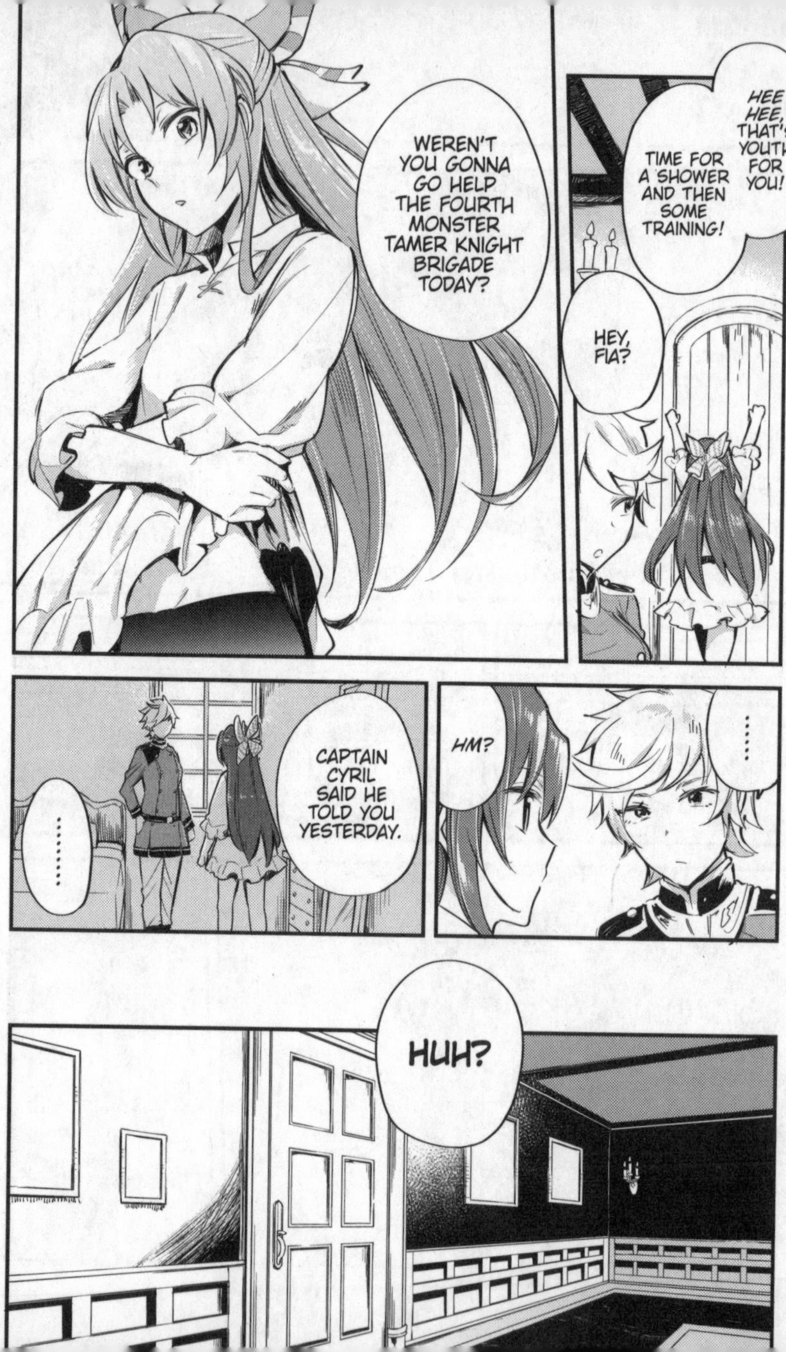
HEE HEE, THAT'S YOUTH FOR YOU!
TIME FOR A SHOWER AND THEN SOME TRAINING!
HEY, FIA?
WEREN'T YOU GONNA GO HELP THE FOURTH MONSTER TAMER KNIGHT BRIGADE TODAY?
......
HM?
CAPTAIN CYRIL SAID HE TOLD YOU YESTERDAY.
......
HUH?

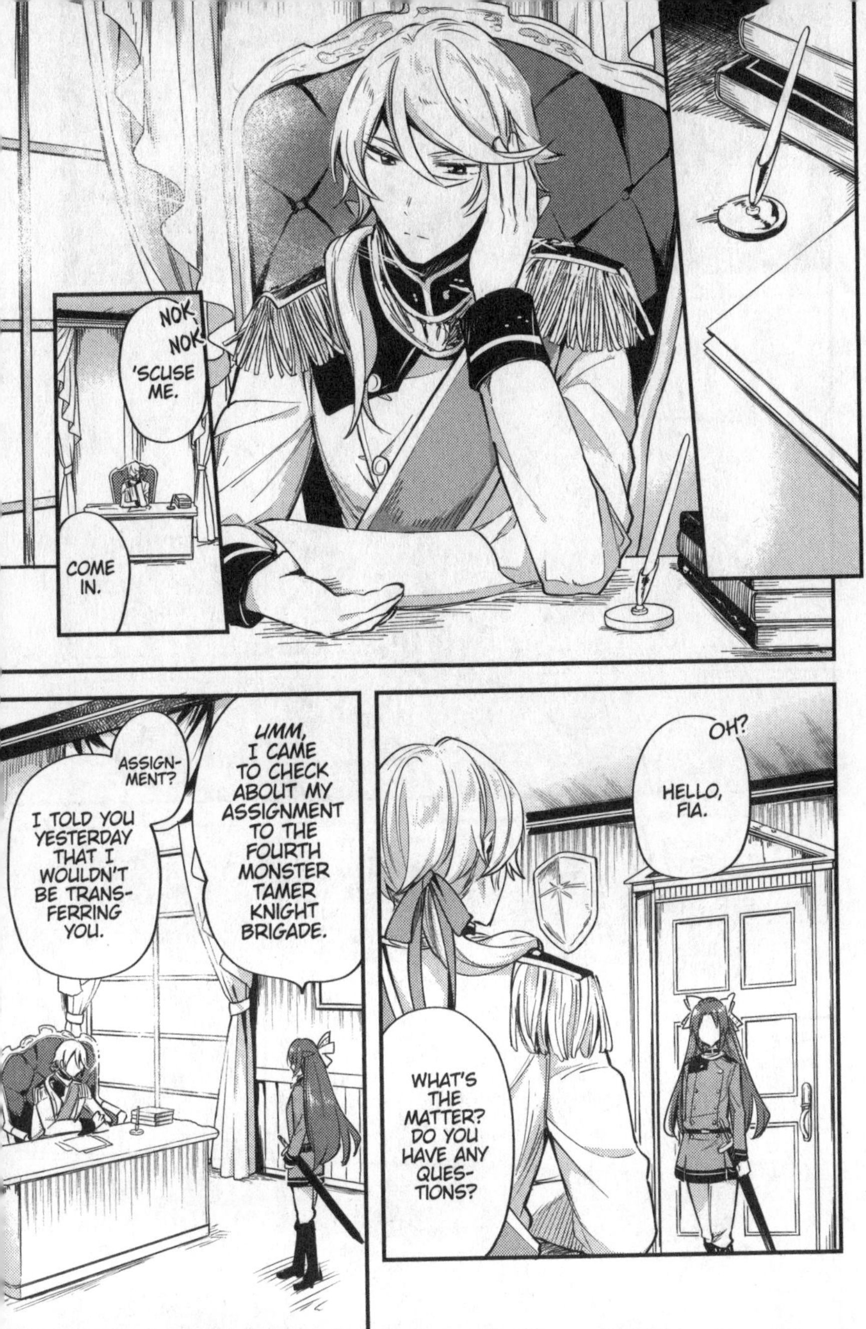
NOK NOK
'SCUSE ME.
COME IN.
OH?
HELLO, FIA.
WHAT'S THE MATTER? DO YOU HAVE ANY QUES-TIONS?
UMM, I CAME TO CHECK ABOUT MY ASSIGNMENT TO THE FOURTH MONSTER TAMER KNIGHT BRIGADE.
ASSIGN-MENT?
I TOLD YOU YESTERDAY THAT I WOULDN'T BE TRANS-FERRING YOU.

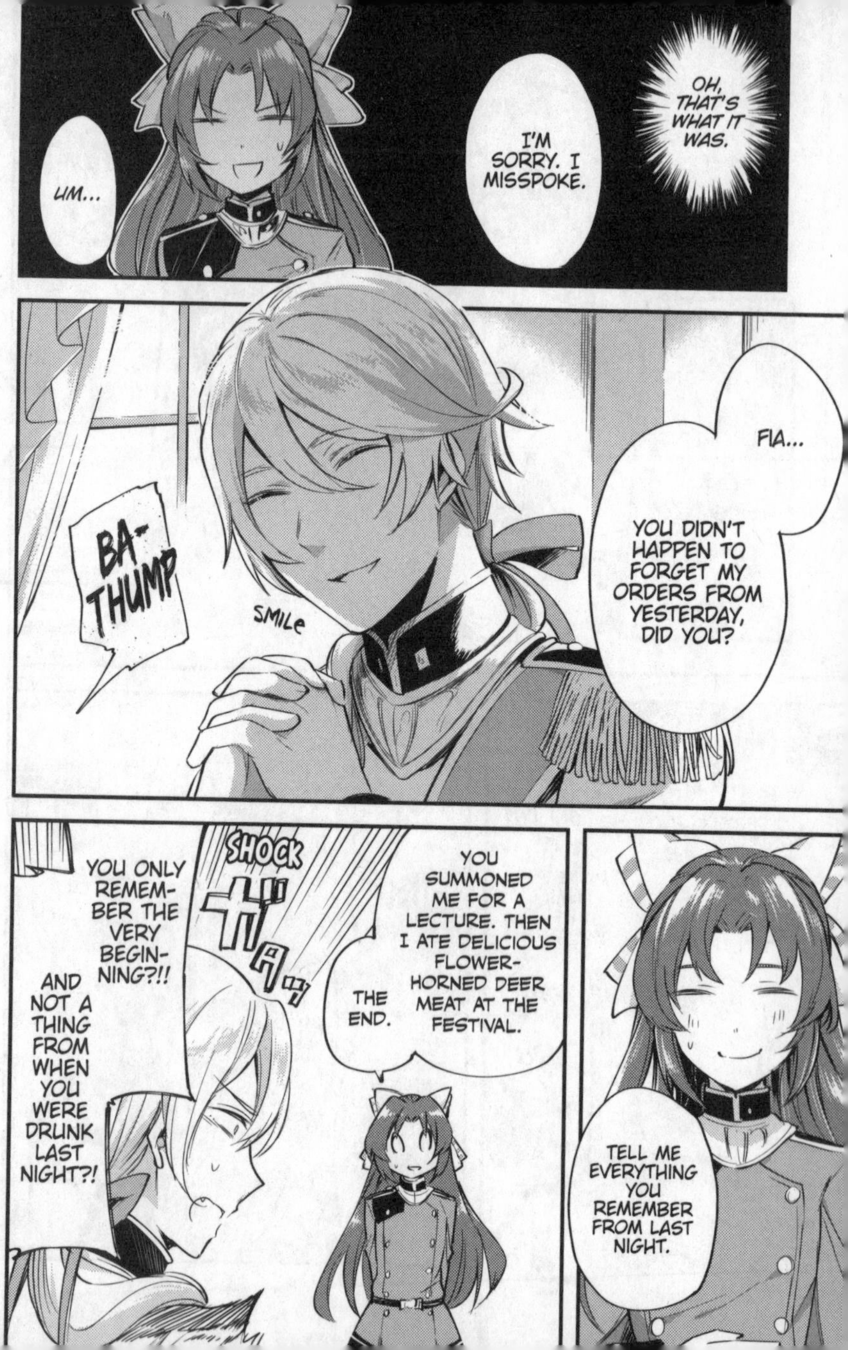
OH, THAT'S WHAT IT WAS.
I'M SORRY. I MISSPOKE.
UM...
FIA...
YOU DIDN'T HAPPEN TO FORGET MY ORDERS FROM YESTERDAY, DID YOU?
SMILE
BA-THUMP
TELL ME EVERYTHING YOU REMEMBER FROM LAST NIGHT.
YOU SUMMONED ME FOR A LECTURE. THEN I ATE DELICIOUS FLOWER-HORNED DEER MEAT AT THE FESTIVAL.
THE END.
SHOCK
YOU ONLY REMEMBER THE VERY BEGINNING?!!
AND NOT A THING FROM WHEN YOU WERE DRUNK LAST NIGHT?!

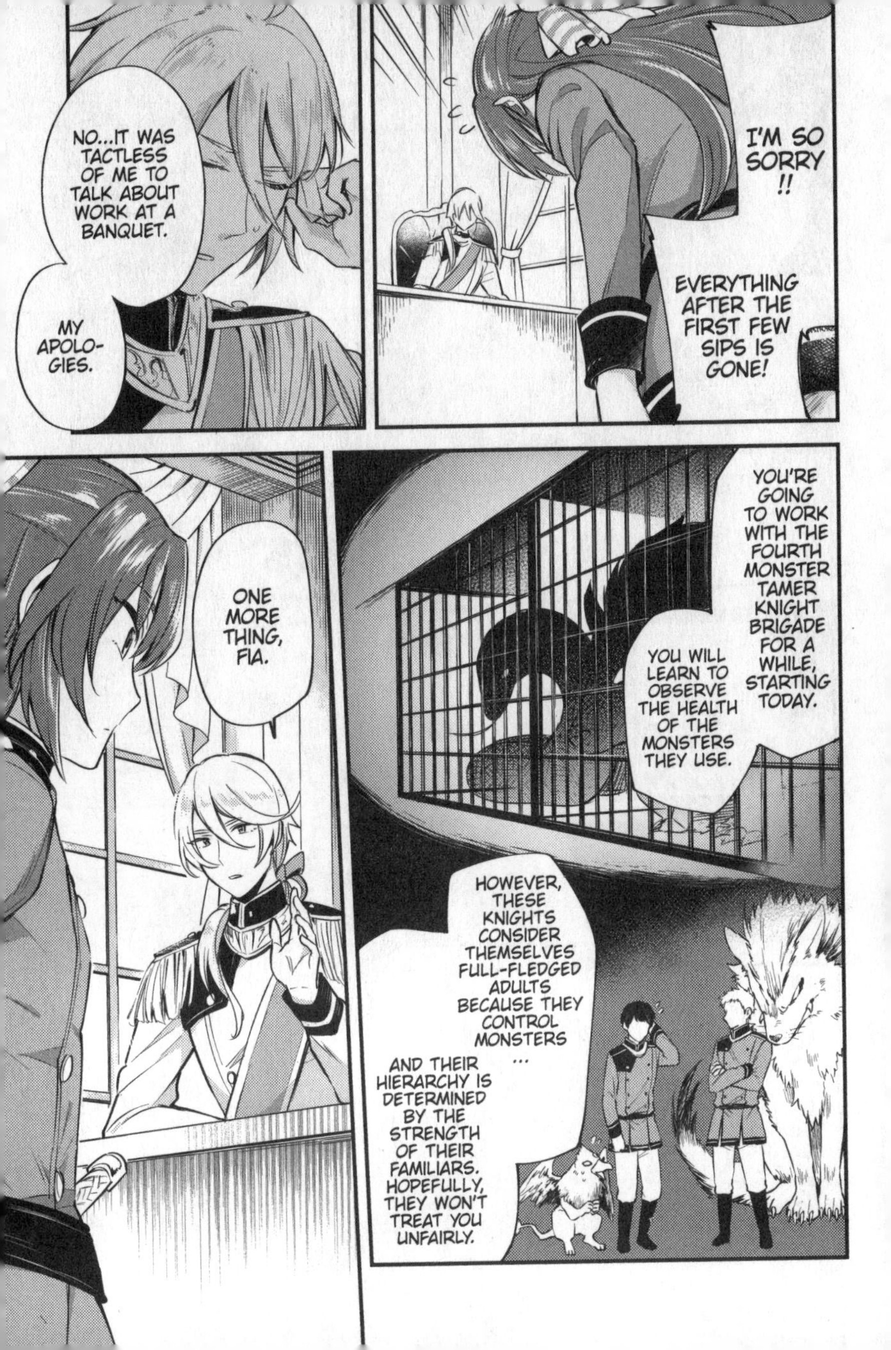
I'M SO SORRY !!
EVERYTHING AFTER THE FIRST FEW SIPS IS GONE!
NO...IT WAS TACTLESS OF ME TO TALK ABOUT WORK AT A BANQUET.
MY APOLOGIES.
YOU'RE GOING TO WORK WITH THE FOURTH MONSTER TAMER KNIGHT BRIGADE FOR A WHILE, STARTING TODAY.
YOU WILL LEARN TO OBSERVE THE HEALTH OF THE MONSTERS THEY USE.
HOWEVER, THESE KNIGHTS CONSIDER THEMSELVES FULL-FLEDGED ADULTS BECAUSE THEY CONTROL MONSTERS ...
AND THEIR HIERARCHY IS DETERMINED BY THE STRENGTH OF THEIR FAMILIARS. HOPEFULLY, THEY WON'T TREAT YOU UNFAIRLY.
ONE MORE THING, FIA.

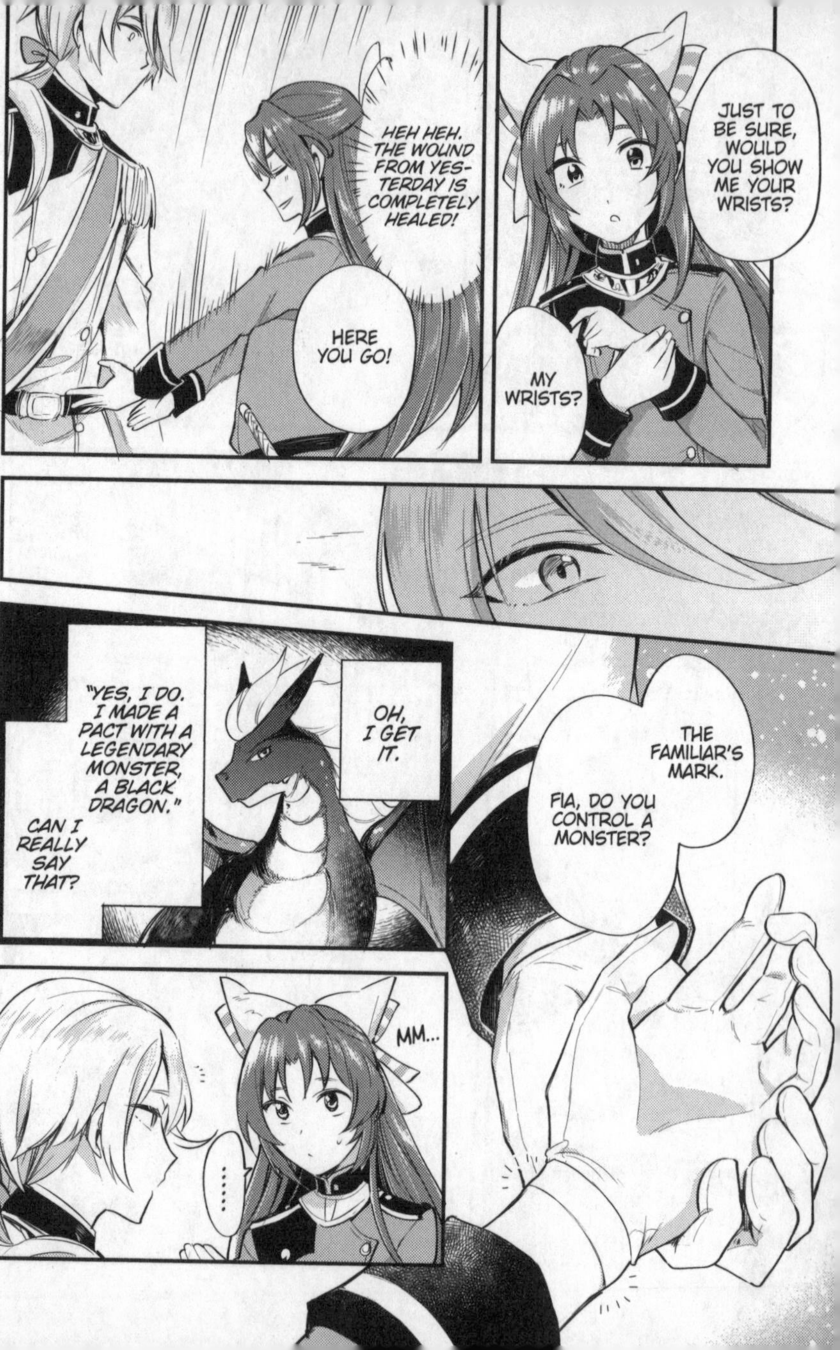
JUST TO BE SURE, WOULD YOU SHOW ME YOUR WRISTS?
MY WRISTS?
HEH HEH. THE WOUND FROM YES-TERDAY IS COMPLETELY HEALED!
HERE YOU GO!
THE FAMILIAR'S MARK.
FIA, DO YOU CONTROL A MONSTER?
OH, I GET IT.
"YES, I DO. I MADE A PACT WITH A LEGENDARY MONSTER, A BLACK DRAGON."
CAN I REALLY SAY THAT?
MM...
......

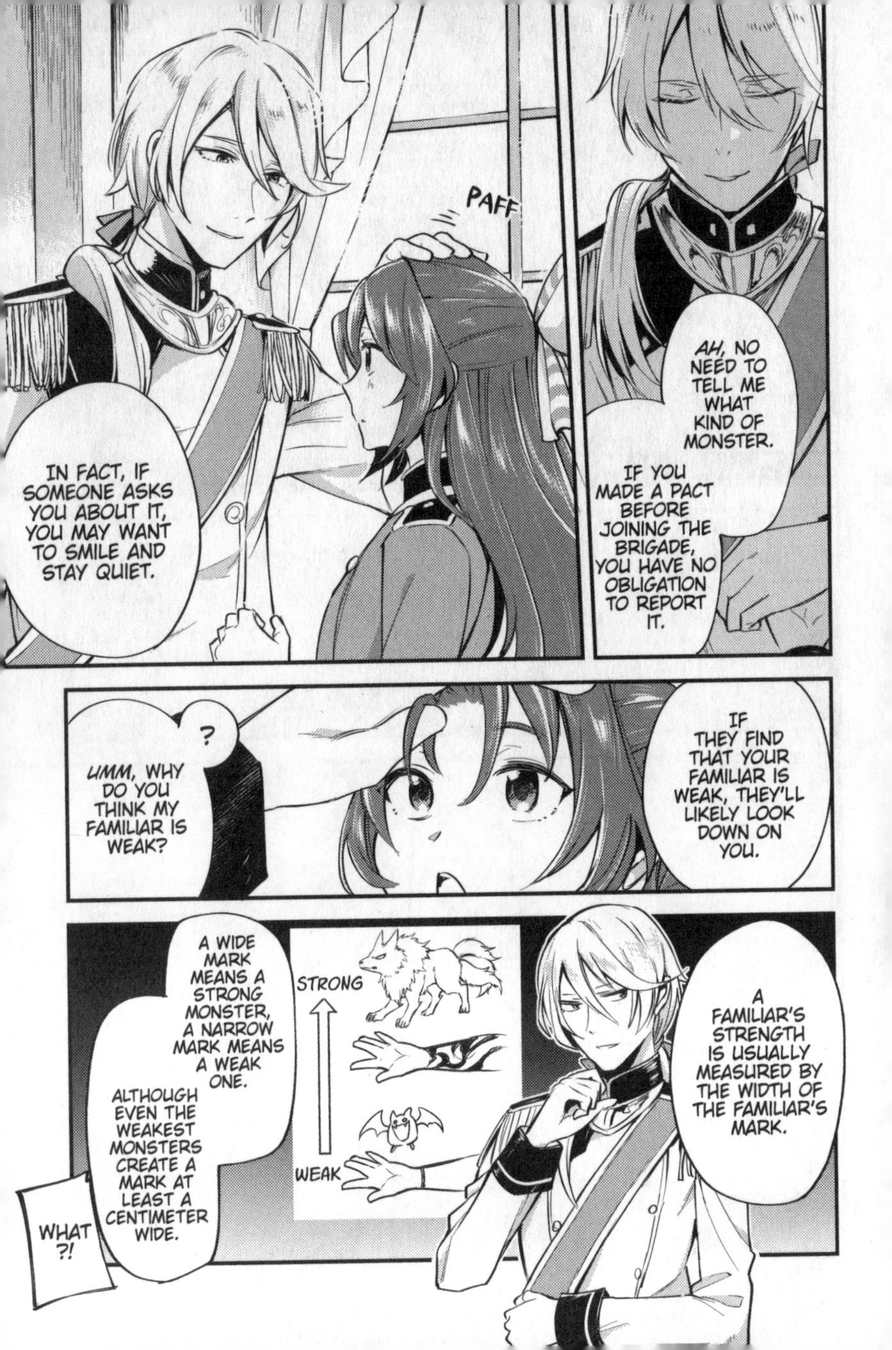
AH, NO NEED TO TELL ME WHAT KIND OF MONSTER.
IF YOU MADE A PACT BEFORE JOINING THE BRIGADE, YOU HAVE NO OBLIGATION TO REPORT IT.
PAFF
IN FACT, IF SOMEONE ASKS YOU ABOUT IT, YOU MAY WANT TO SMILE AND STAY QUIET.
IF THEY FIND THAT YOUR FAMILIAR IS WEAK, THEY'LL LIKELY LOOK DOWN ON YOU.
?
UMM, WHY DO YOU THINK MY FAMILIAR IS WEAK?
A FAMILIAR'S STRENGTH IS USUALLY MEASURED BY THE WIDTH OF THE FAMILIAR'S MARK.
STRONG
WEAK
A WIDE MARK MEANS A STRONG MONSTER, A NARROW MARK MEANS A WEAK ONE.
ALTHOUGH EVEN THE WEAKEST MONSTERS CREATE A MARK AT LEAST A CENTIMETER WIDE.
WHAT ?!

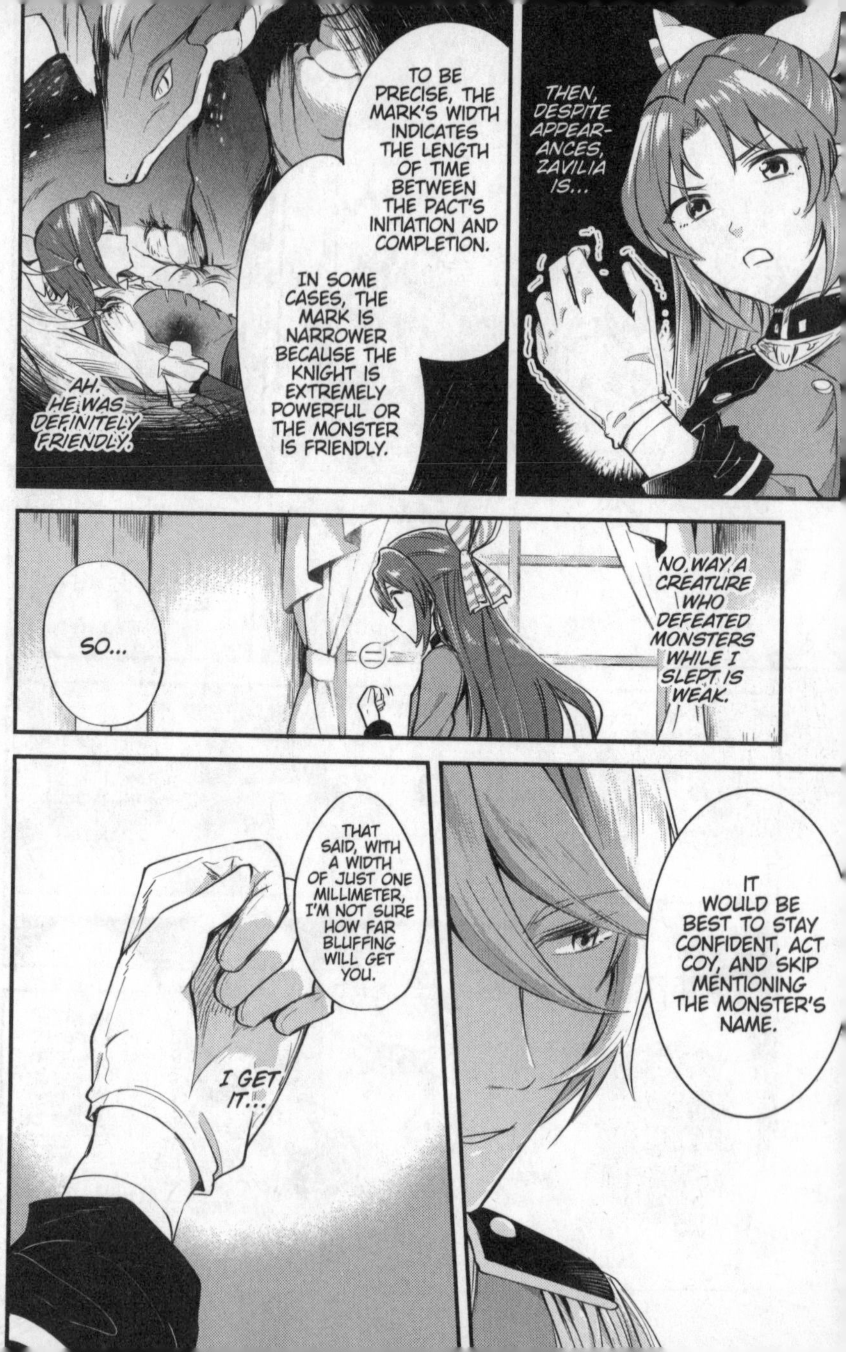
THEN, DESPITE APPEARANCES, ZAVILIA IS...
TO BE PRECISE, THE MARK'S WIDTH INDICATES THE LENGTH OF TIME BETWEEN THE PACT'S INITIATION AND COMPLETION.
IN SOME CASES, THE MARK IS NARROWER BECAUSE THE KNIGHT IS EXTREMELY POWERFUL OR THE MONSTER IS FRIENDLY.
AH. HE WAS DEFINITELY FRIENDLY.
NO WAY A CREATURE WHO DEFEATED MONSTERS WHILE I SLEPT IS WEAK.
SO...
IT WOULD BE BEST TO STAY CONFIDENT, ACT COY, AND SKIP MENTIONING THE MONSTER'S NAME.
THAT SAID, WITH A WIDTH OF JUST ONE MILLIMETER, I'M NOT SURE HOW FAR BLUFFING WILL GET YOU.
I GET IT...

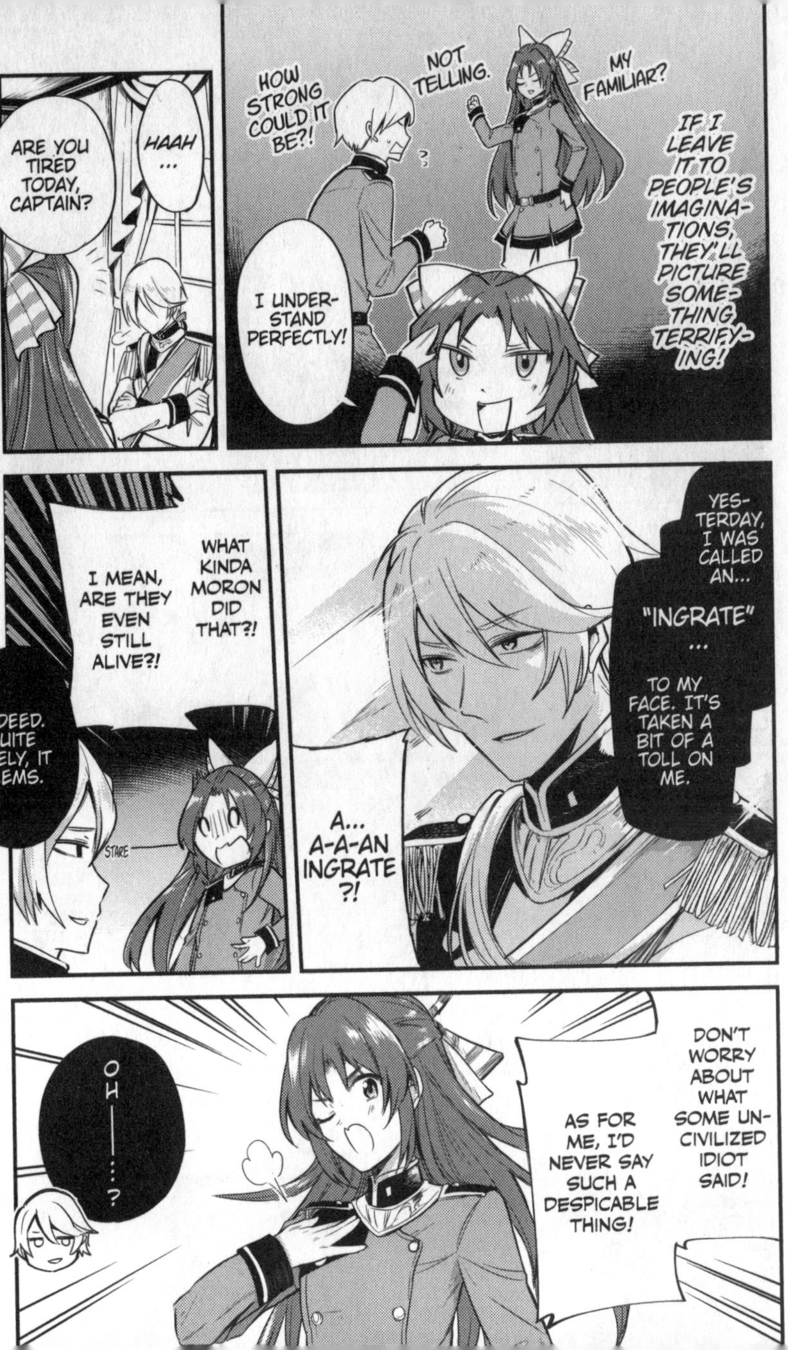
MY FAMILIAR?
NOT TELLING.
HOW STRONG COULD IT BE?!
IF I LEAVE IT TO PEOPLE'S IMAGINATIONS, THEY'LL PICTURE SOMETHING TERRIFYING!
I UNDERSTAND PERFECTLY!
HAAH ...
ARE YOU TIRED TODAY, CAPTAIN?
YESTERDAY, I WAS CALLED AN...
"INGRATE" ...
TO MY FACE. IT'S TAKEN A BIT OF A TOLL ON ME.
A... A-A-AN INGRATE?!
WHAT KINDA MORON DID THAT?!
I MEAN, ARE THEY EVEN STILL ALIVE?!
INDEED. QUITE LIVELY, IT SEEMS.
STARE
DON'T WORRY ABOUT WHAT SOME UNCIVILIZED IDIOT SAID!
AS FOR ME, I'D NEVER SAY SUCH A DESPICABLE THING!
OH——...?

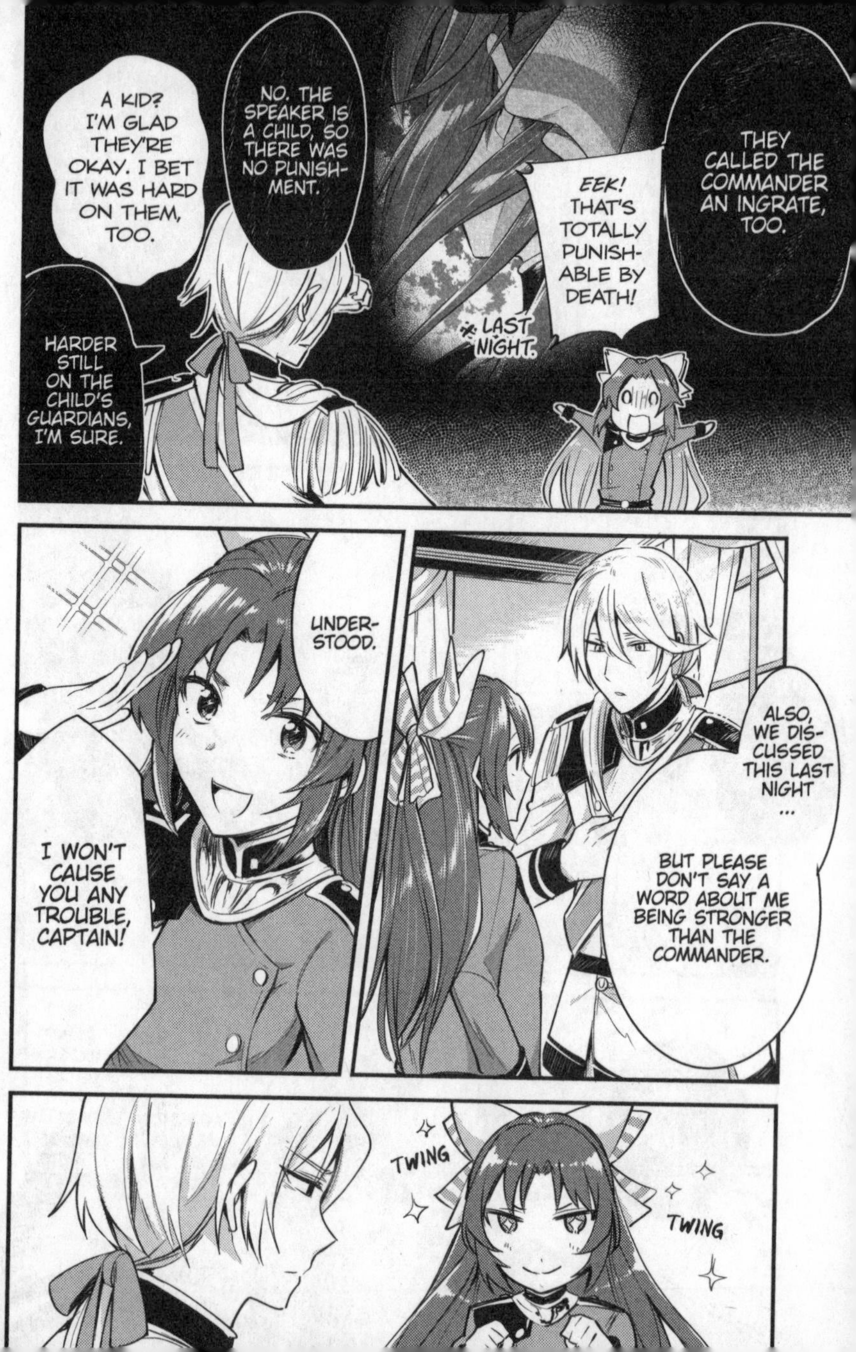
THEY CALLED THE COMMANDER AN INGRATE, TOO.
EEK! THAT'S TOTALLY PUNISHABLE BY DEATH!
*LAST NIGHT.
NO. THE SPEAKER IS A CHILD, SO THERE WAS NO PUNISHMENT.
A KID? I'M GLAD THEY'RE OKAY. I BET IT WAS HARD ON THEM, TOO.
HARDER STILL ON THE CHILD'S GUARDIANS, I'M SURE.
ALSO, WE DISCUSSED THIS LAST NIGHT ...
BUT PLEASE DON'T SAY A WORD ABOUT ME BEING STRONGER THAN THE COMMANDER.
UNDERSTOOD.
I WON'T CAUSE YOU ANY TROUBLE, CAPTAIN!
TWING
TWING

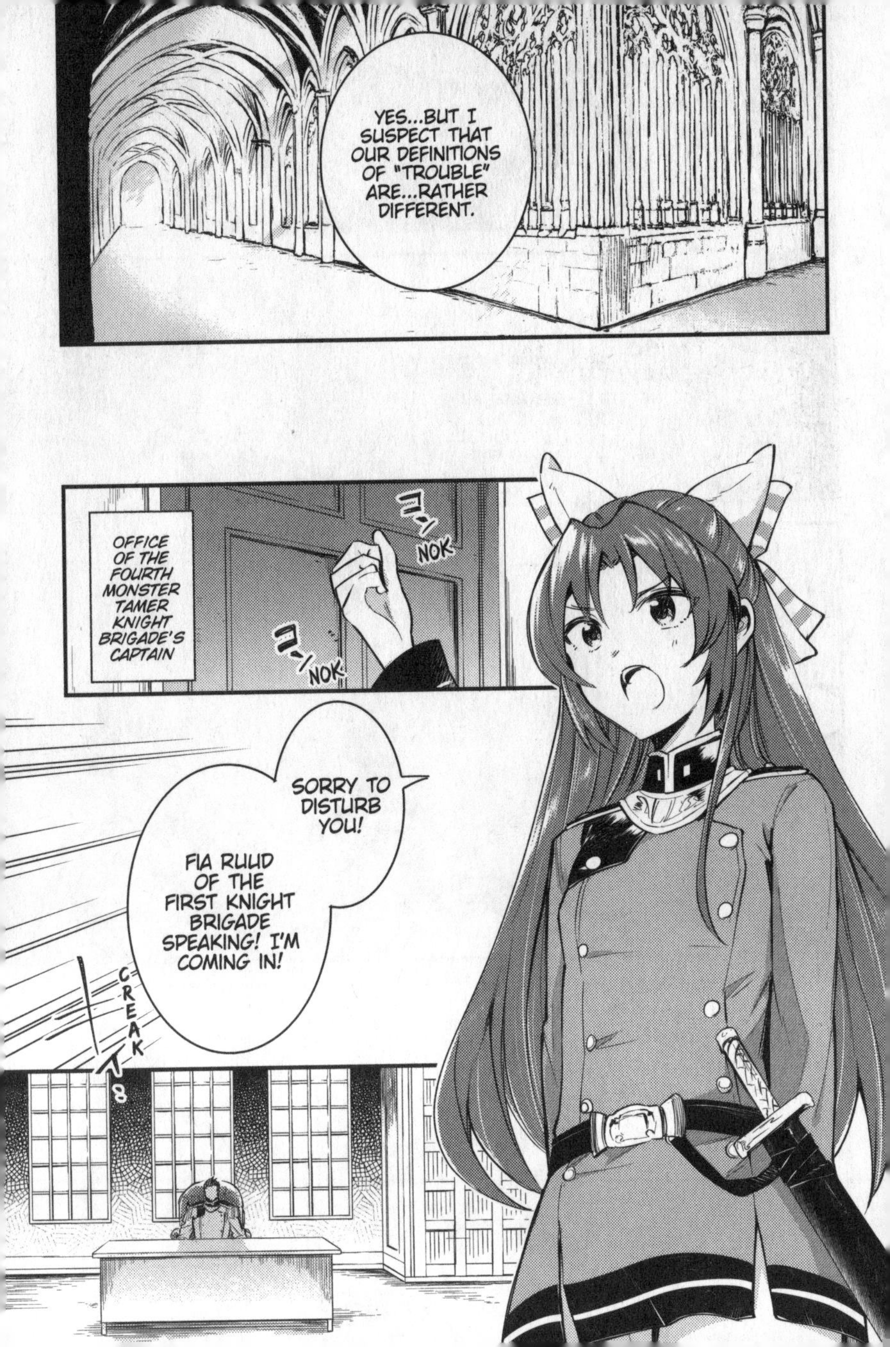

YES...BUT I SUSPECT THAT OUR DEFINITIONS OF "TROUBLE" ARE...RATHER DIFFERENT.
NOK
NOK
OFFICE OF THE FOURTH MONSTER TAMER KNIGHT BRIGADE'S CAPTAIN
SORRY TO DISTURB YOU!
FIA RUUD OF THE FIRST KNIGHT BRIGADE SPEAKING! I'M COMING IN!
CREAK

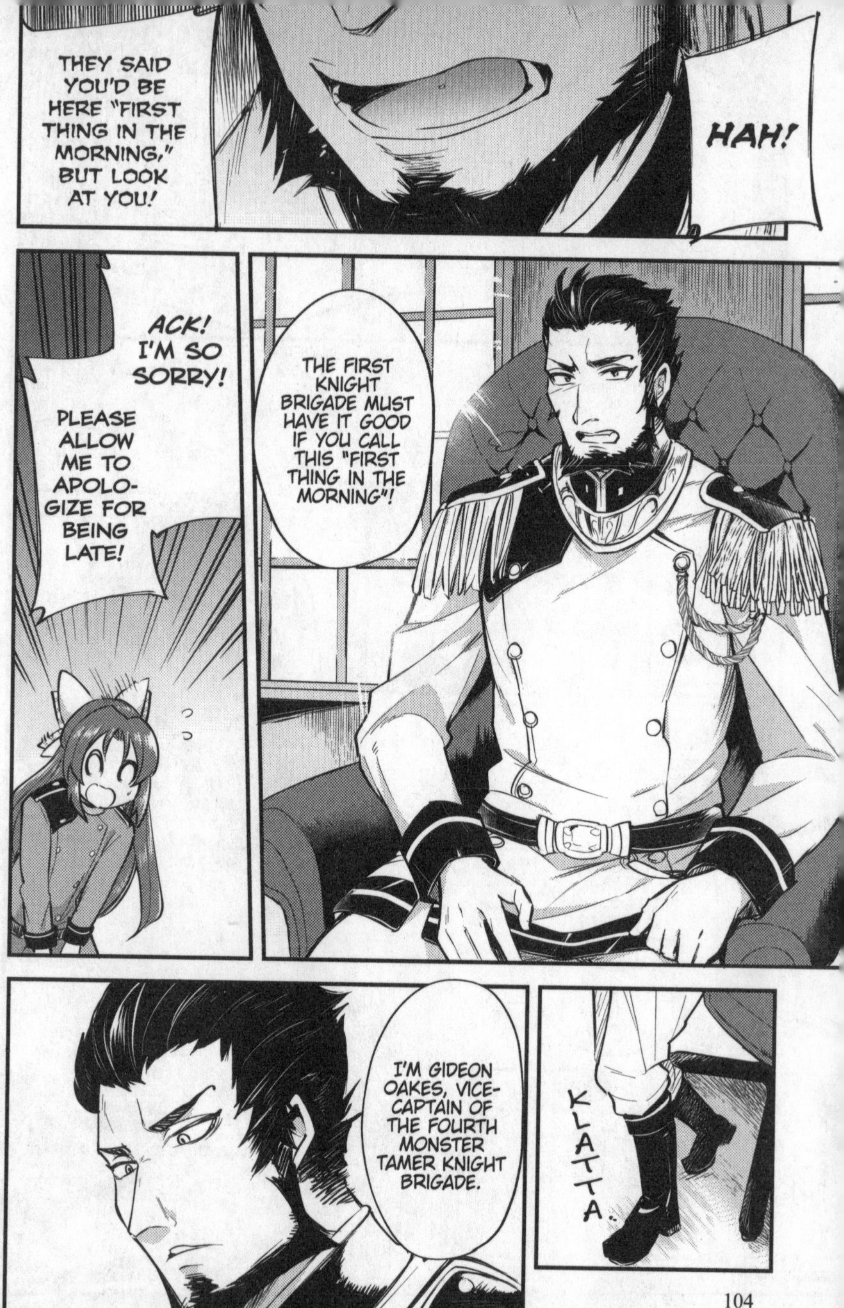
HAH!
THEY SAID YOU'D BE HERE "FIRST THING IN THE MORNING," BUT LOOK AT YOU!
THE FIRST KNIGHT BRIGADE MUST HAVE IT GOOD IF YOU CALL THIS "FIRST THING IN THE MORNING"!
ACK! I'M SO SORRY!
PLEASE ALLOW ME TO APOLOGIZE FOR BEING LATE!
KLATTA
I'M GIDEON OAKES, VICE-CAPTAIN OF THE FOURTH MONSTER TAMER KNIGHT BRIGADE.

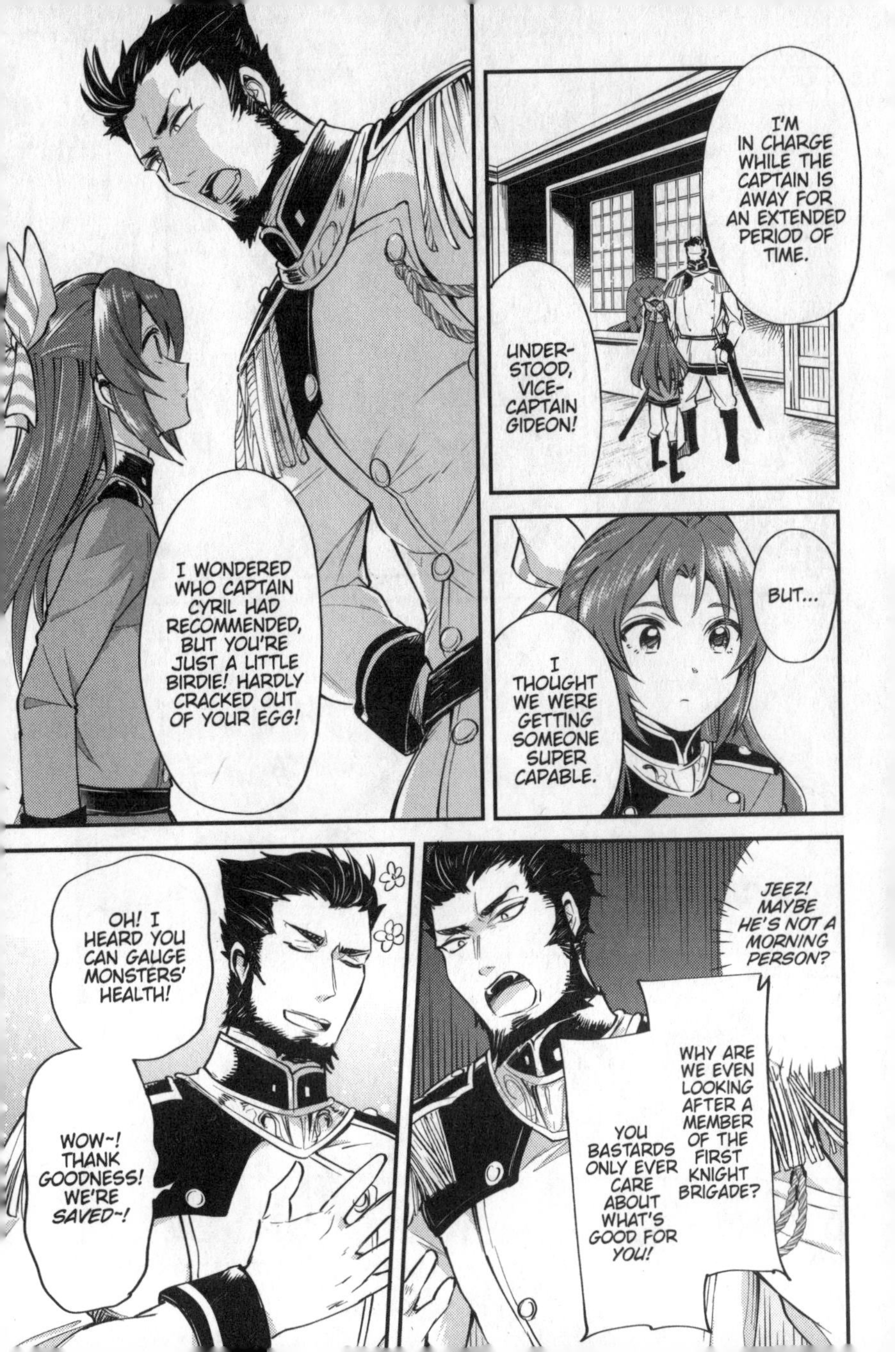
I'M IN CHARGE WHILE THE CAPTAIN IS AWAY FOR AN EXTENDED PERIOD OF TIME.
UNDER-STOOD, VICE-CAPTAIN GIDEON!
BUT...
I THOUGHT WE WERE GETTING SOMEONE SUPER CAPABLE.
I WONDERED WHO CAPTAIN CYRIL HAD RECOMMENDED, BUT YOU'RE JUST A LITTLE BIRDIE! HARDLY CRACKED OUT OF YOUR EGG!
JEEZ! MAYBE HE'S NOT A MORNING PERSON?
WHY ARE WE EVEN LOOKING AFTER A MEMBER OF THE FIRST KNIGHT BRIGADE?
YOU BASTARDS ONLY EVER CARE ABOUT WHAT'S GOOD FOR YOU!
OH! I HEARD YOU CAN GAUGE MONSTERS' HEALTH!
WOW~! THANK GOODNESS! WE'RE SAVED~!

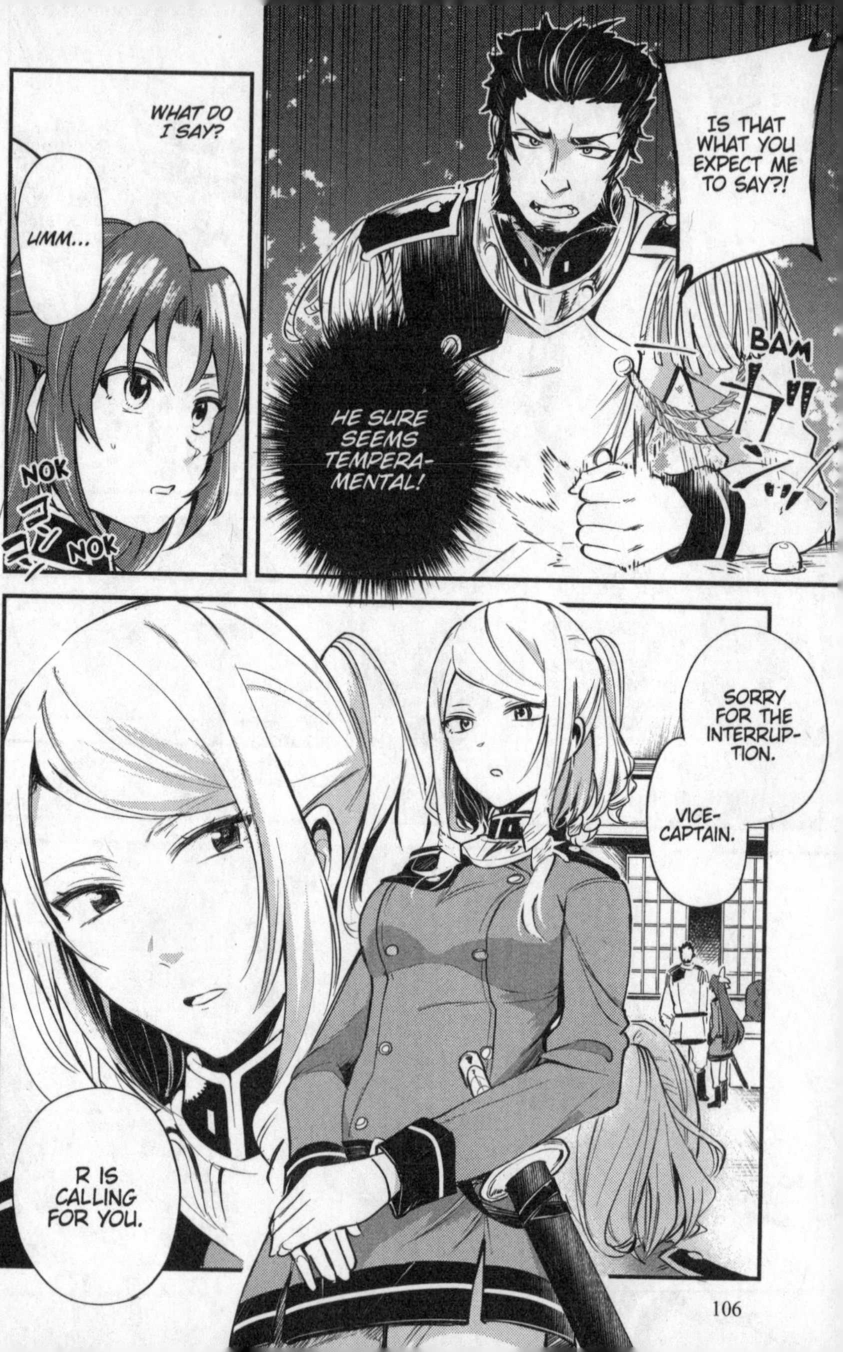
IS THAT WHAT YOU EXPECT ME TO SAY?!
BAM
HE SURE SEEMS TEMPERA-MENTAL!
WHAT DO I SAY?
UMM...
NOK
NOK
SORRY FOR THE INTERRUP-TION.
VICE-CAPTAIN.
R IS CALLING FOR YOU.

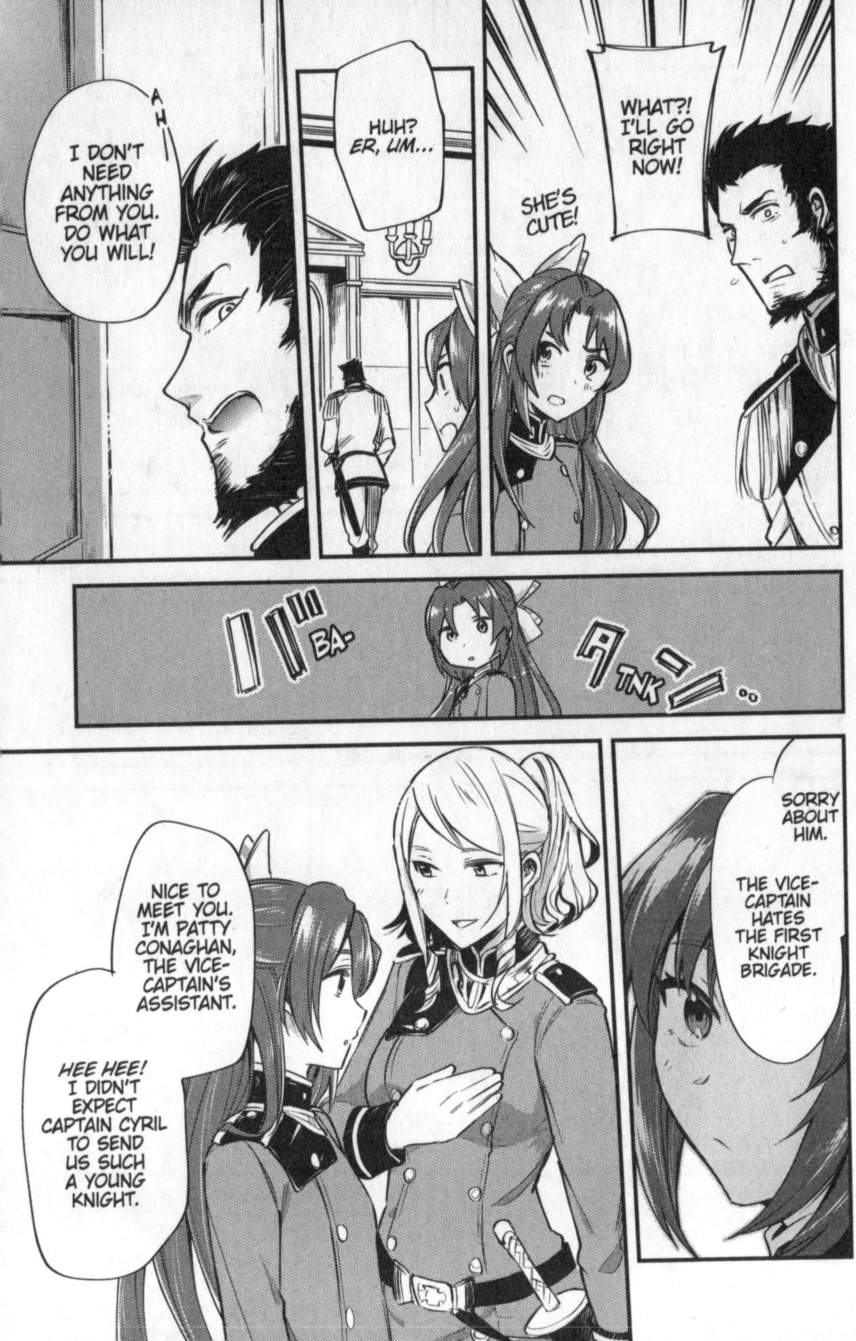
WHAT?! I'LL GO RIGHT NOW!
SHE'S CUTE!
HUH? ER, UM...
AH
I DON'T NEED ANYTHING FROM YOU. DO WHAT YOU WILL!
BA-
TNK
SORRY ABOUT HIM.
THE VICE-CAPTAIN HATES THE FIRST KNIGHT BRIGADE.
NICE TO MEET YOU. I'M PATTY CONAGHAN, THE VICE-CAPTAIN'S ASSISTANT.
HEE HEE! I DIDN'T EXPECT CAPTAIN CYRIL TO SEND US SUCH A YOUNG KNIGHT.

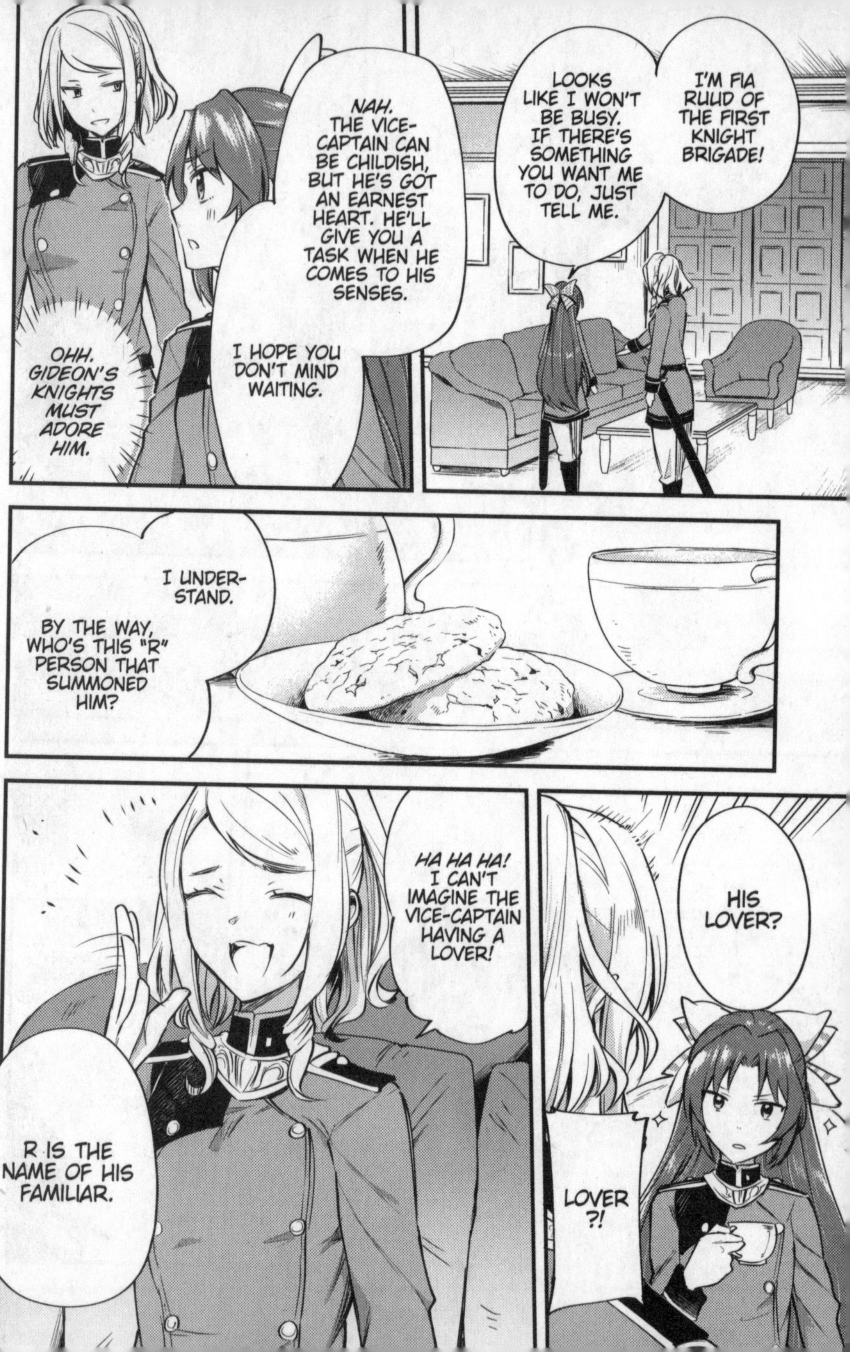
I'M FIA RUUD OF THE FIRST KNIGHT BRIGADE!
LOOKS LIKE I WON'T BE BUSY. IF THERE'S SOMETHING YOU WANT ME TO DO, JUST TELL ME.
NAH. THE VICE-CAPTAIN CAN BE CHILDISH, BUT HE'S GOT AN EARNEST HEART. HE'LL GIVE YOU A TASK WHEN HE COMES TO HIS SENSES.
I HOPE YOU DON'T MIND WAITING.
OHH. GIDEON'S KNIGHTS MUST ADORE HIM.
I UNDER-STAND.
BY THE WAY, WHO'S THIS "R" PERSON THAT SUMMONED HIM?
HIS LOVER?
LOVER ?!
HA HA HA! I CAN'T IMAGINE THE VICE-CAPTAIN HAVING A LOVER!
R IS THE NAME OF HIS FAMILIAR.

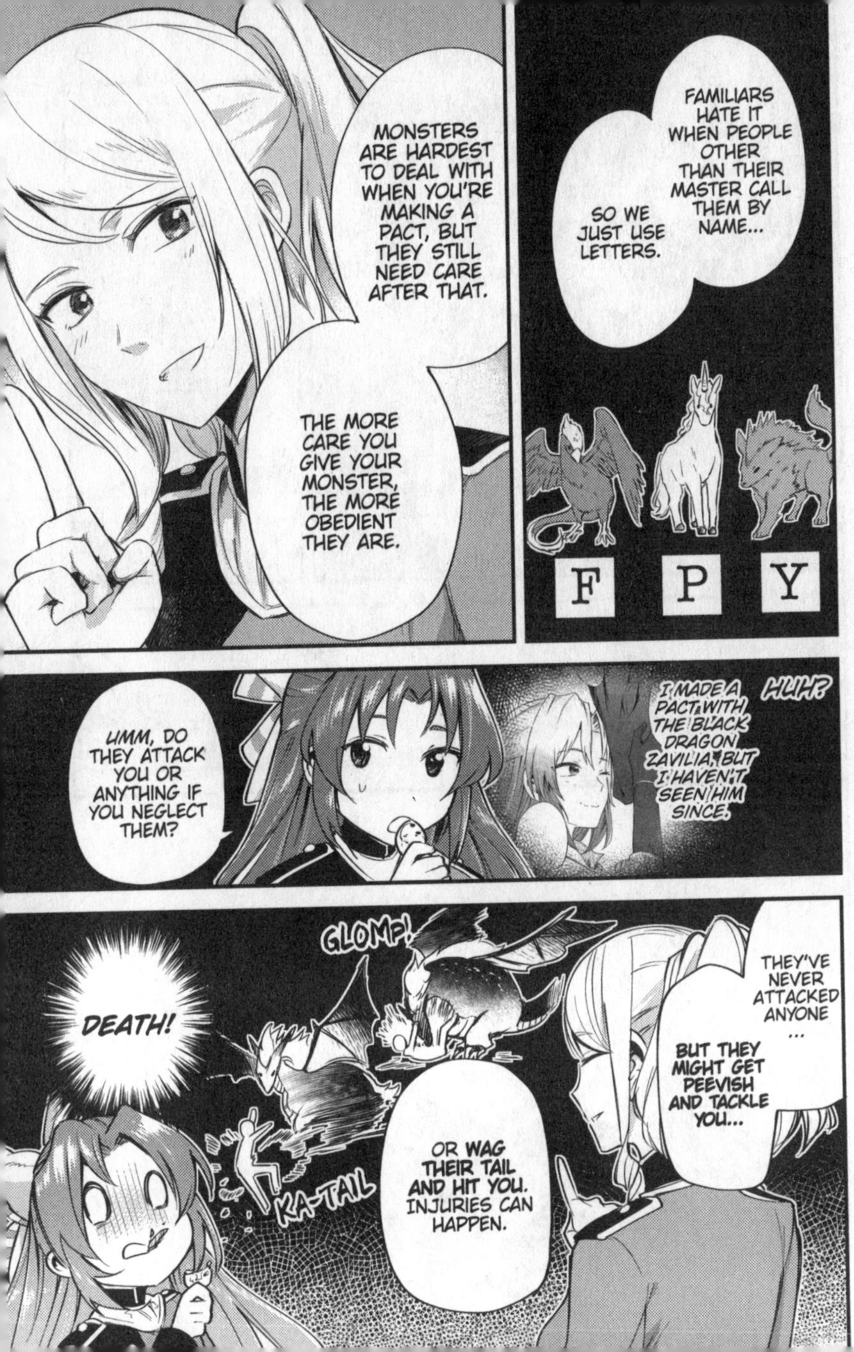
FAMILIARS HATE IT WHEN PEOPLE OTHER THAN THEIR MASTER CALL THEM BY NAME...
SO WE JUST USE LETTERS.
F
P
Y
MONSTERS ARE HARDEST TO DEAL WITH WHEN YOU'RE MAKING A PACT, BUT THEY STILL NEED CARE AFTER THAT.
THE MORE CARE YOU GIVE YOUR MONSTER, THE MORE OBEDIENT THEY ARE.
HUH?
I MADE A PACT WITH THE BLACK DRAGON ZAVILIA, BUT I HAVEN'T SEEN HIM SINCE.
UMM, DO THEY ATTACK YOU OR ANYTHING IF YOU NEGLECT THEM?
THEY'VE NEVER ATTACKED ANYONE ...
BUT THEY MIGHT GET PEEVISH AND TACKLE YOU...
GLOMP!
OR WAG THEIR TAIL AND HIT YOU. INJURIES CAN HAPPEN.
KA-TAIL
DEATH!

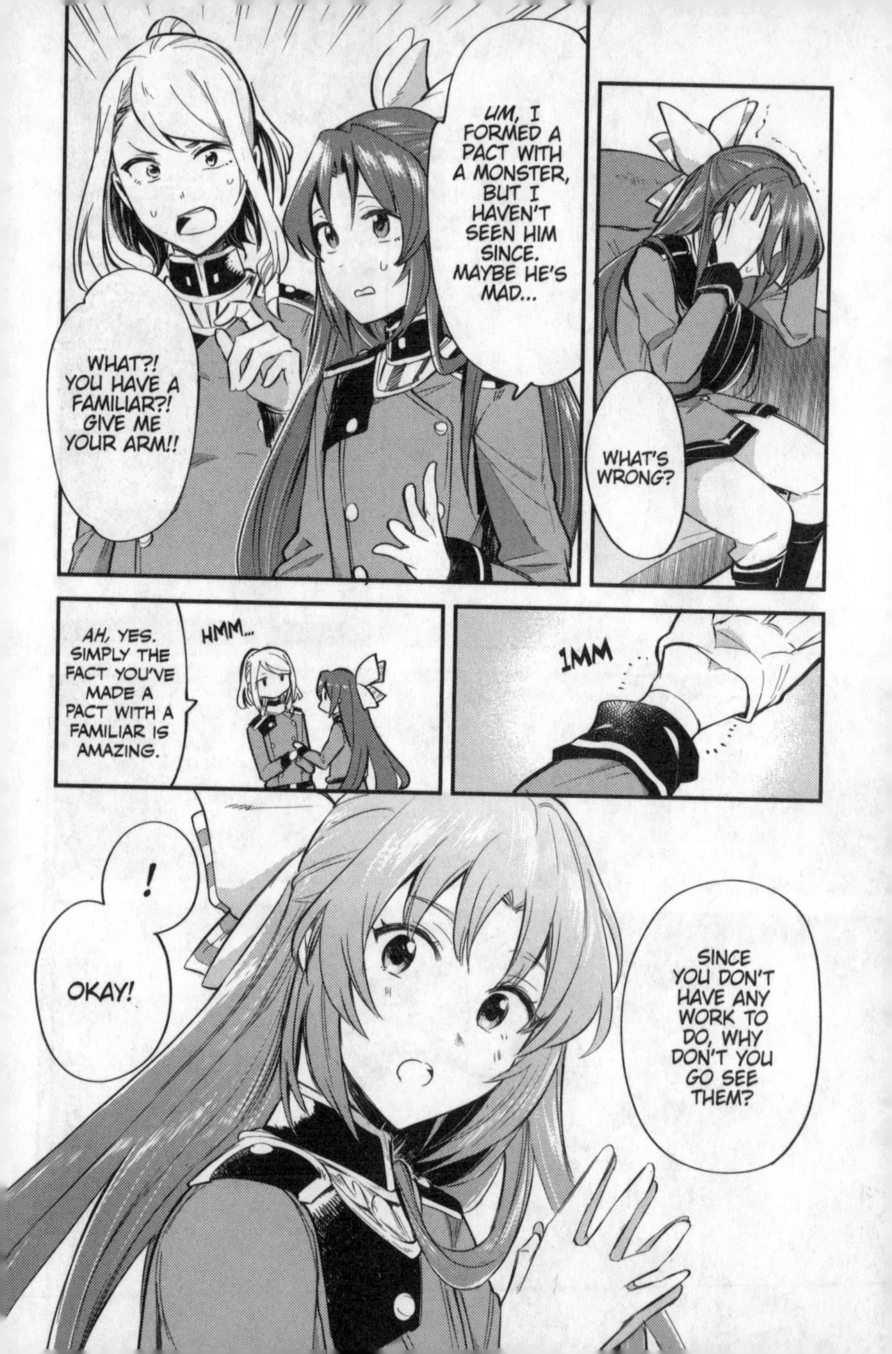
WHAT'S WRONG?
UM, I FORMED A PACT WITH A MONSTER, BUT I HAVEN'T SEEN HIM SINCE. MAYBE HE'S MAD...
WHAT?! YOU HAVE A FAMILIAR?! GIVE ME YOUR ARM!!
1MM
HMM...
AH, YES. SIMPLY THE FACT YOU'VE MADE A PACT WITH A FAMILIAR IS AMAZING.
SINCE YOU DON'T HAVE ANY WORK TO DO, WHY DON'T YOU GO SEE THEM?
!
OKAY!

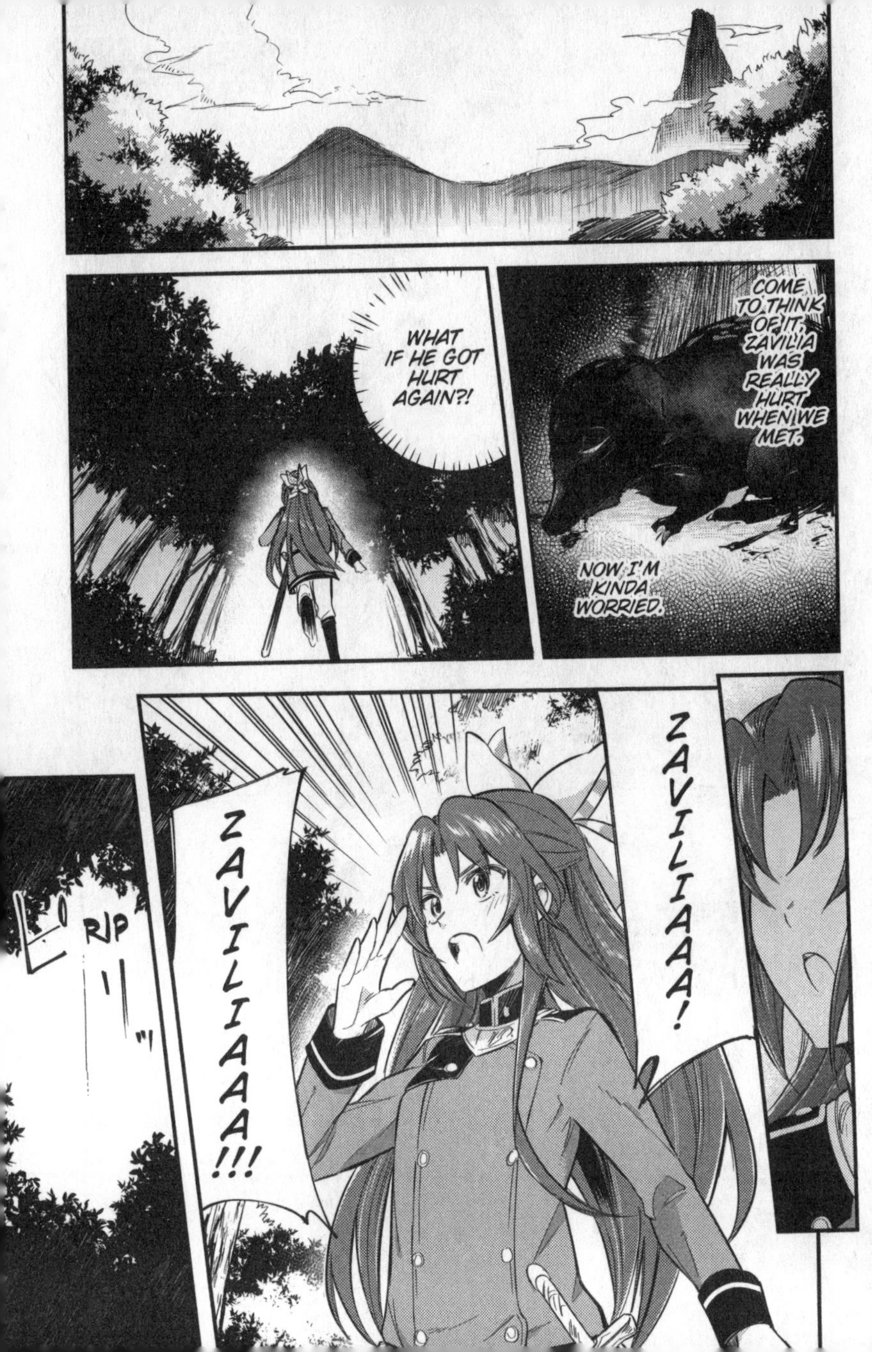
COME TO THINK OF IT, ZAVILIA WAS REALLY HURT WHEN WE MET.
NOW I'M KINDA WORRIED.
WHAT IF HE GOT HURT AGAIN?!
ZAVILIAAA!
ZAVILIAAAA!!!
RIP

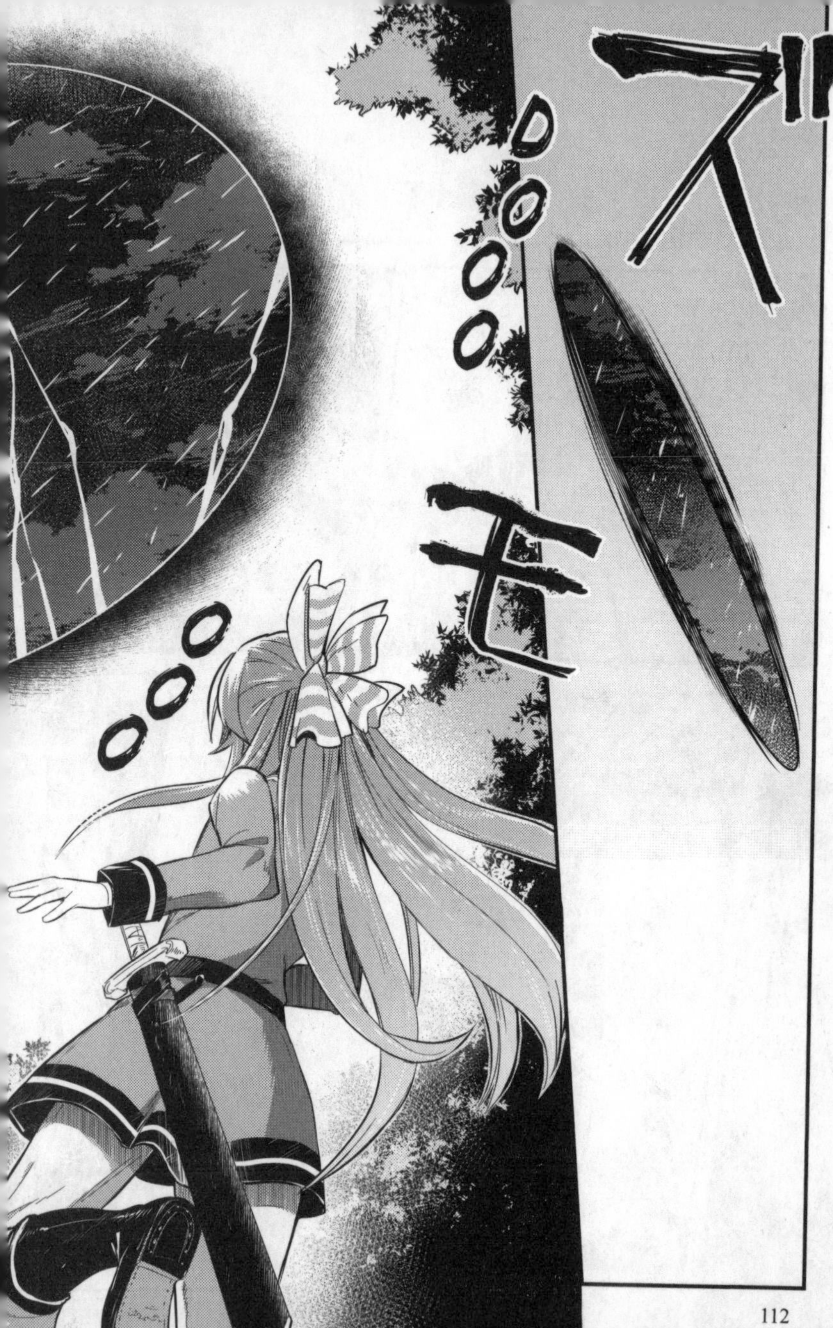
ズ
DOOO
モ
OOO

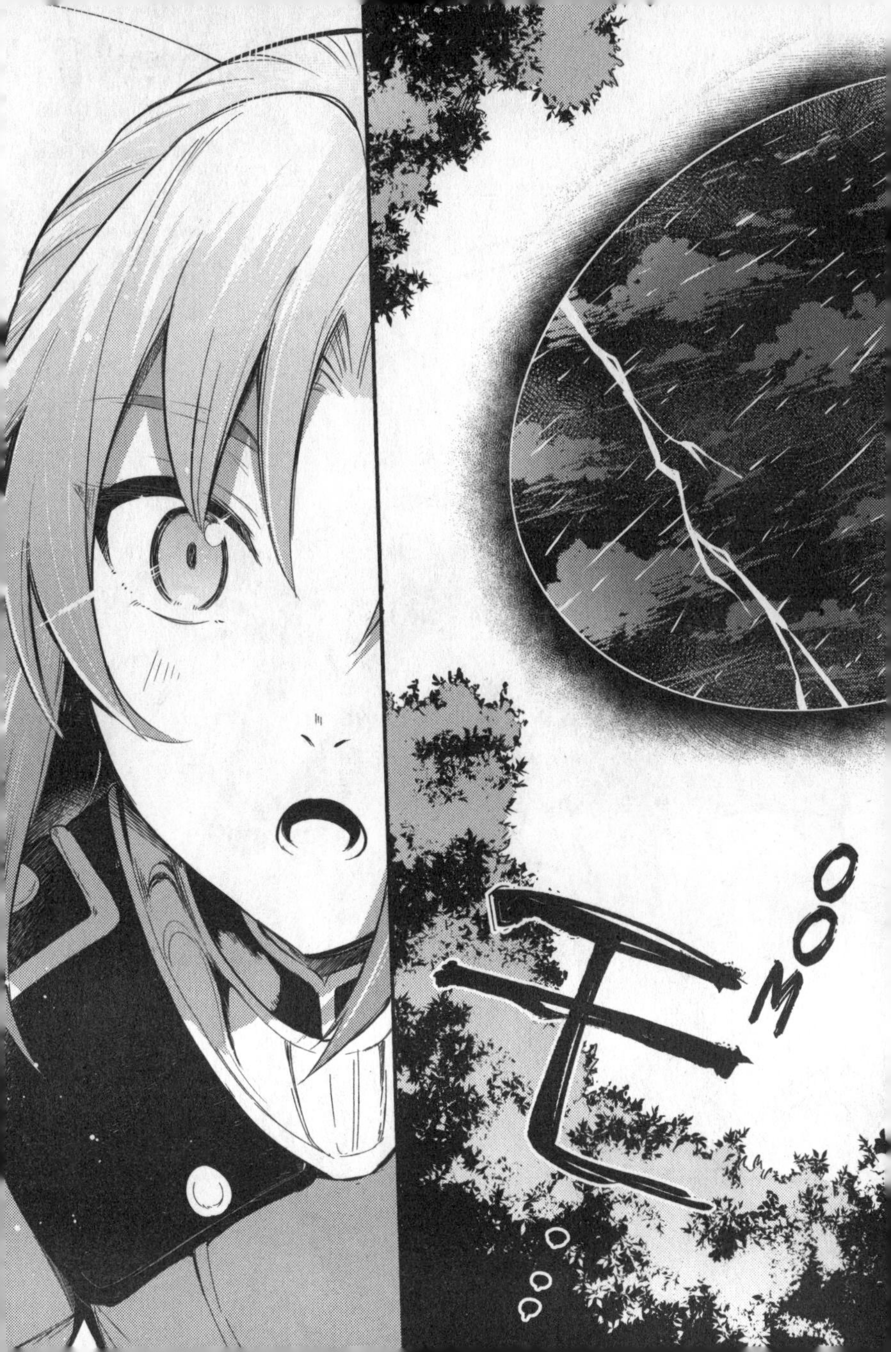
モ
MOO

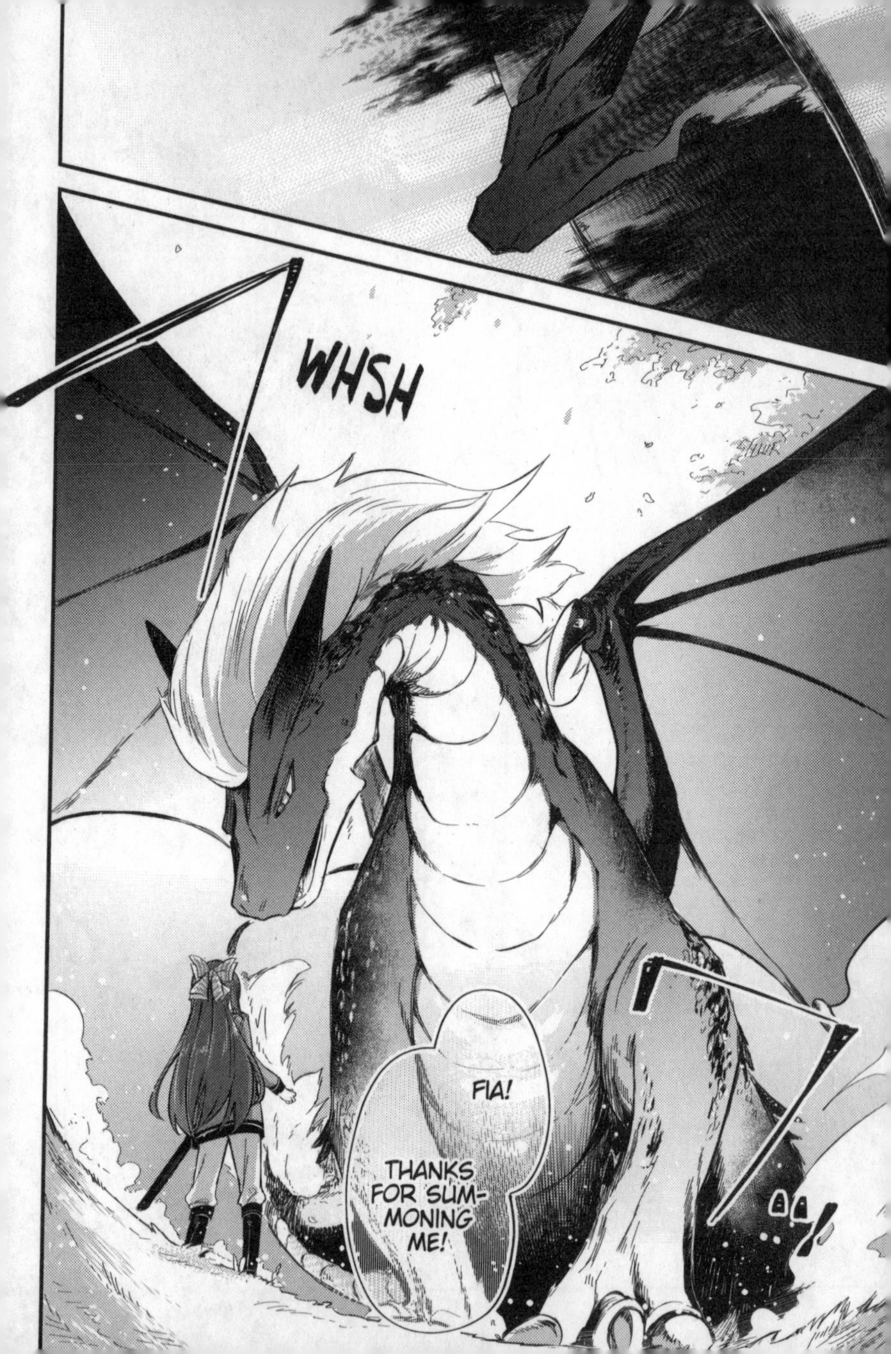
WHSH
SHUK
FIA!
THANKS FOR SUM-MONING ME!

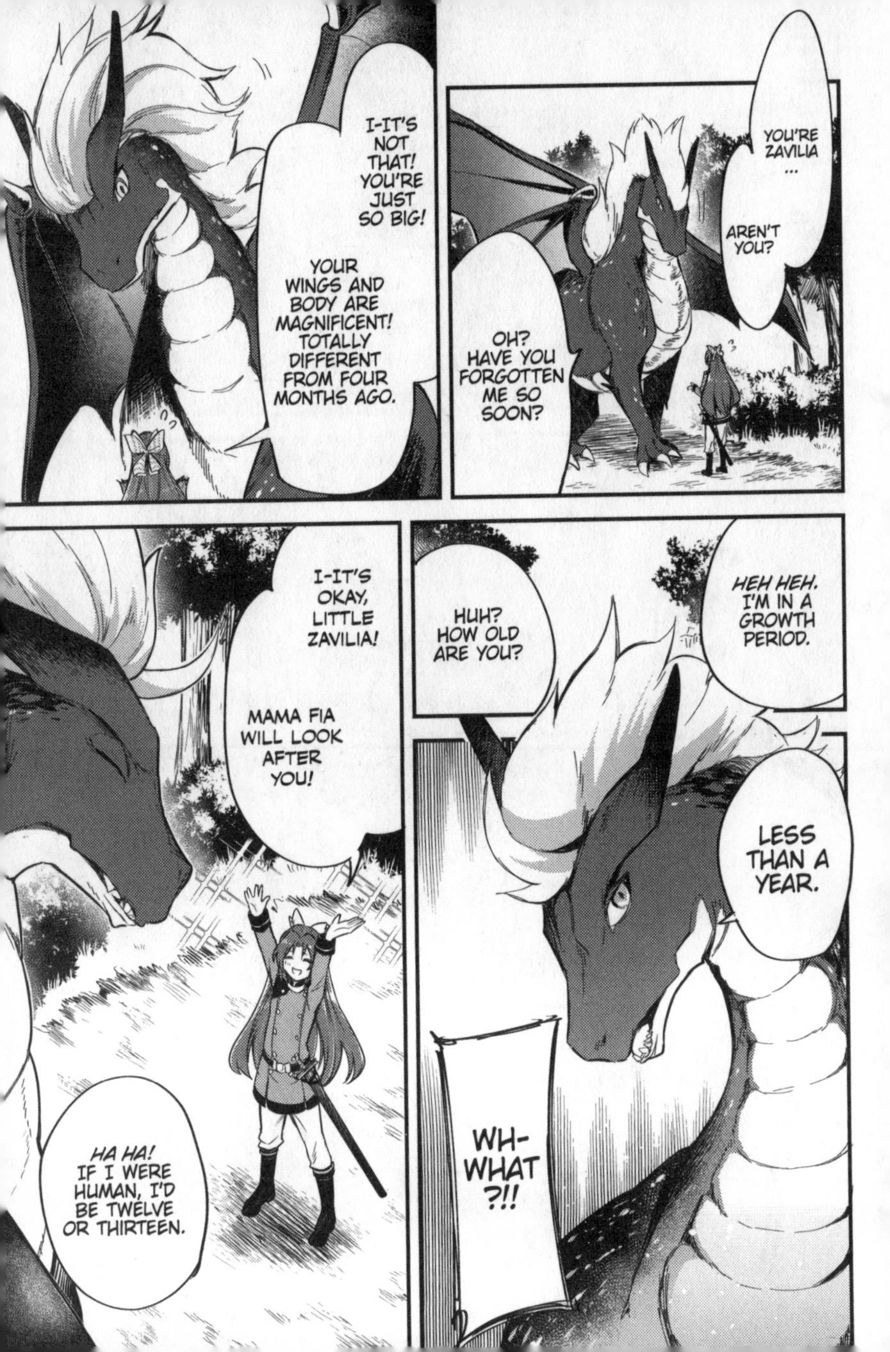
YOU'RE ZAVILIA ...
AREN'T YOU?
OH? HAVE YOU FORGOTTEN ME SO SOON?
I-IT'S NOT THAT! YOU'RE JUST SO BIG!
YOUR WINGS AND BODY ARE MAGNIFICENT! TOTALLY DIFFERENT FROM FOUR MONTHS AGO.
HEH HEH. I'M IN A GROWTH PERIOD.
HUH? HOW OLD ARE YOU?
LESS THAN A YEAR.
WH- WHAT ?!!
I-IT'S OKAY, LITTLE ZAVILIA!
MAMA FIA WILL LOOK AFTER YOU!
HA HA! IF I WERE HUMAN, I'D BE TWELVE OR THIRTEEN.

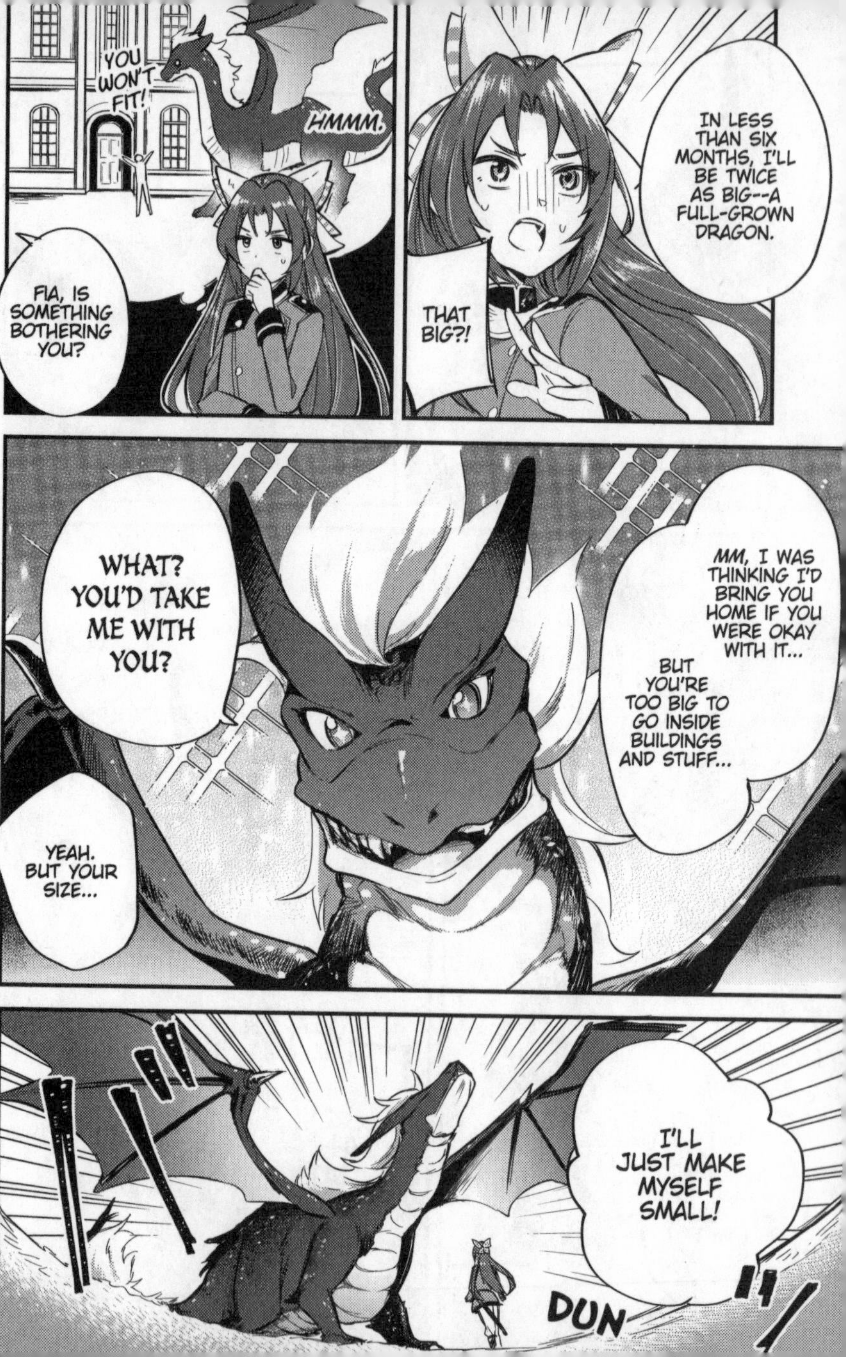
IN LESS THAN SIX MONTHS, I'LL BE TWICE AS BIG--A FULL-GROWN DRAGON.
THAT BIG?!
YOU WON'T FIT!
HMMM.
FIA, IS SOMETHING BOTHERING YOU?
MM, I WAS THINKING I'D BRING YOU HOME IF YOU WERE OKAY WITH IT...
BUT YOU'RE TOO BIG TO GO INSIDE BUILDINGS AND STUFF...
WHAT? YOU'D TAKE ME WITH YOU?
YEAH. BUT YOUR SIZE...
I'LL JUST MAKE MYSELF SMALL!
DUN

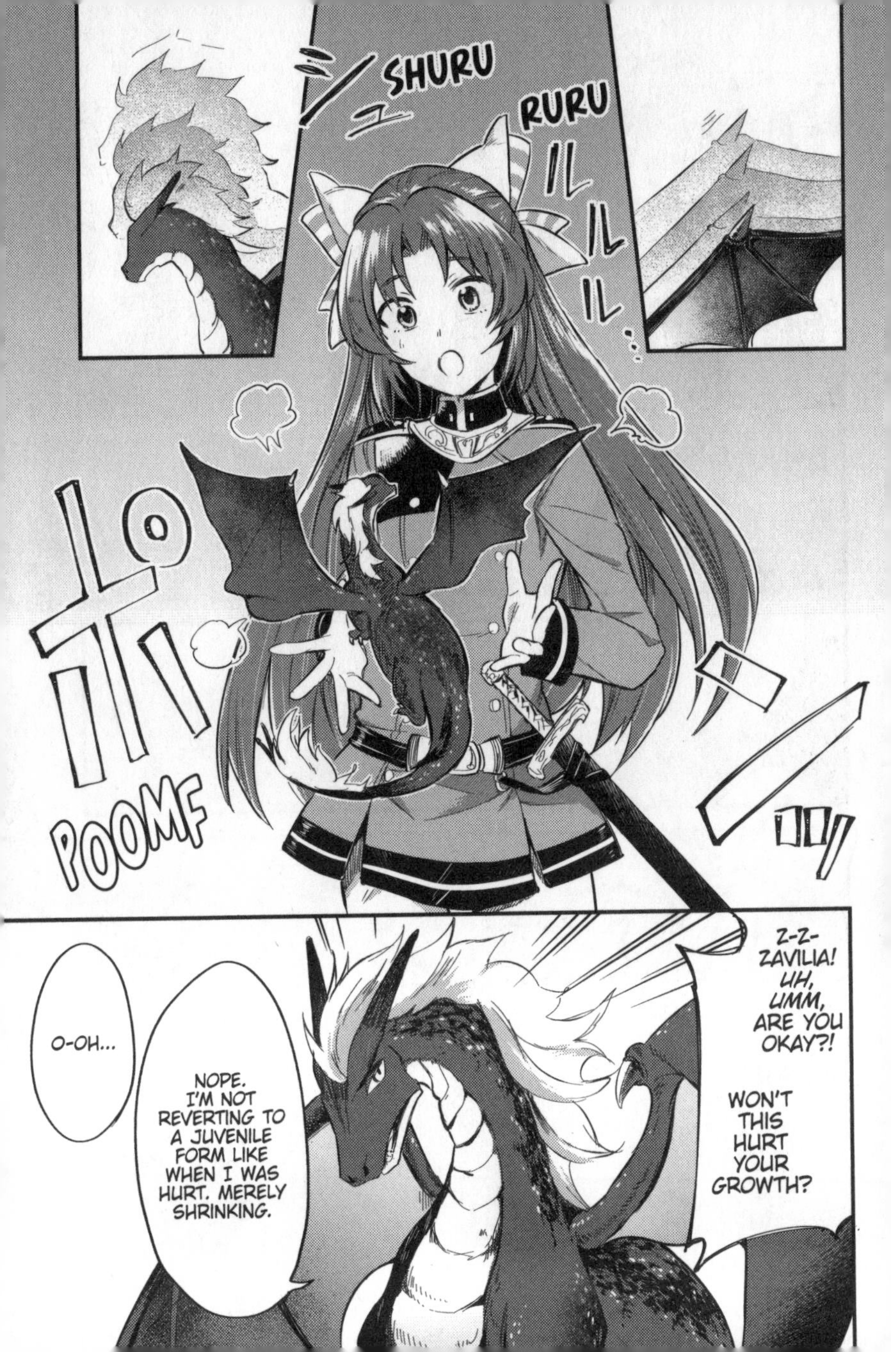
SHURU
RURU
POOMF
Z-Z-ZAVILIA! UH, UMM, ARE YOU OKAY?!
WON'T THIS HURT YOUR GROWTH?
NOPE. I'M NOT REVERTING TO A JUVENILE FORM LIKE WHEN I WAS HURT. MERELY SHRINKING.
O-OH...

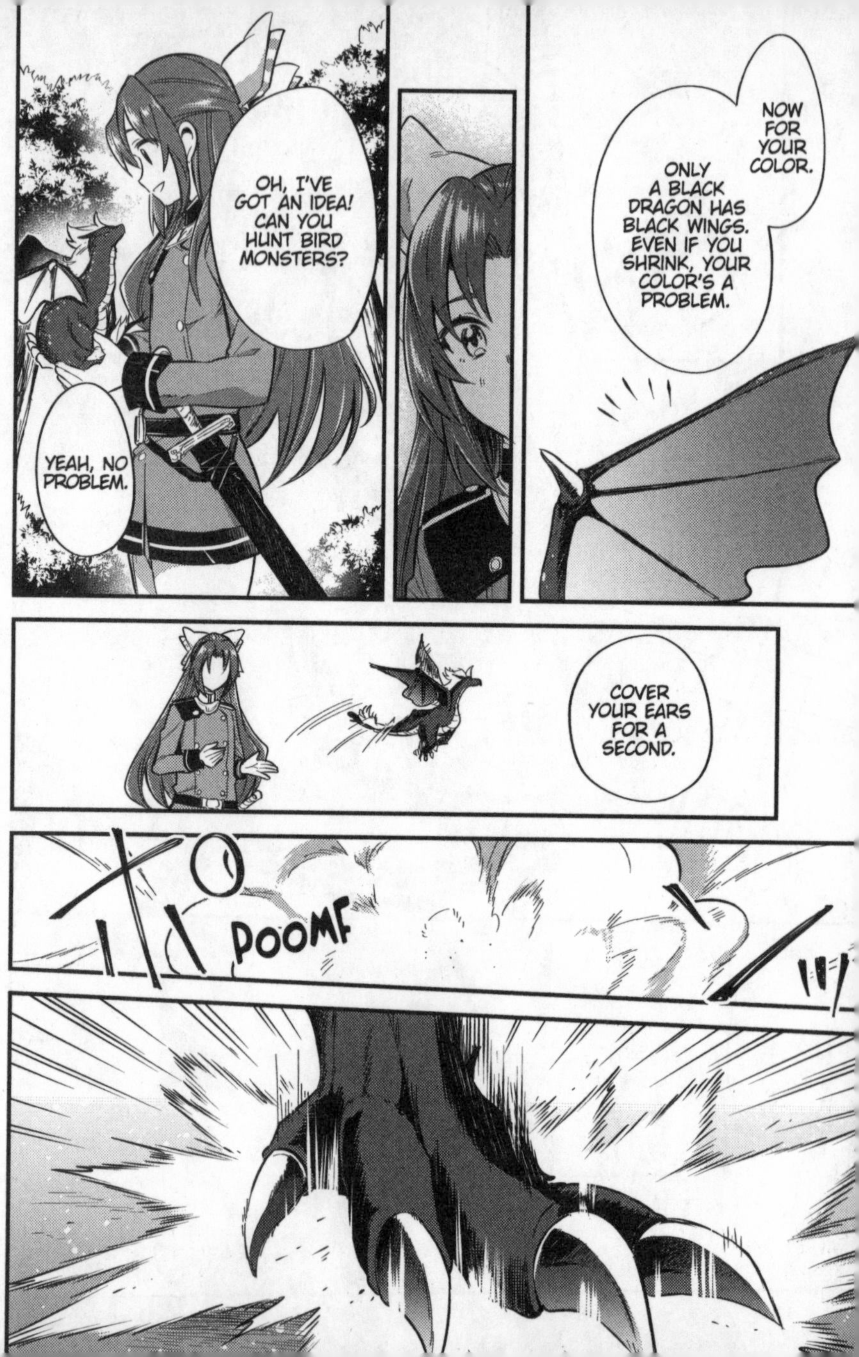
NOW FOR YOUR COLOR.
ONLY A BLACK DRAGON HAS BLACK WINGS. EVEN IF YOU SHRINK, YOUR COLOR'S A PROBLEM.
OH, I'VE GOT AN IDEA! CAN YOU HUNT BIRD MONSTERS?
YEAH, NO PROBLEM.
COVER YOUR EARS FOR A SECOND.
POOMF

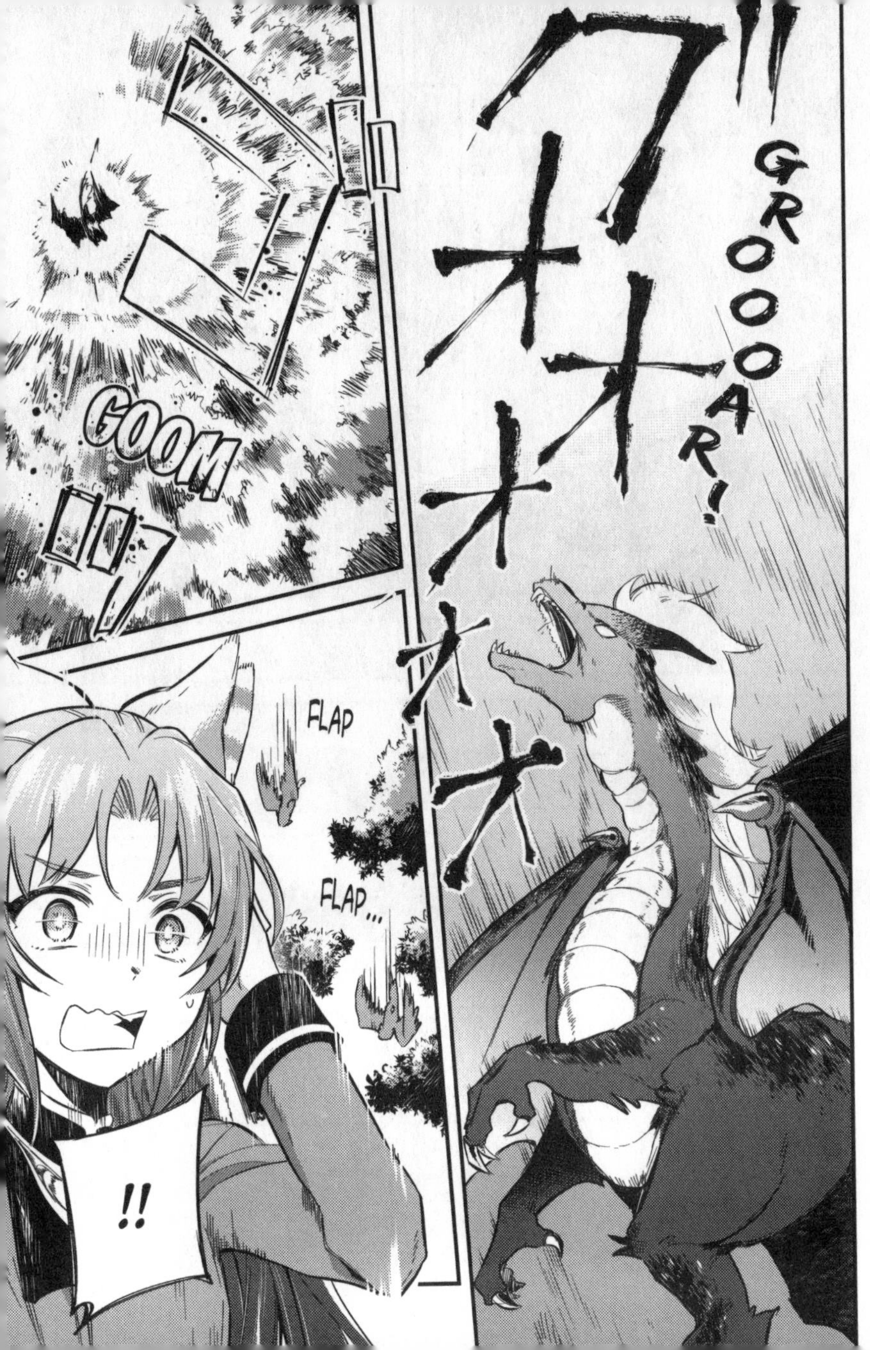
グオオオオ
GROOOAR!
GOOM
FLAP
FLAP...
!!

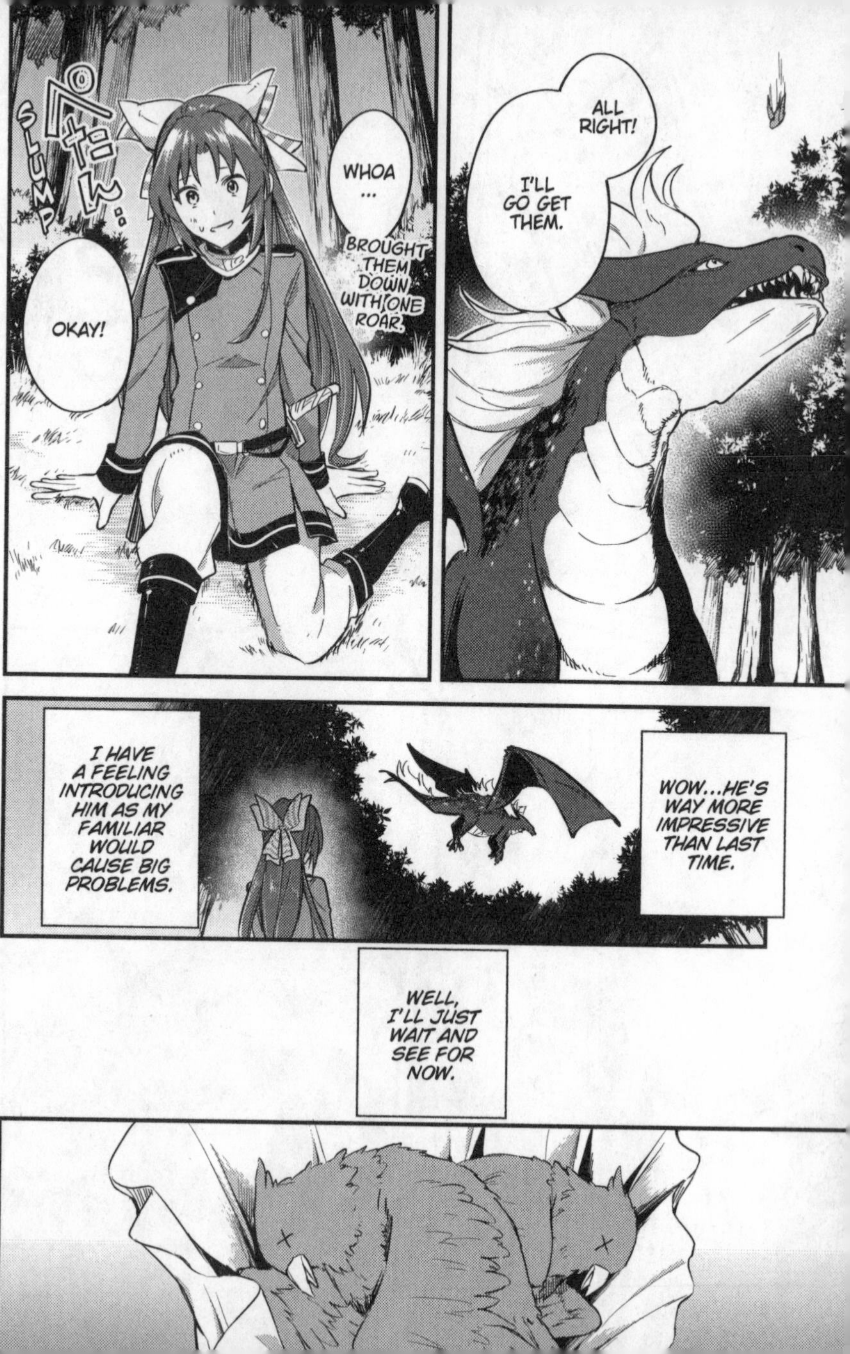
ALL RIGHT!
I'LL GO GET THEM.
WHOA...
BROUGHT THEM DOWN WITH ONE ROAR.
ぺたん...
SLUMP
OKAY!
WOW...HE'S WAY MORE IMPRESSIVE THAN LAST TIME.
I HAVE A FEELING INTRODUCING HIM AS MY FAMILIAR WOULD CAUSE BIG PROBLEMS.
WELL, I'LL JUST WAIT AND SEE FOR NOW.

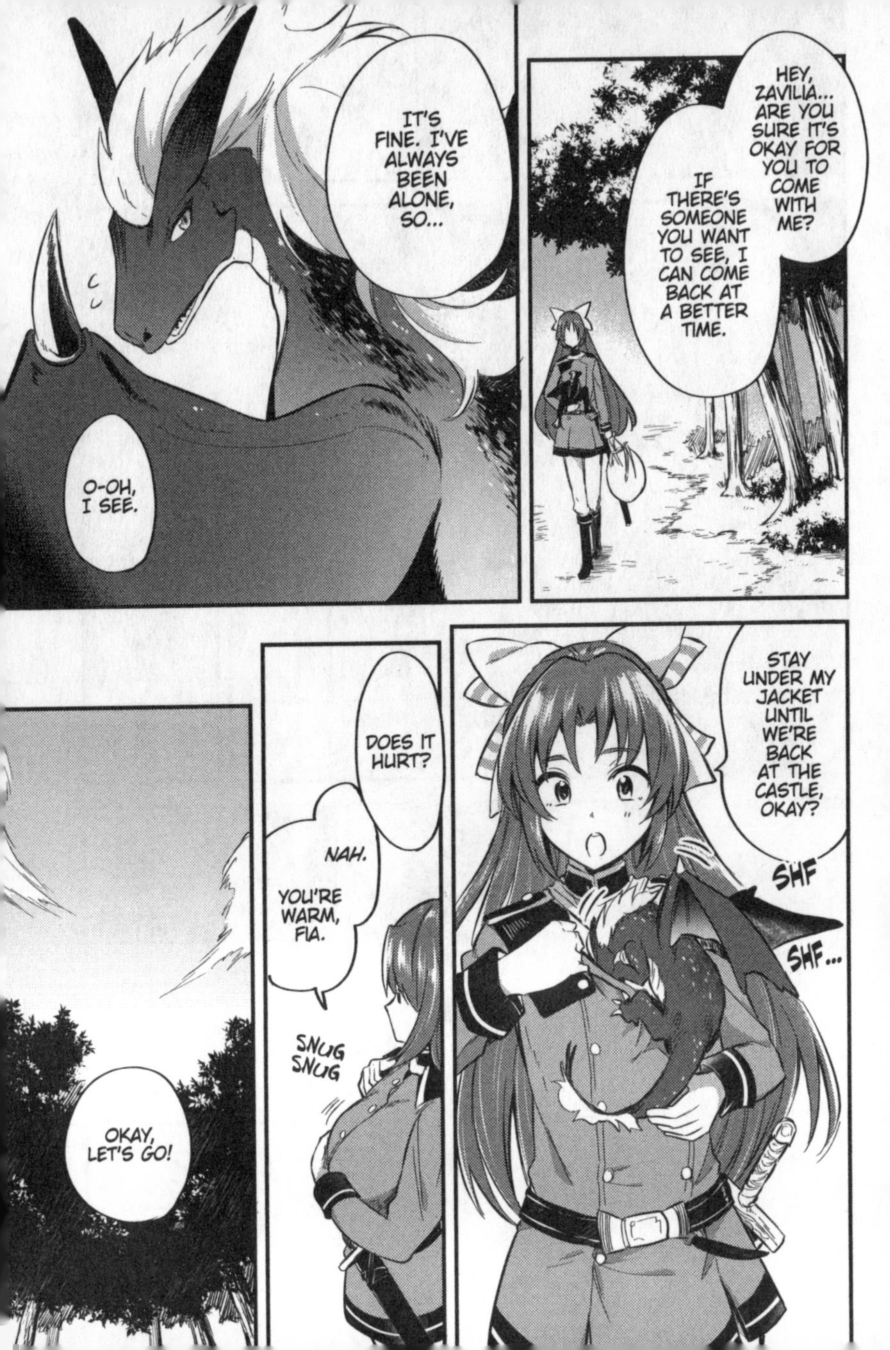
HEY, ZAVILIA... ARE YOU SURE IT'S OKAY FOR YOU TO COME WITH ME?
IF THERE'S SOMEONE YOU WANT TO SEE, I CAN COME BACK AT A BETTER TIME.
IT'S FINE. I'VE ALWAYS BEEN ALONE, SO...
O-OH, I SEE.
STAY UNDER MY JACKET UNTIL WE'RE BACK AT THE CASTLE, OKAY?
SHF
SHF...
DOES IT HURT?
NAH.
YOU'RE WARM, FIA.
SNUG SNUG
OKAY, LET'S GO!

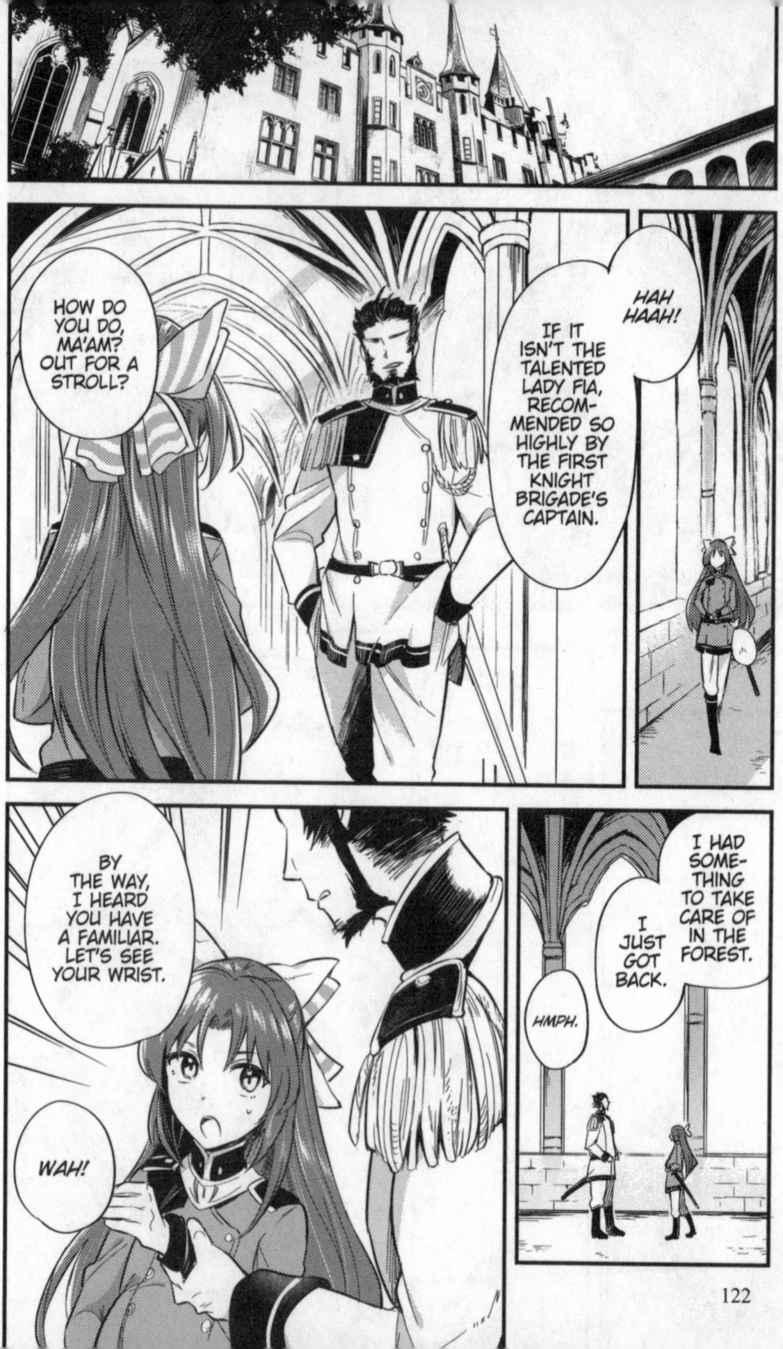
HAH HAAH!
IF IT ISN'T THE TALENTED LADY FIA, RECOMMENDED SO HIGHLY BY THE FIRST KNIGHT BRIGADE'S CAPTAIN.
HOW DO YOU DO, MA'AM? OUT FOR A STROLL?
I HAD SOMETHING TO TAKE CARE OF IN THE FOREST.
I JUST GOT BACK.
HMPH.
BY THE WAY, I HEARD YOU HAVE A FAMILIAR. LET'S SEE YOUR WRIST.
WAH!

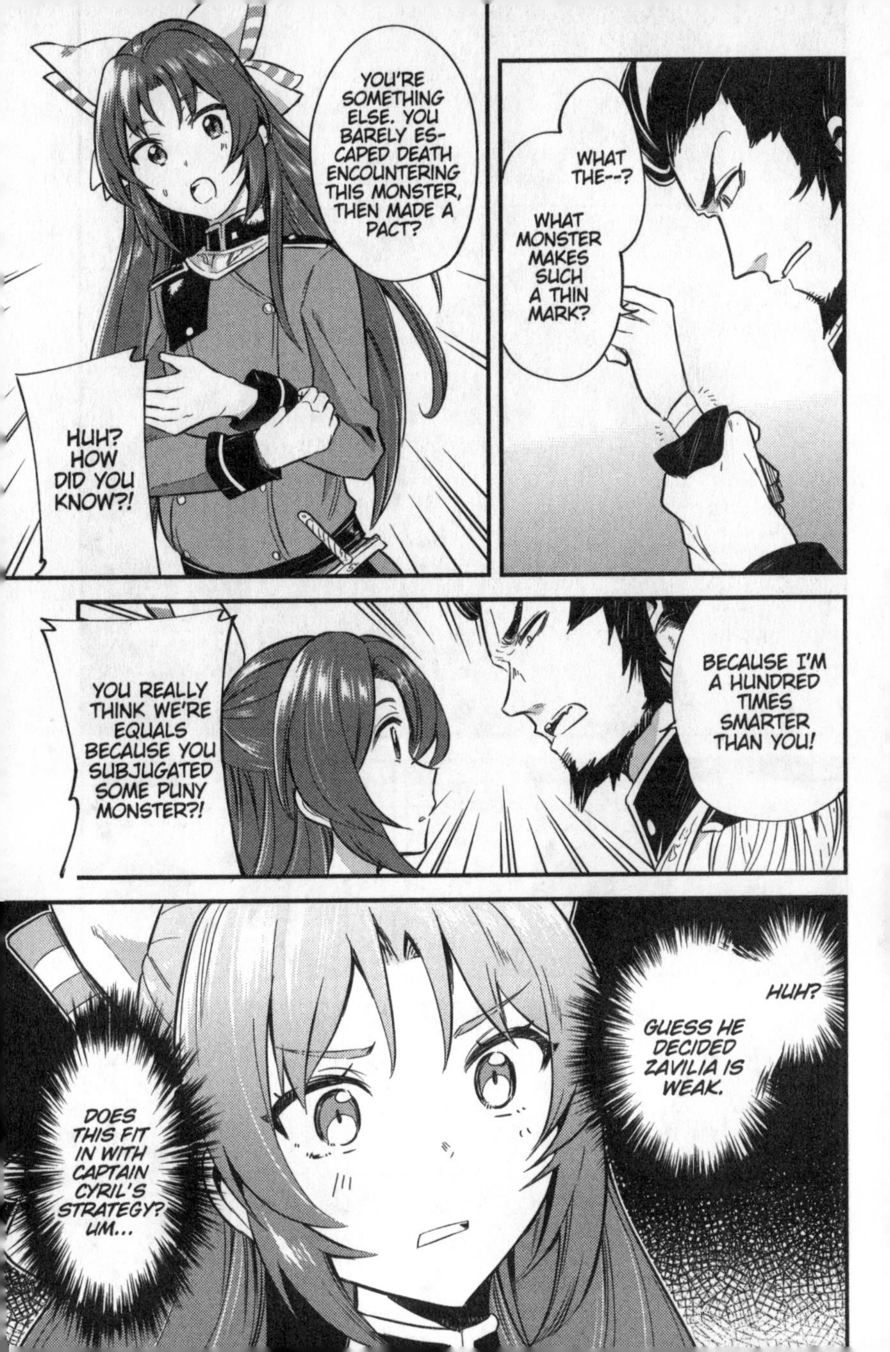
WHAT THE--?
WHAT MONSTER MAKES SUCH A THIN MARK?
YOU'RE SOMETHING ELSE. YOU BARELY ES-CAPED DEATH ENCOUNTERING THIS MONSTER, THEN MADE A PACT?
HUH? HOW DID YOU KNOW?!
BECAUSE I'M A HUNDRED TIMES SMARTER THAN YOU!
YOU REALLY THINK WE'RE EQUALS BECAUSE YOU SUBJUGATED SOME PUNY MONSTER?!
HUH?
GUESS HE DECIDED ZAVILIA IS WEAK.
DOES THIS FIT IN WITH CAPTAIN CYRIL'S STRATEGY? UM...

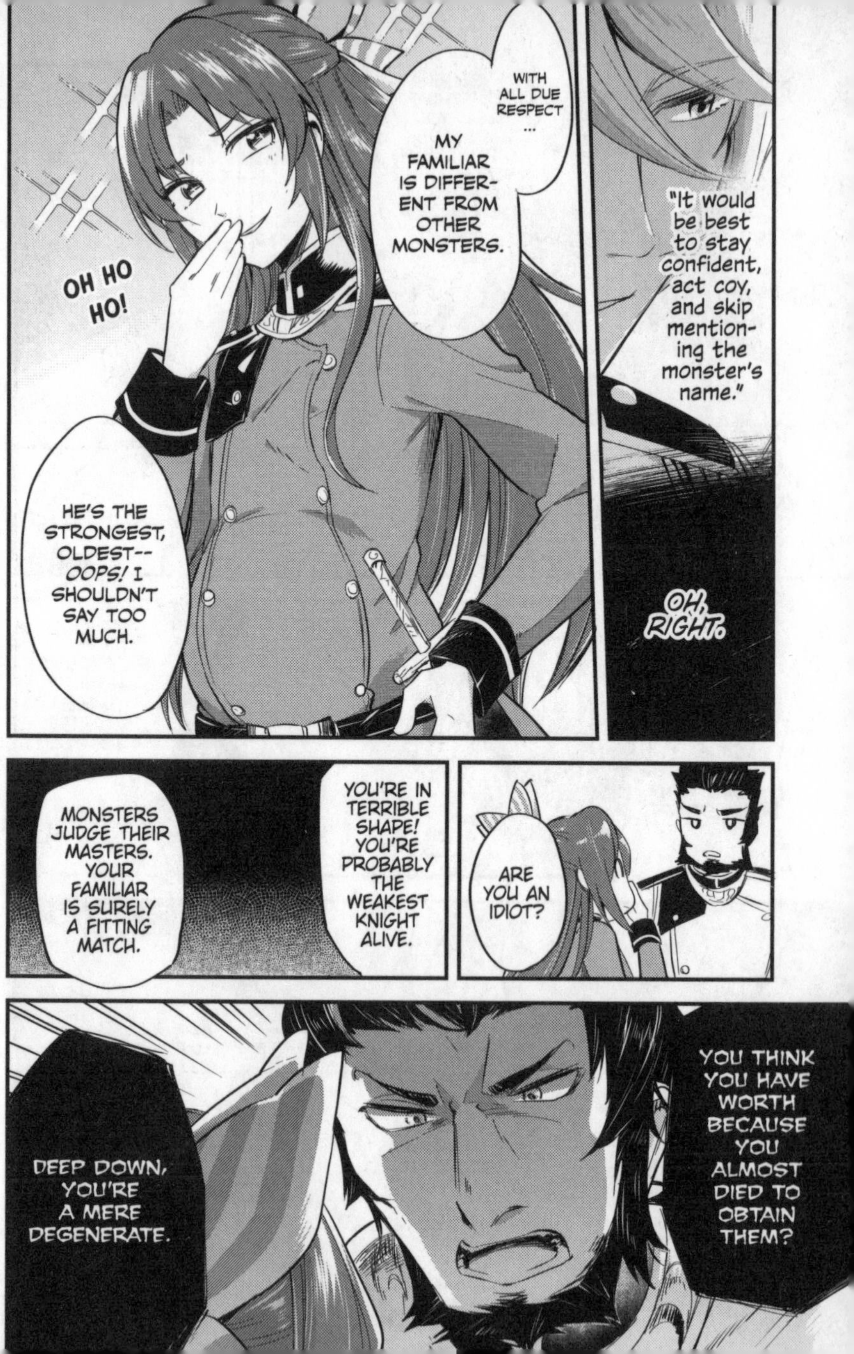
"It would be best to stay confident, act coy, and skip mentioning the monster's name."
OH, RIGHT.
WITH ALL DUE RESPECT ...
MY FAMILIAR IS DIFFERENT FROM OTHER MONSTERS.
OH HO HO!
HE'S THE STRONGEST, OLDEST-- *OOPS!* I SHOULDN'T SAY TOO MUCH.
ARE YOU AN IDIOT?
YOU'RE IN TERRIBLE SHAPE! YOU'RE PROBABLY THE WEAKEST KNIGHT ALIVE.
MONSTERS JUDGE THEIR MASTERS. YOUR FAMILIAR IS SURELY A FITTING MATCH.
YOU THINK YOU HAVE WORTH BECAUSE YOU ALMOST DIED TO OBTAIN THEM?
DEEP DOWN, YOU'RE A MERE DEGENERATE.

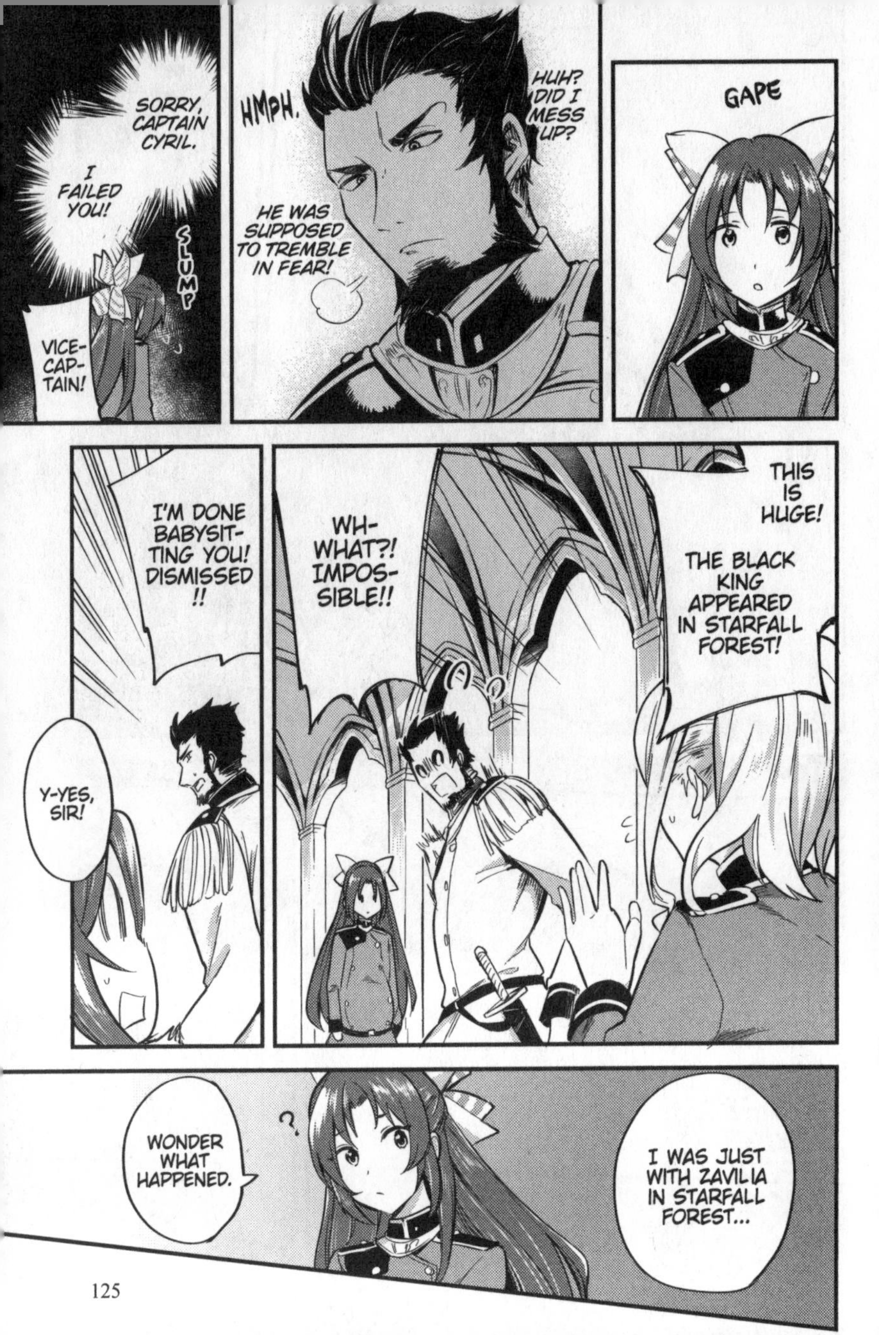
GAPE
HUH? DID I MESS UP?
HMPH.
HE WAS SUPPOSED TO TREMBLE IN FEAR!
SORRY, CAPTAIN CYRIL.
I FAILED YOU!
SLUMP
VICE-CAPTAIN!
THIS IS HUGE!
THE BLACK KING APPEARED IN STARFALL FOREST!
WH-WHAT?! IMPOSSIBLE!!
I'M DONE BABYSITTING YOU! DISMISSED!!
Y-YES, SIR!
I WAS JUST WITH ZAVILIA IN STARFALL FOREST...
WONDER WHAT HAPPENED.

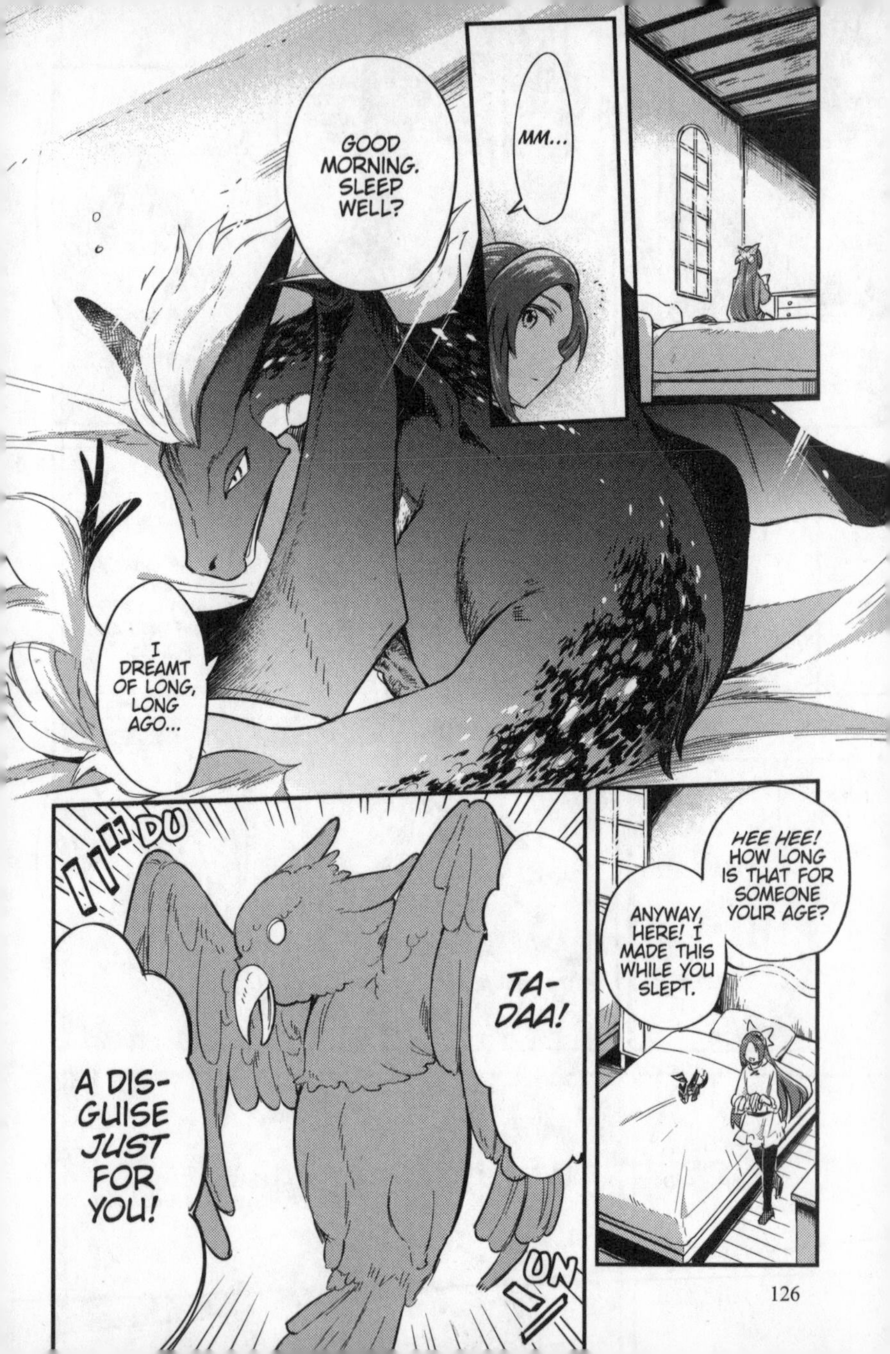
MM...
GOOD MORNING. SLEEP WELL?
I DREAMT OF LONG, LONG AGO...
HEE HEE! HOW LONG IS THAT FOR SOMEONE YOUR AGE?
ANYWAY, HERE! I MADE THIS WHILE YOU SLEPT.
TA-DAA!
DU
UN
A DIS-GUISE JUST FOR YOU!

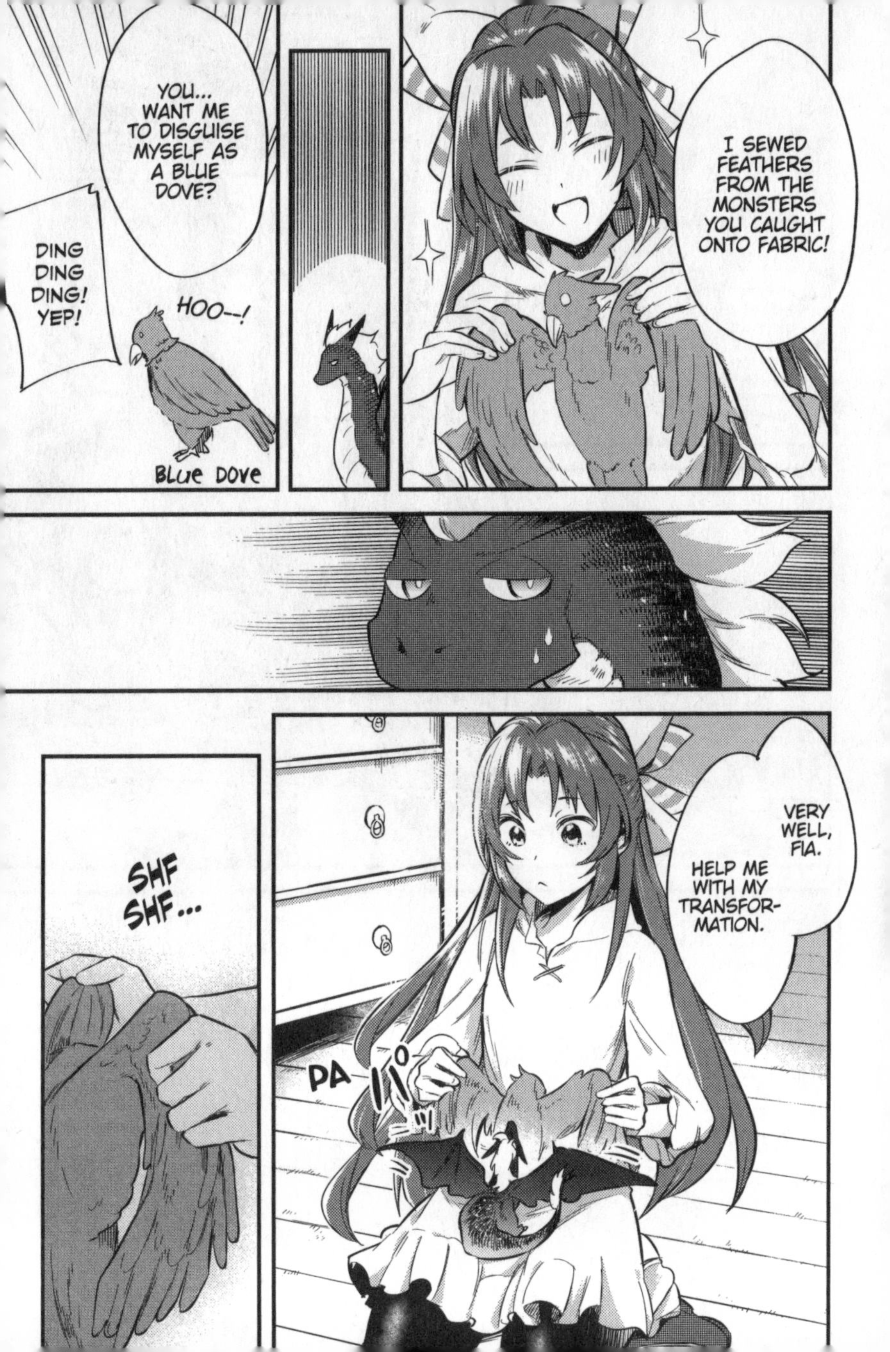
I SEWED FEATHERS FROM THE MONSTERS YOU CAUGHT ONTO FABRIC!
YOU... WANT ME TO DISGUISE MYSELF AS A BLUE DOVE?
DING DING DING! YEP!
HOO--!
Blue Dove
VERY WELL, FIA.
HELP ME WITH MY TRANSFOR-MATION.
PA
SHF SHF...

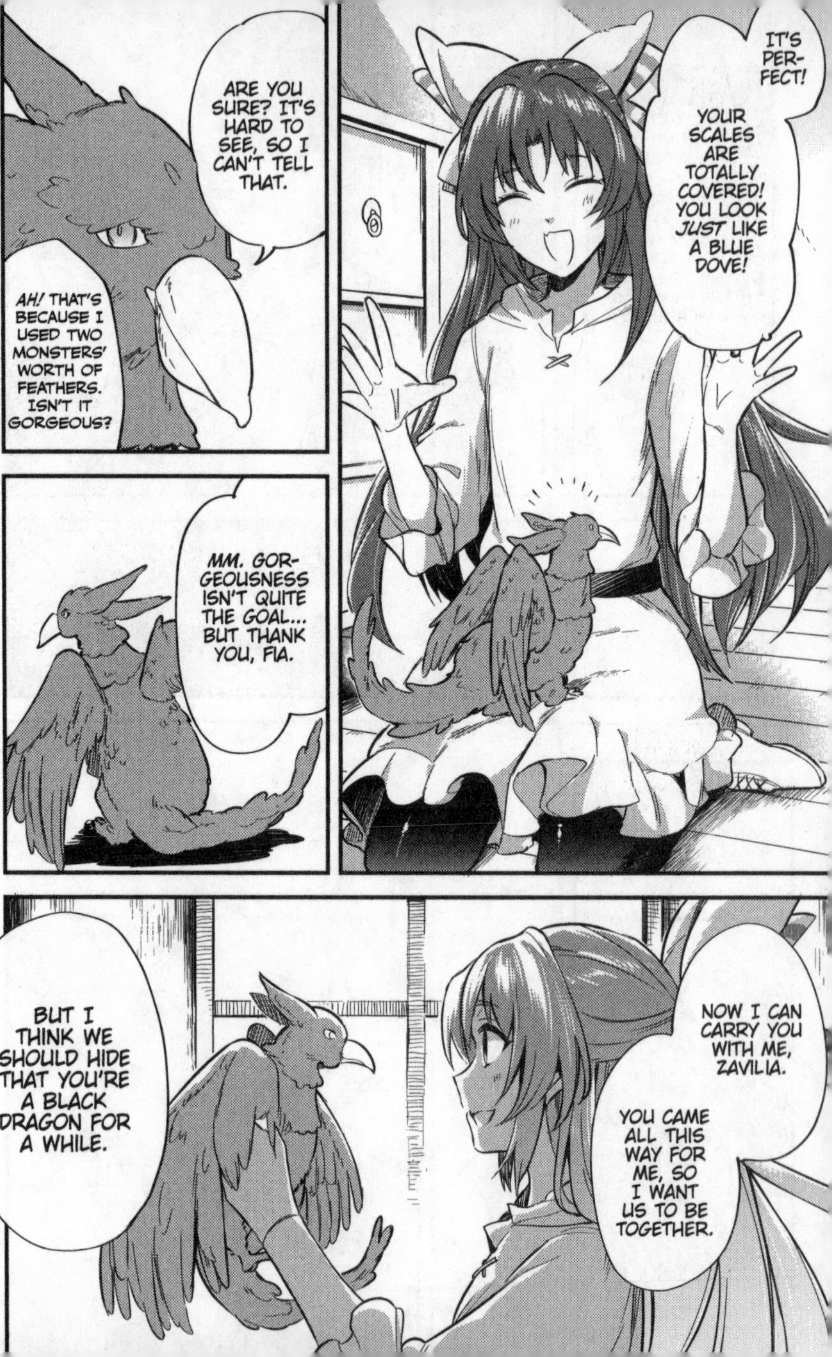
IT'S PER-FECT!
YOUR SCALES ARE TOTALLY COVERED! YOU LOOK JUST LIKE A BLUE DOVE!
ARE YOU SURE? IT'S HARD TO SEE, SO I CAN'T TELL THAT.
AH! THAT'S BECAUSE I USED TWO MONSTERS' WORTH OF FEATHERS. ISN'T IT GORGEOUS?
MM. GOR-GEOUSNESS ISN'T QUITE THE GOAL... BUT THANK YOU, FIA.
NOW I CAN CARRY YOU WITH ME, ZAVILIA.
YOU CAME ALL THIS WAY FOR ME, SO I WANT US TO BE TOGETHER.
BUT I THINK WE SHOULD HIDE THAT YOU'RE A BLACK DRAGON FOR A WHILE.

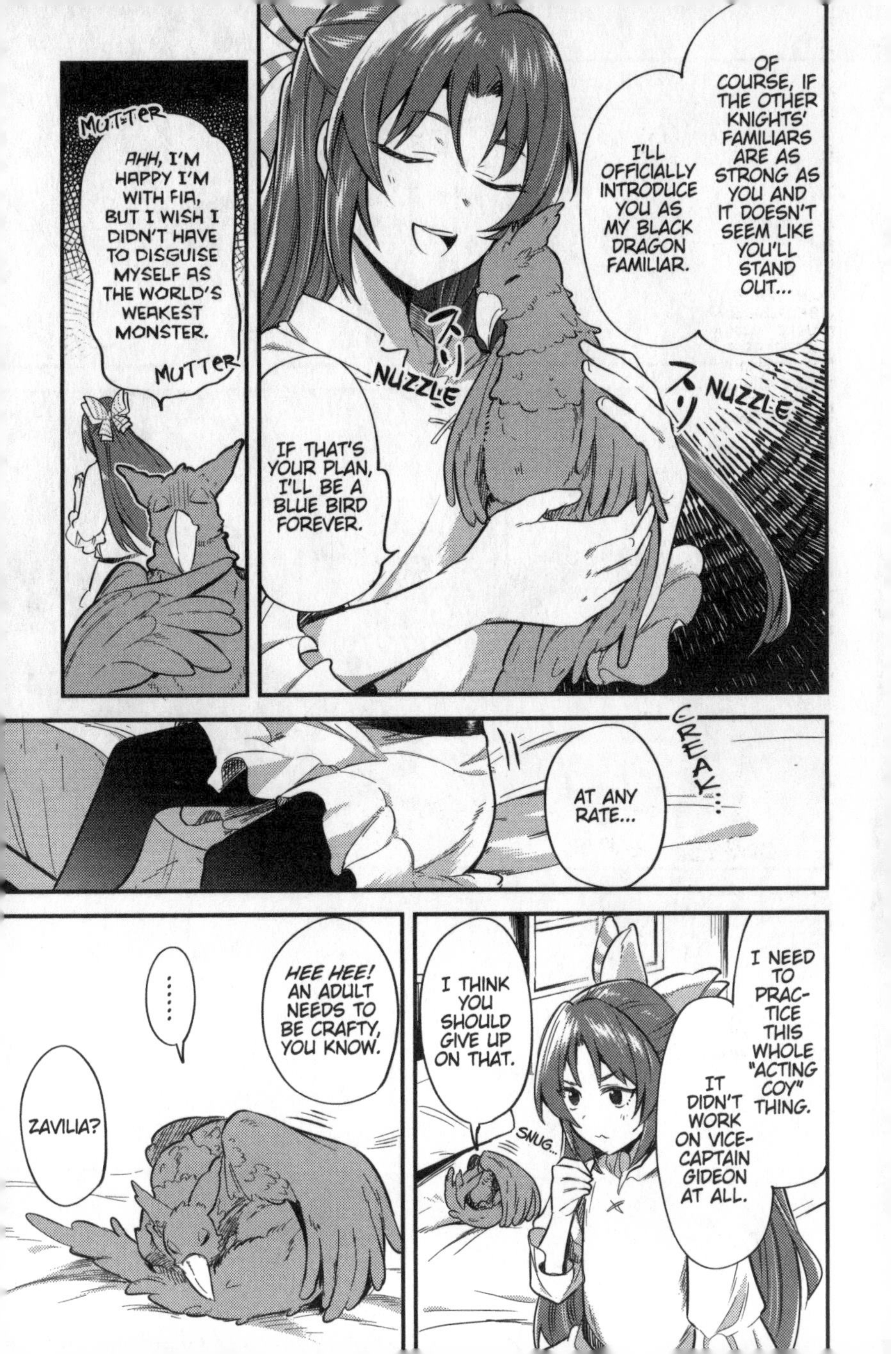
OF COURSE, IF THE OTHER KNIGHTS' FAMILIARS ARE AS STRONG AS YOU AND IT DOESN'T SEEM LIKE YOU'LL STAND OUT...
I'LL OFFICIALLY INTRODUCE YOU AS MY BLACK DRAGON FAMILIAR.
スリ NUZZLE
スリ NUZZLE
IF THAT'S YOUR PLAN, I'LL BE A BLUE BIRD FOREVER.
MUTTER
AHH, I'M HAPPY I'M WITH FIA, BUT I WISH I DIDN'T HAVE TO DISGUISE MYSELF AS THE WORLD'S WEAKEST MONSTER.
MUTTER
CREAK...
AT ANY RATE...
I NEED TO PRACTICE THIS WHOLE "ACTING COY" THING.
IT DIDN'T WORK ON VICE-CAPTAIN GIDEON AT ALL.
SNUG...
I THINK YOU SHOULD GIVE UP ON THAT.
HEE HEE! AN ADULT NEEDS TO BE CRAFTY, YOU KNOW.
......
ZAVILIA?

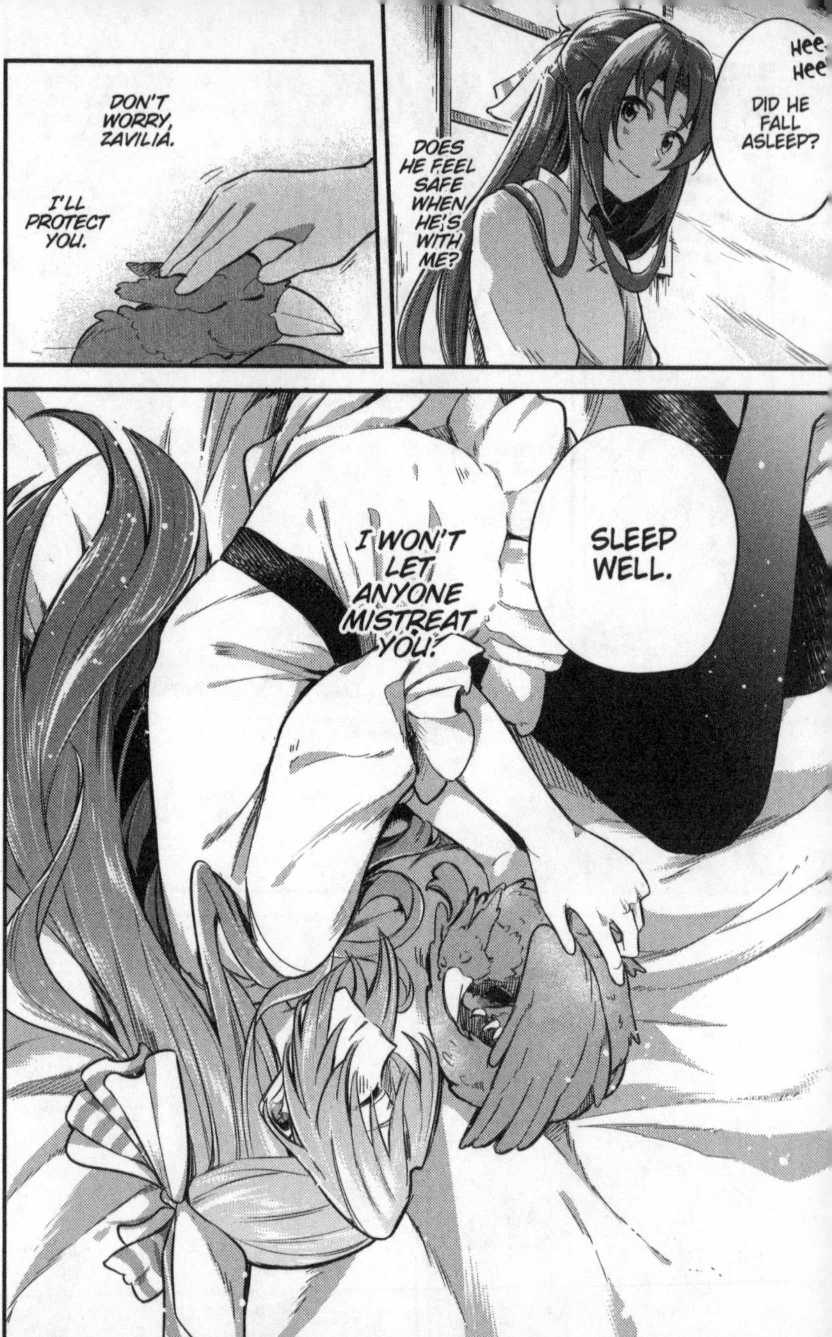
Hee-Hee
Did he fall asleep?
Does he feel safe when he's with me?
Don't worry, Zavilia.
I'll protect you.
Sleep well.
I won't let anyone mistreat you.

A Tale of the
Secret
Saint

A Tale of the
Secret
Saint

Book 8: Monster Tamer Knight Brigade: Part II

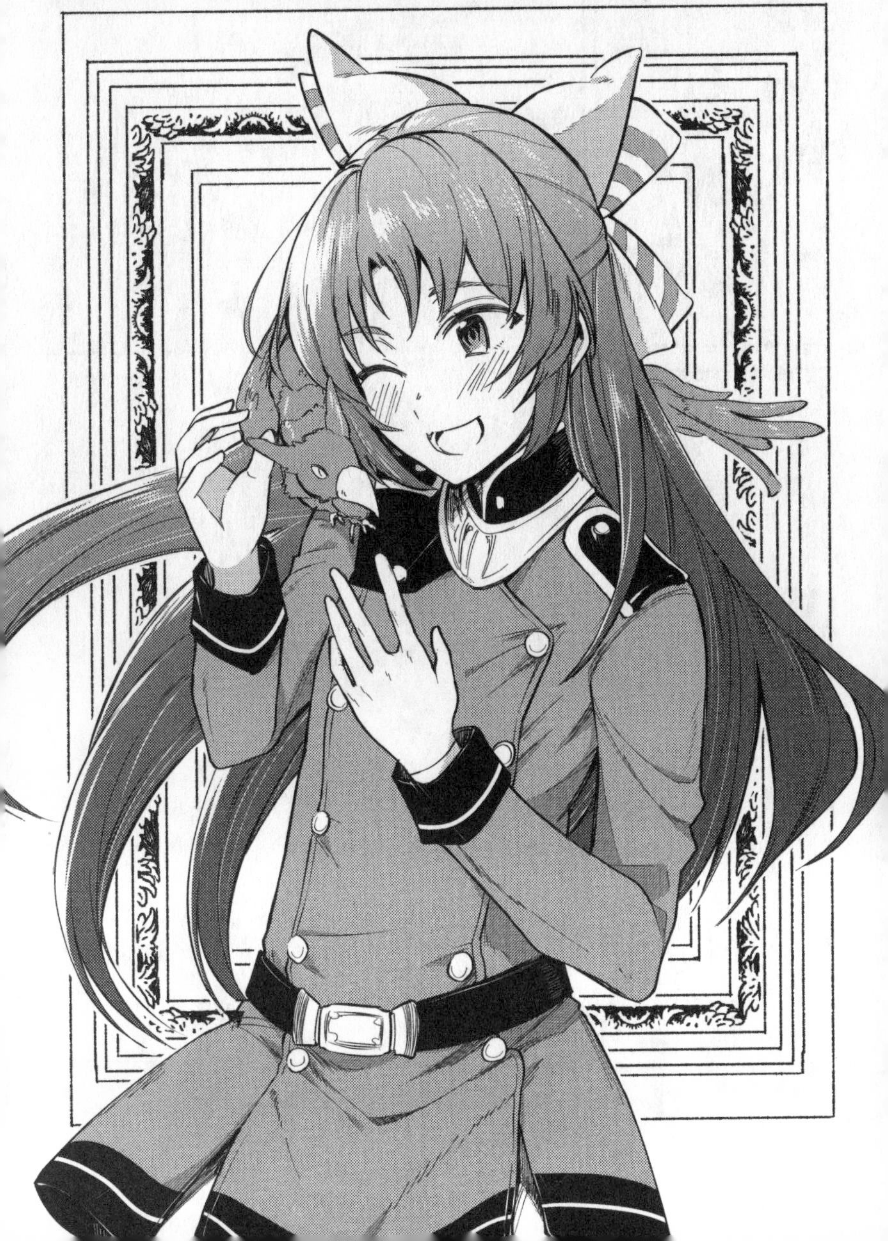

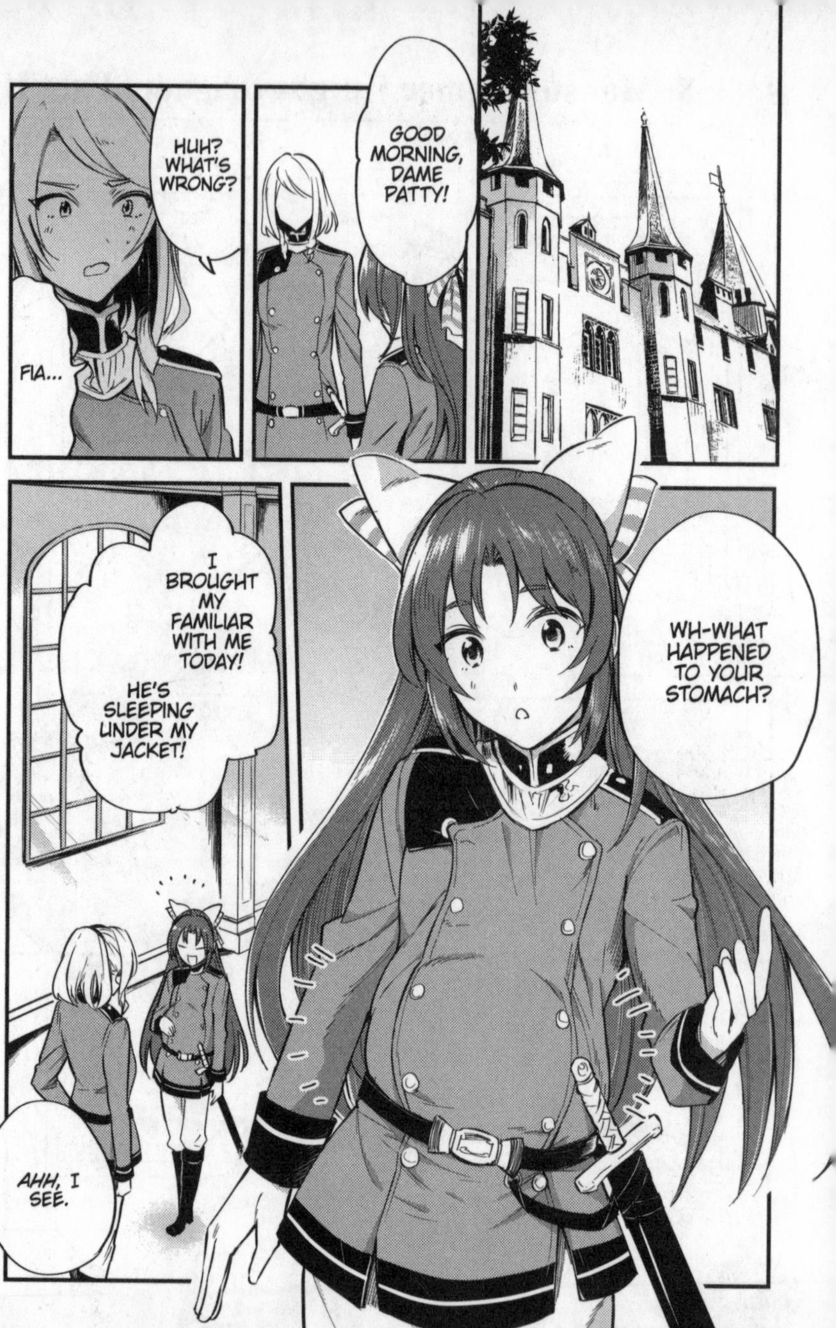
GOOD MORNING, DAME PATTY!
HUH? WHAT'S WRONG?
FIA...
WH-WHAT HAPPENED TO YOUR STOMACH?
I BROUGHT MY FAMILIAR WITH ME TODAY!
HE'S SLEEPING UNDER MY JACKET!
AHH, I SEE.

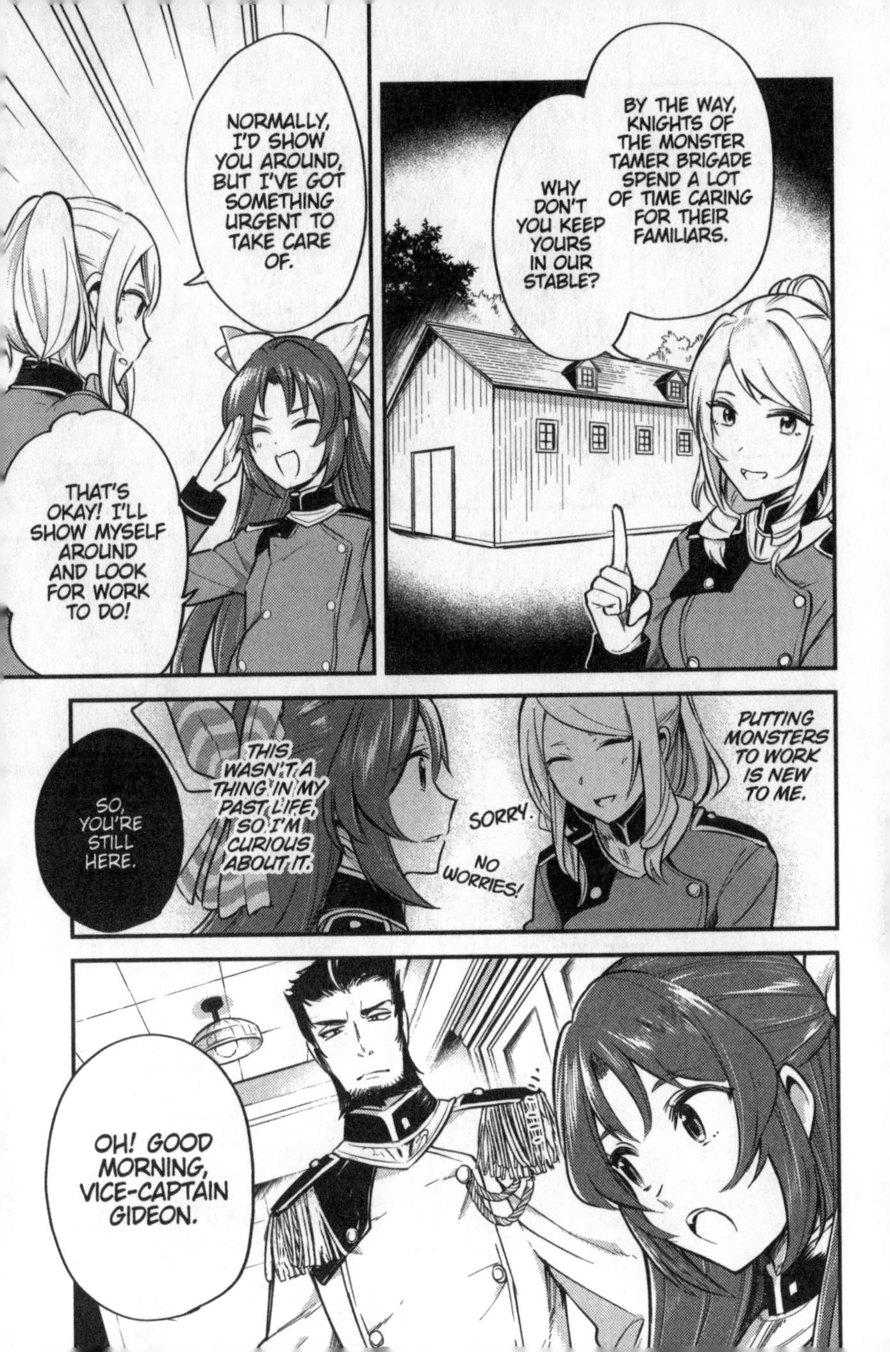
BY THE WAY, KNIGHTS OF THE MONSTER TAMER BRIGADE SPEND A LOT OF TIME CARING FOR THEIR FAMILIARS.
WHY DON'T YOU KEEP YOURS IN OUR STABLE?
NORMALLY, I'D SHOW YOU AROUND, BUT I'VE GOT SOMETHING URGENT TO TAKE CARE OF.
THAT'S OKAY! I'LL SHOW MYSELF AROUND AND LOOK FOR WORK TO DO!
PUTTING MONSTERS TO WORK IS NEW TO ME.
SORRY.
NO WORRIES!
THIS WASN'T A THING IN MY PAST LIFE, SO I'M CURIOUS ABOUT IT.
SO, YOU'RE STILL HERE.
OH! GOOD MORNING, VICE-CAPTAIN GIDEON.

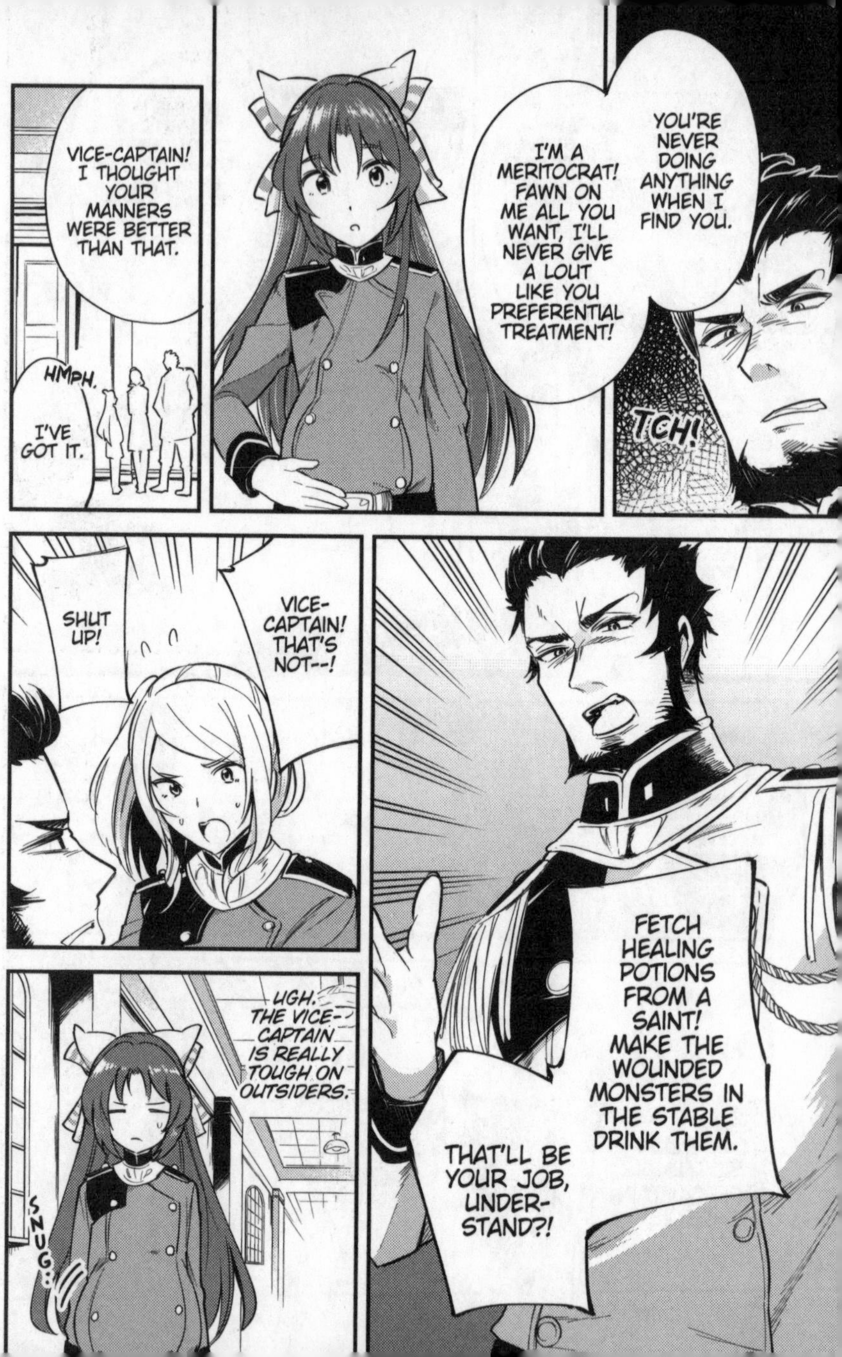

YOU'RE NEVER DOING ANYTHING WHEN I FIND YOU.
I'M A MERITOCRAT! FAWN ON ME ALL YOU WANT, I'LL NEVER GIVE A LOUT LIKE YOU PREFERENTIAL TREATMENT!
TCH!
VICE-CAPTAIN! I THOUGHT YOUR MANNERS WERE BETTER THAN THAT.
HMPH.
I'VE GOT IT.
FETCH HEALING POTIONS FROM A SAINT! MAKE THE WOUNDED MONSTERS IN THE STABLE DRINK THEM.
THAT'LL BE YOUR JOB, UNDER-STAND?!
VICE-CAPTAIN! THAT'S NOT--!
SHUT UP!
UGH. THE VICE-CAPTAIN IS REALLY TOUGH ON OUTSIDERS.
SNUG...

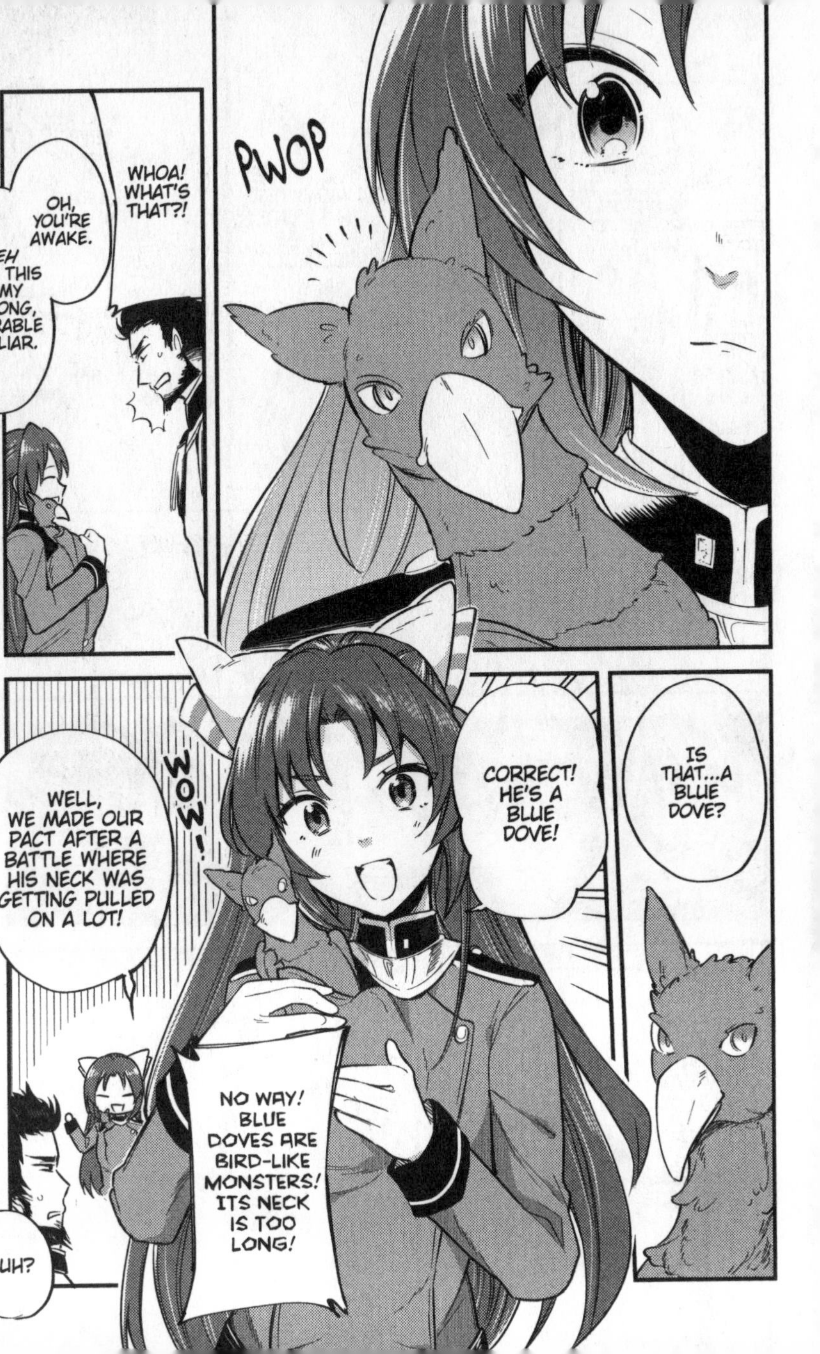
PWOP
WHOA! WHAT'S THAT?!
OH, YOU'RE AWAKE. HEH HEH! THIS IS MY STRONG, ADORABLE FAMILIAR.
IS THAT...A BLUE DOVE?
CORRECT! HE'S A BLUE DOVE!
WOW!
WELL, WE MADE OUR PACT AFTER A BATTLE WHERE HIS NECK WAS GETTING PULLED ON A LOT!
NO WAY! BLUE DOVES ARE BIRD-LIKE MONSTERS! ITS NECK IS TOO LONG!
HUH?

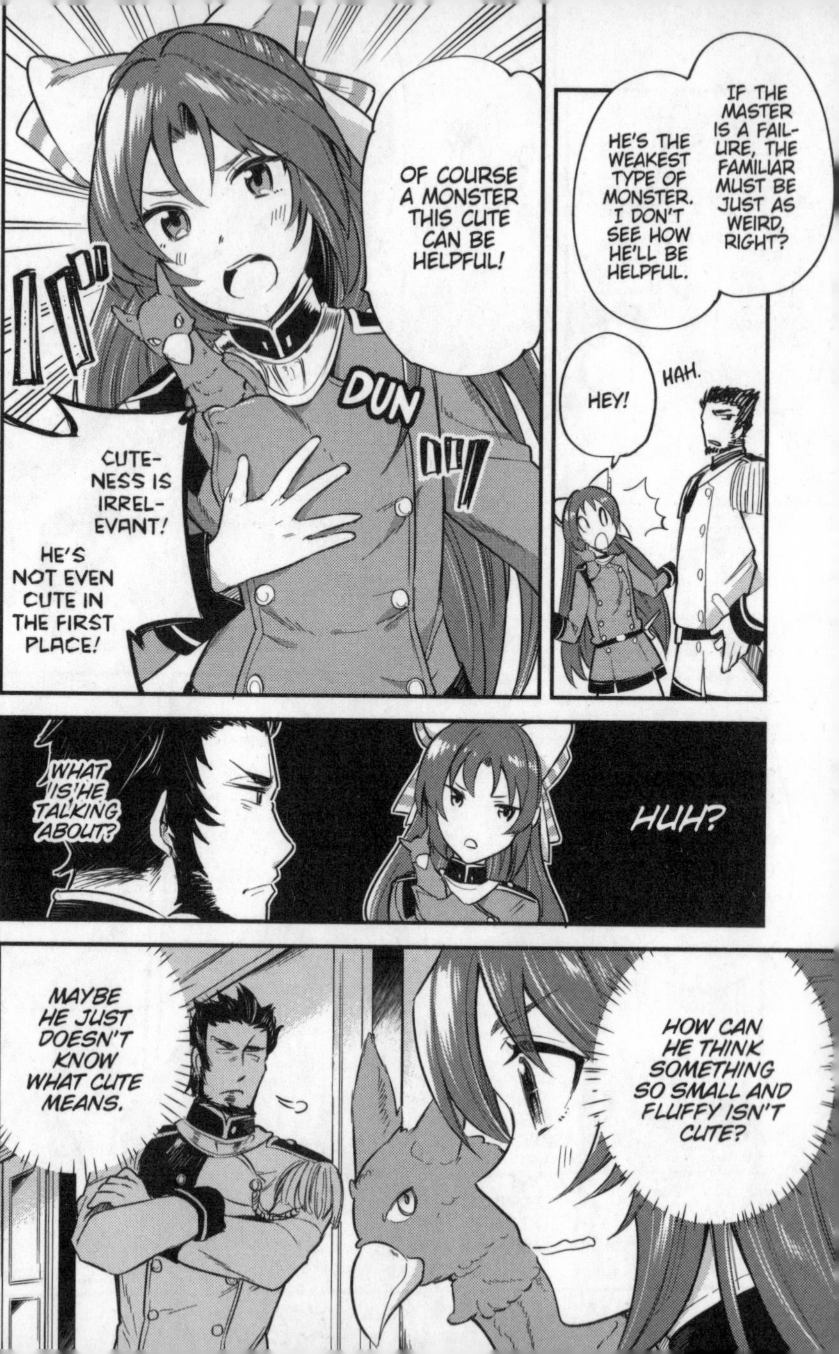
IF THE MASTER IS A FAILURE, THE FAMILIAR MUST BE JUST AS WEIRD, RIGHT?
HE'S THE WEAKEST TYPE OF MONSTER. I DON'T SEE HOW HE'LL BE HELPFUL.
HAH.
HEY!
OF COURSE A MONSTER THIS CUTE CAN BE HELPFUL!
DUN
CUTENESS IS IRRELEVANT!
HE'S NOT EVEN CUTE IN THE FIRST PLACE!
HUH?
WHAT IS HE TALKING ABOUT?
HOW CAN HE THINK SOMETHING SO SMALL AND FLUFFY ISN'T CUTE?
MAYBE HE JUST DOESN'T KNOW WHAT CUTE MEANS.

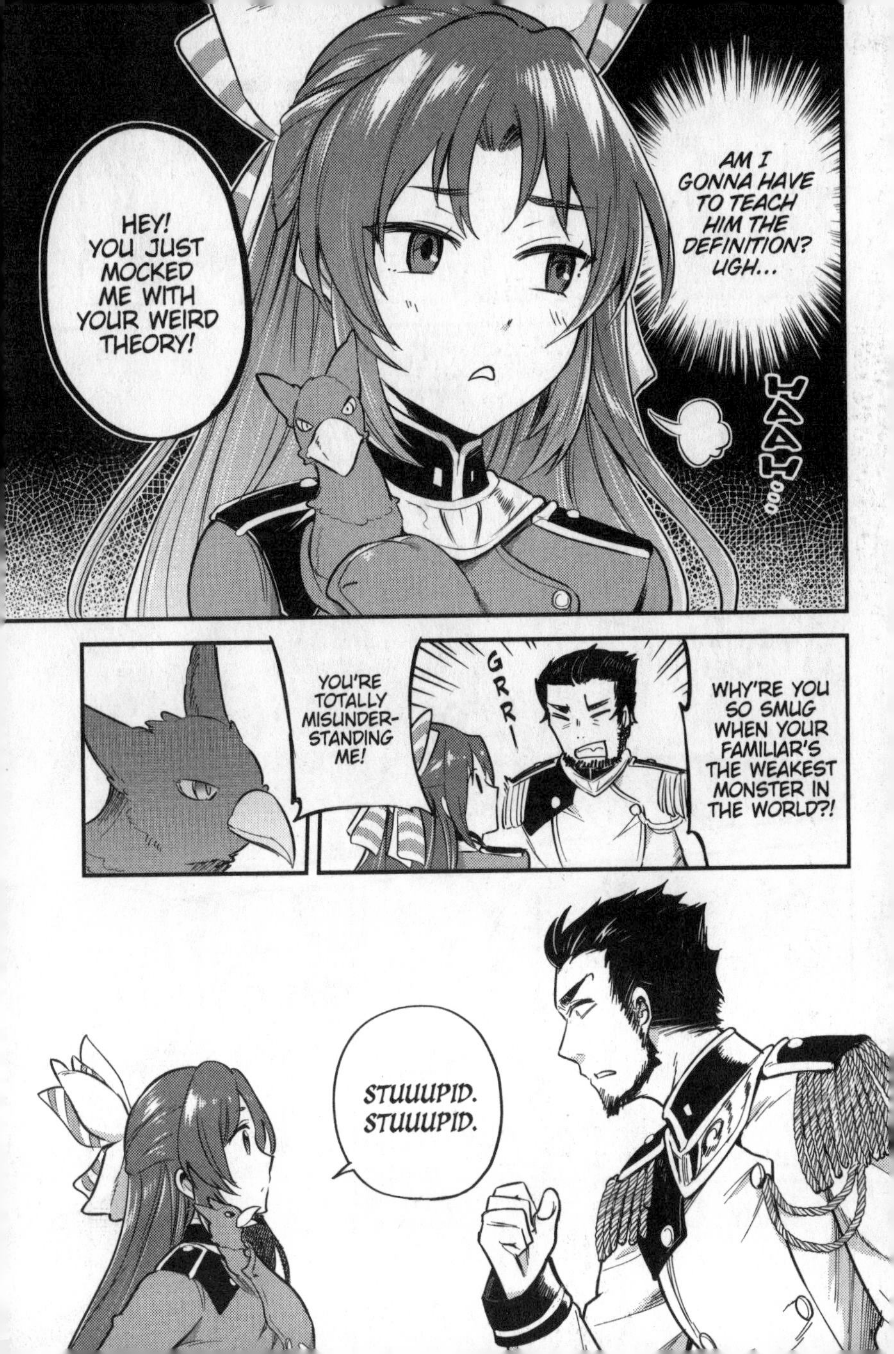
AM I GONNA HAVE TO TEACH HIM THE DEFINITION? UGH...
HAAAH...
HEY! YOU JUST MOCKED ME WITH YOUR WEIRD THEORY!
WHY'RE YOU SO SMUG WHEN YOUR FAMILIAR'S THE WEAKEST MONSTER IN THE WORLD?!
GRR!
YOU'RE TOTALLY MISUNDER-STANDING ME!
STUUUPID. STUUUPID.

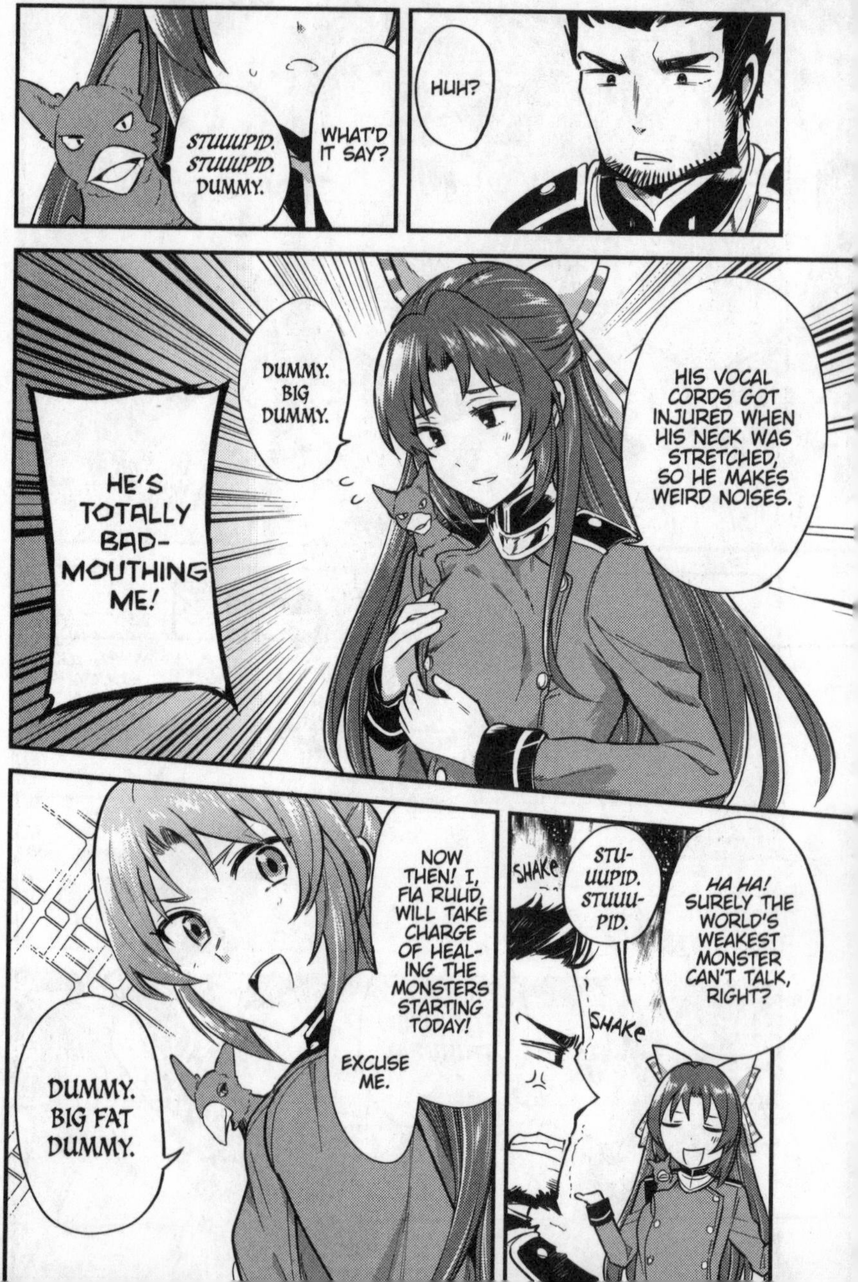
HUH?
WHAT'D IT SAY?
STUUUPID. STUUUPID. DUMMY.
HIS VOCAL CORDS GOT INJURED WHEN HIS NECK WAS STRETCHED, SO HE MAKES WEIRD NOISES.
DUMMY. BIG DUMMY.
HE'S TOTALLY BAD-MOUTHING ME!
HA HA! SURELY THE WORLD'S WEAKEST MONSTER CAN'T TALK, RIGHT?
STU-UUPID. STUUU-PID.
SHAKE
SHAKE
NOW THEN! I, FIA RUUD, WILL TAKE CHARGE OF HEAL-ING THE MONSTERS STARTING TODAY!
EXCUSE ME.
DUMMY. BIG FAT DUMMY.

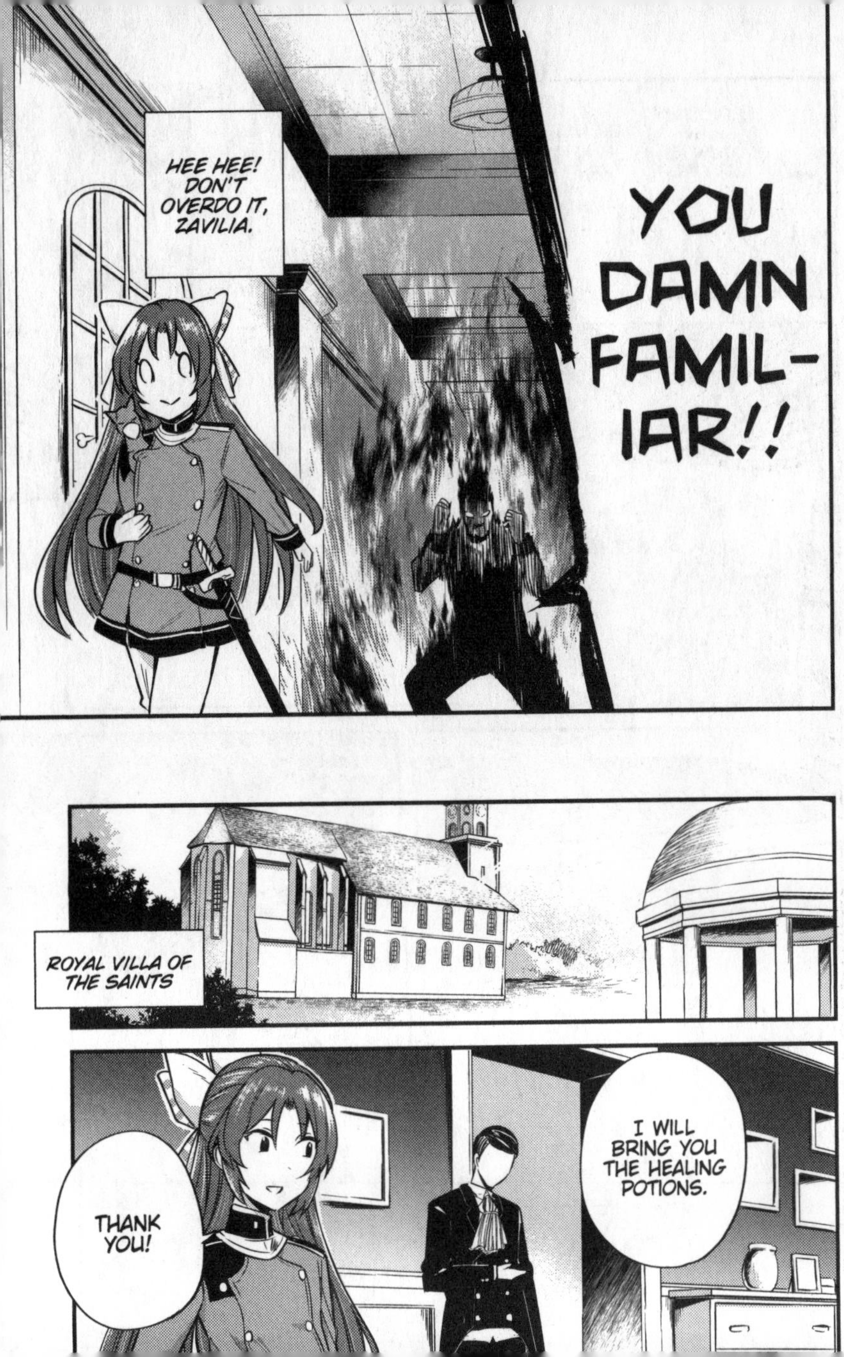
YOU DAMN FAMIL-IAR!!
HEE HEE! DON'T OVERDO IT, ZAVILIA.
ROYAL VILLA OF THE SAINTS
I WILL BRING YOU THE HEALING POTIONS.
THANK YOU!

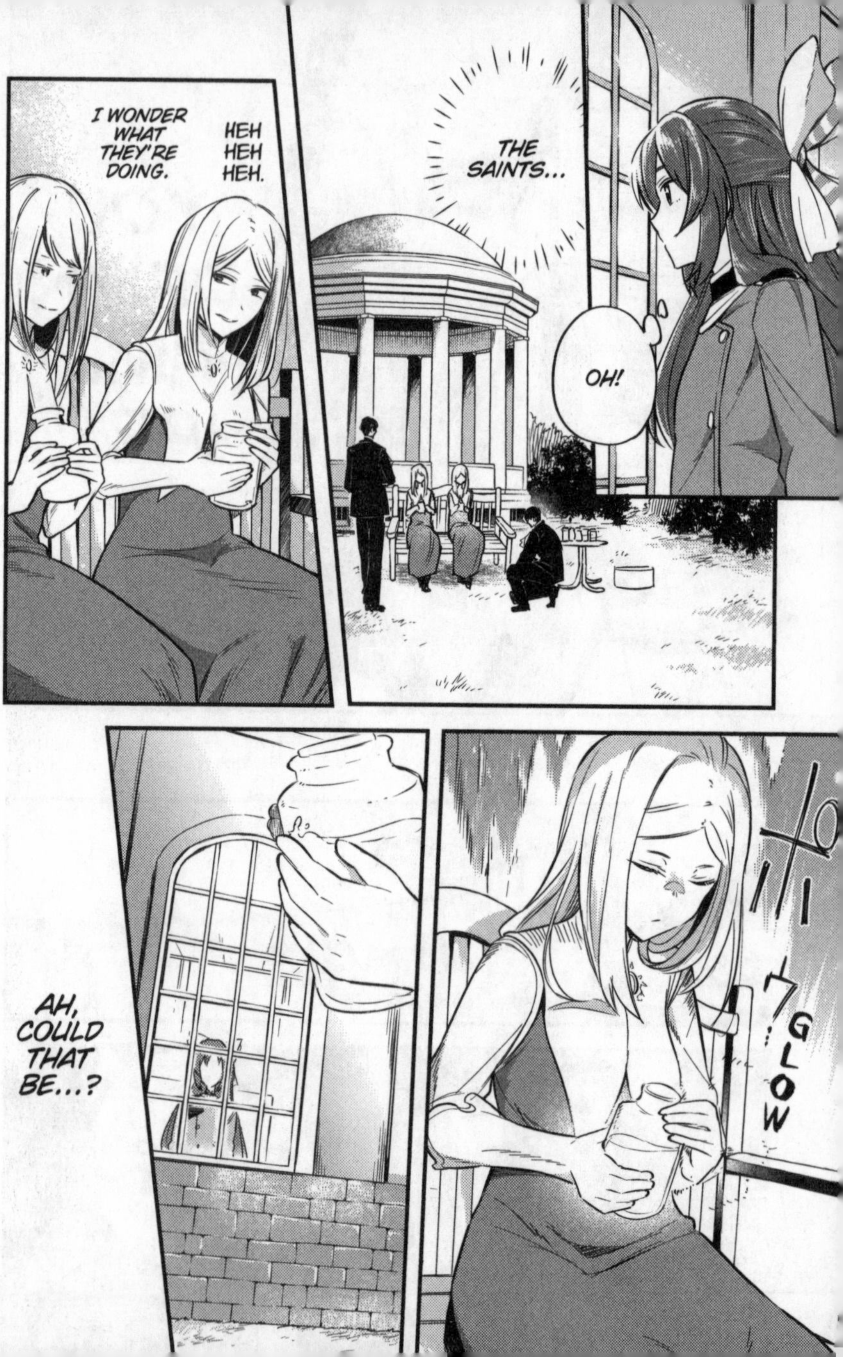
OH!
THE SAINTS...
HEH HEH HEH.
I WONDER WHAT THEY'RE DOING.
GLOW
AH, COULD THAT BE...?

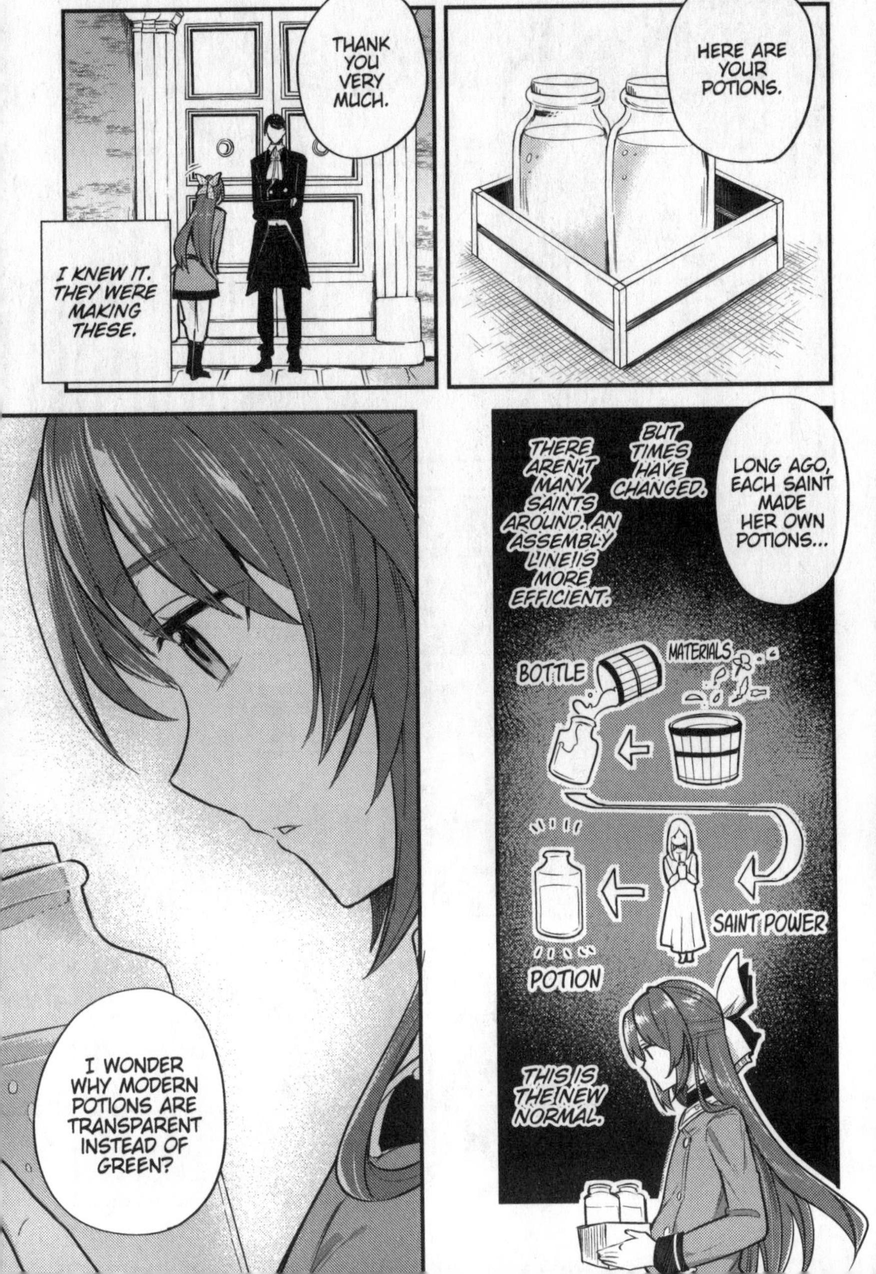
HERE ARE YOUR POTIONS.
THANK YOU VERY MUCH.
I KNEW IT. THEY WERE MAKING THESE.
LONG AGO, EACH SAINT MADE HER OWN POTIONS...
BUT TIMES HAVE CHANGED.
THERE AREN'T MANY SAINTS AROUND. AN ASSEMBLY LINE IS MORE EFFICIENT.
MATERIALS
BOTTLE
SAINT POWER
POTION
THIS IS THE NEW NORMAL.
I WONDER WHY MODERN POTIONS ARE TRANSPARENT INSTEAD OF GREEN?

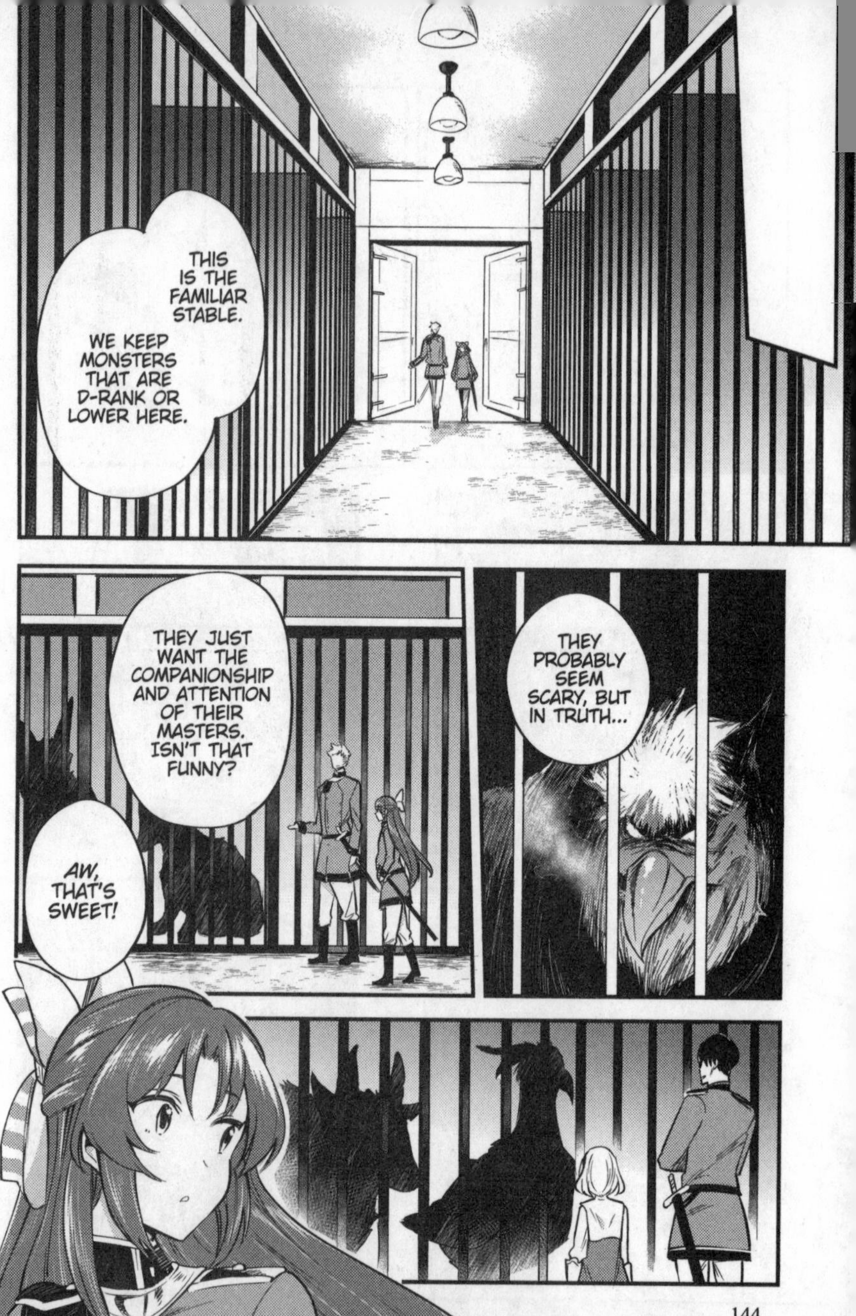
THIS IS THE FAMILIAR STABLE.
WE KEEP MONSTERS THAT ARE D-RANK OR LOWER HERE.
THEY PROBABLY SEEM SCARY, BUT IN TRUTH...
THEY JUST WANT THE COMPANIONSHIP AND ATTENTION OF THEIR MASTERS. ISN'T THAT FUNNY?
AW, THAT'S SWEET!

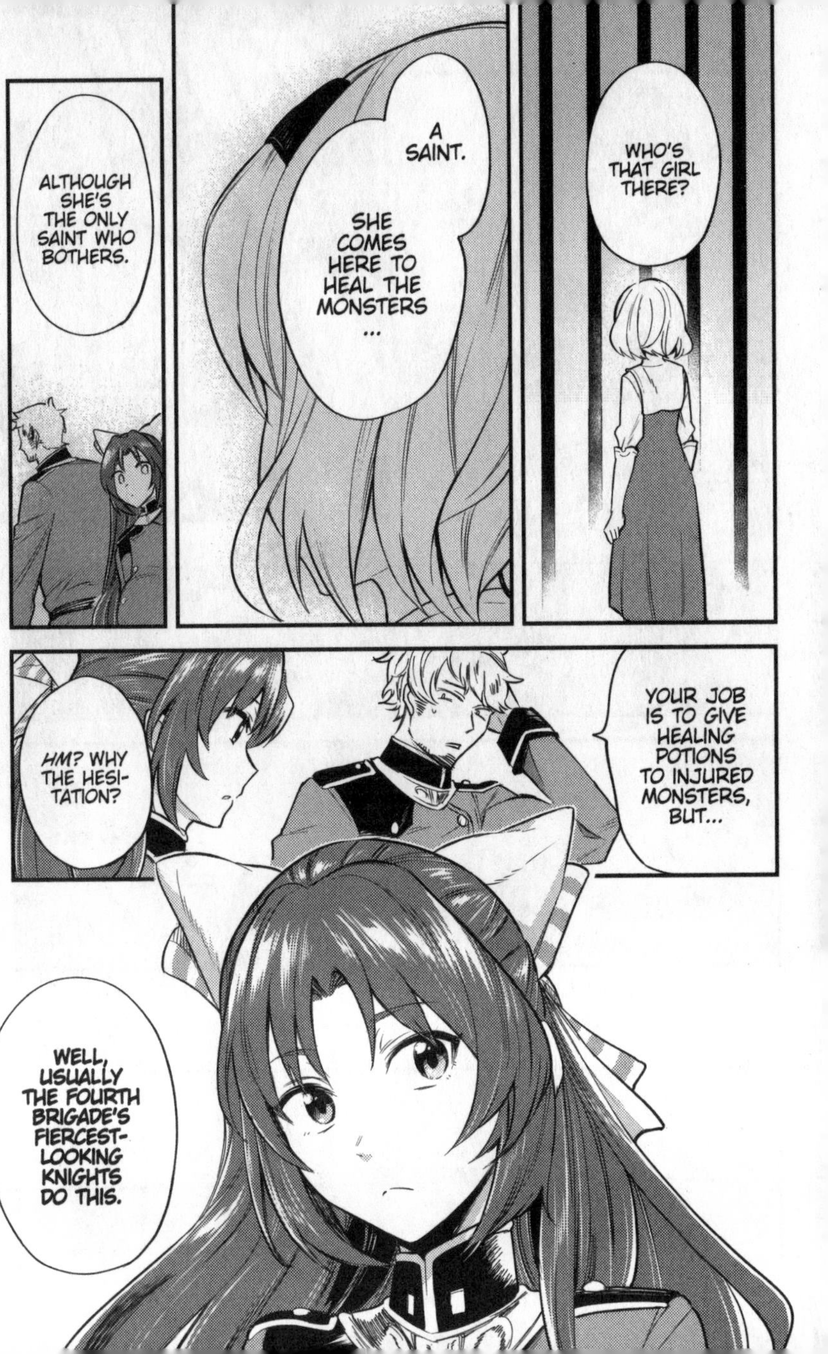
WHO'S THAT GIRL THERE?
A SAINT.
SHE COMES HERE TO HEAL THE MONSTERS ...
ALTHOUGH SHE'S THE ONLY SAINT WHO BOTHERS.
YOUR JOB IS TO GIVE HEALING POTIONS TO INJURED MONSTERS, BUT...
HM? WHY THE HESI-TATION?
WELL, USUALLY THE FOURTH BRIGADE'S FIERCEST-LOOKING KNIGHTS DO THIS.

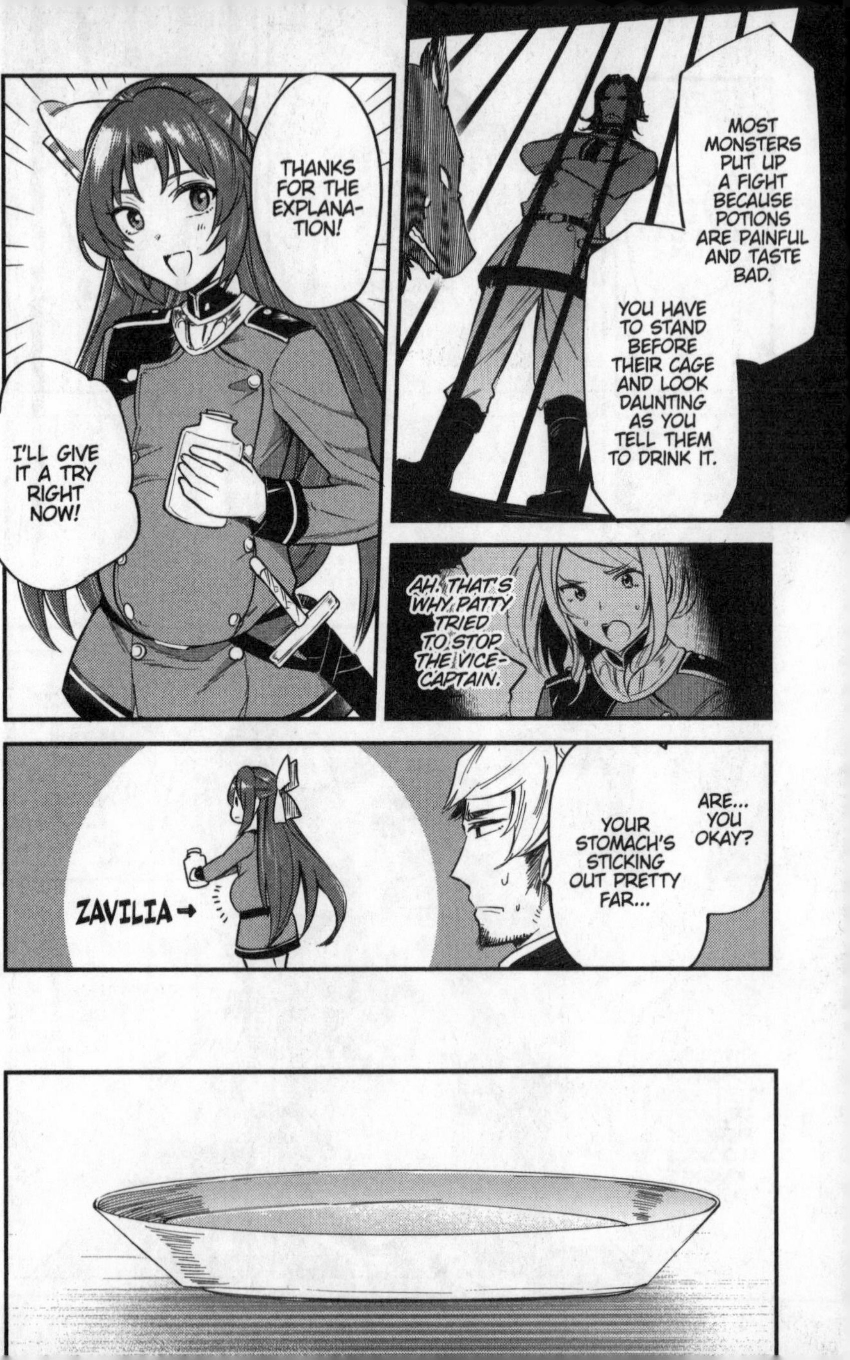
MOST MONSTERS PUT UP A FIGHT BECAUSE POTIONS ARE PAINFUL AND TASTE BAD.
YOU HAVE TO STAND BEFORE THEIR CAGE AND LOOK DAUNTING AS YOU TELL THEM TO DRINK IT.
AH. THAT'S WHY PATTY TRIED TO STOP THE VICE-CAPTAIN.
THANKS FOR THE EXPLANA-TION!
I'LL GIVE IT A TRY RIGHT NOW!
ARE... YOU OKAY?
YOUR STOMACH'S STICKING OUT PRETTY FAR...
ZAVILIA →

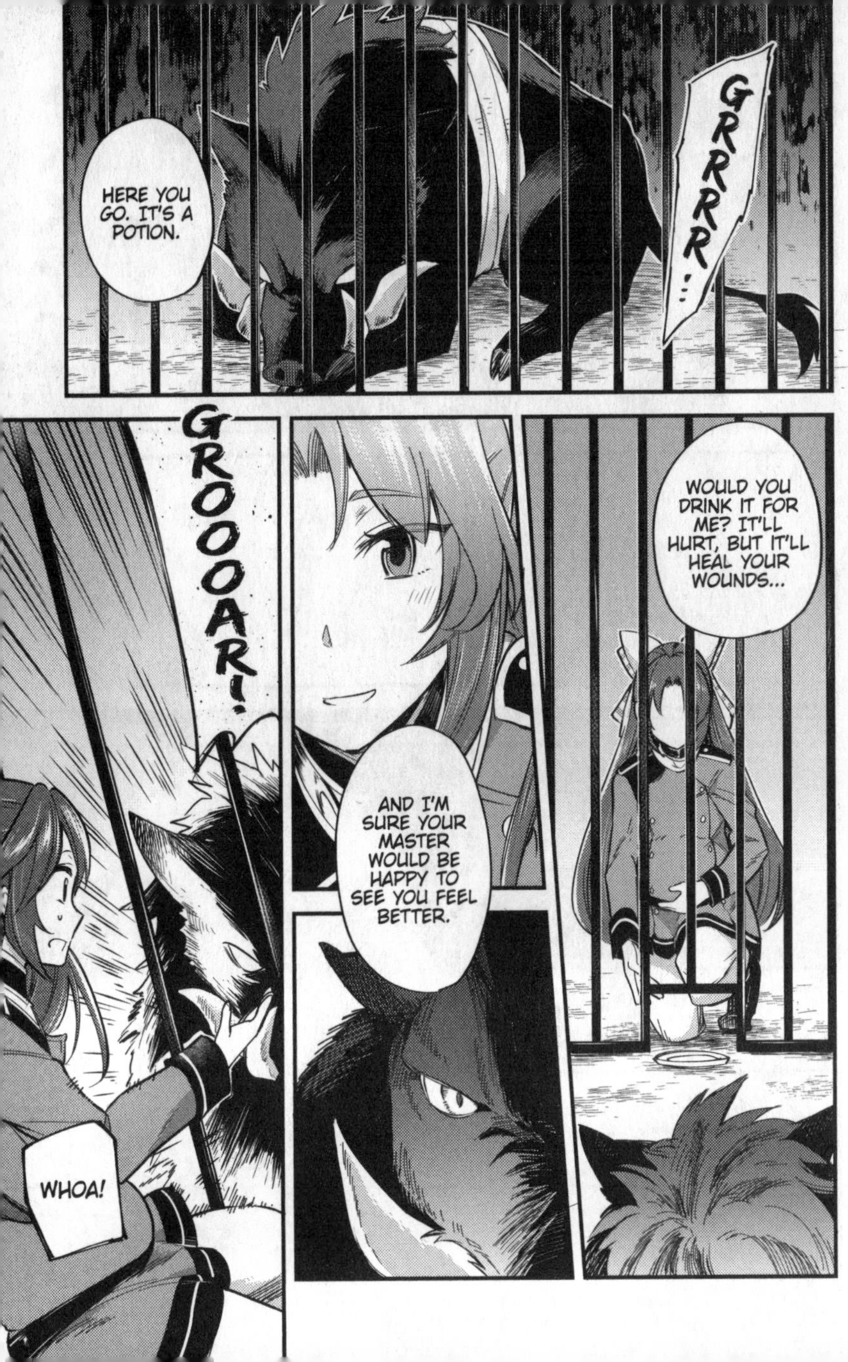
HERE YOU GO. IT'S A POTION.
GRRRR...
WOULD YOU DRINK IT FOR ME? IT'LL HURT, BUT IT'LL HEAL YOUR WOUNDS...
AND I'M SURE YOUR MASTER WOULD BE HAPPY TO SEE YOU FEEL BETTER.
GROOOAR!
WHOA!

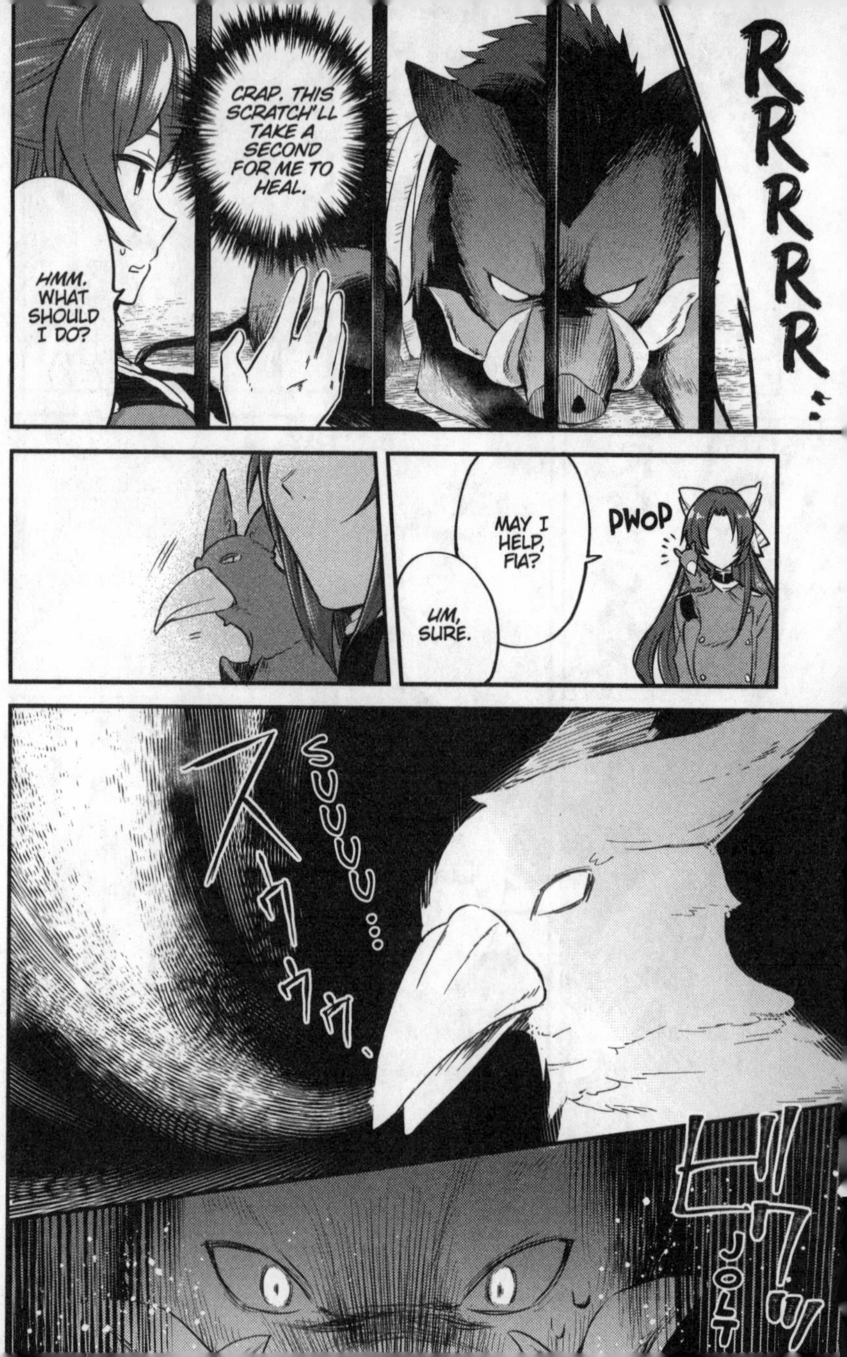
RRRRR.
CRAP. THIS SCRATCH'LL TAKE A SECOND FOR ME TO HEAL.
HMM. WHAT SHOULD I DO?
PWOP
MAY I HELP, FIA?
UM, SURE.
SUUUU...
JOLT

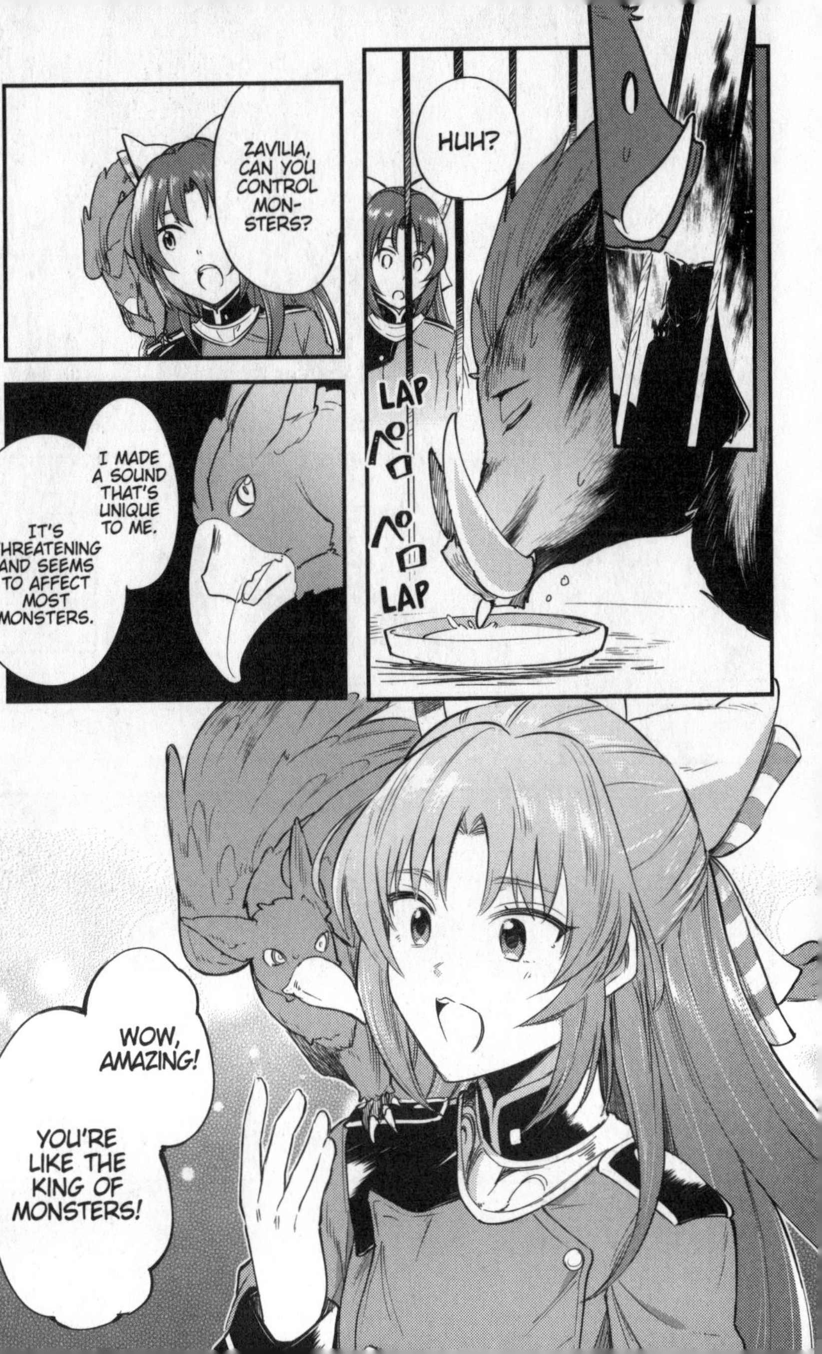
HUH?
LAP
ペロ
ペロ
LAP
ZAVILIA, CAN YOU CONTROL MON-STERS?
I MADE A SOUND THAT'S UNIQUE TO ME.
IT'S THREATENING AND SEEMS TO AFFECT MOST MONSTERS.
WOW, AMAZING!
YOU'RE LIKE THE KING OF MONSTERS!

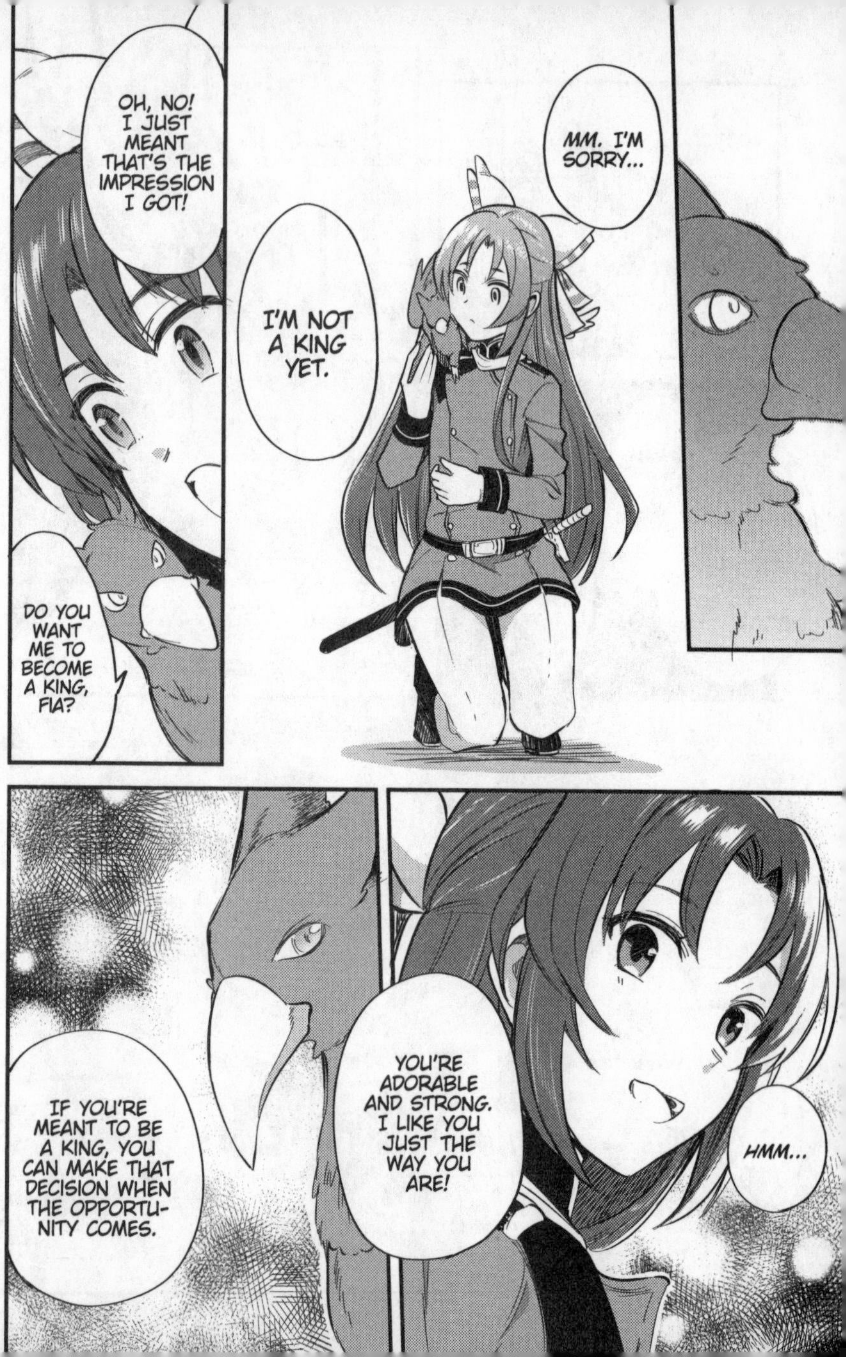
MM. I'M SORRY...
I'M NOT A KING YET.
OH, NO! I JUST MEANT THAT'S THE IMPRESSION I GOT!
DO YOU WANT ME TO BECOME A KING, FIA?
HMM...
YOU'RE ADORABLE AND STRONG. I LIKE YOU JUST THE WAY YOU ARE!
IF YOU'RE MEANT TO BE A KING, YOU CAN MAKE THAT DECISION WHEN THE OPPORTU-NITY COMES.

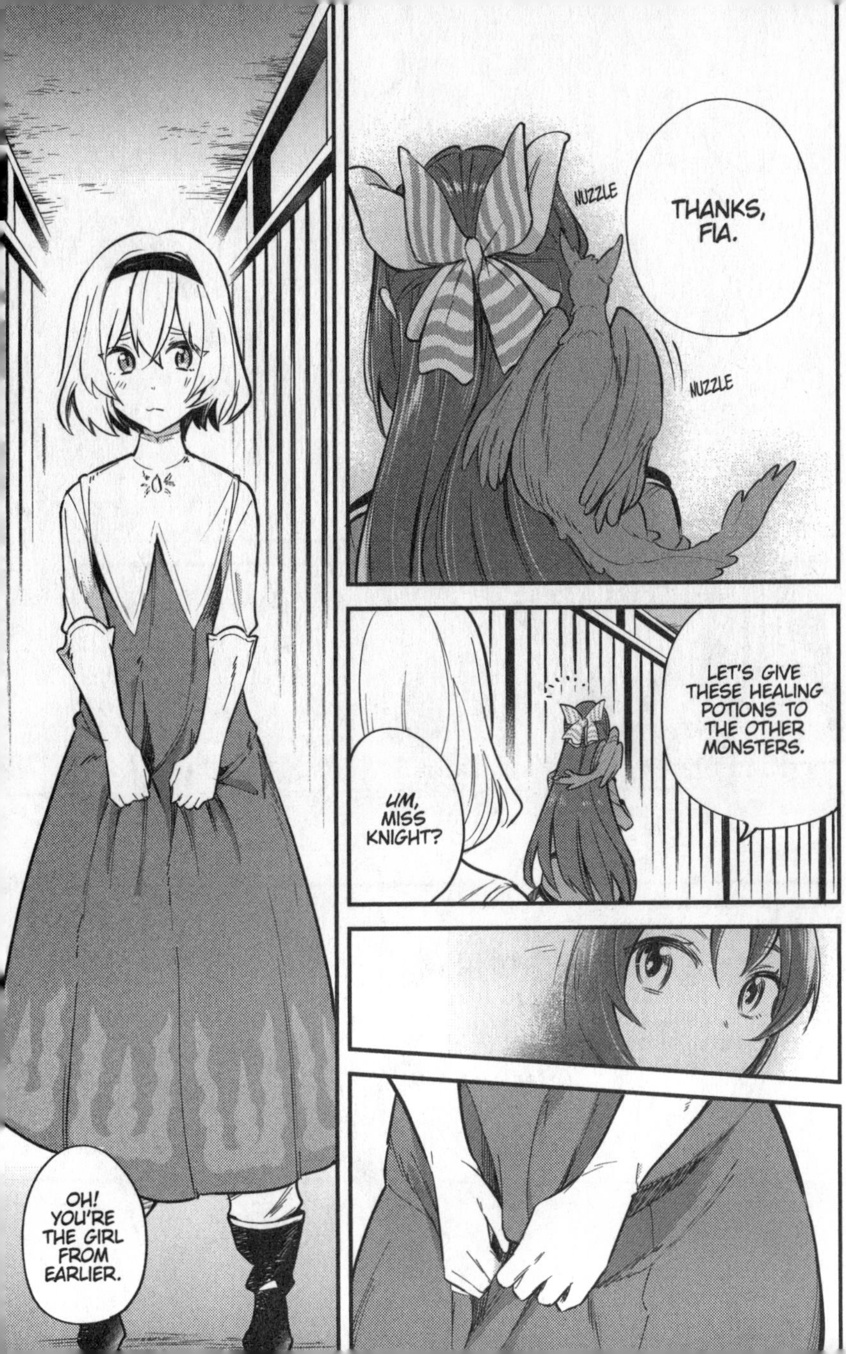
THANKS, FIA.
NUZZLE
NUZZLE
LET'S GIVE THESE HEALING POTIONS TO THE OTHER MONSTERS.
UM, MISS KNIGHT?
OH! YOU'RE THE GIRL FROM EARLIER.

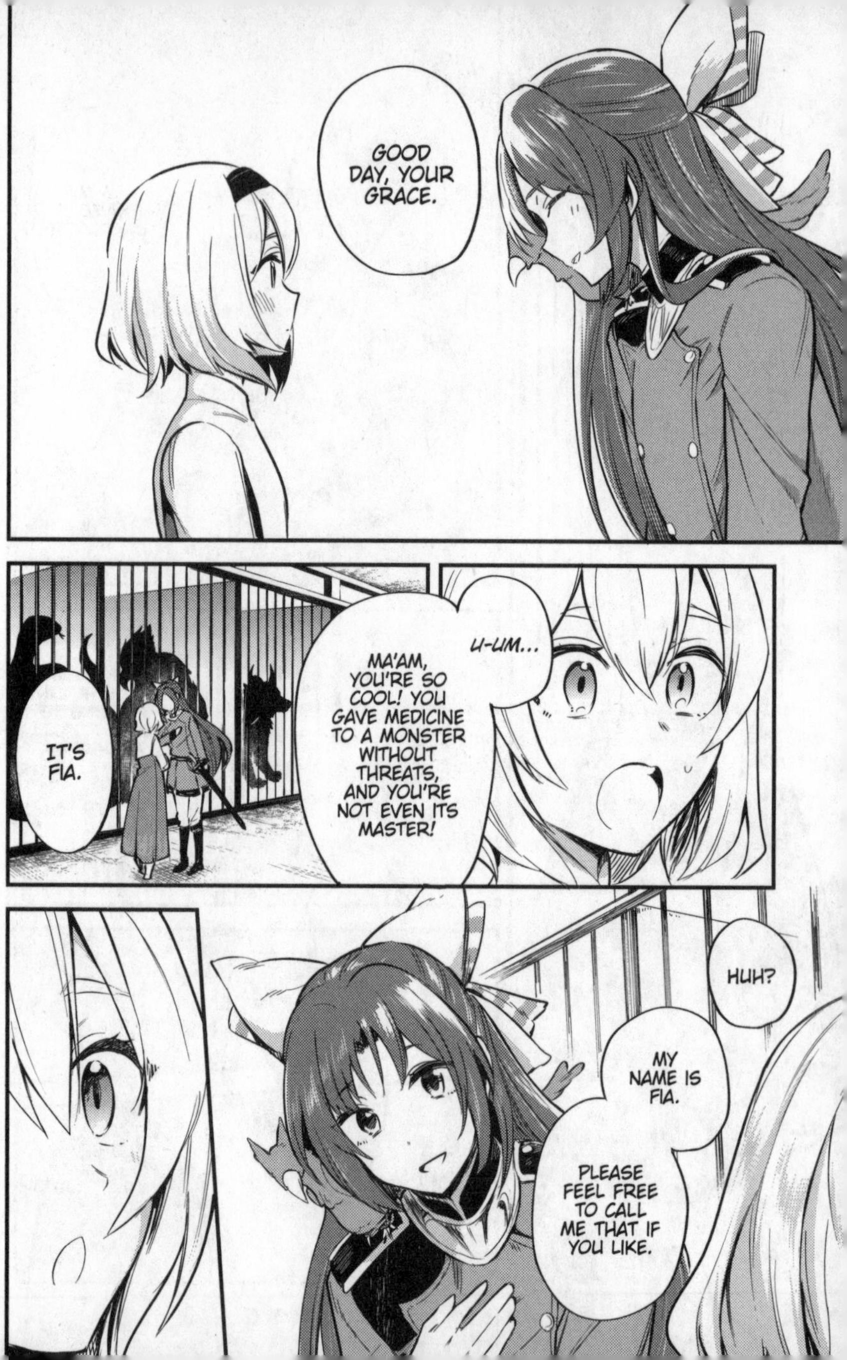
GOOD DAY, YOUR GRACE.
U-UM...
MA'AM, YOU'RE SO COOL! YOU GAVE MEDICINE TO A MONSTER WITHOUT THREATS, AND YOU'RE NOT EVEN ITS MASTER!
IT'S FIA.
HUH?
MY NAME IS FIA.
PLEASE FEEL FREE TO CALL ME THAT IF YOU LIKE.

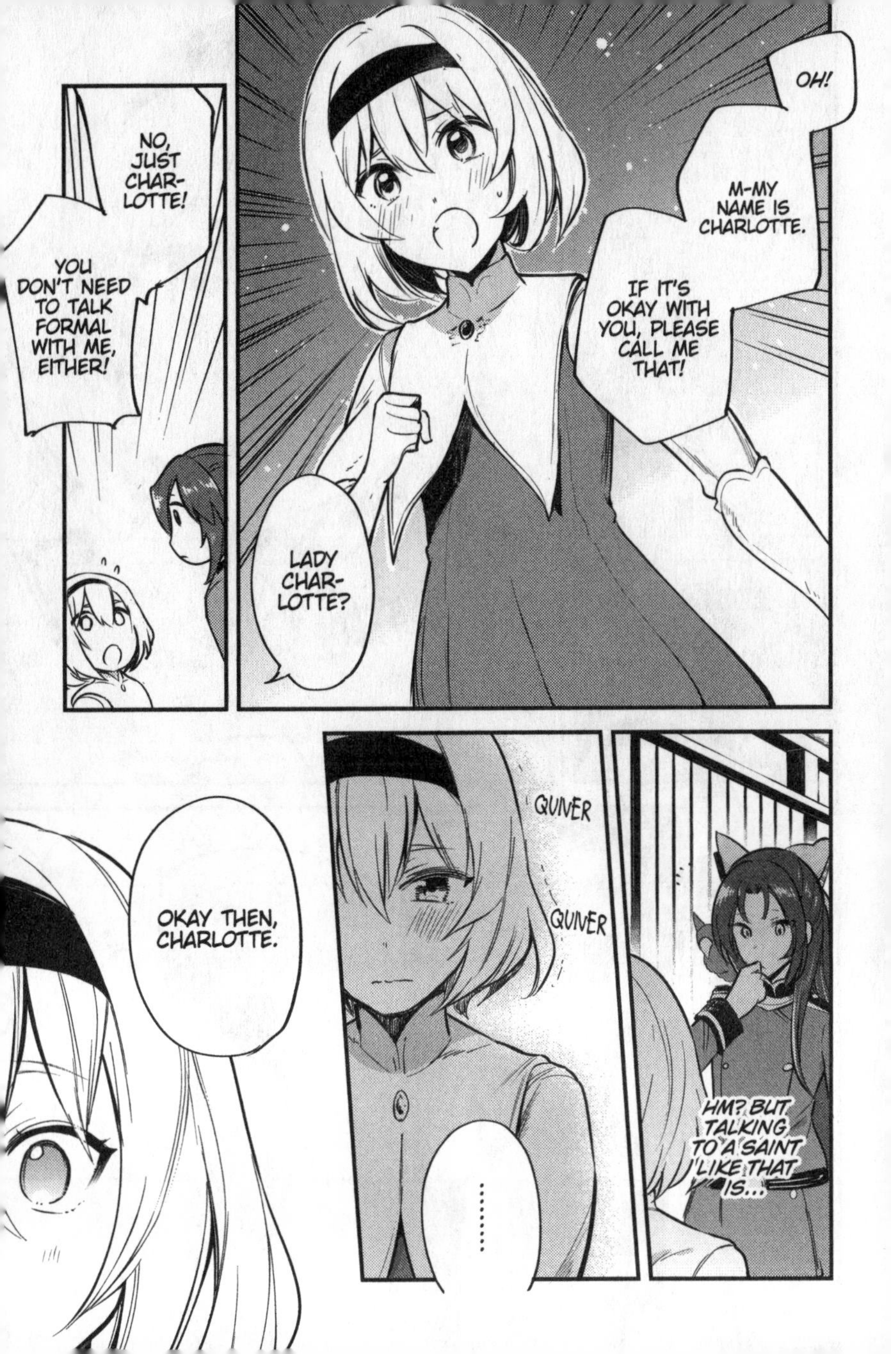
OH!
M-MY NAME IS CHARLOTTE.
IF IT'S OKAY WITH YOU, PLEASE CALL ME THAT!
LADY CHAR-LOTTE?
NO, JUST CHAR-LOTTE!
YOU DON'T NEED TO TALK FORMAL WITH ME, EITHER!
HM? BUT TALKING TO A SAINT LIKE THAT IS...
QUIVER
QUIVER
......
OKAY THEN, CHARLOTTE.

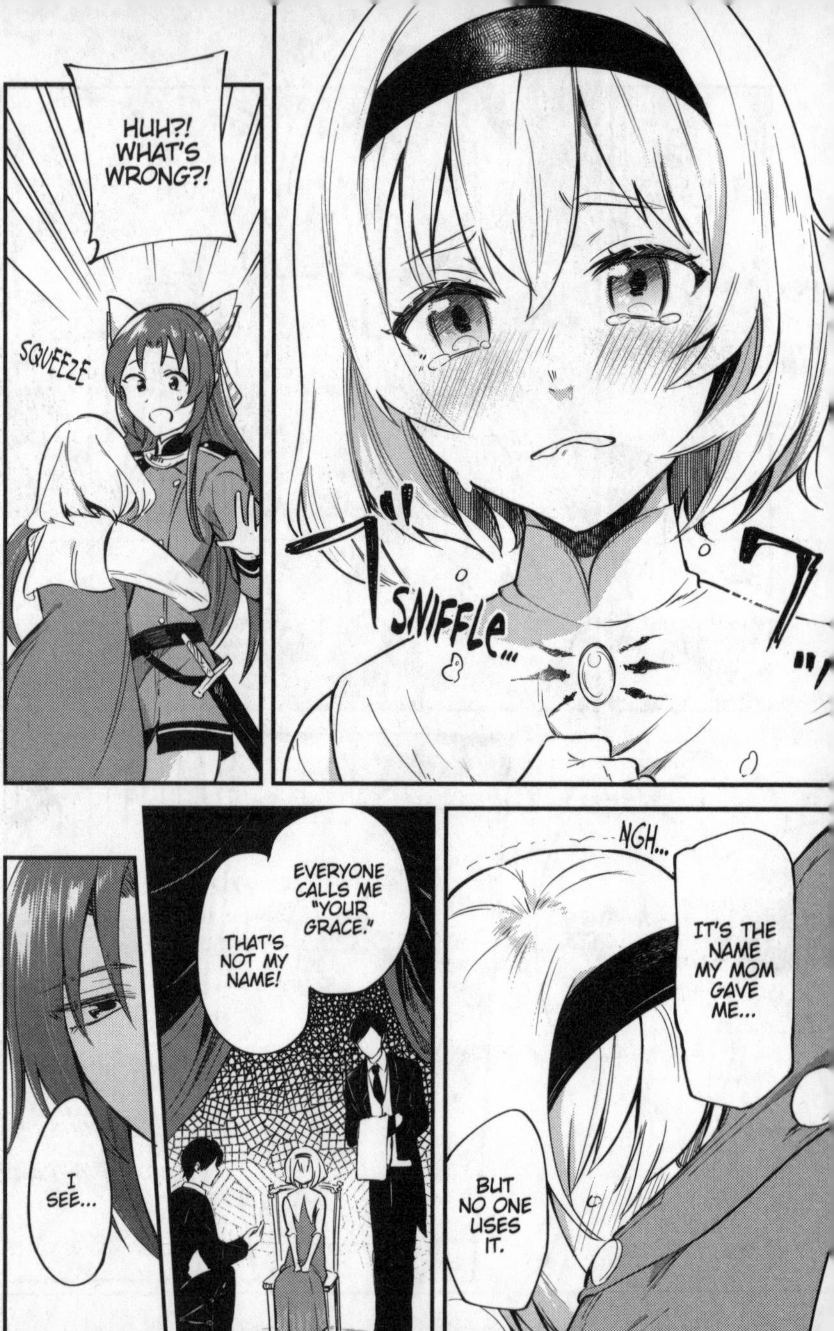
SNIFFLE...
HUH?! WHAT'S WRONG?!
SQUEEZE
NGH...
IT'S THE NAME MY MOM GAVE ME...
BUT NO ONE USES IT.
EVERYONE CALLS ME "YOUR GRACE."
THAT'S NOT MY NAME!
I SEE...

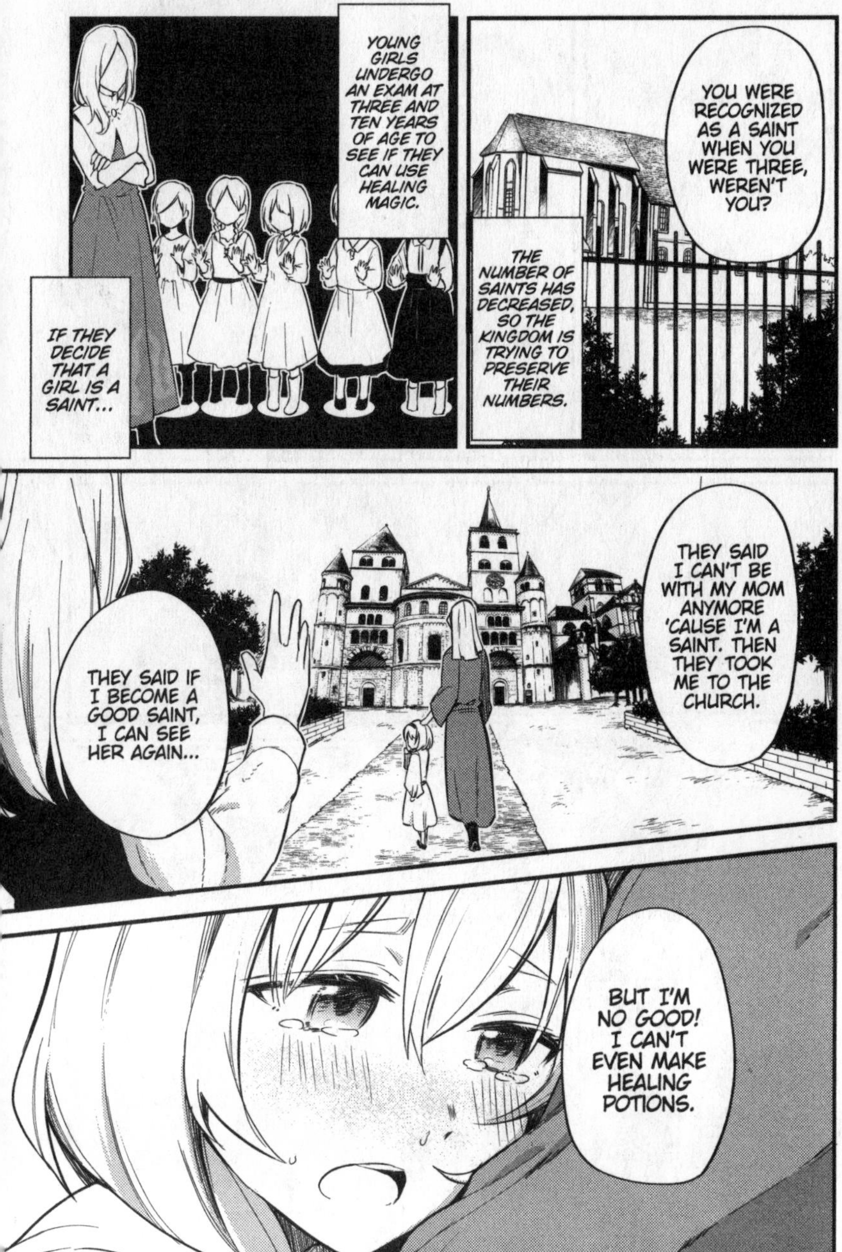
YOU WERE RECOGNIZED AS A SAINT WHEN YOU WERE THREE, WEREN'T YOU?
THE NUMBER OF SAINTS HAS DECREASED, SO THE KINGDOM IS TRYING TO PRESERVE THEIR NUMBERS.
YOUNG GIRLS UNDERGO AN EXAM AT THREE AND TEN YEARS OF AGE TO SEE IF THEY CAN USE HEALING MAGIC.
IF THEY DECIDE THAT A GIRL IS A SAINT...
THEY SAID I CAN'T BE WITH MY MOM ANYMORE 'CAUSE I'M A SAINT. THEN THEY TOOK ME TO THE CHURCH.
THEY SAID IF I BECOME A GOOD SAINT, I CAN SEE HER AGAIN...
BUT I'M NO GOOD! I CAN'T EVEN MAKE HEALING POTIONS.

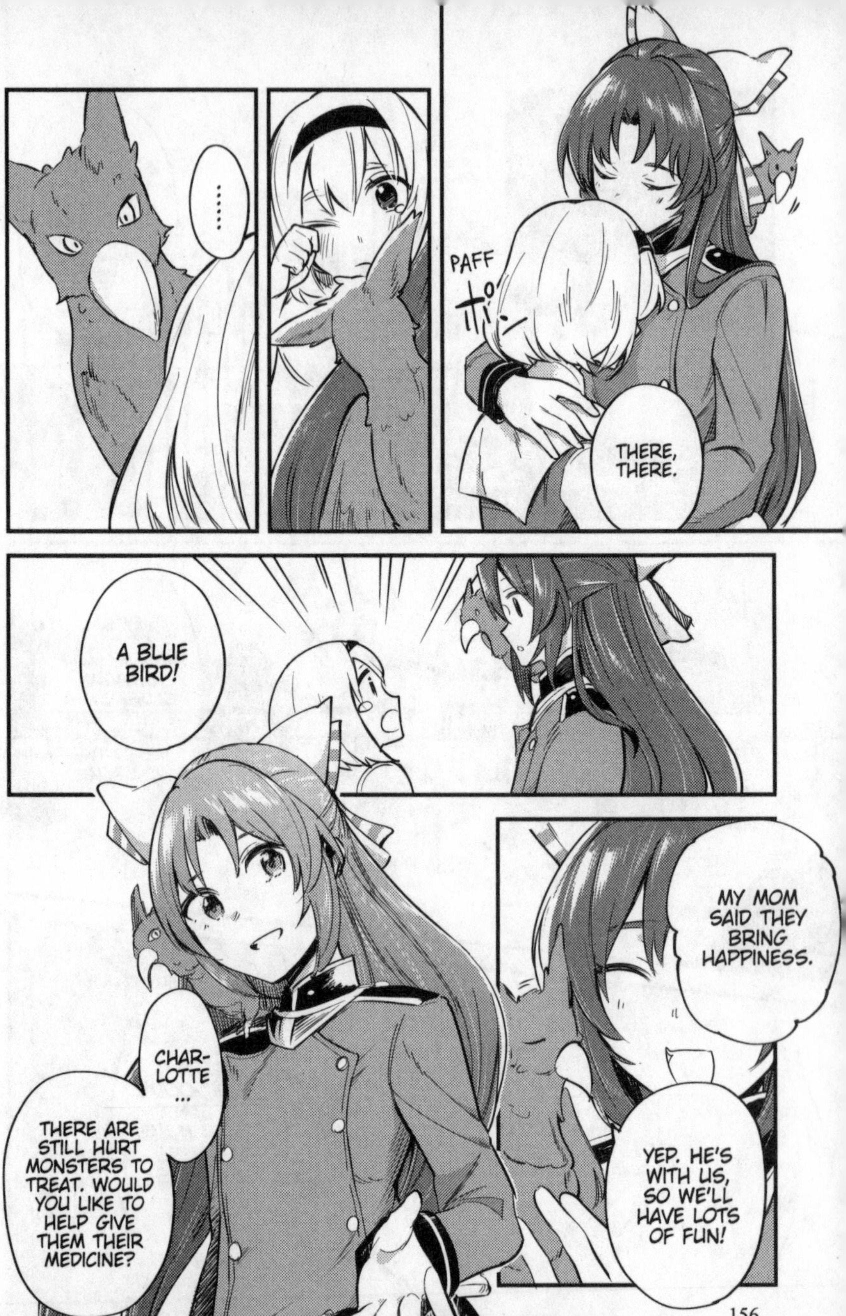
PAFF
THERE, THERE.
......
A BLUE BIRD!
MY MOM SAID THEY BRING HAPPINESS.
YEP. HE'S WITH US, SO WE'LL HAVE LOTS OF FUN!
CHAR-LOTTE ...
THERE ARE STILL HURT MONSTERS TO TREAT. WOULD YOU LIKE TO HELP GIVE THEM THEIR MEDICINE?

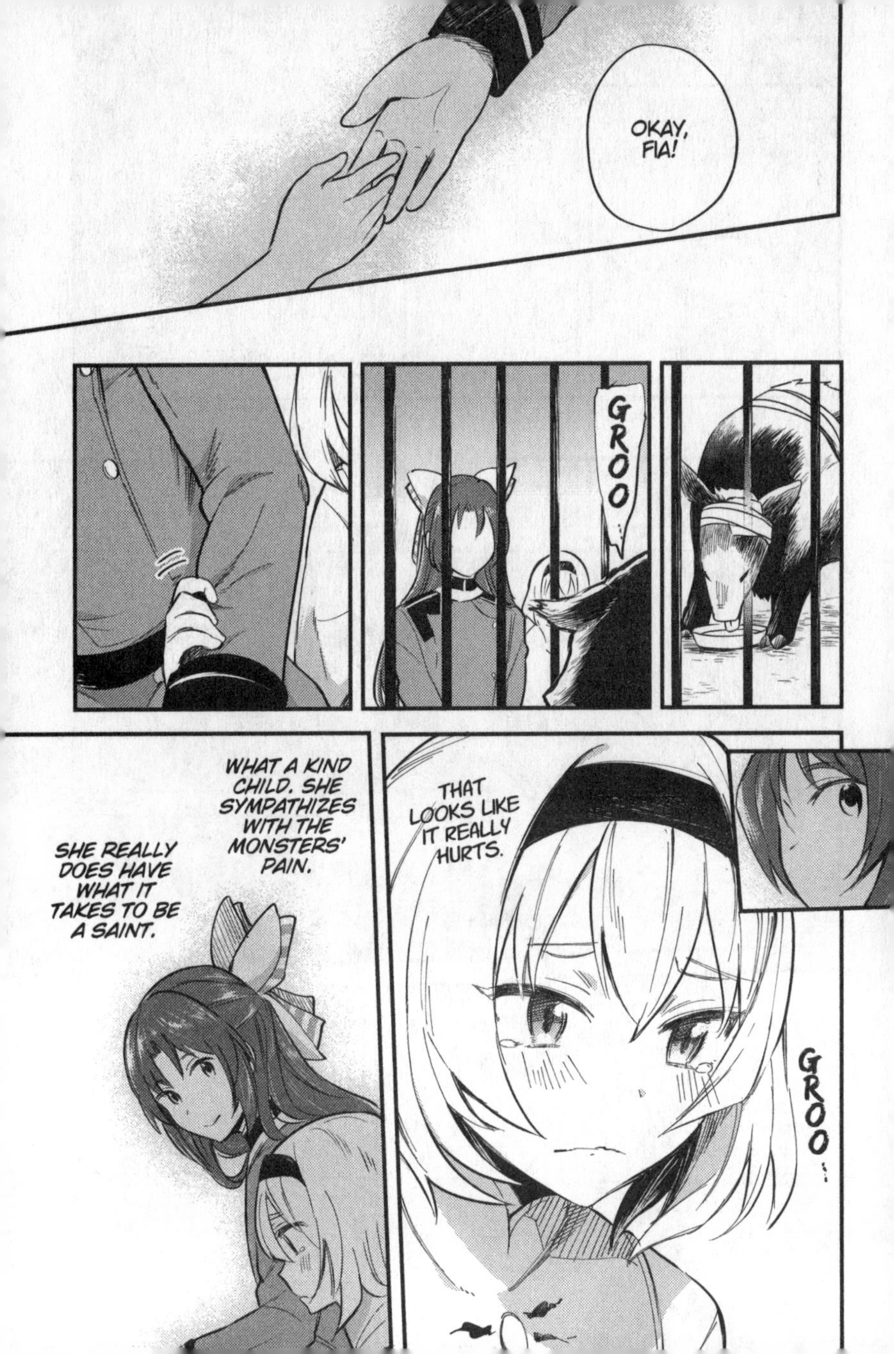
OKAY, FIA!
GROO...
THAT LOOKS LIKE IT REALLY HURTS.
GROO...
WHAT A KIND CHILD. SHE SYMPATHIZES WITH THE MONSTERS' PAIN.
SHE REALLY DOES HAVE WHAT IT TAKES TO BE A SAINT.

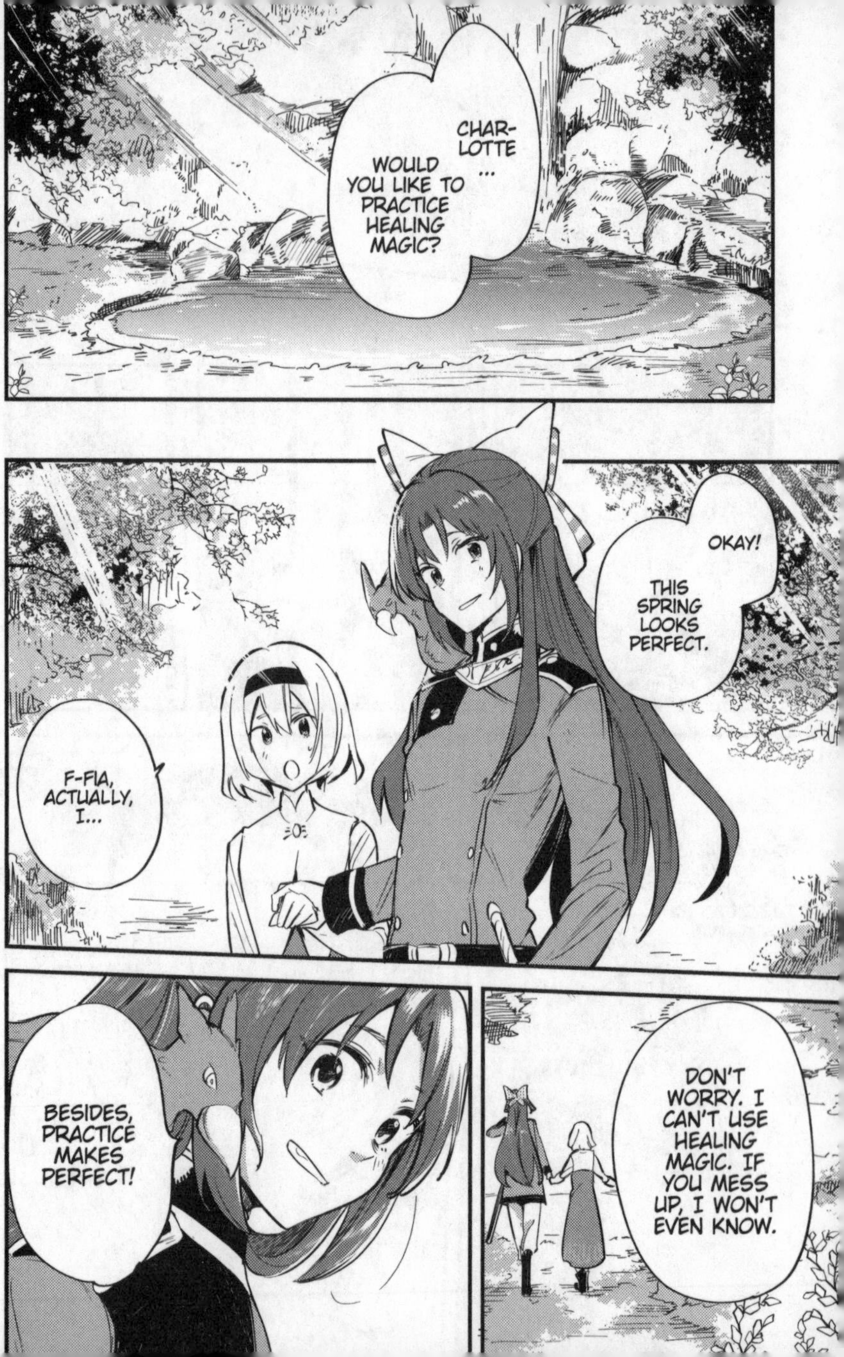
CHAR-LOTTE ... WOULD YOU LIKE TO PRACTICE HEALING MAGIC?
OKAY!
THIS SPRING LOOKS PERFECT.
F-FIA, ACTUALLY, I...
DON'T WORRY. I CAN'T USE HEALING MAGIC. IF YOU MESS UP, I WON'T EVEN KNOW.
BESIDES, PRACTICE MAKES PERFECT!

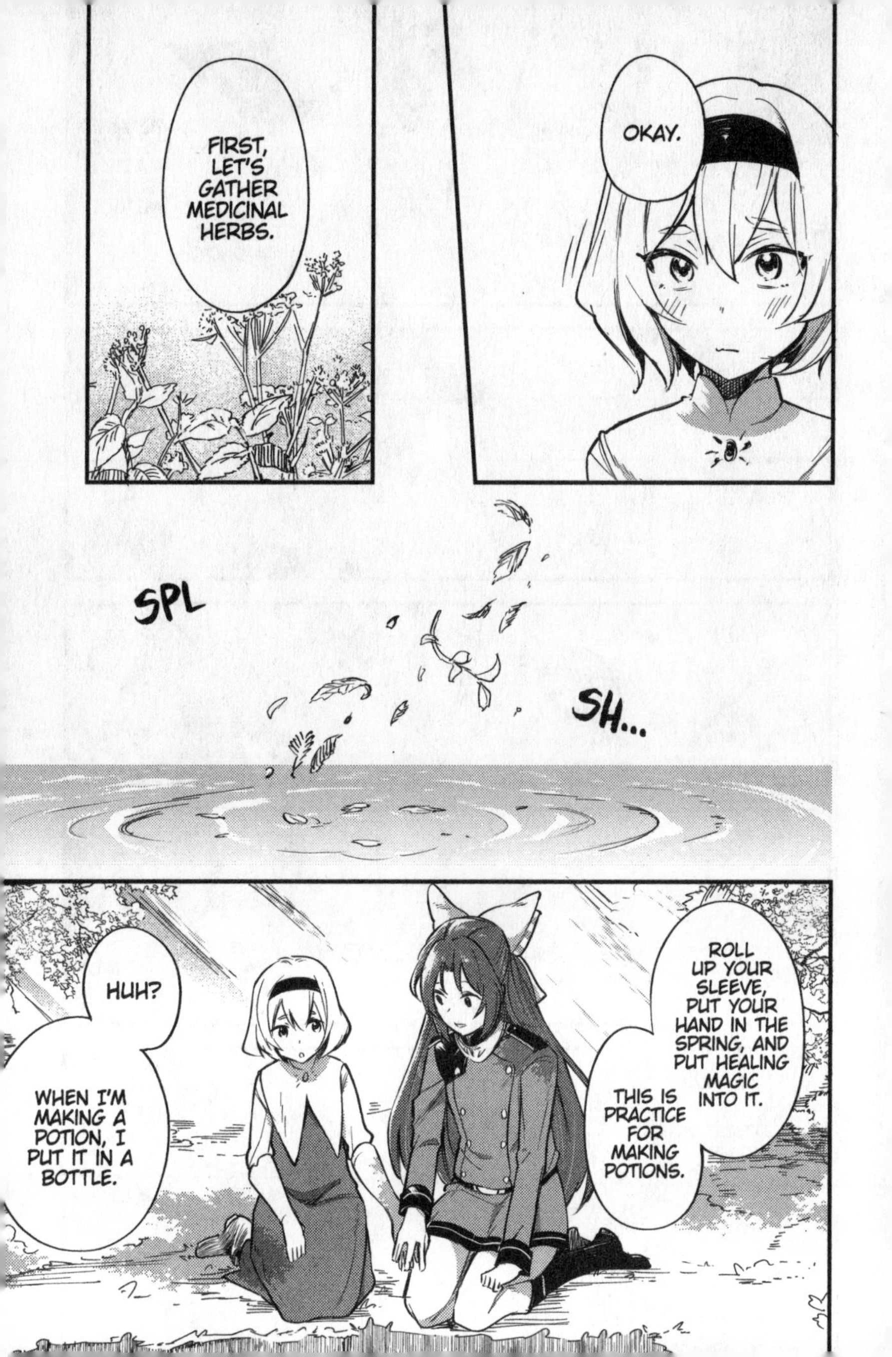
OKAY.
FIRST, LET'S GATHER MEDICINAL HERBS.
SPL
SH...
ROLL UP YOUR SLEEVE, PUT YOUR HAND IN THE SPRING, AND PUT HEALING MAGIC INTO IT.
THIS IS PRACTICE FOR MAKING POTIONS.
HUH?
WHEN I'M MAKING A POTION, I PUT IT IN A BOTTLE.

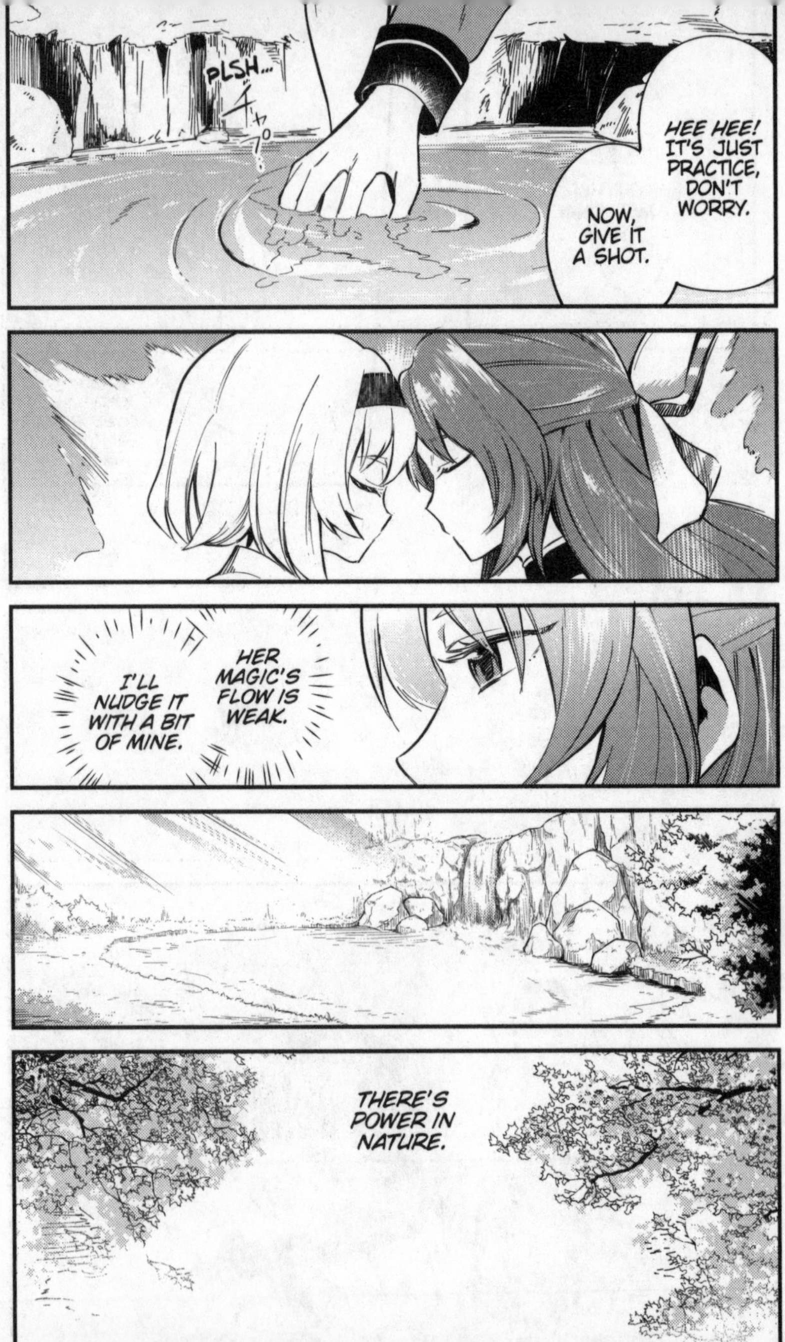
HEE HEE! IT'S JUST PRACTICE, DON'T WORRY.
NOW, GIVE IT A SHOT.
PLSH...
HER MAGIC'S FLOW IS WEAK.
I'LL NUDGE IT WITH A BIT OF MINE.
THERE'S POWER IN NATURE.

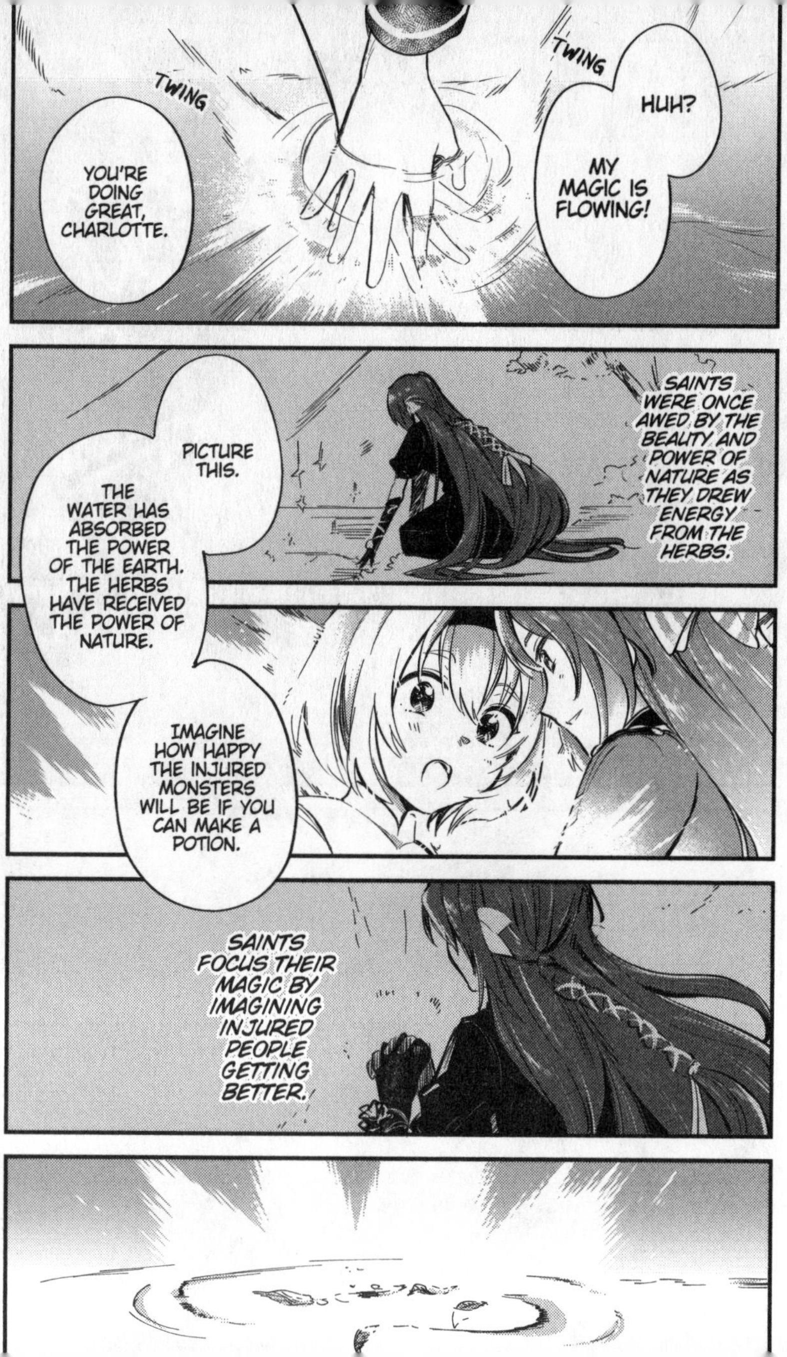
TWING
HUH?
MY MAGIC IS FLOWING!
TWING
YOU'RE DOING GREAT, CHARLOTTE.
SAINTS WERE ONCE AWED BY THE BEAUTY AND POWER OF NATURE AS THEY DREW ENERGY FROM THE HERBS.
PICTURE THIS.
THE WATER HAS ABSORBED THE POWER OF THE EARTH. THE HERBS HAVE RECEIVED THE POWER OF NATURE.
IMAGINE HOW HAPPY THE INJURED MONSTERS WILL BE IF YOU CAN MAKE A POTION.
SAINTS FOCUS THEIR MAGIC BY IMAGINING INJURED PEOPLE GETTING BETTER.

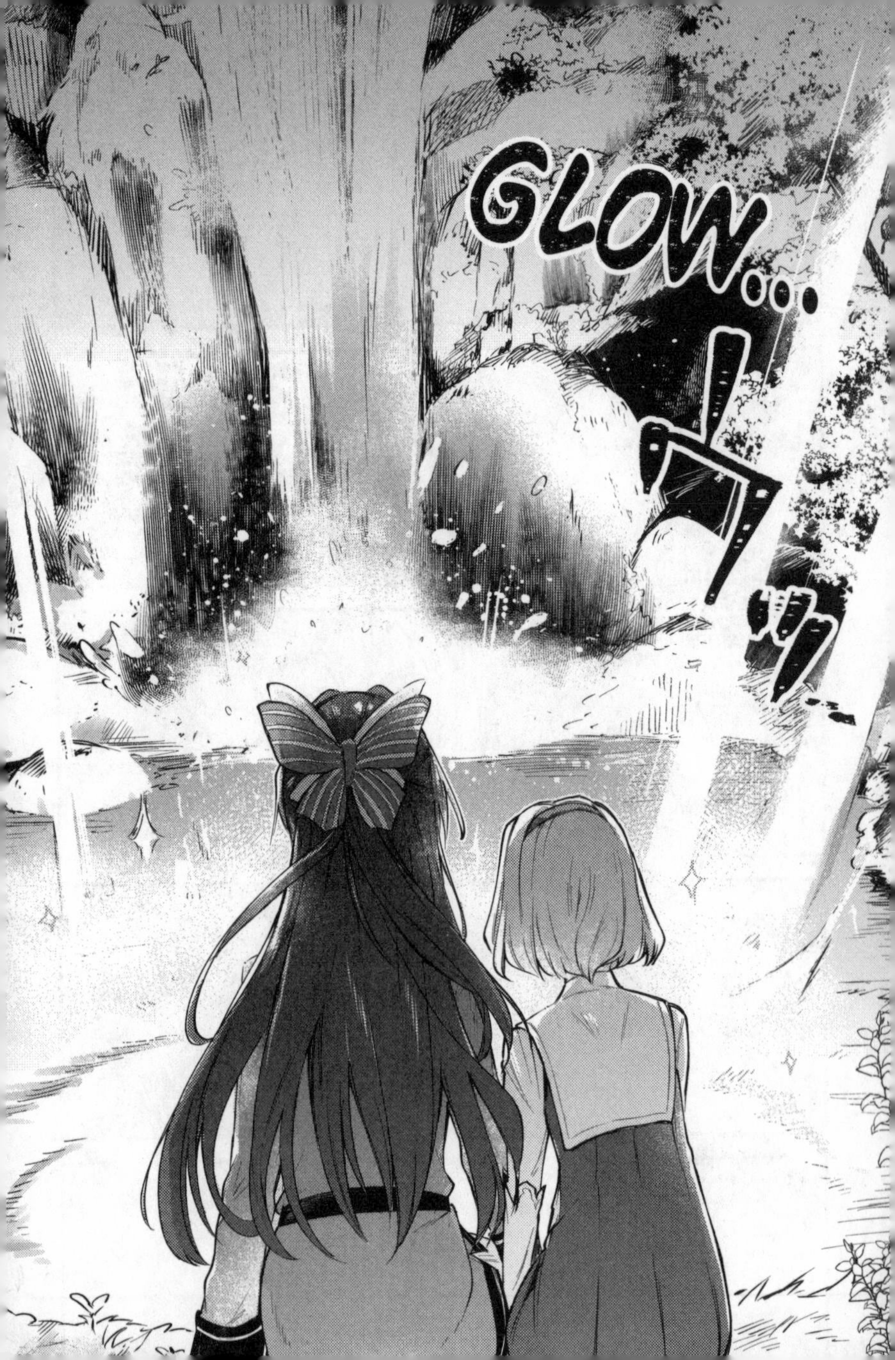
GLOW...

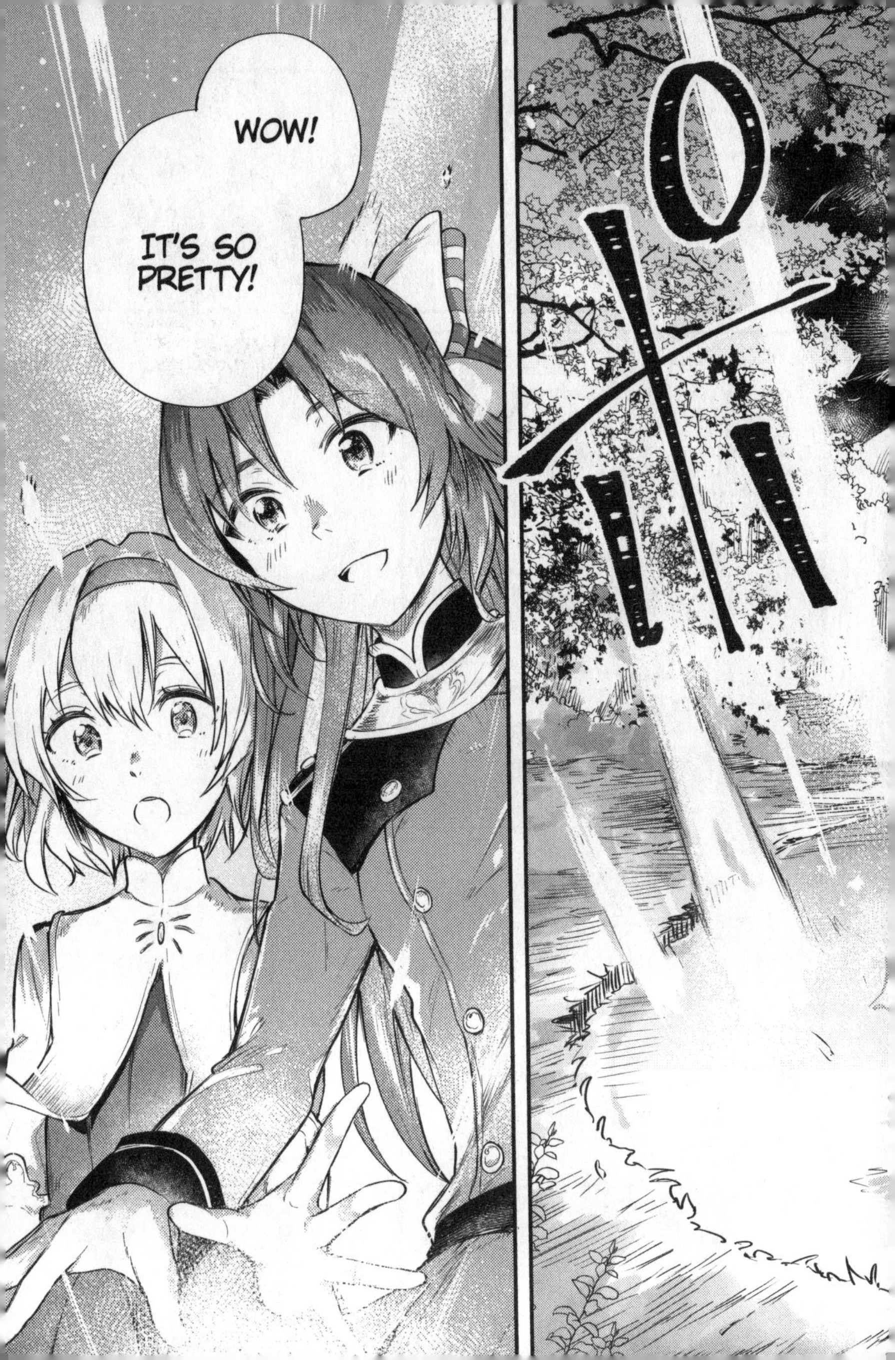
WOW!
IT'S SO PRETTY!

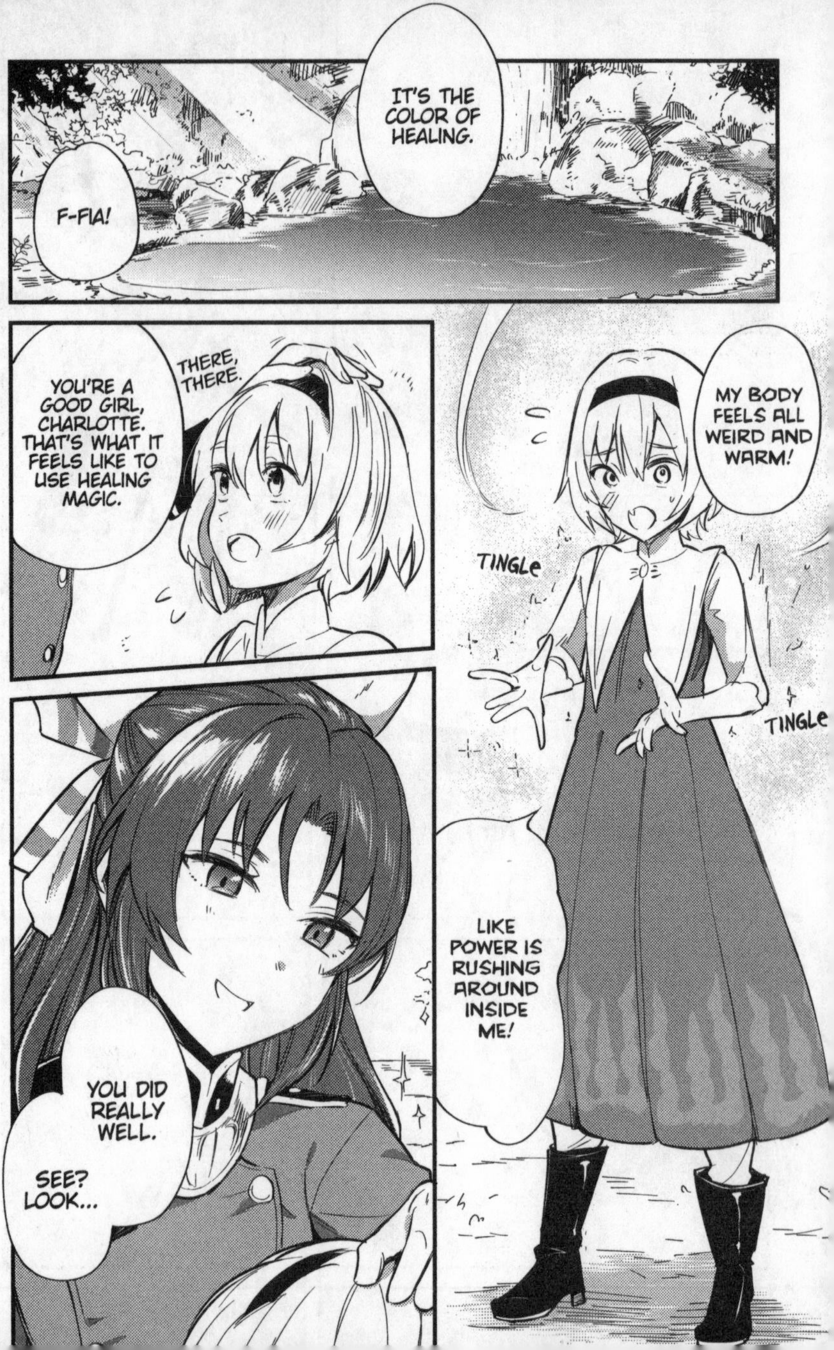
IT'S THE COLOR OF HEALING.
F-FIA!
MY BODY FEELS ALL WEIRD AND WARM!
TINGLE
TINGLE
LIKE POWER IS RUSHING AROUND INSIDE ME!
THERE, THERE.
YOU'RE A GOOD GIRL, CHARLOTTE. THAT'S WHAT IT FEELS LIKE TO USE HEALING MAGIC.
YOU DID REALLY WELL.
SEE? LOOK...

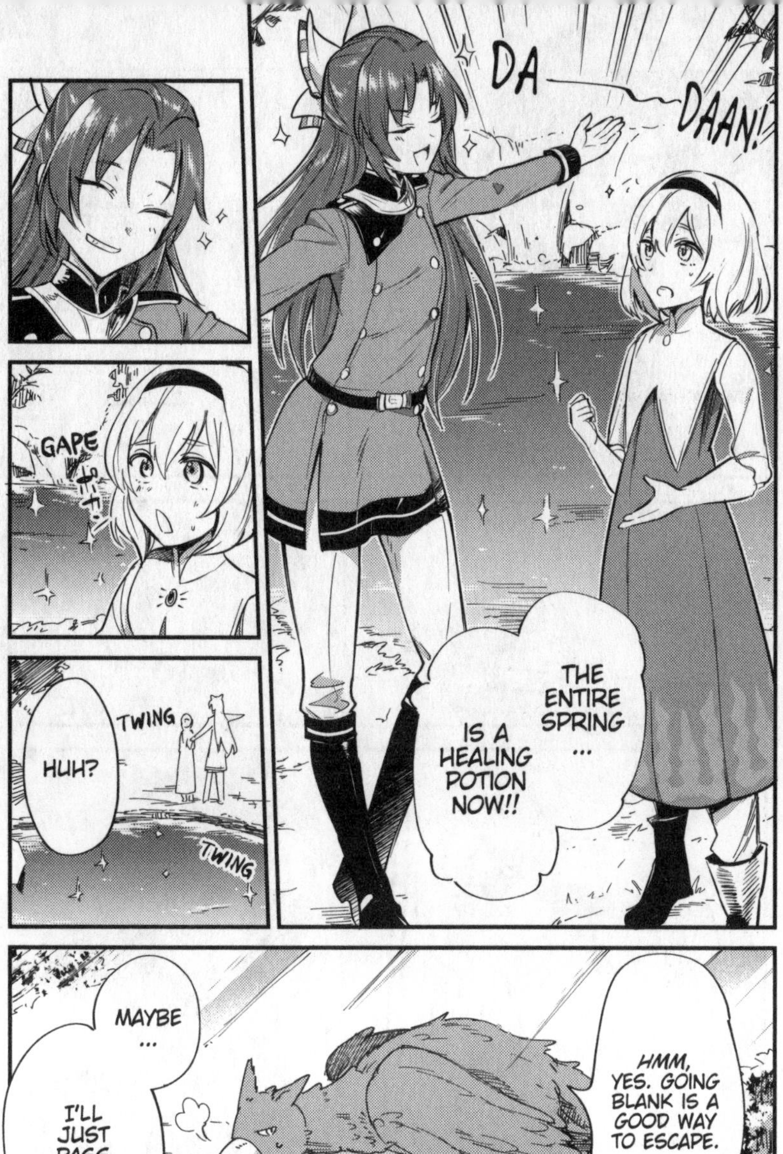
DA
DAAN!!
THE ENTIRE SPRING ...
IS A HEALING POTION NOW!!
GAPE
HUH?
TWING
TWING
HMM, YES. GOING BLANK IS A GOOD WAY TO ESCAPE.
MAYBE ...
I'LL JUST PASS OUT.

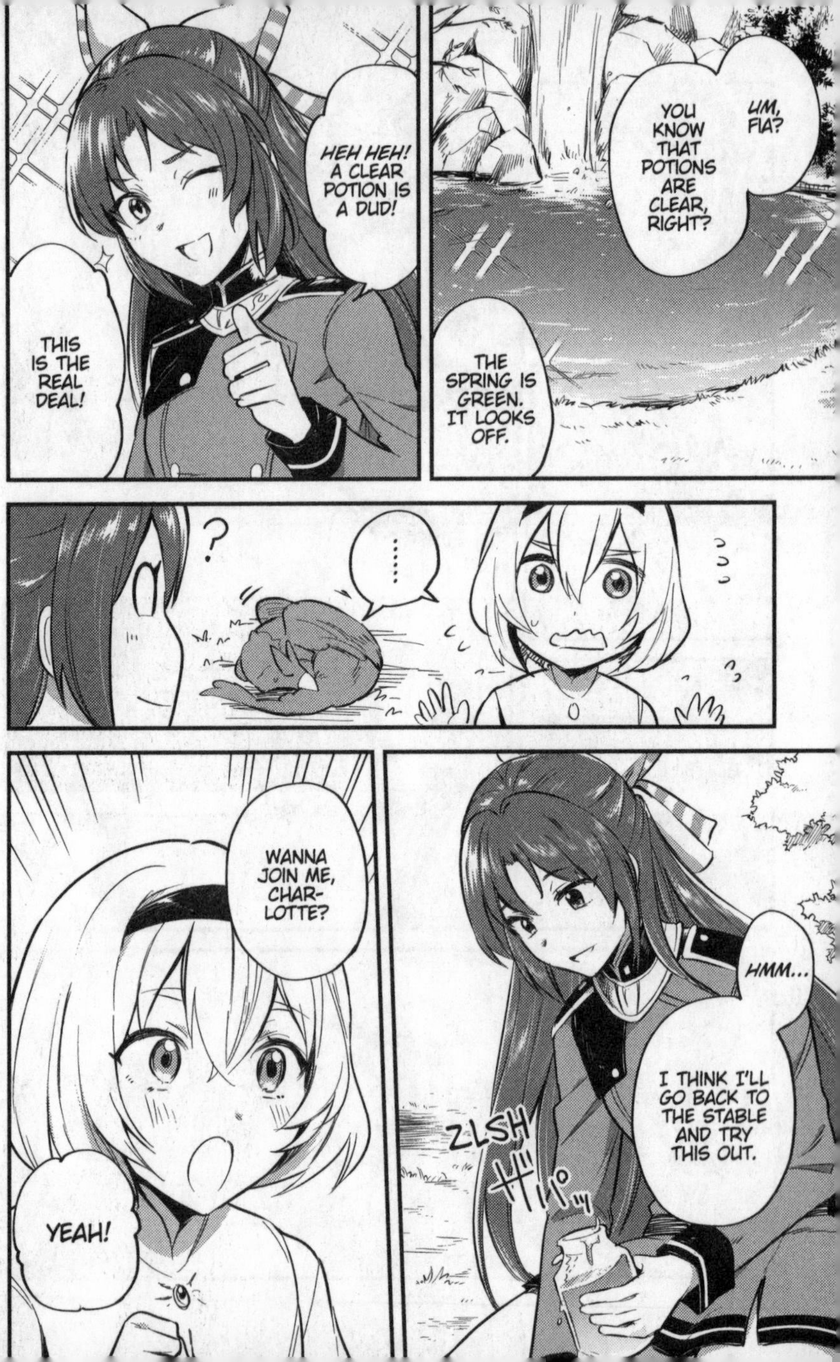
UM, FIA?
YOU KNOW THAT POTIONS ARE CLEAR, RIGHT?
THE SPRING IS GREEN. IT LOOKS OFF.
HEH HEH! A CLEAR POTION IS A DUD!
THIS IS THE REAL DEAL!
?
......
HMM...
I THINK I'LL GO BACK TO THE STABLE AND TRY THIS OUT.
ZLSH
ザパッ
WANNA JOIN ME, CHARLOTTE?
YEAH!

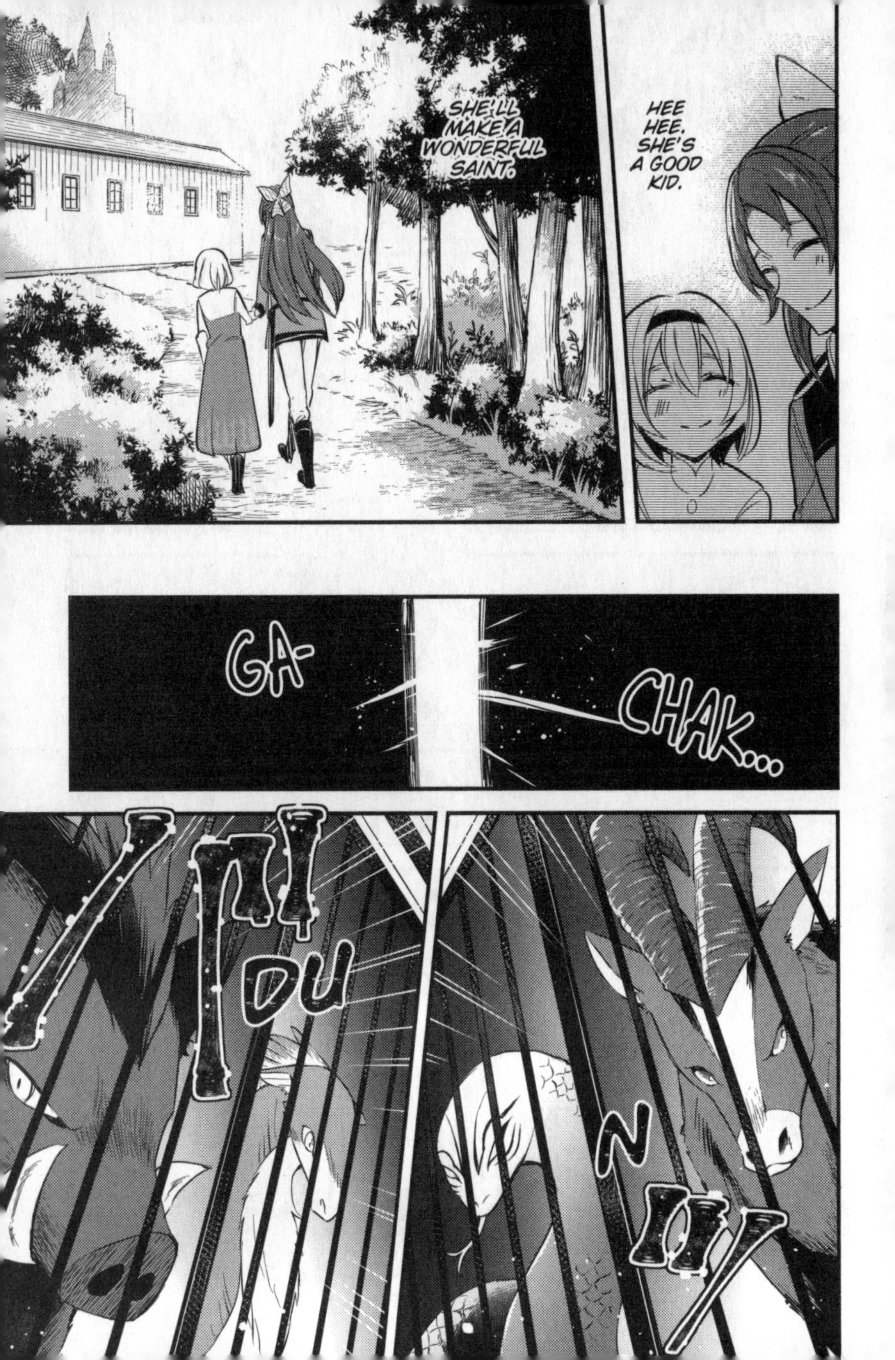
HEE HEE. SHE'S A GOOD KID.
SHE'LL MAKE A WONDERFUL SAINT.
GA-CHAK...
DU
N

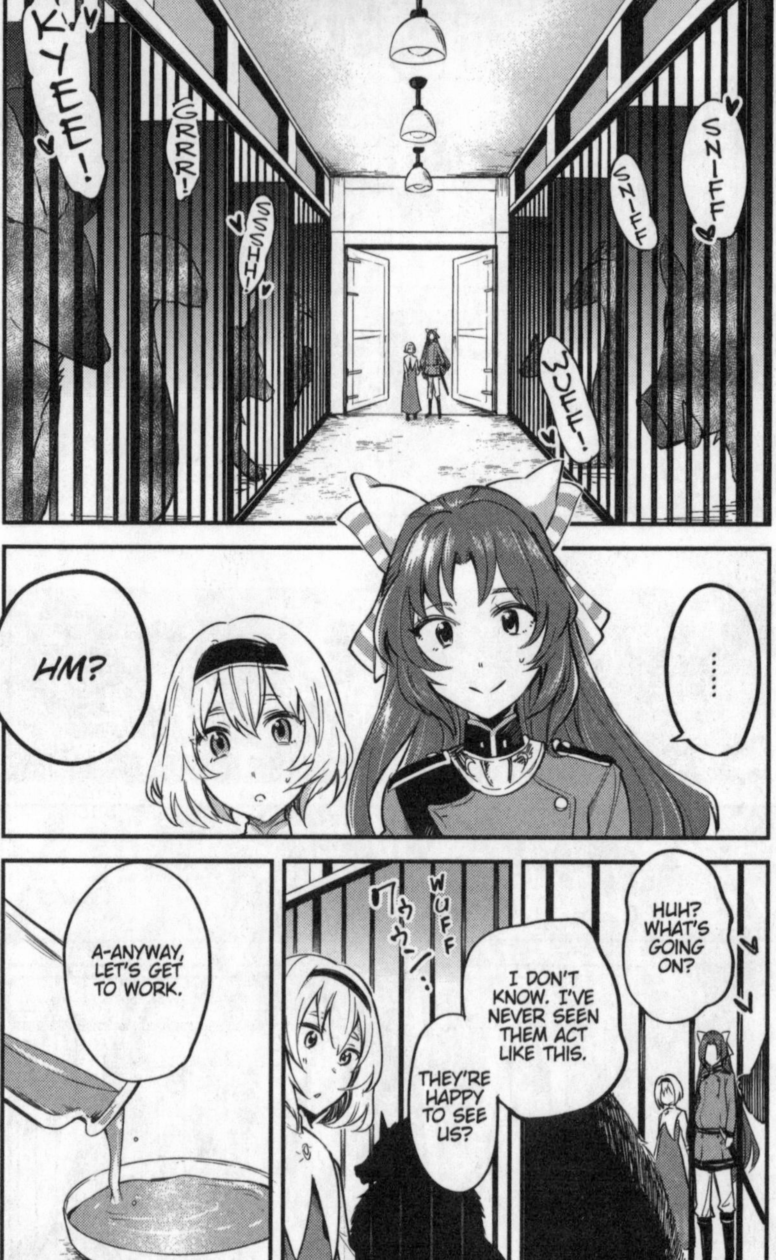
SNIFF
SNIFF
KYEEE!
GRRR!
SSSHH!
WUFF!
......
HM?
HUH? WHAT'S GOING ON?
I DON'T KNOW. I'VE NEVER SEEN THEM ACT LIKE THIS.
WUFF
THEY'RE HAPPY TO SEE US?
A-ANYWAY, LET'S GET TO WORK.

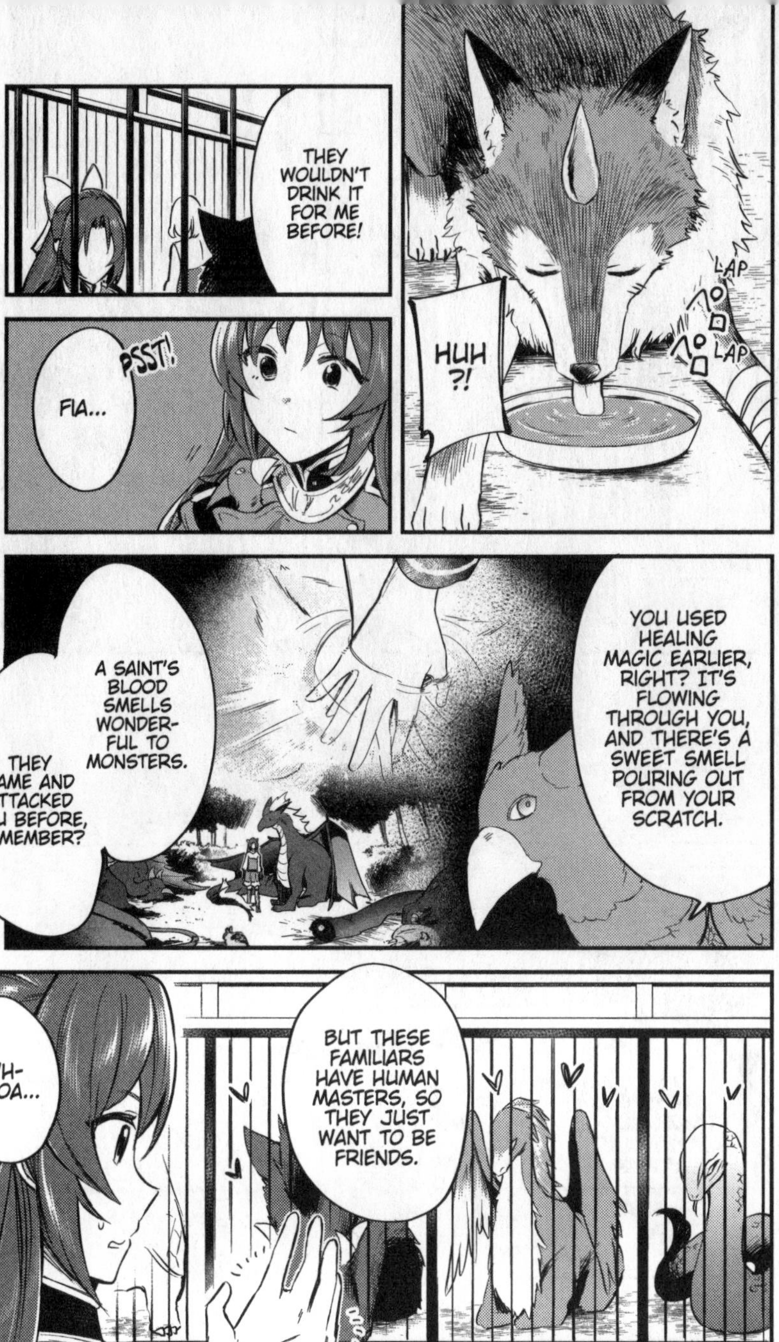
LAP
LAP
HUH ?!
THEY WOULDN'T DRINK IT FOR ME BEFORE!
PSSST!
FIA...
YOU USED HEALING MAGIC EARLIER, RIGHT? IT'S FLOWING THROUGH YOU, AND THERE'S A SWEET SMELL POURING OUT FROM YOUR SCRATCH.
A SAINT'S BLOOD SMELLS WONDERFUL TO MONSTERS.
THEY CAME AND ATTACKED YOU BEFORE, REMEMBER?
BUT THESE FAMILIARS HAVE HUMAN MASTERS, SO THEY JUST WANT TO BE FRIENDS.
WH-WHOA...

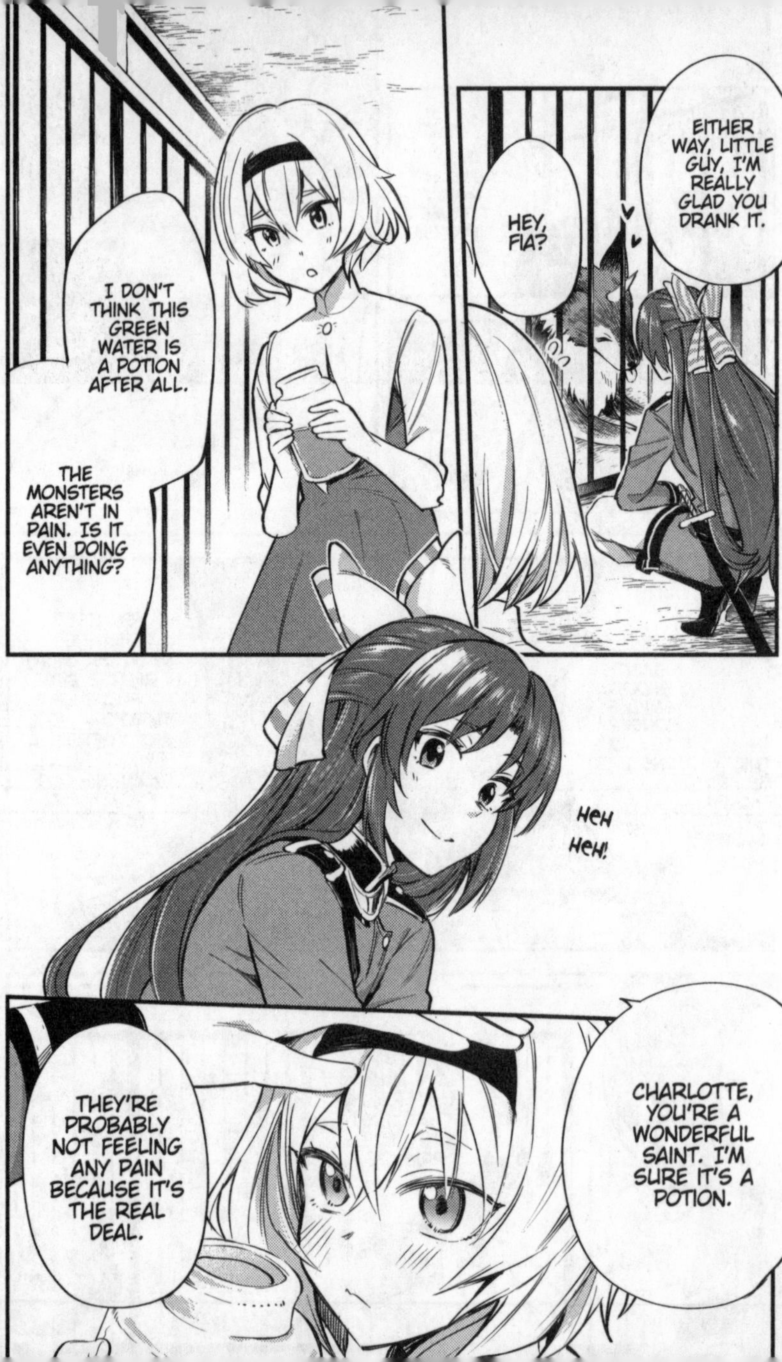
EITHER WAY, LITTLE GUY, I'M REALLY GLAD YOU DRANK IT.
HEY, FIA?
I DON'T THINK THIS GREEN WATER IS A POTION AFTER ALL.
THE MONSTERS AREN'T IN PAIN. IS IT EVEN DOING ANYTHING?
HEH HEH!
CHARLOTTE, YOU'RE A WONDERFUL SAINT. I'M SURE IT'S A POTION.
THEY'RE PROBABLY NOT FEELING ANY PAIN BECAUSE IT'S THE REAL DEAL.

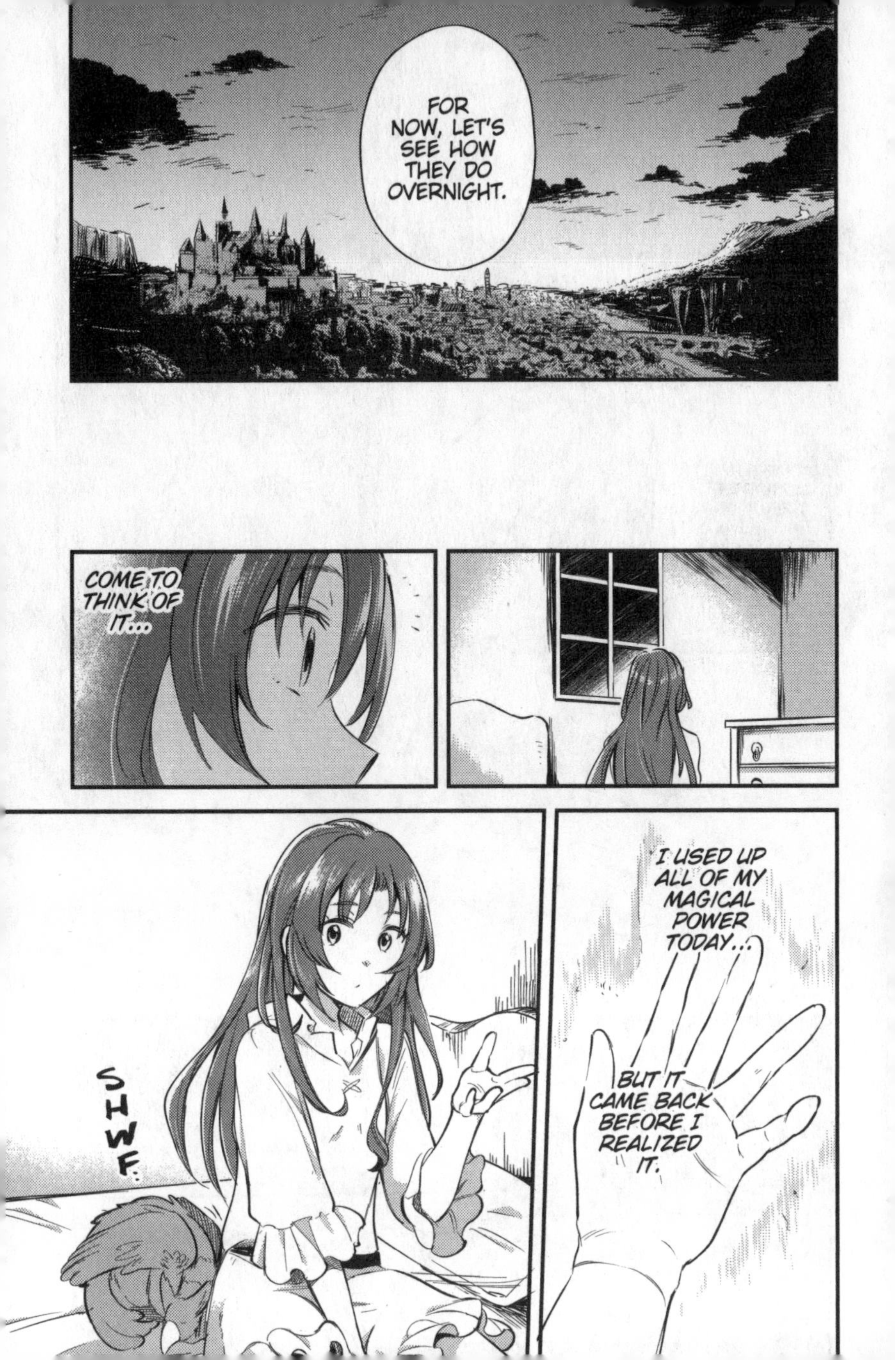
FOR NOW, LET'S SEE HOW THEY DO OVERNIGHT.
COME TO THINK OF IT...
I USED UP ALL OF MY MAGICAL POWER TODAY...
BUT IT CAME BACK BEFORE I REALIZED IT.
SHWF.

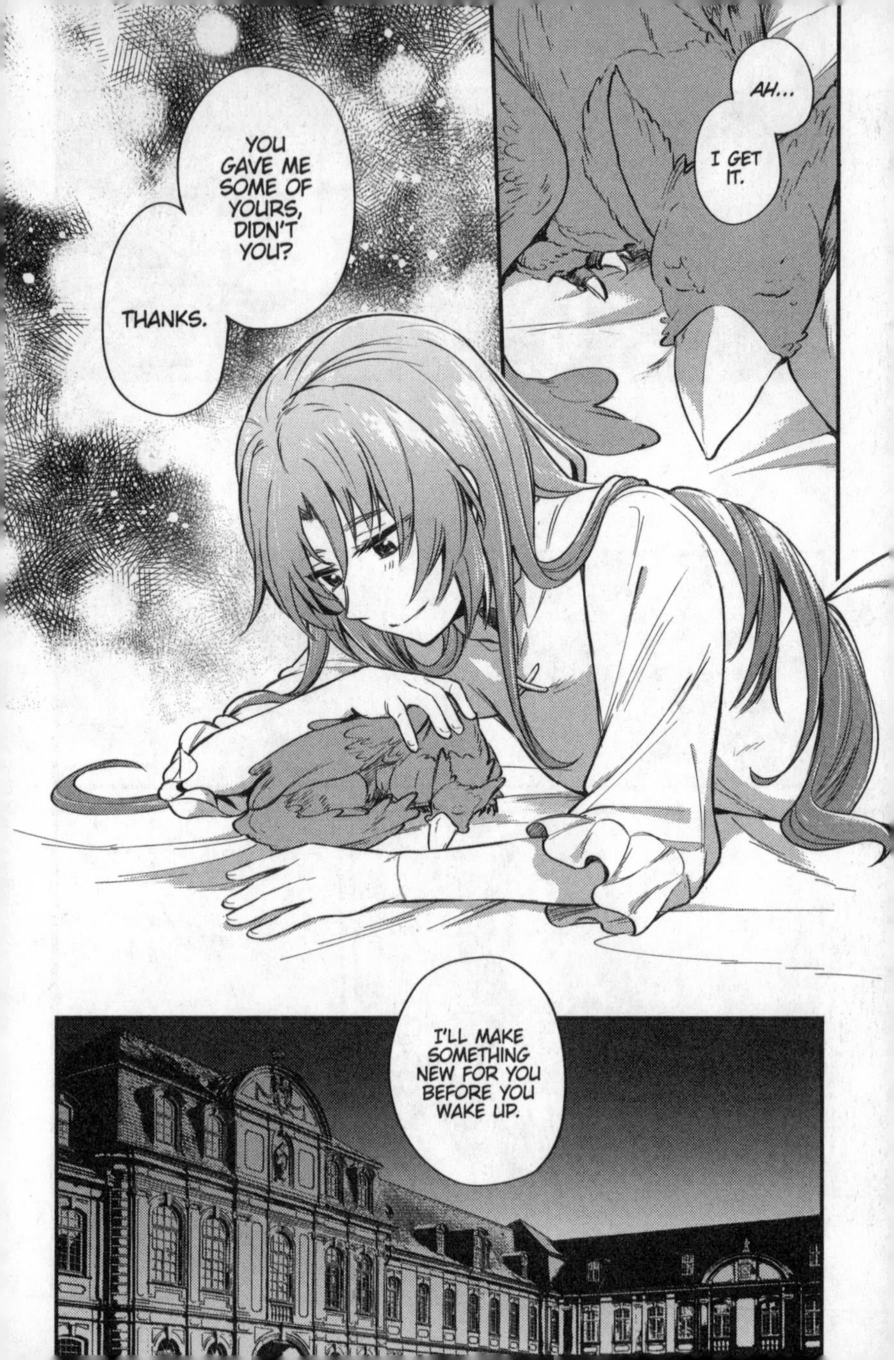
AH...
I GET IT.
YOU GAVE ME SOME OF YOURS, DIDN'T YOU?
THANKS.
I'LL MAKE SOMETHING NEW FOR YOU BEFORE YOU WAKE UP.

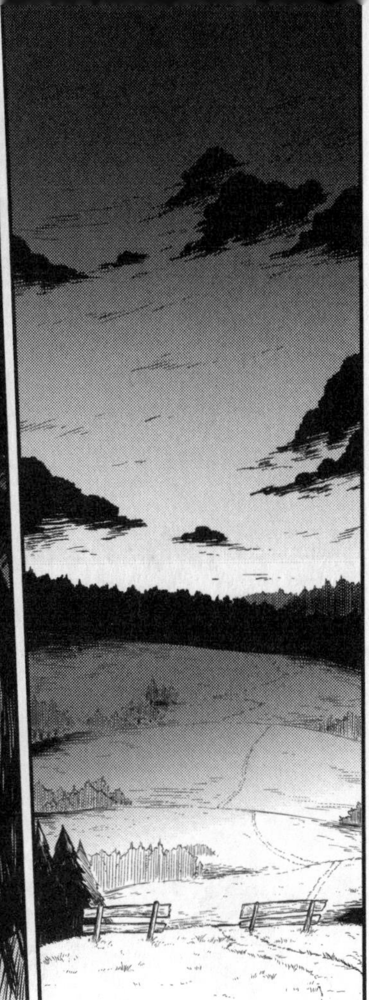

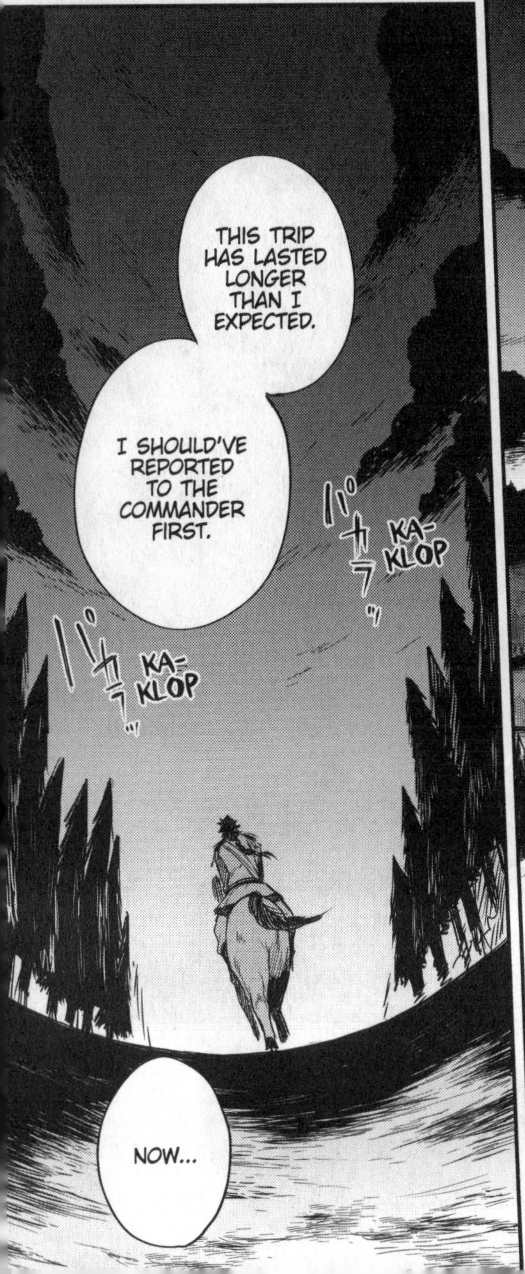

THIS TRIP HAS LASTED LONGER THAN I EXPECTED.
I SHOULD'VE REPORTED TO THE COMMANDER FIRST.
KA-KLOP
KA-KLOP
NOW...

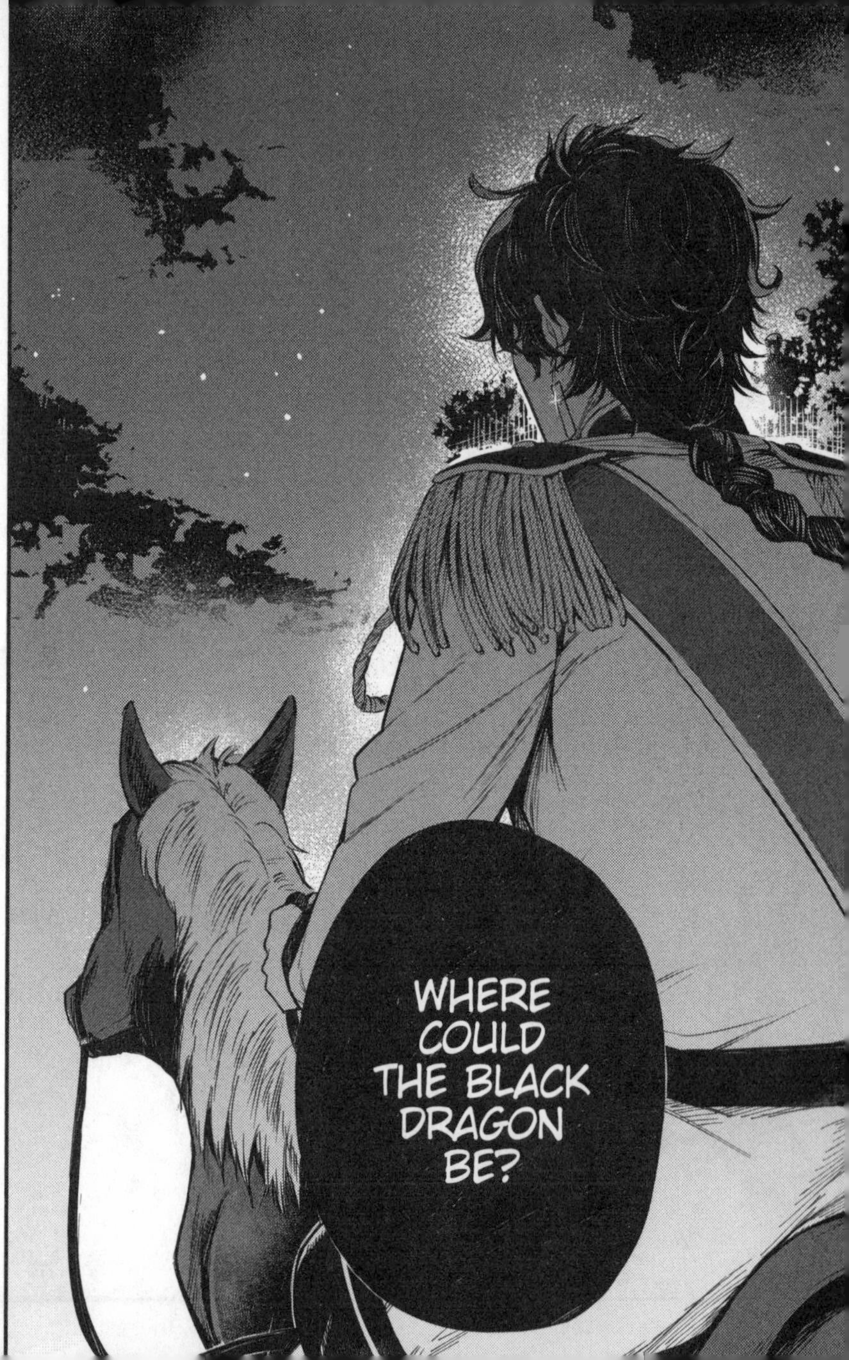
WHERE COULD THE BLACK DRAGON BE?

A Tale of the
Secret
Saint

Fia's Evaluation by the Knight Brigades' Top Three

Author: **Touya**

After eating their fill of monster meat at the meat festival, four members of the Knight Brigade were enjoying a leisurely time sipping wine in Commander Saviz's room.

Commander Saviz calmly tilted his glass back and noticed, just as First Knight Brigade Captain Cyril and Second Knight Brigade Captain Desmond did: Fia was drifting off into the world of dreams.

Her eyes were closed even as she sat upright. Her head swayed a few times, then her eyes opened wide in surprise. She gave a forced cough, as though to prove she was still awake…and promptly fell asleep again, starting the cycle over.

To be fair, Fia had only just joined the adult world, having finally come of age. As a result, her body wasn't used to alcohol yet. Moreover, she was enjoying some quiet time in a comfortable room; it made sense that she would get sleepy. But…

"Amazing," Desmond said, as he gave the sleeping Fia a sidelong glance. "Fia really is a top dog if she can sleep so soundly around us. And not just around you and me, two—though I hesitate to say it— peerless Knight Brigade Captains, otherwise known as 'the Dragon and the Tiger'! She's sleeping in the presence of Commander Saviz, the very head of the Knight Brigade!"

Cyril shot Desmond a cold glance. "*You're* the one who's amazing. You're a fledgling captain, yet you have the audacity to sit with Commander Saviz and call yourself a peerless knight. I can't help but sigh."

"Huh? No, no, I said I was hesitant about it! Anyway, you're one to talk. Fia's a member of your brigade, right, Cyril? This's all because you're too soft on her. She's dozing off in front of Commander Saviz because of *you*!"

"Oh? An interesting theory." Cyril wore a charming smile as he spoke. "In that case, you must have a similar influence on your own brigade. Funny thing—every single one of them is unmarried despite being of the proper age. I suppose that's because your fiancée left you, right?"

The chill that ran down Cyril's spine was as unpleasant as Desmond's smile was radiant. "Stop trying to reopen old wounds, Cyril! Fellow knights who trust each other with their lives shouldn't treat each other like this."

"My point holds. If your warped view of women puts my knights at a disadvantage, I will not hold my tongue. Besides, Fia put in a hard day's work; I couldn't possibly expect her to do any better. She's more than earned her right to rest."

As he spoke, Cyril nimbly removed his jacket and draped it over the sleeping Fia's shoulders. He gazed at her a moment, expression kind, before putting his hands on her shoulders and drew her close, until her head rested gently upon his shoulder. Soon enough, she was snoring softly, sound asleep.

Cyril chuckled. "She looks so peaceful." He paused a moment, then said, "You know, seeing her this close makes it even harder to believe that such a young girl took command and conquered a monster from the abyss. Because of her, we didn't lose a single knight."

Commander Saviz nodded slightly. "Yes, she's full of surprises. Desmond, Fia is beloved by the spirits. After the monster was felled, the spirits helped her. They changed the flavor of a fruit from bitter to sweet."

"What?!" Desmond blurted.

The commander paid him no mind. "Regrettable, isn't it? If Fia could use healing magic, she could've become an outstanding saint. When I said as much, she told me—and I quote—

'I've already been given everything I need.' This young knight has integrity."

Even though it was Commander Saviz himself saying it, Desmond felt a twinge of doubt. After all, women throughout the country longed to become saints. And why not? If a woman became a saint, her worth skyrocketed. Everyone knelt before her and idolized her as an incomparable being. She could take her pick of aristocratic grooms. Could there really be a woman who wasn't fixated on the idea of becoming one of those most-revered saints? Desmond's doubt mingled with his deep distrust of women. No, he couldn't believe it.

As he stared at the sleeping Fia, she opened her mouth with a soft *aah* and, eyes still closed, chomped Cyril's shoulder through his shirt.

"Hah?!"

A young girl had her teeth around the shoulder of the strongest knight in the kingdom!

With an expression of utter astonishment, Desmond gazed at his colleague. Even Cyril's eyes widened in shock.

Desmond looked back at Fia in disbelief.

As for Fia, she made little whimpering sounds, her teeth still on Cyril's shoulder.

"Tough…the meat is tough! Hmph, this was supposed to be tender, delicious meat…but the meat got tough because Captain Cyril lectured me too long!" She gnawed on his shoulder, muttering.

Cyril remained frozen in surprise for another moment, then pulled himself together and began the oh-so-delicate process of attempting to remove his shoulder from Fia's mouth.

"Fia, I wasn't lecturing you earlier," he said, very seriously addressing the drunk, half-asleep girl. "I was merely gathering information. And you see, they began cooking *after* we were finished, so it had no influence over the meat's toughness. Finally, what you're chewing right now isn't monster meat, but your captain's shoulder."

"Aww…why isn't my captain's meat tender and juicy? It's so tough…"

"Of course it is. Your captain's meat isn't for eating, it's for battling monsters. It should be tough."

"But fighting monsters is my job too, and *my* meat is tender."

"Err…certainly, that's my own fault. Starting tomorrow, I'll rearrange the training schedule to include more abdominal exercises."

Fia didn't seem to fully comprehend what Cyril had said. She smiled in apparent relief and plopped into his lap. Before long, she was once again snoring softly.

The three men, caught completely off guard by what just happened, simply gazed in silence at the peacefully sleeping Fia.

Saviz's mouth curved into a smile. "When I said Fia is full of surprises, I didn't realize how right I was. I've never seen anyone gnaw on you, Cyril!" he teased. "The way you sat there with your mouth hanging open, helpless and dumbfounded... Fia's impression of you was 'tough.' Ha! How excellent."

"I'm glad you found it funny, Commander. Laugh as much as you like," Cyril said, though he didn't look the least bit amused.

Desmond let out a sigh, as if unable to hide his true feelings. "Amazing... It's said that dreams are unconscious expressions of one's state of mind, but I can't believe eating delicious meat influences Fia more than saving countless knights or being loved by the spirits. She's a top dog, she's upstanding, and she's...the strongest?! I've never seen anyone munch on the strongest knight in the kingdom before."

The Knight Brigades' top three exchanged silent glances, and then breathed a collective sigh. No one could deny what Desmond said. Every one of them felt that, in a sense, it was true.

***

Thus it was that Fia was described as "a top dog, upstanding, and the strongest (when it comes to non-work-related behavior)" in her knight evaluation record.

A Tale of the Secret Saint

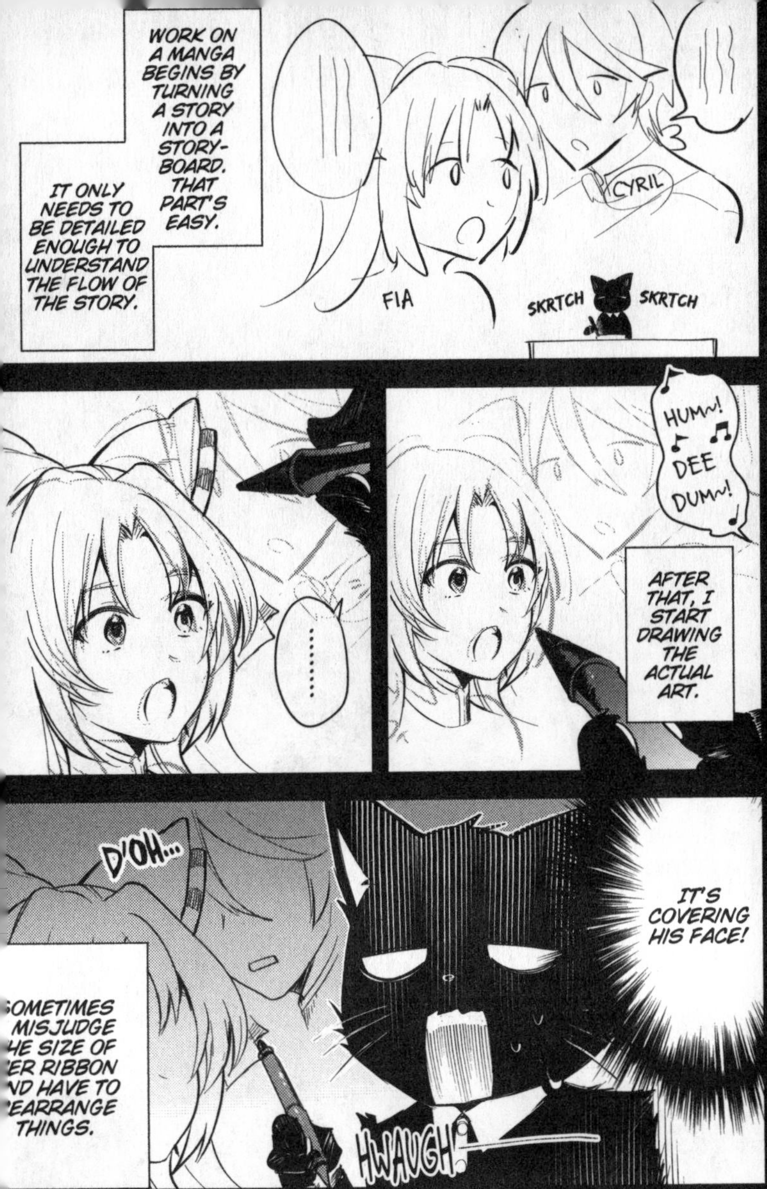
WORK ON A MANGA BEGINS BY TURNING A STORY INTO A STORY-BOARD. THAT PART'S EASY.
CYRIL
IT ONLY NEEDS TO BE DETAILED ENOUGH TO UNDERSTAND THE FLOW OF THE STORY.
SKRTCH SKRTCH
FIA
HUM~! ♪ ♫ DEE DUM~!
AFTER THAT, I START DRAWING THE ACTUAL ART.
……
IT'S COVERING HIS FACE!
D'OH...
SOMETIMES MISJUDGE HE SIZE OF ER RIBBON ND HAVE TO EARRANGE THINGS.
HWAUGH

Special Thanks

U MOKUBA-SAN ASAI SORA-SAN TAKAHASHI-SAN (EDITOR) TAKAHASHI-SAN (DESIGNER)

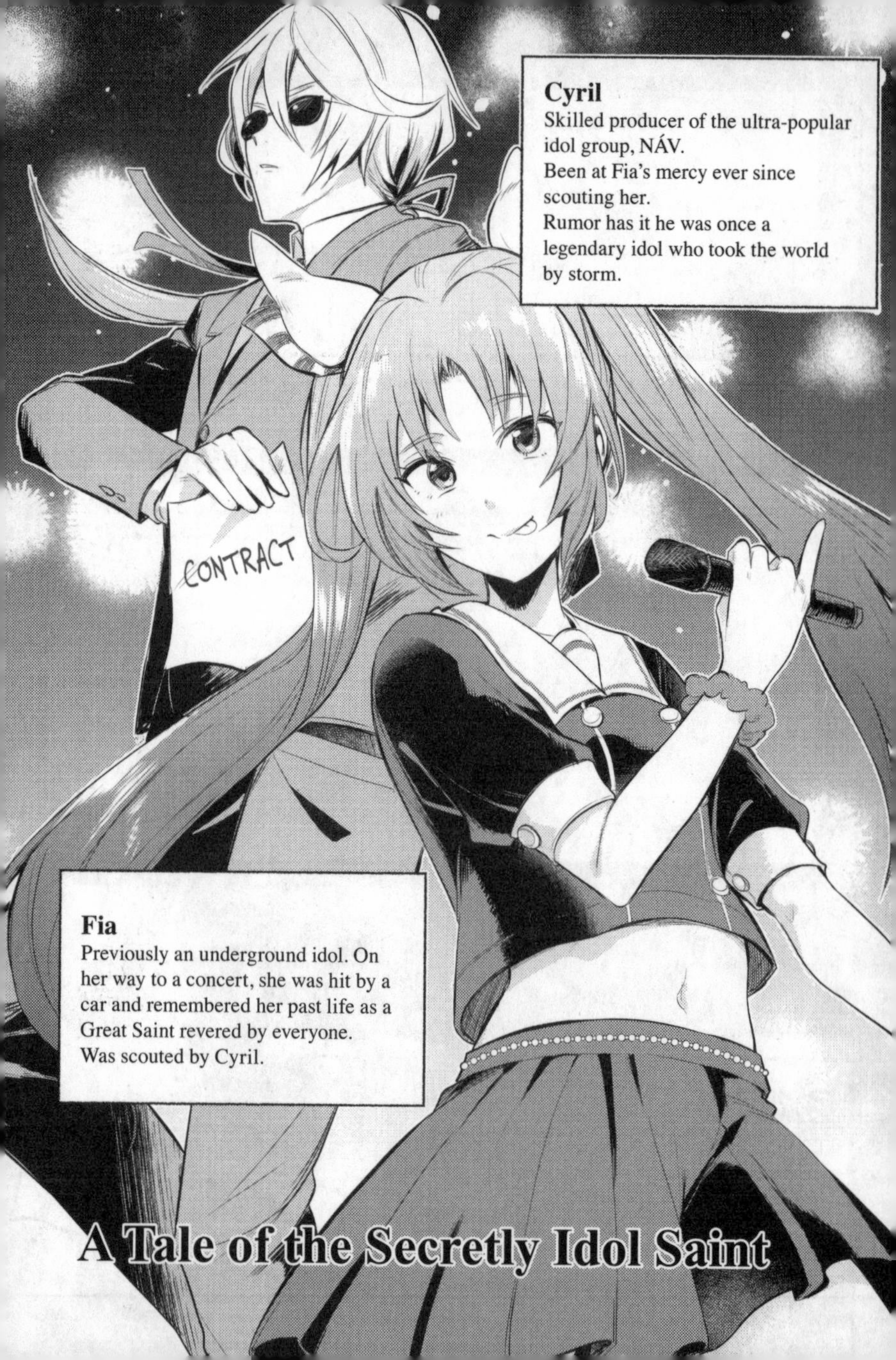
Cyril
Skilled producer of the ultra-popular idol group, NÁV.
Been at Fia's mercy ever since scouting her.
Rumor has it he was once a legendary idol who took the world by storm.
CONTRACT
Fia
Previously an underground idol. On her way to a concert, she was hit by a car and remembered her past life as a Great Saint revered by everyone.
Was scouted by Cyril.
A Tale of the Secretly Idol Saint

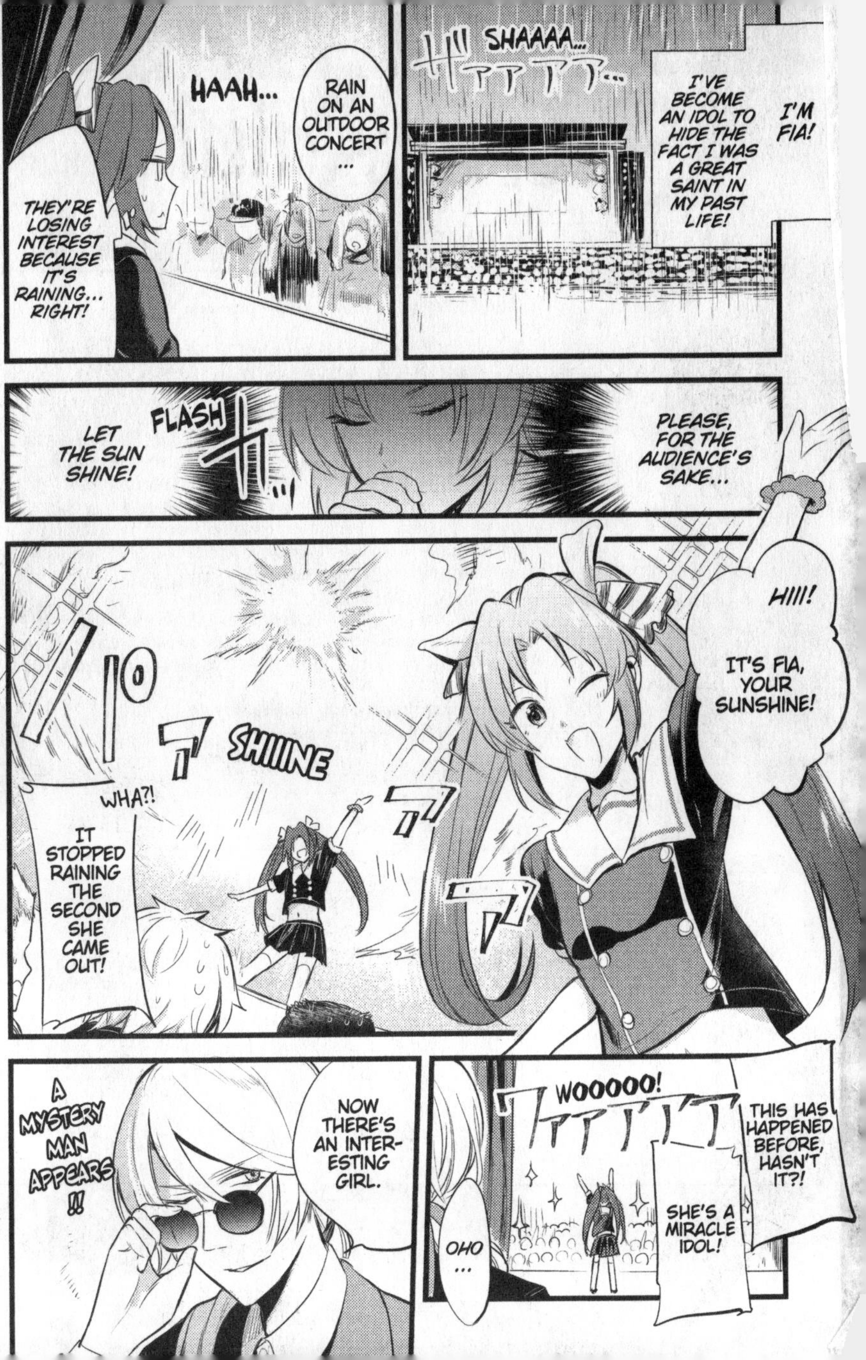
SHAAAA...
I'M FIA!
I'VE BECOME AN IDOL TO HIDE THE FACT I WAS A GREAT SAINT IN MY PAST LIFE!
RAIN ON AN OUTDOOR CONCERT ...
HAAH...
THEY'RE LOSING INTEREST BECAUSE IT'S RAINING... RIGHT!
PLEASE, FOR THE AUDIENCE'S SAKE...
FLASH
LET THE SUN SHINE!
HIII!
IT'S FIA, YOUR SUNSHINE!
SHIIINE
WHA?!
IT STOPPED RAINING THE SECOND SHE CAME OUT!
THIS HAS HAPPENED BEFORE, HASN'T IT?!
WOOOOO!
SHE'S A MIRACLE IDOL!
OHO ...
NOW THERE'S AN INTERESTING GIRL.
A MYSTERY MAN APPEARS!!

SEVEN SEAS ENTERTAINMENT PRESENTS

A Tale of the Secret Saint
VOLUME 2

art by **MAHITO AOBE** story by **TOUYA** character design by **CHIBI**

TRANSLATION
Erin Husson

ADAPTATION
Matthew Birkenhauer

LETTERING
Rina Mapa

COVER DESIGN
Hanase Qi

LOGO DESIGN
George Panella

PROOFREADER
B. Lillian Martin

ASSISTANT EDITOR
Jenn Grunigen

EDITOR
Kristiina Korpus

PREPRESS TECHNICIAN
Melanie Ujimori

PRINT MANAGER
Rhiannon Rasmussen-Silverstein

PRODUCTION ASSOCIATE
Christa Miesner

PRODUCTION MANAGER
Lissa Pattillo

MANAGING EDITOR
Julie Davis

ASSOCIATE PUBLISHER
Adam Arnold

PUBLISHER
Jason DeAngelis

Tensei Sita Daiseijyo ha, Seijyo dearukotowo hitakakusu Vol. 2

Originally published in Japan in 2020 by EARTH STAR Entertainment, Tokyo.
English translation rights arranged with EARTH STAR Entertainment, Tokyo, through TOHAN CORPORATION, Tokyo.

Seven Seas press and purchase enquiries can be sent to Marketing Manager Lianne Sentar at press@gomanga.com. Information regarding the distribution and purchase of digital editions is available from Digital Manager CK Russell at digital@gomanga.com.

ISBN: 978-1-63858-104-8
Printed in Canada
First Printing: February 2022
10 9 8 7 6 5 4 3 2 1

READING DIRECTIONS

This book reads from ***right to left***, Japanese style. If this is your first time reading manga, you start reading from the top right panel on each page and take it from there. If you get lost, just follow the numbered diagram here. It may seem backwards at first, but you'll get the hang of it! Have fun!!

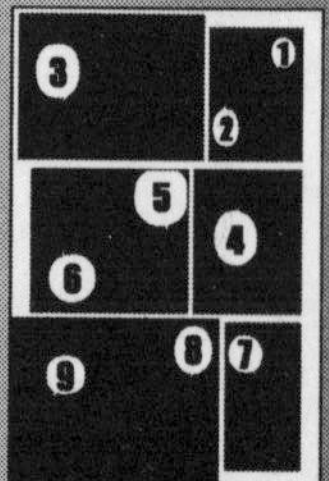
1
2
3
4
5
6
7
8
9

Follow us online: www.SevenSeasEntertainment.com